Hollywood Babylon Strikes Again!

BLOOD
MOON
Productions, Ltd.

OTHER BOOKS BY DARWIN PORTER

BIOGRAPHIES
Steve McQueen, King of Cool, Tales of a Lurid Life
Paul Newman, The Man Behind the Baby Blues
Merv Griffin, A Life in the Closet
Brando Unzipped
The Secret Life of Humphrey Bogart
Katharine the Great: Hepburn, Secrets of a Lifetime Revealed
Howard Hughes: Hell's Angel
Jacko, His Rise and Fall (The Social and Sexual History of Michael Jackson)

Coming Soon:
Humphrey Bogart, the Making of a Legend
The Kennedys, All the Gossip Unfit to Print
Frank Sinatra: The Boudoir Singer
AND IN COLLABORATION WITH ROY MOSELEY
Damn You, Scarlett O'Hara: The Private Lives of Vivien Leigh and Laurence Olivier

FILM CRITICISM
50 Years of Queer Cinema--500 of the Best GLBTQ Films Ever Made (2010)
Blood Moon's Guide to Recent Gay & Lesbian Film--Volume Two (2007)
Blood Moon's Guide to Recent Gay & Lesbian Film--Volume One (2006)
Best Gay and Lesbian Films- The Glitter Awards, 2005

NON-FICTION
Hollywood Babylon-It's Back!

NOVELS
Butterflies in Heat
Marika
Venus (a roman à clef based on the life of Anaïs Nin)
Razzle-Dazzle
Midnight in Savannah
Rhinestone Country
Blood Moon
Hollywood's Silent Closet

TRAVEL GUIDES
Many editions and many variations of *The Frommer Guides* to
Europe, the Caribbean, California, Georgia and The Carolinas, Bermuda, and The Bahamas

Hollywood Babylon Strikes Again!

Volume Two of Blood Moon's Babylon Series

Another Overview of Exhibitionism, Sexuality, and Sin
as Filtered through 85 years of Hollywood Scandal

BY DARWIN PORTER AND DANFORTH PRINCE

HOLLYWOOD BABYLON STRIKES AGAIN!

Volume Two of Blood Moon's Babylon Series

Manufactured in the United States of America

ISBN 978-1-936003-12-9
First printing June 2010
Second Printing October 2010
Cover designs by Richard Leeds (www.bigwigdesign.com)
Videography and publicity trailers by Piotr Kajstura
Distributed in North America and Australia
through the National Book Network (www.NBNbooks.com)
and in the U.K. through Turnaround (www.turnaround-uk.com)

Blood Moon acknowledges the National Book Network
for their savvy guidance in the presentation and marketing of this book.

DEDICATION

THIS BOOK IS DEDICATED TO ANYONE
WHO HAS EVER BEEN EMBARRASSED
BY ANY ASPECT
OF A CAREER IN THE ENTERTAINMENT BUSINESS.

REST IN PEACE

Memories of a Lost Civilization

"Grauman's Chinese Theater stands a couple of miles from the Paramount lot. It has passed into other hands since the death of Sid Grauman, but the name persists. In the absence of some sort of film-industry museum, a cultural enterprise undreamed of by the primitives who ran the big studios, the theater has become Hollywood's Louvre and its Pantheon.

Visitors buy souvenirs from old extras in cowboy boots and worn buckskins, walk through a wax museum, and solemnly study the indentations formed in the pinkish-tan concrete of the forecourt by the hands and feet of scores of movie stars, beginning in 1927 with Norma Talmadge and Mary Pickford. The autocratic DeMille placed his bootprints in the wet concrete, Betty Grable her celebrated and rather overrated legs, and Jayne Mansfield her breasts, creating declivities in which mosquitoes breed after a heavy rain.

From Grauman's depart the limousines that carry tourists past the homes of the stars in Beverly Hills and Bel Air. I made the excursion one Saturday afternoon in company with two honeymooning young couples from places like Deathball City, Ind., and New Acne, Neb. The driver, who bore a passing resemblance to Elvis Presley, turned out to be an aspiring actor from Brentwood, L.I., named Chuck Cavanagh. He told me that he had decided on a screen career after losing his job as a jet-engine mechanic at Los Angeles International Airport, and had recently worked as an extra on Lepke, a nineteen thirties gangland saga.

As we rolled through winding, hilly lanes, past opulent, palm-fringed homes, many of them reflecting the taste of people who have made a lot of money in a short time, Chuck briefed us on the latest gossip of the film capital. Vivacious Debbie Reynolds and shoe magnate Harry Karl had finally called it quits, he reported. She was being squired around town by Glenn Ford. Priscilla Presley was not lacking for friends since the breakup of her marriage.

We rolled by the mansion of Hugh Hefner, the Playboy man, which was fenced with wire mesh to keep the Bunnies from getting out and breeding all over the place; the Sammy Davis Jr. house, protected by a 20-foot fence and patrolled by armed guards because of kidnapping threats by Arab terrorists and, at the summit, Pickfair, where Mary Pickford, in her 80s, lives as a virtual recluse.

Chuck divided the stars into the friendlies and the unfriendlies. Doris Day was a friendly, he said. A couple of days previously, out bicycling, she had agreed to pose for a photograph with one of his tourists and had dispensed autographs with a liberal hand. Barbra Streisand was an unfriendly, as was Robert Young. 'We saw him standing in front of his house,' he said, 'and he wouldn't even wave back at us.'

'Gee, I never see anybody,' said one of the honeymooners. 'I guess I'm not that lucky.'

Passing Pat Boone's house, it seemed that her luck had changed. Through an open gate, a man in a flowered shirt could be seen placing suitcases in the trunk of a car. 'Is that him?' she asked. 'I think it is,' exclaimed the other young woman. Cavanagh, ever obliging, stopped the car. She lowered the window and waved. The man turned. It might have been Pat Boone's Filipino gardener, but it wasn't Pat Boone.

'I could've told you it wasn't him,' said one of the young husbands. 'You wouldn't see Pat Boone loading his own suitcases like that.'"

—**Tom Buckley**

WHAT WOULD LOUIS B. MAYER HAVE DONE WITH
CRUISE, LOHAN & GIBSON?

"Ah, the Golden Age of Hollywood. Where stars were stars—other worldly and untouchable—and a selection of discreet broads were readily available to help a not-gay man get his rocks off. It's a relief that Jimmy Stewart and, most of all, Louis B. Mayer are not alive today to witness the antics of the present crop of Hollywood's finest. What would they make of Tom Cruise jumping up and down on Oprah's couch screaming, 'Whaaooo!' What advice would they give 'teen queen' Lindsay Lohan as she is drunkenly and very publicly scraped off the sidewalk, offering indecent photo opportunities to the expectant paparazzi? And you can be sure they would have an uncompromising view on Mel Gibson, who added to the A-list implosion after his drunken, anti-Semitic and sexist remarks to police officers who leaked it to the press. Our culture is changing: once, we viewed actors like Stewart as heroes and role models; now we live in a society defined by gossip rags such as Heat and Grazia, determined to show that celebrities have zits and beer bellies like the rest of us."

—Mark Hooper

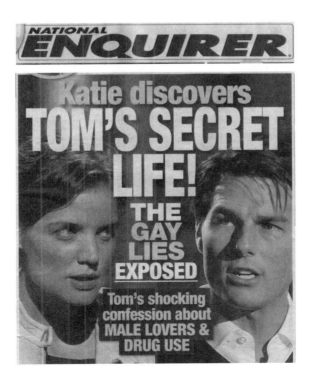

HOLLYWOOD: CITY OF BROKEN DREAMS

"In the center of the field was a gigantic pile of sets, flats and props. While he watched, a 10-ton truck added another load to it. This was the final dumping ground. He thought of Janvier's Sargasso Sea. Just as that imaginary body of water was a history of civilization in the form of a marine junkyard, the studio lot was one in the form of a dream dump. A Sargasso of the imagination! And the dump grew continually, for there wasn't a dream afloat somewhere which wouldn't sooner or later turn up on it, having first been made photographic by plaster, canvas, lath, and paint. Many boats sink and never reach the Sargasso, but no dream ever entirely disappears. Somewhere it troubles some unfortunate person and some day, when that person has been sufficiently troubled, it will be reproduced on the lot."

—**Nathanael West,** *The Day of the Locust*

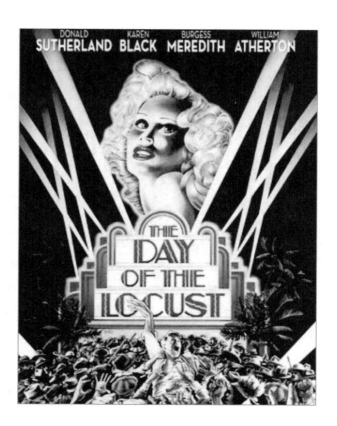

CONTENTS

THE WHOREHOUSES
OF BABYLON

Naughty

Brothels

of Golden Age Yesteryear

"How'd you like to f*** a movie star?"

The "madams" of Hollywood—in some cases a male—were to some degree inspired by the notorious Polly Adler, who operated the most famous bordello in New York City during the 1920s and 30s. She wrote about her exploits in her autobiography, *A House Is Not a Home*, which was made into an atrocious movie in 1964 starring Shelley Winters and Robert Taylor.

The madams of Hollywood were far less famous and celebrated than Adler. But although they operated under shrouds of secrecy, and shielded from members of the general public, they were nonetheless widely gossiped about within Hollywood. Here's an overview of some of them:

The House of Francis
"WE CATER TO ALL DESIRES"

Before she established her own whorehouse in Los Angeles, Miss Lee Francis was a working prostitute "going from house to house—I never liked to stay in one bordello too long," she claimed. Eventually, her cathouse, which operated from more than one address during its heyday, closing down and reopening, depending on the degree to which it was being harassed by the police and local politicians during any particular era, became the busiest and most successful in Los Angeles.

One of her first customers was the legendary John Barrymore. But what transpired with him was relatively conservative. In fact, his visit was unremarkable considering his status as a major-league star.

Although Francis whored around in San Francisco and Reno, it was in Los Angeles that she became known as "the madam with the most-est," particularly during the period in the 1930s when she operated in Hollywood from a location at 8439 Sunset Boulevard.

Inspired by the example of thousands of other madams, Francis paid off the police and any petty politicians on the take. She estimated that "about half of what I earned went to bribe cops and crooked politicians—have you ever met any other kind?"

But whereas other famous American madams—especially Polly Adler in New York or Sally Sanford

"I've lived a notorious life," said **Lee Francis**, the West Coast's most famous bordello keeper. "I made a lot of money, and it sure as hell beat typing for some fat boss with a fat cigar. At least I had some of the biggest VIPs in California calling me 'madam,' and that's a term of respect. I specialized in white gals, but if the client wanted them oriental or black, that could be arranged. I had to pay 40 percent of my profits to the police and politicians—and those occasional vice squad 'raids.' But until 1940, no arrests were ever made. In the middle of the Depression, some of my gals hauled in $1,000 a week. That was a fortune back then, and is still pretty good pay."

in San Francisco—got the headlines. Francis deliberately shunned any notoriety. "We like to keep it quiet," she once told George Raft. "Our clients are so famous they don't need any more publicity."

Since her establishment was so well known, and since what she called "the blue noses" systematically reported her establishment to the police, she was subjected to frequent raids by the vice squad. Remarkably, none of her clients and none of her girls was ever arrested in these raids. They were just for show.

She was rumored to have treated the vice squad to Russian caviar and French champagne during their periodic raids. She also gave them "rain checks," which entitled them to return on a quieter night to sample the prostitute of their choice.

Francis had a motto: "We can satisfy all desires." That wasn't quite true. She claimed she didn't hire underage girls, even though many of her customers took her motto seriously and asked for girls under twelve. One john requested a five-year-old.

Francis was very clear about not wanting to face any child molestation charges, but Errol Flynn, one of her best customers, claimed that he seduced many a 15- or 16-year-old at the House of Francis. These girls deliberately made themselves up to look much older.

Wall Street executives, many of them flying to the coast to check on their studio investments, were Francis' biggest spending customers. She entertained them in style in her deluxe on-site restaurant. Service was by topless waitresses. Within her brothel were at least eight bars, and her private bedrooms, or so she boasted, were more luxurious than those within any five-star hotel.

During her first years in business, Francis had learned that many of her patrons not only preferred their whores to be young but also, as she put it, "women of color."

"I never could understand the attraction of a white man to a black woman, but I catered to their desires. I didn't really hire black, black, but 'high yaller' gals as they were called. One statuesque, golden brown woman turned out to be one of my most popular gals. I guess the men who came to my place had beautiful white blonde goddesses at home and preferred someone exotic when 'dining out.'"

One visiting sheik from the Middle East called to inform her that he wanted to seduce 24 blondes during his brief stay in Los Angeles. Francis couldn't round up that many real blondes and consequently asked several of her prostitutes to dye both their pubic hair and the hair crowning their head.

For a roll on any of Francis's deluxe mattresses, and in the midst of the Depression, each of the girls was paid the staggering sum of $1,000, the highest price ever reported for a girl in the House of Francis. In most cases, faced with the economic hardships of that era, many would have settled happily for a $50 bill.

By 1929, Francis had become a celebrated fixture in town, eventually evolving into one of its leading tourist attractions. When the "Baltimore Oracle," H.L. Mencken, first arrived in Hollywood, he borrowed a custom-made Rolls-Royce from cowboy star Tom Mix and drove over to meet Francis. He didn't want to meet such A-list movie stars as Pola Negri, Gloria Swanson, or Norma Talmadge. Much more compelling was his fixation about meeting "the madam."

He later reported that Francis "was the epitome of graciousness and a fine lady indeed." He also claimed—falsely or oth-

As has been revealed in so many biographies, **Clark Gable** *(left)* and **Errol Flynn** *(right)* both harbored bisexual desires. "At my house, they fooled around only with my gals," said Madam Lee Francis. "But I wasn't above arranging a boy or a boy and a gal combo if either Errol or Clark desired that. Boy/girl whores were shipped to private homes. Such action didn't take place under my roof. You have to realize that every woman or girl in Hollywood was throwing herself at both Clark or Errol. They got tired of the same old, same old. No one should condemn them for wanting to spice up their sex lives. If a diner has nothing but caviar every night, he might want to dig into a steak with mashed potatoes for a change of pace."

erwise—that he played a few tunes for her on the piano in her parlor. "She complimented me on my playing, and I did not venture upstairs to sample all the goodies I knew were waiting there."

Actors, especially Errol Flynn and Clark Gable, frequented the establishment at least once a week. The well-hung Flynn was a great lover, and all the in-house whores signed up to take him on.

Even though he was the King of Hollywood, Gable didn't manage to convince the girls that he was also a competent lover off-screen.

None of the girls ever wanted to go to bed with him a second time, asserting that he was "a lousy lay," apparently in agreement with his longtime "gal pal," Joan Crawford, who loved Gable but not so much after she was pressured to take him into her boudoir. "We got over that as soon as I could," she told her gay pal, William Haines, "so we could get back to the living room and resume our drinking."

In her memoirs, Francis wrote about her friendship with Gable. "He never once set foot in my establishment," she claimed. Based on her friendship with him, she was, of course, working hard to protect his reputation.

Observers reported that Gable's custom-made Duesenberg coupe was often parked in front of the House of Francis. There were only two such Duesenberg's in the world, the white one belonging to Gable and a black one owned by Gary Cooper.

"Gary never came to my place," Francis said. "With that club he had swinging, his phone was ringing day and night. Both men and women wanted to see what all the excitement was about."

In contrast, Gable often preferred prostitutes, even though he could virtually have his pick of any of the leading ladies at MGM. [As such, he more or less sampled them one by one.] When Gable was hot and horny, he often called Francis to send a working girl over to his dressing room on the lot at MGM.

"With a prostitute, you can always pat her ass and send her back to Francis," Gable told the Hollywood columnist, Adela Rogers St. Johns, his oldtime friend and former sex partner from way back during his early days in Hollywood. Then, with wry humor, he continued, "A local whore once said to me—'And they call you the King of Hollywood. Maybe a young prince would be more apt.'"

Sometimes Irving Thalberg, who at the time was running MGM along with Louis B. Mayer, would show up at the House of Francis with three or four of his important male stars. They usually included Gable, who might also be accompanied by Robert Taylor, Mickey Rooney (allegedly), and Spencer Tracy.

Of delicate constitution, Thalberg wouldn't actually take on one of the girls himself. He had Norma Shearer at home, and she was more than he could handle. Instead, he sat in Francis' lavishly decorated lobby reading the trade papers while

John Gilbert *(left)* and **Spencer Tracy** *(right)* were frequent customers at the House of Francis. "I welcomed Jack with open arms, although he brought a certain baggage with him," said Lee Francis. "I shuddered every time that old drunk Tracy showed up, fearing he'd wreck my joint. Jack was a drunk too, but didn't tear up the place. He died in 1934. He was only 40 years old, a victim of alcoholism. During his last few months, Marlene Dietrich came back into his life as his nursemaid. In fact, I heard she was in bed with him the night he died. Jack was sweet and died young. Tracy was mean and died old. The old goats seemed to live forever, as the good ones die off."

"my boys" carried on upstairs.

On many a Saturday night, the "Three Jacks" showed up—John Gilbert, John Colton, and John Conway. Conway and Gilbert came for the action. But Colton, an alcoholic homosexual, didn't want any girl. He always made a deal with the other two Jacks to watch them in the saddle.

Colton (1887-1946) was a famous playwright of his day. He is chiefly remembered for his 1925 play *Shanghai Gesture*. In 1941 Josef von Sternberg turned it into a movie starring Gene Tierney in Oriental makeup and hunky Victor Mature.

Colton is also known for his 1923 play *Rain*, which he co-authored with Clemence Randolph. In separate productions, both Gloria Swanson and Rita Hayworth brought the character he created, a prostitute named Sadie Thompson, to the screen.

Conway (1887-1952) was a film director and producer. He often directed Gable in such features as *Boom Town* (1940), *Honky Tonk* (1941), and *The Hucksters* (1947).

Gilbert, of course, was the leading matinee idol of the Silents and the highly publicized lover of Greta Garbo.

Spencer Tracy was Francis's most dreaded client. A closeted homosexual, he also liked to seduce young female prostitutes. Regrettably, he always arrived drunk. "There are happy drunks and there are mean drunks," Francis said. "Tracy was a mean drunk. Once he got so belligerent that he wrecked my lobby and beat one of the girls. I would have had him arrested but I was in too delicate a position. I barred him from my premises, but he kept coming back for more trouble. He knew I couldn't call the police, so I had to put up with this old drunk. He slapped my face when I told him one night, 'Why don't you go over to the boy whorehouse? I think you'd be happier with a young guy.'"

MGM became such a heavy patron of the House of Francis that the studio opened a personal charge account for clients they would send over, notably East Coast distributors or "the money boys" from Wall Street. Every week, MGM bigwig

A forgotten figure today, **Kay Francis** (1905-1968) was the number one female star at Warner Brothers and the highest paid American film actress during the peak of her career from 1930 to 1936. Her striking dark beauty, plus her deep and supple voice, made her ideal for sound. Of course, there was that minor speech impediment which earned her the nickname of *"Wavishing Kay Fwancis."*

Once her decline came, the descent was rapid. She married five times and had a bevy of affairs with both men and women. Francis also had a taste for young women, especially those selected by Lee Francis at her bordello. Incidentally, Lee and Kay shared only a name—they were not related.

Howard Strickling (*left figure in photo, right*) was the keeper of the secrets at MGM. Here he is sharing confidences with silent screen star **John Gilbert**, who tried desperately to get Greta Garbo to marry him. She jilted him at the altar.

Strickling hushed up so many career-ruining scandals at MGM that he was known as "The Fixer." If anything went wrong at MGM, a star called Strickling for a bail-out. "He often went to the police and paid anybody off he had to so nothing came of it," said James Stewart. Some of Strickling's cover-ups included the murder of Paul Bern (husband of Jean Harlow), the drug addictions of Judy Garland, the murder of Ted Healy (creator of *The Three Stooges*) by Wallace Beery, and the adoption of an unmarried Loretta Young of her own child, fathered by the married Clark Gable on the set of *Call of the Wild*.

Howard Strickling sent Francis a check on his personal account, from which Mayer later reimbursed him. Although Strickling was officially listed as an MGM publicist, his real job involved covering up the indiscretions of the studio's male and female stars.

Strickling's checks, of course, never bounced. Not so with many of Francis's other clients. "I have received a total of more than $47,000 in bad checks from some of the most important, famous, and wealthy celebrities in the world. I have such checks in my possession from matinee idols, from movie producers, from political bigwigs, from European noblemen—from every strata of the social scene."

From all reports, Francis was a fascinating conversationalist. John Garfield liked to stop in after work for long talks with her before heading to one of the upstairs rooms for his whore *du jour*.

Francis also claimed that many of her male customers had a "strong homosexual streak in them, of which they are not consciously aware, or which they try to fight. Such men will marry but fail to find any happiness with their wives. They'll come to my house and have my girls, but there, too, the pleasure is not tremendous. Some of the men like their wives to cheat, even encourage it, getting an indirect sort of thrill from the contact of another man with someone they have already possessed."

Not all my clients were men," Francis later said. "Many lesbians, some of them big stars like Kay Francis, came to my house to be entertained with one of my gals. Many of them were not stars, but married society women. This sort of woman is usually sex hungry because she has married, for instance, an older, rich man, or perhaps her husband spends all his energy with a mistress."

"A famous director, who made some of our outstanding earlier epics, had a noted lesbian daughter," Francis claimed. "She used to stride into the house, pick one of the prettiest and most feminine girls and take her upstairs, just like a man. Later she'd come down, stop for a drink and leave. My girls didn't mind, and I understand she was very generous with them."

Francis later claimed that her most bizarre customer was not Tracy but the blonde bombshell Jean Harlow, who died of uremic poisoning in 1937.

She had been Spencer Tracy's lover, but she'd also had affairs with Gable, Howard Hawks, Howard Hughes, William Powell, James Stewart, and even gangster Bugsy Siegel.

"What is not known is that Harlow liked to go to bed with prostitutes," Francis alleged. "She came to my establishment and took away two or three gals a week, for which she paid me one hundred dollars each, which was twice the going rate. The girls didn't really want to go because they said Harlow liked her sex rough. Sometimes she'd show up and take some of my male customers after having drinks with them in the lobby. But she paid for every guy she took away from my

The blonde bombshell of the 1930's **Jean Harlow** (1911-1937) seduced some of the biggest names in Hollywood, including Howard Hughes, Clark Gable, and mobster Bugsy Siegel. She also picked up a lot of traveling salesmen, taxi drivers, and other assorted flotsam.

Her second husband, Paul Bern, reportedly had a very small penis and was impotent as well. His death became one of the most scandalous in Hollywood history. If he couldn't satisfy Harlow, she saw that her third husband, cinematographer Harold Rosson, was man enough for the job. Male friends who'd seen him in the shower nicknamed him "Long Dong."

house."

Francis later and very discreetly installed peepholes in some of her rooms. She got the idea from Jack Colton who liked to watch Gilbert and "The Other Jack," Conway.

"I found out there were a lot of voyeurs in Hollywood," Francis said. "After the Production Code came in, you couldn't see much action on the screen. A lot of guys, and women too, wanted to watch their favorite star in action off screen. Flynn told me he had installed such peepholes at his private home. I got good money by allowing 'fans' to watch Gable, Bob Taylor, Tyrone Power, Johnny Weismuller, among several others, in action. The stars never found out that they were putting on a show and not getting paid for it. I collected the money, however, for my old age retirement."

After endless police raids over the decade, the one that did her house in occurred on January 16, 1940. "You're a sly one," she told the arresting officer. "In thirty-one years in the business, this is the first time anyone ever got me."

She was charged with operating a house of ill repute in a spacious apartment with nine bedrooms on Sunset Boulevard, a few steps from Ciro's, a popular celebrity-haunted restaurant and bar. "I was sentenced to thirty days in the slammer," as she so colorfully said. But since Francis turned out to be such a "model inmate," a lenient judge reduced her term to just twenty-one days.

When she got out of prison, she spent time composing her memoirs, which she entitled *Ladies on Call*. They were published in 1965, and in 1987 reissued in a version entitled *Hollywood Madam*.

The sprawling Venetian-inspired building which sheltered Francis, her girls, and the trade they plied during the 1930s was later, for a time, owned by rock star Rod Stewart.

Women We Wish We'd Known
Women We Think Are Cool

POLLY ADLER

"THE BEST GODDAMN MADAM IN AMERICA"

(1900-1962)

RIP

Born in Russia at the turn of the 20th century, **Polly Adler** emigrated to the United States on the eve of World War I. Raped while working as a mill girl in a Brooklyn factory, she became pregnant and had her kid aborted. Turning her back on her orthodox Jewish upbringing, she became involved with mobster Dutch Schultz and began to secure girls for gangsters. In 1920 she opened her first bordello.

Throughout the roaring 20s and into the Depression Era 30s, even through the early years of World War II, Polly ran America's most famous whorehouse. Patrons such as Robert Benchley made her place a second home, and the notorious mayor of New York, Jimmy Walker, called regularly. She shifted her brothels from apartment to apartment, before retiring in 1944. On the West Coast, she wrote an international bestseller, *A House Is Not a Home* (1953), which was made into a movie after her death, with Shelley Winters playing Adler.

"I Wanna Fuck Joan Crawford"

An Oft-Repeated Request from Clients at MGM's Bordello

Aware of the river of profits that the House of Francis was making, MGM, with the approval of Louis B. Mayer, decided to open its own bordello. Evocative of Twelve Oaks in *Gone With the Wind,* the brothel stood north of Sunset Strip. Built in the Greek Revival style, the sprawling mansion had broad verandahs and stately white columns associated with the antebellum South.

"In its bar you could meet some of the biggest names in Hollywood," said Joan Crawford, who often dropped in "to drink with the fellows." A gourmet restaurant with a top chef from Hong Kong served dinner nightly. Upstairs were fourteen lavishly appointed suites, each rather gaudily decorated, usually in reds, purples, or "pussy pink."

MGM's Howard Strickling hired a very beautiful blonde named "Billie Bennett" to run the operation. She was a dead-ringer for Mae West, and even talked like her, using a version of West's famous line. When a male customer would leave, Bennett would say, "Come back and see me sometime." Within two weeks of its launch, the bordello became known as "Mae's House."

When West herself heard of this, she was furious. She feared that many of the clients, especially those who had had one drink too many, would think that the real Mae West was running the joint. "After all," West said, "I was known for doing some pimping for the boys in New York, and my fans might have thought I've reverted to my old profession, the oldest profession in the world."

The starlets for Mae's House were supplied by Frank Orsatti (1893-1947), longtime best pal of Louis B. Mayer. Irving Thalberg referred to Orsatti as "Mayer's pimp and chief bootlegger." Although a teetotaler himself, Mayer demanded to be cut in for a percentage of the bootleg action for the liquor consumed within the brothel. Orsatti later became an actor's agent.

Strickling always called Billie when a VIP, perhaps an investment executive from Wall Street or a major distributor of MGM products, informed the studio that he'd be in town and needed entertainment. One night, Strickling phoned to tell her that the major distributor of

If men couldn't get the real thing, they settled for **Joan Crawford**'s lookalike, who was employed in the notorious bordello actually run under the auspices of MGM, with Louis B. Mayer's blessing.

Irving Thalberg, his chief executive, was a frequent visitor, but he stayed downstairs enjoying music and the liquor, as his heart made it difficult for him to engage in strenuous activity such as intercourse.

A rumor—never confirmed—claimed that the real Crawford sometimes filled in for her lookalike, but only if the johns were "very, very special." She grew used to hearing a familiar compliment: "You're a dead-ringer for Crawford, the spitting image. God damn it, your surgeon was good. I can't believe it."

MGM movies in Mexico City was flying into Los Angeles.

"He wants to fuck Jean Harlow," Strickling said. "Jean's a good sport and would do it for us, but she told me she got an infection down below. She blames Clark Gable for giving it to her."

Billie had an idea. "Why don't you get that gal who doubled for Jean Harlow to fill in for her tonight?" she asked. "The Spic from South of the Border wouldn't know the difference."

Strickling thought that was a good idea, and summoned the would-be actress into his office. Once a thousand dollar bill—and this was during the Depression—was waved in front of her, she agreed to a gig at "Mae's House" for that night. MGM's wardrobe and makeup departments were enlisted to work on the young woman with the goal of transforming her into Harlow. Her hair was already platinum blonde. Once she arrived at Mae's, she told the madam that there was one thing that might give her away. "I'm sorta ginger down there," she confessed. "Maybe this *mexicano* creep wants me to be platinum all over."

"We get a lot of requests for blondes," Billie told her, inviting her into a private room. There she presented a bottle of peroxide to the young actress and told her to go to work. "There's only one problem," Billie said. "When the guy goes down on you, he's gonna get a mouth full of peroxide."

The evening between the Harlow stand-in and the Mexican honcho went so successfully—he really believed that he was fucking the real Jean Harlow—that Billie came up with an idea. She pitched it to Strickling, who went for it.

She proposed engaging a corps of out-of-work actresses, each of whom desperately needed the money, to impersonate various stars in various states of undress. She asked an assortment of her customers which women they'd most like to bed, and the names that surfaced near the top included Joan Crawford, Alice Faye, Marlene Dietrich, Carole Lombard, Ginger Rogers, and Barbara Stanwyck.

"**Billie Bennett**" (God knows what her real name was) was said to be a dead ringer for Mae West. Billie's origins are unknown but she ingratiated herself with the MGM hierarchy and was asked to run a whorehouse just for the studio's male stars. Billie learned to impersonate the voice of West better than any female impersonator in the years to come.

West was horrified by the association of her likeness with the bordello and called Louis B. Mayer to protest. He informed her, "Now, now, Mae, let's don't make trouble. If you sue for libel, we'll have to reveal to the world that you were a bit of madam in New York, pimping chorus girls to the guys. And what about the rumor you pimped Cary Grant to men?" West slammed down the phone on Mayer, but until the day the bordello was eventually shut down, she never again protested.

Surprisingly, Mae West was not on that list. [One wonders what the reaction of Miss West would have been had she known.] Also notably absent from the list were two really big stars, Greta Garbo and Katharine Hepburn. "I think most men would be intimidated to take Hepburn or Garbo to bed," Billie said. "Frankly, they're mostly lez anyway."

To Billie's surprise, many men specifically requested child star Shirley Temple. Strickling, however, wasn't at all surprised that Shirley's name came up. "Deep down in their hearts, many men would like to go to bed with a twelve-year-old girl, even a ten-year-old," he said. "But there's no way MGM is going to sell children into sex."

Shortly thereafter, as part of their ongoing dialogues, Billie called Strickling: "I've found the girl. She just turned eighteen, but she looks no more than thirteen, especially when I dress her up as Shirley." If she could provide guarantees that the girl was "of legal age," Strickling agreed to cooperate.

Billie later told Strickling that business was booming as regards men requesting Shirley. "She's doing more business than Crawford or Dietrich. In fact, I'm considering finding at least two more young gals to impersonate Little Miss *Rebecca of Sunnybrook Farm.* According to the gal I hired, most men who come to bed her, tell her, 'I want you to suck my lollipop.' I guess Shirley's 'On the Good Ship Lollipop' number got to 'em."

Soon John Barrymore, Clark Gable, Errol Flynn, Robert Montgomery, Johnny Weissmuller, Douglas Fairbanks Jr., Spencer Tracy, and others were transferring their sexual patronage from the House of Francis to Mae's (aka Billie's) House.

Throughout the early 1930s, during the height of the Depression, Billie's house flourished. "Isn't it the dream of all men to fuck a movie star?" Billie asked. Some of her young women even had themselves surgically altered to look more like the movie star they were imitating.

Strickling even arranged for nightly visits from an MGM makeup artist, and often sent a shipment of the actual wardrobes that various stars had worn in recent pictures. At one point Billie had seven different hairdressers and makeup men—oddly never a woman—"getting my gals ready for the night's entertainment in my basement rooms," Billie claimed.

"Men simply want to sleep with movie stars," said Ted McIlvenna of the Institute for the Advanced Study of Human Sexuality. "And the stronger the desire, the stronger the fantasy."

"My all-time best paying customer was Groucho Marx, although I'd heard that he was a bit stingy," Billie later said.

Charlie Chaplin, according to Billie, became a regular. "He liked them real young," she claimed. "He told me, 'the most beautiful form of life is the very young girl just starting to bloom.' Naturally, Shirley Temple was his favorite. Charlie always claimed he possessed a twelve-inch penis which he referred to as 'the eighth wonder of the world.' One of my gals told me Charlie was big, but not in the eighth wonder of the world category."

Billie's house operated smoothly, albeit with an occa-

THIS IS NOT A BROTHEL THERE ARE NO PROSTITUTES AT THIS ADDRESS

A large blowup of a picture similar to the one above decorated the main lounge of Mae's House. "I wanted to put men in the mood while they were having their drinks and making their choice of gal for the evening."

When Billie had to move her house of prostitution, her former rental was taken over by an evangelical group. When johns started knocking on their door at all hours of the night, the staff inside posted the sign above.

The real **Shirley Temple** is seen here sucking on a big lollipop. The lookalike Shirley Temple, at her peak, took on eight johns in one night. When the real Shirley Temple was being interviewed by MGM producer Arthur Freed in his office, he exposed his penis to her. But, in spite of that, her name was linked only to her two husbands—the philandering John Agar, a fellow actor, and her businessman husband of long duration, Charles Black. In spite of her relatively clean sexual record, Louise Brooks, a silent screen star, called her, "A swaggering, tough little slut."

sional mishap. "My gal impersonating Alice Faye almost got split open by Milton Berle. He didn't have a cock between his legs—more like a tree trunk. I had to take her to the hospital to get her sewn up. After she recovered, she told me never to send her a client who was more than eight inches. That was no problem for me. Nearly all my clients had less than eight inches. I should know since I sampled many of them myself, especially that adorable George Montgomery. Dinah Shore later made off with that hunk of man herself."

As far as it is known, only one male MGM star was ever coerced into proving his mettle within Billie's brothel, and that was Jimmy Stewart. Louis B. Mayer kept hearing stories about Stewart's early days in New York. Both director Joshua Logan and actor Broderick Crawford had spread the word that in those early days Henry Fonda and Stewart had been lovers.

For some reason, Stewart was not known as a ladies' man, even though in time he had affairs with some of the biggest names in Hollywood, even Katharine Hepburn. To his list of seductions might be added over the years June Allyson, Olivia de Havilland, Marlene Dietrich, Jean Harlow, Rita Hayworth, Ginger Rogers, Margaret Sullavan, Loretta Young, Lana Turner, Norma Shearer, Grace Kelly, and Jeanette MacDonald.

During the late 30s, however, many of those affairs had not yet unfolded. Others were conducted so discreetly during the 30s that Mayer didn't hear about them. Stewart wasn't a kiss-and-tell kind of guy.

"I keep hearing he's a homo," Mayer quizzed Strickling. "and we've got to do something about it. I want Jimmy to prove to me he's not a homo."

Mayer summoned Stewart into his office and demanded that he visit Billie's brothel, stressing that it lay close to the edge of the MGM lot. "Get your ass over there and get those rocks off with at least two of those broads," Mayer ordered Stewart.

Stewart, rising to the task, performed nobly. One of Billie's whores even claimed, "I'd do him for free."

Apparently, Mayer had never heard of bisexuality. He believed that if it could be ascertained that Robert Taylor was screwing a woman, it was impossible that this handsome matinee idol might also get plugged by Errol Flynn, Howard Hughes, etc.

Charlie Chaplin's favorite refrain might have been, "Thank God for little girls." As Gloria Swanson once sarcastically remarked, "Charlie likes his girls so young you'll find him hanging out in maternity wards." He also seduced older women willing to submit to him.

Charlie was a world class john at various brothels. He told Orson Welles, "Whores don't judge you. Like everyone else's, my sex life goes in cycles. Sometimes I'm potent; other times disappointing." With Mae West, he was always potent.

"Now," she said, "Chaplin was short, and his nose was average, but his pecker was really big-time."

The big name stars really fell for **James Stewart**. For the 1939 *Destry Rides Again*, Marlene Dietrich claimed she and the actor started having sex when they met for wardrobe fittings. She also claimed that she became pregnant from their first sexual encounter and later had an abortion. On the set of *The Philadelphia Story* 1940), he seduced **Katharine Hepburn**. She liked his "soft-spoken manly charm," and vowed to make him "forget the charms of Ginger Rogers and Olivia de Havilland."

Charles Higham, in his biography of Louis B. Mayer, *Merchant of Dreams*, claimed that "Billie Bennett was generous. When an actor was in trouble, or an executive was desperate for money, she would always take care of them, with generous loans."

The breakout of World War II dimmed business for the bordellos. "Christ," Billie protested. "You had practically every virgin from New York to San Francisco giving it away. All of them seemed willing to surrender their honeypots to men going overseas, perhaps to remind them of what was waiting for them back home when they defeated the damn Japs and Hitler."

In looking back over her career, Billie said, "I sold illusions just like MGM movies did. My johns believed they were sleeping with real stars. That's how realistic my girls were. It was a wonderful, golden time in Hollywood. I operated a great Pleasure Palace. Many of my gals, who had come to Hollywood to become movie stars, in some strange way lived out their fantasies at my bordello. For a few nights at least, they got to be Barbara Stanwyck, Joan Crawford, or Carole Lombard."

"Most of them got married during the war years and settled down into roles as dutiful housewives, especially during the post-war years," Billie said. "Their husbands and children, for the most part, never knew exactly what mama had really been doing during her Hollywood days."

Billie Bennett, or so it was reported in an article in *The New York Times*, died sometime in 1951.

But did the whorehouse madam really die in 1951? Could the *Times* reporter have confused the prostitute Billie Bennett with the American film actress, Billie Bennett of the silent era, who appeared in 52 films between 1913 and 1930, and who died in Los Angeles in May of 1951?

"STUD SERVICE FOR SALE"
Male Bordellos
of Hollywood

Even though it flourished in hundreds of manifestations, female prostitution was illegal everywhere in America during the so-called Golden Age of Hollywood. But so was homosexuality, even more so, and when it was uncovered, it was punished even more severely.

The male bordellos that flourished in Los Angeles during the 1930s, therefore, were in double jeopardy. Their "male madams" had to be far more secretive than the directors of the relatively better-publicized "House of Francis" and the MGM-backed bordello, both of which regularly paid off the police.

The male brothels didn't have restaurants, bars, and lavishly decorated boudoirs. Most of them came and went with little longevity, and most of them operated within private mansions in the Hollywood Hills, their addresses discreetly communicated only to a chosen few.

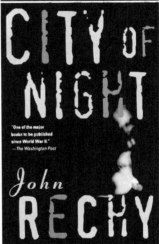

They operated under the guise of private parties. Such all-male gatherings were still subjected to raids, even when men joined each other in private homes without options or potentialities for intra-male sex. In other words, it was dangerous for a man to invite ten or twelve males over for a "legitimate" Saturday night barbecue.

"Homosexual men in the 1930s lived in a virtual police state and could be arrested at any time," claimed director James Whale, of *Frankenstein* fame.

Sergeant David Hancoff, a key player in the Los Angeles Vice Squad, reported that in the 1930s most male hustlers operated independently of any "madam." They were free agents operating out of their own homes. Many of them regularly scheduled appointments with a select list of clients; other "johns" were picked up on the streets, in Griffin Park, or in bars, although actual gay bars were illegal and could be subjected to raids. Few hustlers in those days wanted to share half their earnings with any pimp. Even so, there were several male brothels that emerged and soon after disappeared over the years.

Out-of-work actors were eager targets to be recruit-

John Rechy, born in 1934, the son of a Scottish father and a Mexican-American mother, became a literary sensation in 1963 when he published his pioneering hustler novel *City of Night*. Several producers attempted to film the novel but nothing came of it. "We can't shoot a movie about a male whore," said a Paramount official. Of course, then along came *Midnight Cowboy* which won Best Picture of the Year in 1969.

City of Night was the story of a lonely male hustler who desperately seeks to find love on the bright neon streets of New York, New Orleans, and Los Angeles. "Youngman," the main character of the novel, has sex with, among others, another hustler, a sadist, and a bed-ridden old man. Its stark depiction of hustling has never been equaled.

ed as hustlers. Many of them were exclusively homosexual, some were bisexual, and others were "gay for pay," with girlfriends or wives at home. Many of the patrons of male bordellos were married men. These bisexuals had to be extra careful. If a man had a name in movies, he had to operate in total secrecy. If arrested in a raid, it would in most cases be a career breaker.

Literature on the female brothels of Los Angeles is scant enough. As regards the male brothels, there is even less documentation. For the most part, homosexual prostitution was simply not recorded. However, some recorded data does exist.

In his book, *Thicker 'n Thieves*, Sergeant Charles F. Stoker, a policeman, claimed that one of the most successful male whorehouses was run by a man named "Little Brother," although there was nothing little about him. His actual name was Ward Kris. Growing up in Kansas, he eventually married and fathered two children before deserting his family and heading for the greater thrills of Los Angeles. There, he wanted to break into the movies.

Although he was handsome enough to be a movie star, so were thousands of other young men. He began to hustle and proved so successful at it that he could no longer handle all his male clients. He met two or three other hustlers, and they pooled their investment funds and talents, opening a male whorehouse together and recruiting other handsome, well-endowed young men to staff it.

Throbbing Hearts, Throbbing ???

After the success of Billie Bennett's female star lookalike prostitutes, it was inevitable that a male madam would try to pull the same stunt with men. A very unofficial survey was taken, and a rough list compiled. Getting the most votes was **Robert Taylor** *(left)*, the matinee idol of the 1930s. He was known as Hollywood's pretty boy. When he signed to co-star with Joan Crawford in *The Gorgeous Hussy*, in 1936, studio wags wondered, "Which is the gorgeous?" Taylor had numerous affairs with men, including Howard Hughes. His co-star in *Camille* (1936), **Greta Garbo,** found him "so beautiful—and so dumb."

Tyrone Power *(second photo from left)* came in a close second. He and Taylor had been lovers. The one person he fell in love with was not Judy Garland and certainly not Robert Taylor, but Errol Flynn. "He wanted me to do unspeakable things to him," Flynn told his cronies.

Don Ameche (second from right) came in a surprise third on this unofficial list. The male madam thought it would be Errol Flynn (he came in fifth). Ameche with his mustache enjoyed a certain following in the 30s. Calling the telephone the "Don Ameche" became popular slang in the 30s and 40s because of the actor's role in *The Story of Alexander Graham Bell (1939)*. When Ameche heard about his lookalike, he protested. "Why do homosexuals want to go to bed with me? I've been a happily married man since 1932." "It's the mustache," Tyrone Power jokingly answered him. "Also, word is that you give great rim jobs." "Exactly what is a rim job?" Ameche asked.

Placing fourth, **Mickey Rooney** on the far right should be remembered for what he was, not what he looked like in the 21st Century, where he's been compared to something you discover when you open an old coffin. In the 1930s he appealed to men who wanted a teenage boy. In fact, Mickey once confessed that, "I was a fourteen-year-old boy for thirty years."

"Their place was heavily draped and thickly carpeted," according to Sergeant Stoker's account. "Drinks were placed on low tables on the floor. The room abounded with pillows. People lay in corners of the room, in which smoke from marijuana resembled the Los Angeles atmosphere on a smoggy day. Little Brother and his 'waiters' were clad in costumes which reminded one of a scene from *The Arabian Nights*—baby silk pants, embroidered blouses, and turbans around their heads."

Inspired by Billie Bennett's use of look-alike prostitutes, Noah Thomas, coming from either Ohio or Indiana, ran a very special bordello in the 1930s, catering to specific tastes. He recruited young men who resembled male movie stars popular during that era, including "Clark Gable," "Robert Taylor," "Errol Flynn," "Tyrone Power," "Don Ameche," and—would you believe it—"Mickey Rooney."

It must be understood that the real Mickey Rooney at the time had a certain cuteness and vitality to him and was arguably the biggest box office attraction in America. At least he managed to snare Ava Gardner, and even Rock Hudson once expressed a desire to go to bed with him.

Another intriguing "bordello" of the 1930s, if it could be called that, was operated by a single performer, Jean-Pierre Roux, who for some reason was nicknamed "Pupu." The son of a French father and a stunningly "brown belle" Creole woman from Martinique, Pupu grew into an exotic creature himself. He stood nearly six feet, four inches and had a sculpted physique. In his native Martinique, he became legendary for his endowment, often appearing in private stag shows for visiting mixed audiences of men and women.

A Hollywood director (name unknown) convinced Pupu that he could make far more money hustling his wares to both men and women in Hollywood. Pupu was bisexual, but once he arrived in Los Angeles he became more or less homosexual, since he found himself far more popular with his male clients than any female clients he might attract.

Although he occasionally brought in other hustlers, often mulatto, too, he mostly operated as a one-man bordello with himself as the star attraction.

Because of contacts made with that director, Pupu catered only to male movie stars of the 1930s, the ones who had the most to lose career-wise if their homosexuality became known.

Among the stars he entertained were lovers Cary Grant

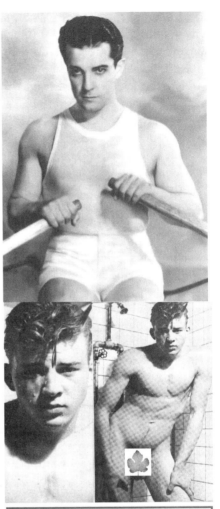

Silent screen star **Ramon Novarro** *(top photo)* was paddling toward disaster. His notorious patronage of male hustlers would lead to his death on the night of October 39, 1968. He picked up two male hustlers, **Paul Ferguson** *(pictured in the two lower photos, above)* and his brother Tom Ferguson. Both brothers believed that Novarro had a large stash of cash in his house. He didn't. When Novarro couldn't produce any significant cash, Paul tied his hands and feet with an electrical cord and mercilessly beat and tortured the former star. The house was ransacked, and Novarro was left to die.

The brothers were tried and convicted of first degree murder and given a life sentence. Tom served six years, and Paul did time for nine. After Paul was released, his violent streak returned and he was again sentenced to jail for the rape of a woman in Missouri.

and Randolph Scott, with whom Pupu indulged in a three-way. Nils Asther was also a faithful client. A Swede, the handsome, suave Asther came to Hollywood during the silent era. He appeared in the famous Joan Crawford flapper film, *Our Dancing Daughters* (1928), and also was romantically teamed with Greta Garbo in *Wild Orchids* (1929) and *The Single Standard* (also 1929). Garbo didn't want to kiss Asther, claiming, "I don't know where your mouth was last night."

The silent screen heartthrob Ramon Novarro, star of MGM's *Ben-Hur*, was the most reliable patron of Pupu and was said to be "utterly fascinated" with the male whore's appendage. Novarro became known in the 1930s for his patronage of hustlers, and eventually was murdered by a pair of them, two brothers, Paul and Tom Ferguson, in 1968.

Among directors, **George Cukor** (1899-1983) was virtually the "patron saint" of male hustlers, certainly their greatest customer. In addition to hustlers supplied by male madams, he picked up sailors from Long Beach, California, if they were young and virile. He had a taste for straight, masculine men whom he paid for their favors.

He once said, "Never under estimate the stupidity of actors." That didn't stop him from seducing a bevy of them, notably Aldo Ray, Anthony Quinn, Peter Lawford, Forrest Tucker, and even young James Dean, among others. Of those actors named, Lawford got the worst score. "Peter was not a good lover—not at all," Cukor said.

Director George Cukor was also turned onto the charms of Pupu, as was another director, Edmund Goulding. A married couple, Lilyan Tashman and Edmund Lowe, visited Pupu at least once a week for a three-way.

The brilliant fashion designer, Adrian, who for a while was married to the lesbian actress Janet Gaynor, touted Pupu's charms to his male friends. Director James Whale, along with his longtime partner, David Lewis, were often seen coming and going from Pupu's apartment.

Pupu, or so it is said, returned to his native Martinique with a "lot of dough." By then, he'd learned American vernacular.

In David Ehrenstein's 1998 book, *Open Secret*, author John Rechy referred to a gay bordello, lying in the hills of Los Feliz, that flourished during the 1950s. Rechy, of course, became notorious for his semi-autobiographical novel, *City of Night*, which remains virtually the definitive portrait of a male hustler's life.

Such gay actors as Anthony Perkins, Rock Hudson, George Nader, and Montgomery Clift led closeted lives during the day, but on certain occasions were seen at this bordello, which was privately nicknamed "the Garden of Delights." Supposedly, it was operated by one Alan Junod, from Augusta, Georgia. When his mother, his last remaining parent, died, he cashed in his inheritance and headed for Hollywood "and a life of flamboyant decadence," as he put it.

In an interview, Rechy recalled, "I was taken there by some people I'd met. It was an extraordinary place, that club. And the most extraordinary thing about it was that one didn't consider it extraordinary. We just accepted it. It was almost like going to a foreign country, because you 'passed through customs' to get to the place. There were two people on the road, kind of 'spotting' things, who would check you out. Then you went up and there was this house that had been converted into a dance hall. I remembered they served soft drinks. No liquor. Men danced with men, and women with women. They had a system of flashing lights that warned when the police were on their way. And that was a signal for lesbians to team up with gay men on the dance floor. Everybody of the opposite gender coupled up. A man dancing with another man or a woman dancing with another woman could get arrested back then—just for doing that."

Within this house, it was understood that social gatherings would not evolve into orgies. Junod discreetly arranged introductions between male hustlers and potential clients. He was an equal opportunity employer, hiring as many lesbian hookers for the ladies as he did male whores for a clientele of usually older men, often producers, directors, and leading men.

Junod was more or less replaced by Robert Bolton, a tall, statuesque, and exceedingly well-built African American who operated a so-called "massage parlor" on Santa Monica Boulevard in the late 60s and early 70s. Male customers at his establishment got massaged all over, especially anally.

Bolton was a famous top man, seducing male movie stars, producers, directors, and in some cases politicians. One such client, who shall go nameless, rose to the heights of power in California.

Unlike Pupu, Bolton eventually didn't operate just by himself. At the peak of his popularity, he employed at least fifteen handsome and well-developed young men.

He was very discreet and was never arrested. Clients were given a card and were told, at least on the phone, to give only a number for their request. If they wanted a hustler to perform fellatio on them, they said ONE. If they wanted a 69, they said SIX. If they requested number 10, it meant an "around the world."

In 1945, at the end of World War II, a well-built, curly-haired blond from southern Illinois moved to Los Angeles. Shortly thereafter, he opened Scott Richfield's Gas Station at the corner of Fairfax and Hollywood Boulevard. Within eight months, it had become the most popular gas station among gays in Hollywood.

Getting a lube job at Scotty's came to mean something else. He hired as many as a dozen young men to pump gas and to escort certain gentlemen callers into the back rooms. There, the car owners could perform fellatio on these handsome, strapping former servicemen, or else become passive recipients of sodomy. Scotty hired only "tops."

Nils Asther (1897-1981), a Danish-born Swedish stage and film actor, is seen here making love to **Greta Garbo** in *Wild Orchids* (1929). He proposed to her that same year. Aware that he was a homosexual, she turned him down.

His good looks made him a leading man, playing opposite such legendary women as Pola Negri, Marion Davies, and Joan Crawford. Because of his accent, with the arrival of sound, his career declined. Struggling as an actor, he ended up driving a truck. During his heyday, Asther requested that male madams supply him with young men with "exceptional endowments."

Among the many patrons of the gas station were director George Cukor and the very closeted Spencer Tracy. Robert Taylor often stopped by to get "filled up," and Tyrone Power took some of the young men home with him to "perform the down and dirties," in the words of one gas jockey hustler.

"Most of Scotty's men were gorgeous," or so claimed Vivien Leigh, who visited the gas station accompanied by her friend Cukor. Most of Scotty's men were bisexuals and could accommodate either gender. Sometimes one of the gas jockeys was hired for private sessions at the homes of a married couple.

In his investigation, author Paul Young quotes a source who claimed that "Scotty was smarter than some of his competitors. He refused to accept money from his boys or his clients. He'd only accept gifts: gold watches, silver trinkets, stocks, bonds, you name it. Some of his regular clients, who greatly appreciated his services, even went so far as to give him pieces of property. When he finally retired in the 1970s, he not only had a clean record, but a healthy "investment portfolio."

Another "male madam," Billy Bryars, was said to be the son of a multi-millionaire Texas oilman. According to a book by news reporter Paul Young, *L.A. Exposed*, Bryars, once in Hollywood, devoted his energies to producing gay porn and establishing a bordello at the summit of Laurel Canyon.

In Anthony Summers' provocative book, *Official and Confidential: The Secret Life of J. Edgar Hoover*, the author detailed episodes at the Del Charro Hotel in La Jolla where the FBI chief often went with his longtime lover and assistant director, Clyde Tolson.

Bryars is alleged to have sent strapping young men in a limousine to their hotel suite for "love in the afternoon." Many of these sexual escapades took place under the "no seeing" eyes of FBI agents.

In 1973, Bryars came under surveillance by the Los Angeles Police Department, which was investigating him for alleged trafficking in kiddie porno. During extensive interviews with the police, a number of hustlers were rounded up and interrogated. During the course of the investigation, at least three "boy whores" admitted being delivered to Hoover and Tolson for sexual liaisons.

One tantalizing detail emerged from this investigation. Within the hustler world, Hoover was known as "Mother John," Tolson as "Uncle Mike."

When Howard Hughes didn't have need for their services, **Randolph Scott** and **Cary Grant** made love to each other. "Scott is an Adonis," said Louis B. Mayer upon seeing his screen test. The actor didn't exactly agree. "I suppose I was good looking, not spectacular." In his inarticulate ramblings about homosexuality, he uttered this statement: "If a man is for men, and it's in most walks of life, I can buy that." "Randolph Scott was tall, blond, and handsome," said the actress Anne Baxter. "Who cares if he was Cary Grant's better half or not?" In addition to Grant and Hughes, Scott also had a torrid affair with Gary Cooper in the early days of Hollywood. That we can understand—but Fred Astaire? Both of the photos (right) show the two handsome stars during unguarded private moments in the home they shared in the 1930s.

In addition to Scott and Hughes, Grant's male lovers also included Cooper, along with Noël Coward, playright Clifford Odets, and Cole Porter. Among his first-rate female seductions were the tobacco heiress Doris Duke, Grace Kelly, Ginger Rogers, and Fay Wray of *King Kong* fame.

Cary Grant was once arrested in the men's room of a department store, caught in the act of fellatio with a male employee. A quick police payoff avoided exposure. In 1969 the police appeared at his house based on a complaint filed by a mother that he had picked up her teenage son on the road and propositioned him. Nothing came of the case. The woman, for reasons known only to herself, abruptly dropped the complaint.

[For movie trivia buffs, Grant's first surrendered his cherry at the age of sixteen in New York City. His seducer was Francis Renault, a well-known female impersonator of his day. Later in life, his co-star Marlene Dietrich denied all rumors of an involvement with Grant. "I had no feelings for him—he was a homosexual."]

June Allyson & Van Johnson

Yesterday's Versions of America's Sweethearts

Hollywood at the end of World War II was the right place for **June Allyson** and **Van Johnson**. Together, they reigned as "America's Sweethearts," often starring together in light comedies and musicals.

Thousands of returning servicemen were arriving in Los Angeles from the war zones of the Pacific or the battlefields of Europe, hoping to find work in the movie industry.

Van told his gay pals, "June and I had our pick of these guys. California in the 1940s was heaven itself if you wanted to get screwed. Both June and I wanted that a lot, and we had our fill. If only I could go back and live those glory days again."

June was billed as "The Girl Next Door," Van as "The Boy Next Door," a title he shared with Tom Drake, his occasional lover.

America's two sweethearts were showcased together on screen in the 1944 *Two Girls and a Sailor* co-starring Gloria DeHaven. Starry-eyed young girls flocked to see Van, who also drew more gay fan mail than any other man at MGM. June was "the girl we fought WWII for, and we wanted to come home to her," wrote one G.I.

Louis B. Mayer wasn't satisfied with June and Van being just on-screen lovers. He virtually ordered them to have a romance off screen, the details of which would be played up in the movie magazines.

"THE GIRL NEXT DOOR"

WHO SEDUCED TWO FUTURE U.S. PRESIDENTS

"June Allyson and I appeared on Broadway in <u>Panama Hattie</u>. The scene-stealing bitch could always draw attention to herself if she heard that some V.I.P. like Clark Gable was in the audience. She would trip or fall down as the chorus made its way off stage. That staged act always brought clapping from the audience when she quickly navigated herself up and blew a kiss to the crowd as she made her belated exit."

—Betsy Blair

June had known Van since her Broadway days, and she knew he liked guys. Because she believed that Mayer knew everything, she was shocked that he didn't know that one of his leading stars was a homosexual. Nonetheless, she agreed to date Van, feeling it would be good publicity for America's two sweethearts to be reconfigured as a romantic duo. "After all," June said, "the movies are nothing if not fantasies."

When Van agreed to date her—also for publicity reasons—Mayer smiled in glee. "You're one lucky gal," he told June. "Every bobbysoxer in America is swooning over Van."

June Allyson and **Van Johnson** may have been America's sweethearts in the mid-1940s, but they confined their love-making to what took place in front of the camera. Off camera, they aggressively pursued handsome young men, often the same ones.

"One night Van called me and begged me to go with him to Hedda Hopper's party," Allyson said. The columnist had threatened Van that if he didn't show up with Allyson, she'd hint in her column that he was a homosexual. "The next day in her column, she praised Van but knocked me," Allyson said. "I always got some barb from the bitch. Noting my Peter Pan collars, she once asked if there was something wrong with my neck. The next time I saw her I wore a low cut gown. Even then she attacked me, saying my 'lack of endowment' meant I'd never compete against Kathryn Grayson. Kathryn had the largest boobs at MGM."

All the fan magazines photographed the two "lovers" as they attended premieres together, went to night clubs together, or showed up as a couple at industry functions. Fan magazines announced that their marriage would happen "any day now."

In 1946, the *National Lampoon* defined June as Worst Actress of the Year. Van won an equivalent award as Worst Actor of the Year.

Thousands of returning servicemen did not want a *femme fatale*, dreaming instead of coming home to a girl like June. One sailor in the South Pacific wrote her: "You make me think of the girls in my high school class." A B-29 pilot wrote, "I just like to look at your picture and dream about the States and girls like you." In her heyday, she got more fan mail than two of Hollywood's most sultry beauties, Hedy Lamarr and Lana Turner.

June and Van were brutally honest with each other, each admitting they were "boy crazy."

Often, when Van "discovered" a well-endowed young man who swung both ways, he fixed the guy up on a date with June. There were rumors at MGM that they indulged in three-ways, but Van in later years adamantly denied that.

The Van/June alliance evolved into such a box office draw that their onscreen mating continued in other pictures after her marriage to Dick Powell. The duo appeared together in such movies as *High Barbaree* in 1947, a Navy flyer's life story told in flashback, and *The Bride Goes Wild* in 1948 in which June played an illustrator and Van a children's book author.

Little Ella Geisman, born October 7, 1917 in the Bronx, was too poor to afford dancing lessons, but she saved enough pennies to go see every Fred Astaire and Ginger Rogers movie ever made. After each screening, she'd return home and imitate their dance steps.

Then one day a tree fell on her, as she was riding her bike. Only eight years old at the time, the tree broke half the bones in her body. In her steel brace, she cried out, "Oh, mama, I'll never be a dancer."

Changing her name to June Allyson, little Ella not only learned to walk again, but to dance. She landed roles in Broadway musicals such as *Best Foot Forward* that led to a contract at Metro-Goldwyn-Mayer, where she repeated the role in the movies.

Studio chief Louis B. Mayer said, "She's not pretty. She certainly isn't sexy. She sings fairly well. She doesn't dance all that well, either. But she's got something. Hire her!"

> "I never told any of my real secrets in my auto-biography," **June Allyson** confessed to Van Johnson. "Jimmy Cagney was a great friend of Richard [Dick Powell] when he was married to Joan Blondell. I inherited him as a friend when I married Richard.
>
> "Jimmy got his start as a female impersonator. He often showed up for dinner with us in drag. Out there in America the fans never knew what their favorite stars were doing—even *moi*. Jimmy had the hots for that Audie Murphy boy, the war hero. He chased a lot of other boys, too. Yeah, tough guy Jimmy Cagney! I never wrote such crap in my book. If I'd really spilled the beans on Hollywood, I would have had a best seller."

The various studios already had blonde bombshells like Betty Grable and Lana Turner. What Louis B. Mayer wanted at MGM was The Girl Next Door, a perky archetype, someone wholesome and sweet—or at least someone who appeared wholesome and sweet on the screen.

June's husky voice—"like Jimmy Durante's"—enchanted audiences, as did her pageboy hairdo and Peter Pan collars. At five-foot one-inch, June weighed only 99 pounds.

She never exaggerated her talent. "I have big teeth, I lisp. My eyes disappear when I smile. My voice is funny. I don't sing like Judy Garland or dance like Cyd Charisse. But women identify with me. Our soldiers in World War II desired Betty Grable or Rita Hayworth, but I was the kind of gal they took home to meet mom."

During her Broadway appearance, Dick Powell, the crooner/actor, came backstage with his then-wife, Joan Blondell, to congratulate Allyson on her performance.

From that night on, the Powell/Blondell marriage was all but over. Powell claimed that June was "the cutest thing he'd ever seen." June admitted that Powell "gave me palpitations and shortness of breath just to look at him."

Lucille Ball was one of the stars of *Best Foot Forward*. One day when June was shooting a scene, Desi Arnaz appeared on the set. Lucille introduced Desi to June.

"Before he left that day, Desi asked me for my phone number," June confessed later in life.

"I knew I shouldn't, but I found him dazzling, and I was eager to begin my experiences as a woman."

That weekend Desi came to visit June and stayed until midnight. "I turned her on to sex," Desi later bragged to his gay friend, Cesar Romero, who was in love with Desi at the time. "She couldn't get enough—a true nympho. She wore me out, and I once took on all the gals at Polly Adler's famous bordello in New York."

"If June wore Desi out, that was some accomplishment," Romero claimed. "He could go all night. Never could get enough."

Once "Ricky Ricardo" taught her the joys of sex, June wanted it more and more.

While waiting for Powell to make up his mind, and in between routine pick-ups, June began dating David Rose, who at the time was still married to Judy Garland. Judy had become her friend, and confided in her that she and Rose were separated.

Judy gave her the green light for an affair with Rose but warned her, "He won't go down on me, which is one of my favorite things. Maybe you'll have better luck with him than I did. He's yours. David and I are finished."

By 1945, rumors were already sweeping through Hollywood about what June in her tell-nothing autobiography called "the nymphomaniac thing." She falsely claimed in her 1982 bio that "I was still a virgin when I married," which brought a great laugh to Desi. She admitted that her critics interpreted that "sweet young thing image as a pose and that I really craved sex."

Her critics were right this time. "She's no Goody Two Shoes; she's Goody Round Heels," said her critics—meaning a girl easily toppled backward into bed.

Privately, Mayer ordered her to drop Rose, who had forced Judy to have an abortion. "He's wrong for your image."

Although sleeping around, June continued to pursue Dick Powell, but found him "a hard man to get to the altar." In the interim, she often settled for a quick pick-up. Veronica Lake, no one to cast stones, referred to June as "Motel Betty."

Since her relationship with Van was strictly platonic, June needed a randy, red-blooded, heterosexual male. Van at the time was having a hot affair with the handsome bisexual British actor Peter Lawford. Doing June a favor, he passed Peter Lawford over to her. She found Lawford handsome and charming but she had problems with him in bed.

June complained to Judy that, unlike Judy's former husband Rose, Lawford preferred only oral sex. "Enjoy it," Judy said. "If you want to get fucked, take on one of the grips at MGM. It's best to get them during the day before they go home to their wives."

Both Van and Lawford knew the dashingly handsome Robert Stack, who was seducing, one by one, the leading starlets of Hollywood. For a while Stack had been the toy boy of Howard Hughes. June met him at a party at Lawford's home where he was living with his parents, Sir Sidney and Lady Lawford. Stack asked for June's phone

Desi Arnaz (1917-1986) was candid about his sexual conquests. "I don't take out other broads—I take out hookers. The world was my oyster. What I wanted, I needed only to ask for. Your wife is your wife. Fooling around in no way affects your love for her. A marriage is sacred, and a few peccadilloes mean nothing. My wife has her lovers on the side."

Another actor, Roger C. Carmel, seemed to echo Arnaz's sentiments. "What a lech! Anything from thirteen to thirty, he'd chase after."

number and called her the next day for a date.

"We not only kissed on the first date but made love all night," June told both Van and Judy.

"I know what that's like," Judy said. "I've known Robert as David knew Bathsheba."

After Stack and June had dated for two months, he called her and asked her if a friend of his, visiting from the East Coast, could accompany them on their Saturday night date.

"The more the merrier," she told him. After his arrival at her house, Stack introduced her to a handsome young man, John F. Kennedy.

June ended up spending the entire weekend with both the future president and Stack. It was the wildest weekend of her life, or so she claimed to Van. She found JFK a "God-like Casanova, with tremendous sex appeal."

"He could literally charm the pants off a gal," she claimed. She revealed very personal details. The dashing young man called his penis his "implement," and seemed obsessed with sex. He wanted to enter a girl through both the back and front door. "I'd never had anal sex before until I met him," she said. "At first I resisted but he overcame my reluctance. Frankly, it's not my favorite thing, and it hurts."

June found Stack far more romantic than JFK. "I think Jack doesn't really like women," she later said. "He wants to seduce them and then wants them out of his way while he reads and talks endlessly on the phone. He was sort of a 'Slam, Bam, Thank You, Ma'am' kind of lover. Robert told me that Jack likes the chase more than the conquest. 'He's a hunter,' Robert said. 'Once the act is over, Jack wants to move on to the next conquest.'"

JFK never called June again. Or so she said at the time.

She later revised her story. Although she'd claimed at first that he never called her again, she told a different version after he became president. "Jack got very serious over me. Before he got married, he proposed marriage to me. I turned him down, preferring to stay married to Richard." [She called Dick Powell "Richard." By the time Kennedy had become president, she had long ago married Powell.]

"I know I broke Jack's heart," June later claimed, perhaps falsely. "He married Jackie on the rebound. She was definitely

When **June Allyson** met **Peter Lawford**, she claimed, "We laughed a lot. He reminded me of Jack Kennedy. Both Jack and Peter had the same charm and fun-loving ways. I could not imagine that Jack would one day become the president of the United States. When I met him, I didn't even know that his father had been Ambassador to England. And, of course, I had no idea that Peter would one day become Jack's brother-in-law when he married Patricia."

Dick Powell (1904-1963) looked like part of a romantic duo when he posed with **Joan Blondell**, his second wife. Unknown to most Hollywood biographers, he had an affair with Marion Davies, his co-star in *Hearts Divided*, in 1936. She was the philandering mistress of press baron William Randolph Hearst at the time.

Powell also shacked up with Ruby Keeler, his co-star in *Forty-Second Street* in 1933, and with Ginger Rogers, his co-star in *20 Million Sweethearts* in 1934. He seduced Evelyn Keyes, "Scarlett O'Hara's Little Sister," and also actress/director Ida Lupino. Lupino said he was the most "hygienic" lover she'd ever had.

his second choice. I was the first choice. He told me that repeatedly. Perhaps it's just as well. Jackie made a far better First Lady than I could ever have."

June later said that the most exciting headline she ever read was not about the Nazi or Japanese surrender in 1945, but another tabloid headline: JOAN BLONDELL AND DICK POWELL SEPARATE. In the wake of that article, after many months of delay, Powell and June were married on August 19, 1945 and would remain so until his death from cancer on January 2, 1963.

Throughout the course of her marriage to this much older man, June continued to sleep with other guys. He obviously knew about it because he was a Hollywood insider and must have heard at least some of the gossip.

By the late 40s, June was known as a virtual slut throughout Hollywood, although the mainstream press never picked up on that. At one point, she candidly admitted, "I'm anything but the perfect wife."

Joan Blondell waited for vengeance. Her revenge took the form of a novel she wrote entitled *Center Door Fancy*, published in 1972. In it, the character of Amy was clearly inspired by the life and personality of June Allyson. Joan's choice of the name "Amy," of course, derived from the selfish sister in *Little Women* who steals Jo's boyfriend and marries him herself.

In her novel, Blondell wrote: "Doesn't he know about his Amy? Everybody else does. Her reputation is in the public domain. She's a tramp dressed like a little kid. She was a call girl in New York—exhibitions her specialty."

Ginger Rogers once said about June: "She's the girl every man wants to marry and the girl every woman wants as a friend." That was hardly true. Hollywood wives knew never to leave their husbands alone with June.

Powell and June became best friends with Ronald Reagan and his wife, the Oscar-winning Jane Wyman. June and Powell, but mostly Powell, played a major role in American history when he convinced their mutual friend Reagan to switch his alliance from the Democratic Party to the Republican Party.

Powell accurately predicted that his friend Ronald would one day be either senator or governor from California— "even President of the United States. Ronnie's got the fever in him."

After Reagan's divorce from Wyman in 1949, he had a brief fling with June. As June later admitted to Van, "I was the one who had to seduce Ronnie. It was just a two-week fling. I was mad at Richard [a reference to Powell] at the time, and Ronnie was between engagements. Nothing came of it. We remained friends."

After Reagan married starlet Nancy Davis in March of

Actor **Robert Stack** (right) was "the swinging bachelor of Hollywood." When he was joined by young **Jack Kennedy** on one of his so called "pussy expeditions," there were two swinging bachelors in Tinseltown. Stack once bragged to JFK that his sister-in-law, Lee Radziwill, said, "You kiss better than Farley Granger." Perhaps that was because Granger was secretly gay. Stack had starred with Radziwill during her one disastrous attempt at an acting career.

Yet another actor, the comedian, Jerry Lewis, proclaimed JFK, "One of the great cunt men of all times—except for me."

1952, the friendly quartet continued to gather for dinners, except Nancy had replaced Wyman as one of the foursome guest.

One of the strangest dinners June ever recalled was when the Reagans invited them to dine at their home with Elizabeth Taylor and Eddie Fisher. Fisher had recently left his wife Debbie Reynolds to run off with siren Elizabeth, in the wake of the airplane crash death of Elizabeth's husband, the producer Mike Todd.

"Because of the tension in the room—after all, Eddie and Elizabeth were outcasts in the movie colony—I kept calling Elizabeth 'Debbie' all evening," June said.

At first Elizabeth excused her. But when June made a subsequent slip of the tongue, Elizabeth said. "Why don't you call me George? Just call me George."

June was always falling for her leading man, and often had affairs with them, although there were no sparks between Humphrey Bogart and her when she played opposite him in the 1953 *Battle Circus*.

She was more frequently cast as the wife of James Stewart, beginning with the 1949 *The Stratton Story,* continuing with *The Glenn Miller Story* in 1953 and as Stewart's wife once again in *Strategic Air Command* in 1955.

"We were thrown together on screen so much that it just happened," June told Van, who had remained her confidant. "Jimmy stammered and stuttered on screen, but he was dynamite in bed. That guy knew how to hit the spot."

June later revealed that she felt "honored and in good company," by Stewart's sexual attentions, since he had been previously linked to her girlhood idol, Ginger Rogers, as well as Marlene Dietrich, Olivia de Havilland, Jean Harlow, Katharine Hepburn, Grace Kelly, Rosalind Russell, Lana Turner, Margaret Sullavan, Loretta Young, and even Henry Fonda.

In June's words, one of her leading men became the "love of my life." He was Alan Ladd, a short, blond, good-looking, and rather tight-lipped guy who was born in Arizona in 1913. He eventually drifted to

"*The Stratton Story* tells a touching, human story of triumph over crushing odds with a warmth and sensitive appreciation for sentiment."
— THE NEW YORK TIMES

JAMES STEWART · JUNE ALLYSON
The STRATTON STORY

In *The Stratton Story*, **June Allyson** and **James Stewart** were viewed as a wholesome couple without any particular sexual chemistry. "There was enough chemistry for an explosion when Jimmy crawled into your bed," Allyson told Lucille Ball. "You know, still waters run deep. Some of the men who bragged the most couldn't deliver in bed. Jimmy could. I met him before he married Gloria, his faithful wife. We actually contemplated marriage. The poor dear weighed only 154 pounds when we shacked up, and he stood six feet, four inches tall. I'm an awful cook. If I'd married him, his weight would have dropped down to at least a hundred pounds."

Although the marriage of **Ronald Reagan** and **Jane Wyman** ultimately turned poisonous, there were some happy times, as seen above when they were skating together. Throughout their marriage, neither of them was faithful to each other, Wyman seducing her leading men, Reagan his leading ladies. At least Reagan admitted he had "Leadingladyitis."

When she met Reagan, Wyman actively pursued him but he didn't seem interested at first. She called and invited him "to have cocktails at my place." The future President of the United States rather innocently asked, "What for?"

25

Hollywood where he became a grip at Warner Brothers.

In the beginning he played mostly bit parts; you can catch a glimpse of him as a reporter in the screening room in a scene from Orson Welles' *Citizen Kane* (1941).

He married agent Sue Carol, who pushed him into stardom. From the beginning, she knew he was bisexual but "overlooked" that in pursuit of her greater goal, which was stardom for her husband.

In 1942 he shot to fame as the laconic gunman in *This Gun for Hire*. Just as June had teamed with Van, Ladd's mating with Veronica Lake proved dynamite at the box office in the 1940s.

Ladd came into June's life when they co-starred together in *The McConnell Story* in 1955. This was a weepy fictional biography of a jet test pilot and his understanding wife, a role June had long ago become used to.

"We were both married at the time," June said, "Alan to Sue and me to Richard. We couldn't help ourselves. We fell in love."

The film was a wartime love story about an actual pilot, Captain Joseph McConnell, the most visible and decorated jet pilot fighter of the Korean War. After shooting down 16 enemy MiGs, the pilot met his death in 1954 during a test run of the new, and then experimental, F-86, a nuclear-capable fighter jet. Because of what was later diagnosed as a missing bolt, his plane crashed to earth near Edwards Air Force Base in California. In their roles as McConnell and his wife, both Ladd and Allyson were appropriately brave, courageous, patriotic, and (in Allyson's case) supportive and demure.

In 1950 both Ladd and June were voted America's Favorite Actor and Favorite Actress.

Their affair blossomed, but in the end they decided to go back to their spouses, whom they'd never left, really. "It was the hardest decision that either of us ever made," June said. "Even after we parted, Alan and I still talked for hours on the phone. I loved him until the day he died."

He sent her a recording of "Autumn Leaves," and she played it for years and wept. Tears welled in her eyes when she recalled that he attempted suicide over her on November 1, 1962. He was

"Well, I love her and I never loved you," **Eddie Fisher** told Debbie Reynolds before he ditched her for **Elizabeth Taylor**. As for his new bride, he told his cronies, "Elizabeth is beautiful, a famous Hollywood movie star, but as far as I am concerned, she can also be a pain in the ass, a spoiled brat."

Opinions of Fisher were often not kind. Debbie said, I don't know what to compare him to. He's like an elevator that can't find the floor." Dean Martin said, "The reason I drink is because when I'm sober I think I'm Eddie Fisher."

"What's the worst thing I could do to lose any support I have from the public?" asked Jackie Kennedy. "Run off with Eddie Fisher."

Jerry Lewis, **Dean Martin**'s longtime partner, claimed that, "There was never any stopping my partner, and there was no stopping women once they'd set eyes on him."

Early in their relationship, according to Lewis, Martin established the ground rules, asserting, "A real man has a wife and kids—and whatever he can get on the side."

"And Dean could get plenty," Lewis said. "He was handsome and suave and funny beyond compare, and I wanted to be just like him—to the extent that anatomy allowed. Dean could get women before he had a dime in his pocket. I had to wait."

found in a pool of his own blood, a gun beside him. A .38 caliber bullet had to be removed from his heart. The star survived until January 29, 1964, when he died of an acute overdose of alcohol and sedatives. Dick Powell had died the previous year of cancer.

Helping June get over Ladd was none other than Dean Martin, whom she'd met when he was performing with Jerry Lewis at Slapsie Maxie Rosenbloom's in Hollywood. "She fell for Dean right away," said her blonde bombshell companion Lana Turner. "I heard she became a regular ringsider night after night, even following Dean to Las Vegas. I'd had Dean myself and knew what a lucky gal June was."

Even if Powell hadn't heard any of the gossip, and assuming he could read, he learned of his wife's infidelities in an exposé that blared across the pages of *Confidential* magazine, the leading scandal magazine of the 1950s.

In July 1955, the magazine ran an article: HOW LONG CAN DICK POWELL TAKE IT?

The article claimed that "she is one little book that can't be judged by its cover." It also charged that Powell had been "plucking his pretty bride out of tangles with other men for most of their 10 years of married life."

When this exposé was released, June was at the peak of her popularity. She and Grace Kelly were the only two women on the top ten list of box office stars.

Confidential not only cited Alan Ladd as her love, but also reported on her torrid affair with Martin.

Running a picture of a smiling, waving Martin, D. Loring Taylor in *Confidential* wrote: "When married crooner Dean Martin went to Las Vegas to fill a club date, little June Allyson tagged along, and their after-hours shenanigans raised plenty of eyebrows."

June and Judy often discussed their lost loves over the phone lines. "Judy said it all when she sang about the man who got away," June claimed.

"With Alan and Richard dead, my own life fell apart," June confessed. "I had a series of nervous breakdowns. A disastrous rebound marriage to Richard's hairdresser. I was too much of a coward to commit suicide, so I tried to drink

Alan Ladd was pleased when he first met **June Allyson** in 1954. "At last... a leading lady who could look up to me even when wearing high heels." Within days an infatuation turned to love, and the press got wind of their affair, planting "blind items" in Hollywood columns. Both Allyson and Ladd were supposed to be happily married to other people at the time. When Sue Ladd encountered Allyson at a party, it was rumored that she was tempted to shove her into the swimming pool. Dick Powell took the news of his wife's infidelity calmly—he was used to it. When Sue called him to tell him, "You know my husband is madly in love with your wife," he listened politely. "Isn't everyone?" he asked before putting down the phone.

"When I first met **John Wayne**, he told me that he'd had blow-jobs from only two people in his life—John Ford for one, Marlene Dietrich for another," June Allyson revealed to Van Johnson, who specialized in blow jobs.

"Tell the Duke to come up and see me sometime," Johnson shot back. "Don't bother," Allyson warned him. "There's not enough there to mess up your mouth with." Allyson claimed that Wayne confided to her, "I can't be a philanderer—it makes me feel cheap and dirty. With you, I feel our affair can be clean."

"It was a bit too clean, if you ask me," Allyson said.

myself to death."

She didn't give hairdresser Glenn Maxwell the dignity of even mentioning his name in her autobiography. But she married him on October 13, 1963, divorcing him on April 20, 1965. She charged spousal abuse and also claimed that he'd cashed bad checks to pay for his mounting gambling bills.

"I left him," she later said. "I took him back. I started divorce proceedings. I dropped the proceedings. I did it again. I got the divorce. I remarried him. I left him. I was so confused, so unhappy, so fearful of being alone. I went back. And more and more, I sought relief in wine."

She married Maxwell again on April 17, 1966, divorcing him on March 17, 1970.

She seemed on a downward spiral and a continued descent into alcoholism. Then John Wayne came into her life, inviting her for sails on his yacht *The Blue Goose*. Although she shared The Duke's bed on a few nights, she later confessed, "There was no chemistry there. I loved him dearly, but we decided to be friends, not lovers."

Between husbands, one of her longest romances was with Dirk Wayne Summers, the writer/director. She was unable to lure him into marriage, and she constantly complained about this to Judy. The paparazzi of the 60s often took candid shots of them as they traveled to London, Rome, or Paris. He continued to turn down her proposals.

They were photographed at the deluxe Hotel du Cap Eden-Roc at Cap d'Antibes, sharing the same suite once occupied by Marlene Dietrich and a very young man named John F. Kennedy. In London they stayed at Hugh Hefner's Mayfair penthouse, where everybody had had a tryst before them.

At long last, June fell in love again, this time with Dr. David Ashrow, a dentist. She married him on October 30, 1976. He was at her bedside when she died on July 8, 2006.

In 1985, June had come back into public awareness by becoming the national spokeswoman for Depend, a manufacturer of disposable briefs, undergarments, and pads for adults with bladder control and incontinence issues. Thanks to the barrage of nationwide TV commercials which ensued, she raised national awareness about this once-taboo subject. "I wanted to call attention to this unfortunate condition, but also wanted to let the world know I am still here."

June confided to Judy and Van that autumn was the saddest time in her life, a season for regrets. "When the leaves start to fall, I get out my recording of 'Autumn Leaves,' the one dear, dear Alan sent me. I play it over and over again and cry like it was yesterday. Everybody has a 'What If?' in their lives."

MARRIED TO A STRANGER. Shortly after this picture of the happy couple was taken, **June Allyson** discovered that, contrary to what the movie magazines claimed, Joan Blondell was not **Dick Powell**'s first wife. At the age of 21, he'd married his childhood sweetheart, Mildred Maund, "to prove my manhood," he confessed.

"The studio wanted me to keep the marriage hidden. I was their bachelor star. The gay blade. Available. As a never married bachelor, I attracted more fans who dreamed they might be the gal for me."

In her later years, her career a distant memory, **June Allyson** asked, "What's become of us MGM princesses?" She'd talked to Judy Garland in London, and both of them admitted that each of them was drinking too much.

"Judy was sympathetic about my drinking—she was struggling with uppers and downers herself," Allyson claimed. Although she'd just married another gay husband, Mickey Deans, Garland was talking about her death. "If I ever die, Junie, make sure they put me in a white casket—and that everybody wears white and yellow."

June Wasn't Van's Only Leading Lady

With Elizabeth Taylor

With Lana Turner

Modern Screen

MAY
15¢

DELL

Van Johnson's smiling, freckled face adorned many a movie magazine during his heyday in the 1940s. *Modern Screen*'s cover featured an interview with the star's father, who proclaimed "that's my boy!"

Keenan Wynn said, "Dad got it all wrong. Van was my boy at the time, although I had to share him with others—many others." Wynn's relationship with Johnson "heated up" when they were both cast in *Somewhere I'll Find You*, a WWII drama starring Clark Gable and Lana Turner. "Gable had Lana to fuck at night, and I had Van," Wynn told friends. "A cozy arrangement, wouldn't you say?"

OH, NO!

TELL US THAT IT ISN'T SO!

AMERICA'S BOBBYSOXER'S HEARTTHROB WAS INTO *GUYS!*

"Van Johnson will be a dancer
For his snake hips he'll be known,
You'll soon see him performing
Before the English heir to the throne."

Class prophecy 1934, as predicted in the Rogers High School (Newport, RI) yearbook

When Van Johnson died on December 12, 2008, aged 92, the world took little note of his passing. Only his aging fans, people who attended movies during World War II or during the early 50s, recalled that he, along with his female equivalent June Allyson, was widely known as "America's Sweetheart."

Born one rainy dog day (August of 1916) in Newport, Rhode Island, Van in school became known for his dazzling smile. A shock of red hair crowned suntanned freckled cheeks.

In time, he came to represent the fantasy world that Hollywood in the 1940s and 50s portrayed in such movie mags as *Photoplay*.

When Van was three years old, his mother, Loretta Johnson, abandoned her family and moved back to Brooklyn. As a consequence, his paternal Swedish grand-

Van Johnson was called a "daydreamer" when growing up in Rhode Island. His schoolmates reported that he was shy around girls. "That's because I didn't want anything they had to offer," Johnson later told his gay pals. "I was far more interested in their boyfriends." When he performed with his dance class in a vaudeville show—"and smelled my first greasepaint"—he decided that a show business career was for him. He also found out that it was fairly easy to seduce fellow actors. "Most of them can be had," he later recalled. "Even if they're straight, they're the kind of guys who put on makeup."

Cross-dressing **Dan Dailey,** a gay song-and-dance man, was rumored to have seduced more young actors on the Fox lot than any other performer. "I didn't want to make it with Charles Coburn or Frank Morgan—who would?" he told friends. "But there weren't many who escaped me. I even got John Payne one night. William Lundigan dropped trou for me, and Gene Kelly didn't get away either. But I turned down Jayne Mansfield."

mother came to Newport to take care of him and his father, Charles E. Johnson. Van's father was cold and distant, and Van felt unloved as a child.

In later life, Van claimed, "I hated my father."

He dreamed of Hollywood and collected movie star pictures. His bedroom walls were lined with glossy photographs of Clark Gable, Johnny Weissmuller, George Raft, and James Stewart. His all-time favorite was Cary Grant.

Van's obsession with show business infuriated his father, who was horrified when his son enrolled in Dorothy Gladding's Dancing School. "You'll graduate from it a queer," Charles warned him. Van mowed lawns and shoveled snow in winter to make the $3-a-month tuition.

He had his first sexual encounters at Rhode Island's Quigley Beach Bathhouse where he found summer work, sweeping out the stalls. In some of those stalls he met men who, after he entered, locked the door behind him, inviting him into their beds.

From there, he began to walk the waterfront where he met young sailors from the local naval base. By the time he was seventeen, this love-starved young man had become skilled at both fellatio and bottoming for these horny older boys in blue.

Gable, as a sexual fixation and role model, was soon abandoned when Van discovered the cinematic charms of Spencer Tracy. In later life, he said, "I saw all his movies. They appealed to the drama queen in me. But mostly I went to musicals, seeing anything with Fred Astaire and Ginger Rogers. They were my idols. After seeing *Top Hat* in 1935, I danced all the way home until some street toughs tossed rocks at me."

Saying good-bye to Newport in the autumn of 1935, Van set out for New York with just five dollars in his pockets. He wanted to make it big on Broadway. He arrived by train at Grand Central Station. In the days and weeks ahead, he found many older men willing to take in a strapping, handsome young man. "A pretty boy never has to go hungry in New York," Van later said.

Soon, Van was thrilled to be dancing in a New York show, pulling in $15 a week. The gig ended too soon, and his money ran out. Fortunately, he was soon cast as a male dancer in Leonard Sillman's *New Faces of 1936*.

At this same time, he met another struggling young actor, Keenan Wynn, the son of the famous comic Ed Wynn. In later years, Van confessed to his New York neighbor, Greta Keller, the Austrian chanteuse, that "Keenan and I bonded from that first night. We were lovers on and off for fifteen years."

Keenan introduced Van to Eve Abbott, nicknamed Evie. Born in Buffalo in 1914, she would marry Keenan and have

Johnson's best "gal pal," **June Havoc**, sister of Gypsy Rose Lee, does a burlesque number herself. Havoc offered her house for romantic trysts between Johnson and Gene Kelly, who had also come to Hollywood to break in as a dancer in the movies.

"Van was very neat," she later said. "He always washed the sheets and left them hanging out to dry for me. I think those two dancers really heated up those sheets."

The homosexual lyricist **Lorenz Hart** had his own way of "auditioning" chorus boys on Broadway. Some of his major conquests included a young Desi Arnaz and a young Van Johnson.

Hart frequented the cheap joints around 45th Street and 8th Avenue in Manhattan, rounding up virile young men for his "queer parties," which became notorious in the Broadway area. Arnaz refused to attend. But Johnson was a regular.

two sons with him until their marriage was dissolved in 1947.

"Nobody could dislike this husky hunk of freckled health," Keenan claimed. "Compared to Van, Evie and I were worldly sophisticates." In time, Van, Evie, and Keenan would become Hollywood's tightest threesome.

Van became a Broadway chorus boy dancing at the Roxy Theater, carrying on "notoriously" with the other chorus boys, as asserted by a manager at the time. "He should have been one of my Roxyettes," the manager said sarcastically.

With Keenan out of town, Van took up with cross-dressing Dan Dailey, another Roxy chorus boy. Tall and handsome, Dailey would become the best hoofer in Fox's major musicals of the 40s, twirling around with Betty Grable in such films as *Mother Wore Tights* (1947). Grable often lent Dailey some of her costumes to wear to drag parties in Hollywood.

In January of 1939, Van got a job as one of the "Eight Men of Manhattan," singing and dancing with the great Mary Martin, who later became Queen of Broadway. They appeared together at the Rainbow Room at Rockefeller Center.

Van and Martin went out together, she with her lesbian girl-friend of the moment, Van with his current BF.

She was the first star to urge him to go to Hollywood—"you've got the stuff"—and try for a career in motion pictures.

In August of 1939, the theatrical producer George Abbott cast Van in the chorus line of the Rodgers and Hart musical *Too Many Girls*, in which a rising young Desi Arnaz also appeared. Desi danced a conga, played the bongo drums, and drew wild applause from the audience.

Van Johnson's friend, MGM cutie **Gloria DeHaven**, left her handsome hunk, John Payne, in Hollywood as she and June Allyson landed in New York. They took up with the emerging team of Jerry Lewis and Dean Martin. Martin made off with Allyson and Lewis got De Haven. The New York press dubbed the quartet "The Fun Foursome."

Lorenz Hart, according to Van, was paying the twenty-two-year-old Cuban's bills and "sucking him off regularly. I too was attracted to Desi. He let me give him blow-jobs, and I didn't have to pay, unlike Larry." Hart was called "Larry" by his intimates. "In no time at all Larry was blowing both Desi and me."

Eddie Bracken, who also appeared in the show, claimed that "every chorus boy in the line-up got around to doing Van during the run of the show. He must have had to take vitamins."

When the movies bought the film rights to *Too Many Girls*, Van headed to Hollywood with Desi, along with George Abbott and Eddie Bracken. Bracken claimed that Desi was oversexed, "but Van handled the problem all the way to the L.A."

Since Lucille Ball had also been cast in the movie version of *Too Many Girls*, Desi had no more sexual use for Van, although he became a close friend of the couple.

In 1940 Van returned to Broadway to appear in a small part in *Pal Joey*, starring Gene Kelly. He was also the understudy for Kelly. June Havoc, then 24, also appeared in the show. "I danced with Van on stage. But backstage he was 'dancing' with Gene.

Lucille Ball and **Keenan Wynn** appeared with Spencer Tracy and Katharine Hepburn in the 1945 film *Without Love*. Ball was hip to the Van Johnson/Wynn affair but she maintained a discreet silence about such matters, especially when talking to Wynn's wife. "What boys do together never really bothered me," Ball said. "I never worried if Desi was out with a boy. It's his gals who pissed me off."

Gene, in fact, asked Van to share his dressing room. Everybody in the musical knew what was going on between those two."

Havoc, incidentally, was the sister of the famous stripper, Gypsy Rose Lee, and she and Van became very close friends.

While Van and Kelly were dancing on stage, at the Ethel Barrymore Theater next door, Ethel Merman was starring in *Panama Hattie*, the Cole Porter hit. In the chorus was a young hopeful, June Allyson, who was understudying for the dynamic but unstable Betty Hutton.

So as it happened, America's two future sweethearts were playing in separate plays immediately next door to each other. "Van and I used to hang out together, meet for a hamburger, go to a movie, especially if Alice Faye were in it," June later recalled. "We both promised we'd go to Hollywood and make it big in musicals ourselves. Van was hung up on Spencer Tracy, and I thought Margaret Sullavan was the cat's pajamas."

Back home during a return visit to Newport, Van got a call from Warner Brothers, who wanted to sign him to a six-month contract at $300 a week. "En route by train to Los Angeles, I think I sang 'California, Here I Come' all the way there," he said.

At Warners, the make-up department dyed his hair black. He was told, "Blond men don't make it in Hollywood. The more rugged type is in. Bogie. Errol Flynn."

Warner didn't know what to do with Van. At the end of his contract, the studio let him go. He knocked on the door of other studios, but no one seemed to want a Broadway hoofer. He used Havoc's shoulder to lean on, and even discussed marrying her, but she was too hip for that kind of proposal.

"Van talked only vaguely about marrying me," Havoc said, "but when Keenan Wynn arrived back in town, I knew where my boy was sleeping."

Van looked up Desi and Lucille, who invited him to Chasen's to cheer him up. The future "Lucy and Ricky Ricardo" introduced Van in the restaurant to Billy Grady, head of talent at MGM. Lucille made a strong pitch for Van, and it was because of her that he was soon awarded a $350-a week con-

In February of 1943, Louis B. Mayer announced to the press that he'd cast **Spencer Tracy** and **Irene Dunne** in a major A-list picture, *A Guy Named Joe,* one of the most famous films to come out of World War II. Van Johnson, then a young, relatively new actor in Hollywood, held both of them in awe. Robert Young had been slated to play the juvenile lead, a pilot named Ted Randall, but at the last minute Mayer pulled the plug on Young and cast **Johnson** instead.

Victor Fleming, who'd directed *Gone With the Wind,* had been assigned to direct the picture. "I was scared shitless," Johnson later confessed. "I was in the big league, and I didn't think I could hold my own." Dunne wasn't too happy to have love scenes with a man fifteen years her junior. Fleming introduced Johnson to her as "Mr. Van Warren."

"The God damn director didn't even know my name," Johnson said. An automobile accident that fractured Johnson's skull might have gotten him booted off the picture during recovery—except for one element in his favor. Spencer Tracy demanded that the studio allow him to finish the picture. He uttered a line that became famous throughout Hollywood: "The kid stays in the picture."

In the photos above, **Spencer Tracy** guides **Van Johnson** both in an airplane (top photo) and in the young pilot's onscreen romance (lower photo) with **Irene Dunne**, who was beginning the long twilight of her fabled 1930s movie career.

tract.

He'd found a studio where he'd remain for many a year, working for the tyrannical and homophobic Louis B. Mayer. After he'd settled in, Desi called Van. "Welcome to Hollywood, my friend. It's good to know you're here if one night I want another one of your hot blow-jobs. You're the best! Lucy is no good at it."

Ironically both Keenan and Van were cast in *Somewhere I'll Find You*, starring Clark Gable and Lana Turner.

Van, Keenan, and Evie were seen everywhere together. Hollywood insiders assumed it was a *ménage à trois*.

Van had a lot of boyfriends in those days, according to Havoc. He was seen with Tom Drake, who also became known as "The Boy Next Door" after he appeared in *Meet Me in St. Louis* with Judy Garland.

Van found himself playing a young doctor with Lionel Barrymore in two Dr. Gillespie movies, nothing very special. His big break came when MGM cast him in *A Guy Named Joe* (1943), co-starring Irene Dunne and Van's idol, Spencer Tracy.

After working with Van and Tracy for a few days, Dunne put in a call to Katharine Hepburn, Tracy's "pal." She informed Kate that "the homosexual fool you live with is madly in love with Van Johnson. He follows Van around the set like a lovesick puppy."

During her evenings, Kate saw more and more evidence that Dunne might be right. Tracy had even placed a glossy studio photograph of a beaming Van beside his bed.

Beginning with Van, Tracy began a series of unrequited crushes he'd develop on handsome leading men in pictures.

Director George Cukor had told him that these men were unobtainable, and Tracy instinctively knew that he was right. If Tracy wanted a young man like Van, he'd have to rent a hustler actor who resembled him. There is no evidence, however, that Tracy ever approached Van and made his desires known.

Having rushed prematurely into middle age, Tracy was graying at the temples and had a paunch. His face was often bloated. Although he could still attract women—and would do so for years to come—he found that in the body-conscious male homosexual world, he was viewed as a "john," which Cukor had to explain to him meant a paying customer.

Cukor later said that "Spencer constantly suffered from these crushes on handsome leading men, and he used his lack of satisfaction in love as an excuse to continue his heavy drinking. He was definitely not Van's

Judy Garland appeared with "the boy next door," **Tom Drake**, in the 1944 movie *Meet Me in St. Louis*. "He was a cute kid, and I would have done him," Garland confessed, "but his heart belonged elsewhere—Merv Griffin, Peter Lawford, Van Johnson, you name 'em."

Oddly enough, MGM was grooming Drake to become "The Next Van Johnson."

It was 1948 when the "happy couple," **Evie Wynn Johnson** and her new husband, **Van Johnson**, posed for this picture. Evie had previously been married to Johnson's best friend, **Keenan Wynn**. Many Hollywood columnists, such as Sheilah Graham, predicted the end of Johnson's career. His fans were outraged. "What a dirty trick to pull on your best friend," wrote one "former" fan. A group was formed called the Motion Picture Research Society. It had only one reason to exist—and that was to boycott any picture starring Van Johnson. What the public didn't know was that Wynn and Johnson were lovers. It was an arranged marriage to squash rumors about Johnson's homosexuality.

type, and Spencer would have embarrassed both of them had he pressed sex onto Van. I'm almost certain that Van would have turned him down."

Instead of with sex, Tracy expressed his love for Van by showing extreme loyalty at the sake of his own career.

Van was a great admirer of the acting style of Tracy and admitted to the film's director, Victor Fleming, that he was "sweating gumdrops" at the prospect of playing scenes with the more gifted older actor.

Two weeks into the shooting of *A Guy Named Joe*, Van was driving with Keenan and Evie, and two servicemen—described as "extraordinarily handsome"—to see a special screening of the Tracy/Hepburn film, *Keeper of the Flame*.

Van had just steered his DeSoto convertible into the junction of Clarington Street and Venice Boulevard when another vehicle sped through a red light and crashed into their car, sending it rolling over.

Van's skull was pierced by the clamp positioned in the top center of the metal frame that held the windshield in place, and which locked the convertible's fabric canopy when it was raised. Thrown to the curb, he fractured his skull and suffered mammoth injuries to his face because of the shattering glass.

As later reported by the hospital, "practically the back of his head was peeled off. Fragments of bone had pierced his brain." Not only that, an artery in his neck had been severed.

A Los Angeles policeman, Roger Flynn, rushed to the scene of the accident which had occurred in that city. However, he noticed that Van's body had been tossed across the municipal border into Culver City. The policeman told a hysterical Keenan that he could not come to Van's aid because he was outside of his jurisdiction. For forty-five minutes, Van lay bleeding to death until a Culver City ambulance could be summoned. He lost three quarts of blood.

At Hollywood Presbyterian Hospital, a surgeon closed up the bleeding artery and literally sewed Van's scalp back on before beginning the very delicate work of coping with the cavity in the once handsome actor's skull.

Glenn Clover, a hospital attendant who saw Van wheeled in, later told the press that "he was almost decapitated."

Louis B. Mayer was called and told that Van was dead on arrival at the hospital

On hearing the news, a grief-stricken Tracy rushed to the hospital and offered to give his own blood for the massive transfusions Van required.

As Van lay near death, Tracy met with both Louis B. Mayer and the director, Victor Fleming. Tracy was told that they were contacting both Peter Lawford and John Hodiak as potential replacements for Van.

Worried about the diminishing popularity of **Van Johnson**, MGM cast him in a piece of fluff called *The Bride Goes Wild*. He played Uncle Bumps, a writer of children's books who actually hated kids. Not wanting to take too big a chance on Johnson alone, Louis B. Mayer cast **June Allyson** opposite him. "Maybe their onscreen magic can work one more time," Mayer said.

Even though it included pies in the face *à la* Mack Sennett, the picture was dismal. "My bobbysoxers have grown up and left me," Johnson told Allyson, "I've got to reinvent myself or my career is over. In the meantime, let's go out and find some hung boys to fuck us."

At that point, Tracy became enraged and started screaming denunciations at both Fleming and Mayer.

Tracy threatened to walk off the picture. Amazingly, even though Mayer had briefly considered replacing Tracy himself, the mogul agreed to shut down the picture until Van recuperated. "*If*," as Fleming said, "he recovers."

While Van was in a hospital bed, undergoing a series of painful and difficult operations, Tracy visited him almost daily, bringing flowers, candies, fruit, or books to read.

Kate Hepburn confided her growing concern about Tracy's obsession with Van to her friends, Anderson Lawler and Kenneth MacKenna. "Spencer is consumed with interest in Van's health. He talks about him day and night. If I try to divert him to another subject, he lashes out at me. Naturally, he uses Van's accident to drink even more heavily than before."

The accident occurred on March 30, 1943, and Van returned to the studio on June 28, against his doctor's orders. Tracy was by his side during the remainder of the shoot, and came in to oversee the intricate makeup needed to make Van ready for the camera by concealing a deep gash in his skull and other scar tissue. When Van developed severe headaches every afternoon, Tracy was at his side, with medication, in the same way that Kate administered to Tracy himself. Van's right arm was very weak following the accident.

Ward Bond, also appearing in the film, later said that he could "see Tracy massaging Van's arm for him, helping him regain his strength." Van tired easily, and shooting the film was difficult. When Van's headaches became too severe, and he grew weak and dizzy, Tracy would often demand that Fleming shut down the picture. "As I wrote John Ford, Tracy was like a lioness protecting its cub," Bond recalled.

The film brought major stardom to Van, as wartime audiences flocked to see it. For decades afterward, Van continued to thank Tracy for believing in him and standing by him.

Other joint ventures for the two actors loomed in their future.

In a phone call to her former lover and long-

Married to Ben Gage at the time, **Esther Williams** was having marital problems with her hard-drinking, big-gambling husband when she was cast in MGM's *Easy to Love*. **Van Johnson** would be her co-star. Busby Berkeley was slated to do the big production numbers.

"Same old familiar script," Williams said. "By the time of *Easy to Love*, Van and I were as synchronized as any two swimmers in the pool, having worked together many times before. Through the years, I swam with Van, married him, fought with him, and made love to him—all on camera." What and how much Williams knew about Johnson's private life isn't known. She was discreet in her memoirs.

Esther Williams seductively eyes **John Bromfield** like a *hunk du jour*, but there was no romance between them. She may or not have known that he and Johnson were the real romantic duo during filming—but definitely off screen.

Producer Joe Pasternak walked in on Bromfield while he was taking a shower. "Now I know the reason Van was in love with this stud. He should have hired himself out for porn."

time companion, Laura Harding, Kate said, "Instead of Tracy/Hepburn movies, you're soon going to hear of Tracy/Johnson films."

While filming *Easy to Wed* in 1953, with Esther Williams and pals Lucille Ball and Keenan Wynn, Van fell hard for the handsome actor John Bromfield. "It didn't last," Wynn said. "In those days John was giving it away to all the guys, and didn't want to settle down to become Van's boy."

Back in those days, Van also spent a lot of time going out with Peter Lawford. One day Lady Lawford, Peter's mother, returned home to see Keenan, Evie, and Van in her living room. She promptly left the room and ordered one of her servants to fumigate the place when this "threesome" had departed.

"I don't want homosexuals in our drawing room," she told her son. "If you want them here, then notify me and I will leave while they are here."

It was Lady Lawford herself who told Louis B. Mayer that both her son and Van were gay, and the studio honcho was horrified at the news. MGM at that point maintained a huge investment in Van's career.

In the wake of Lady Lawford's betrayal, Mayer called Van into his office and demanded that "you are to get married—and I mean sooner than later."

It will never be known exactly what transpired between Van and his best friend, Keenan. But a deal was reached. Early in 1947, Evie and Van drove to El Paso, Texas, but in separate cars. In El Paso, they checked into a hotel under assumed names. Van wore a straw hat that concealed most of his face and sunglasses. The next day they drove across the border to Juarez in Mexico, where a quickie divorce terminated the marriage of Evie with Keenan.

That same afternoon, on the winter's day of January 25, 1947, Evie became the first and last Mrs. Van Johnson.

In reacting to the news, Lucille Ball later said, "I couldn't believe it. That sweet kid Desi and I knew had become something else. It looked like he would do anything to protect his star status. But I don't feel sorry for Keenan either. Something about this arrangement stinks. I think Keenan had to agree to it."

After this strange but widely publicized marriage to the wife of his best friend, many young female fans deserted him. Some newspapers called him a "home wrecker." The previous year, in 1946, a popularity poll had defined him as number three at the box office, a higher rating than Clark Gable got when he returned home from the war. Now, however, the bobby-soxers weren't screaming any more. Many of his former fans had grown up and were marrying servicemen returning from the war. Few, if any, seemed to have maintained a crush on Van.

Studio publicist Morgan Hudgins later said, "I think this marriage marked the begin-

Van Johnson (left), **Robert Francis** (center), and **Fred MacMurray** (right) in a tense scene from the box office smash, *The Caine Mutiny* (1954). During the course of the movie, Johnson fell for Francis, a "Golden Boy" of Hollywood who had been promised a big career by his BF, Howard Hughes himself. Like most such promises, Hughes, the billionaire aviator, never delivered.

The picture was a comeback for Johnson, and he was on top again. He wanted a percentage of *Mutiny's* gross. Metro countered with a new contract, but amazingly Johnson turned it down."The only person Van wanted to tie him down and fuck him was Robert Francis," said Edward Dmytryk, the director.

ning of the end of Van's career. He would go on for several years and even have a hit or two, but the peak of his popularity was over."

By 1948, *Screen Guide* was asking, "Is Van Johnson dead at the box office?"

America had moved on in its restless search for another male sweetheart.

In spite of his marriage, one segment of Van's fan base remained loyal. Throughout the 1940s Van had received more gay fan mail than any other star at MGM. Young homosexual men throughout America always had their "gaydar" tuned in on Van. Some of the men mailed him candid shots of themselves with full erections.

Van answered most of his fan letters personally. In a few cases, and although recently married, he enclosed his private phone number. On some occasions when he encountered an exceptionally handsome man with a large endowment, he sent an airline ticket to Los Angeles. Throughout his marriage, he maintained a secret hideaway apartment which he kept for sexual purposes only.

On January 6, 1948, a daughter, Schuyler, was born to Van and Evie. Even after he'd fathered a child, however, he continued to sleep around with young men, often aspirant actors.

As the years went by, Schuyler and her father became alienated. In 2005 she wrote a newspaper *exposé* of her dad for the *Daily Mail* in London.

Van still had some powerful roles in him, appearing in 1948 in *State of the Union* with Katharine Hepburn and his old pal, Spencer Tracy. In the same year he made *Command Decision* with Clark Gable.

Elizabeth Taylor was only a teenager when she was cast in MGM's *The Big Hangover* (1950), co-starring **Van Johnson** in this predictable, silly romantic comedy. Even though still a late teenager, she'd already had experience falling for guys who liked other guys, so she was worldly for her years. She had no illusions about Van Johnson.

He was teamed with Elizabeth once again in the sentimental *The Last Time I Saw Paris* (1954), the last MGM movie he made under contract. It was based on F. Scott Fitzgerald's short story *Babylon Revisited*. Johnson once bragged to Keenan Wynn that "one night I sucked off Nicky Hilton," the former husband of Elizabeth. Did she know? Or, more importantly, did she really care?"

Van's finest motion picture was *Battleground* (1949), a gripping WWII drama of the Battle of the Bulge. One of his last memorable roles was in *The Caine Mutiny* (1954), in which he co-starred with Humphrey Bogart.

During the shoot, he fell in love with Robert Francis, who played the film's handsome young ensign. But Francis was far too interested in playing the field and didn't want to settle down with Van. Also, Howard Hughes was making him better offers. Regrettably, the young actor was soon to die in a plane crash.

Evie and Van Johnson were divorced in 1962 in a bitter proceeding. They had not been "man and wife" for many a year.

Evie later went on record with her reaction to the failure of the marriage. "Mayer decided that unless I married Van, he wouldn't renew Keenan's contract. I was young and stupid enough to let Mayer manipulate me. I divorced Keenan, married Van, and thus became another one of L.B.'s victims."

In 1999 she claimed, "I'm bankrupt—no money—thanks to Van's total lack of appreciation for what I did for him. MGM needed a wife for its Big Star to squash rumors that he was gay. At the time, I was the only woman in Hollywood he could marry and at least guaranteed that his secret would be kept. What could I do? Tell Van's fans that my former husband was fucking him?"

As he aged, his glory days came to an end. Movie roles were far and few between, and most of the films he made were not notable in any way. By the time he appeared in the 1985 *Purple Rose of Cairo*, directed by Woody Allen, Van was virtually an unknown face except to die-hard fans who still remembered him.

He spent some of the last years of his life on the road in dinner theater, where he became a serial seducer of young actors with dreams of making it big in Hollywood like he did. But eventually, even these gullible actors figured out that Van could do nothing for them.

During his final years, he was reduced to paying hustlers to visit his penthouse apartment on East 53rd Street in New York City.

When Van died, he was living in relative obscurity in an assisted-living center in Nyack, New York. Only days before his death on December 12, 2008 he told a nurse, "I don't think I'll make it to Christmas."

It seemed that when **Robert Francis** arrived in town, "all the gay fellows wanted a piece of him," said Vampira, the ghoulish TV host of horror movies.

"Robert believed in sharing what he had with the likes of Paul Newman and Tony Perkins, and so many others. That is, when he wasn't flying high with Hughes, his sugar daddy. He was a true Apollo. Robert was a very sweet boy, and I heard he fucked like a rabbit. He was in such demand. It broke my heart when he died young in an airplane crash. He also broke a lot of male hearts in Hollywood as well. Today his affairs would be splashed all over the tabloids, but back then everything was hush-hush."

"No memoir was more aptly titled than **Lady May Crawford**'s *Mother Bitch*. She was the suffocating mother of Peter Lawford. She not only informed homophobic Louis B. Mayer that Peter was a homosexual, but she denounced her in-laws as well, referring to the Kennedys as "those barefoot Irish peasants." She liked JFK, however, but claimed he "always had his mind down between his legs."

In her memoirs, Lady Crawford wrote this about her son: "Homosexual Peter tried hard to be thought one—by being persistently with Van Johnson."

Even though they lived together for a time, she continued to denounce her son, especially when he married Patricia Kennedy and he became "The First Brother-in-Law."

She referred to her son as "The White House pimp. What a bastard. Peter was such a big mistake! I guess I always knew he should have been born a girl. That's why I dressed him in girl's clothing for years."

"Jackie Kennedy put up with a lot, "Lady Lawford continued. "When she saw a photo of JFK at a Beverly Hills whorehouse, she cried, 'I won't stay with him!' Old Joe Kennedy then quickly offered her a check for one million dollars to remain married to Jack. Jackie was a clever girl—such a businesswoman. She told Joe Kennedy, 'Make it tax free and it's a deal.'"

Good Night, Sweetheart!

In his latter years, all of **Van Johnson**'s boy friends had aged, died, or gone away, and he was reduced to paying male hustlers both at his penthouse apartment on East 53rd Street in New York City and on the road when he toured. When he was offered the starring role in the homosexual play, *La Cage aux Folles*, he said, "I demand the more masculine role. I won't appear in drag." He got his wish, but he nonetheless had to dance in the play. "Gene Kelly I'm not, but I can still shake my buns." His hustlers agreed.

Playing gay every night in some ways helped liberate this 68-year-old star. But Johnson never came out publicly, although he freely talked to his friends like the author Darwin Porter. Johnson told him, "Don't even ask me to pen my memoirs. There may be some teenagers still left from the 1940s who still view me as their romantic hero. It's wrong to take people's illusions from them."

In his Manhattan penthouse, Johnson lived the good life, referring to himself as "the male Doris Day. I made a lot of money. As a tight-fisted Yankee, I invested it well. I have my first buck, believe it or not. Most of my money is tied up in real estate investments."

In contrast, his divorced wife, Evie, and his daughter, Schuyler, no longer lived grandly in Beverly Hills. Because of diminishing finances, they were foced to settle into a dreary tract house in Los Angeles' Coldwater Canyon. "A grip at the studio had a big paycheck compared to what I had to live on," Evie claimed. "I was one of the most important hostesses in Hollywood when I lived with Van. After the divorce, no one would return my calls. I phoned that bitch, **June Allyson**, who had pretended to be such a friend—the hypocrite. The nympho never called back—too busy fucking pickups, I guess."

Homage to America's Sweethearts
Van Johnson & June Allyson

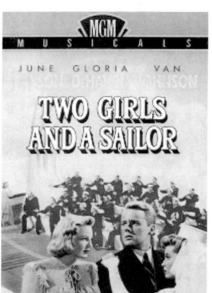

Hollywood's Prince of Darkness
Walt Disney

As has been revealed by a number of controversial biographies, **Walt Disney**, the creator of Mickey Mouse, Dumbo, Cinderella, Donald Duck, Snow White, and Mr. Mickey Mouse had a dark side to his personality.

An anxiety-ridden, chain-smoking alcoholic and lifelong anti-Semite, Disney was a special informant for the FBI in Hollywood, rooting out communists and "subversive" Jews.

According to dozens of sources, he was also a homosexual, and was outed by several underground newspapers after his death.

These included Bill Dakota's *Hollywood Star*, the editor publishing his notarized affidavit *(see the image to the right)* wherein he insisted that his allegations were true.

IT ALL STARTED WITH
A MOUSE

On a winter's day in Chicago in December 5, 1901, a boy was born who would change the entertainment world forever. He was Walter Elias Disney. He came into the world just a few days after occupancy of the White House had passed to "that damned cowboy" [his father's words], meaning Teddy Roosevelt.

His parents were Elias and Flora Disney. An itinerant ne'er do-well, Elias ruled his household with the motto: "Spare the rod, spoil the child."

Growing up in such a brutal household was very rough on young Walt, and those early brutalities may have scarred him for life. When Walt was very young, Elias chased Walt and his older brother, Roy, out of bed at 3:30 in the morning to deliver newspapers.

Growing up on a farm, young Disney became acquainted with sex by watching the animals fornicate. But throughout his youth he expressed no interest in sex himself. He confided to his brother Roy that adolescent girls held no interest for him—in fact, he considered them a nuisance. "They bore me," Walt said. "Their interests are not my own."

Filled with insecurities, and dreading his father's beatings, Walt became a compulsive bed-wetter. "Roy and I slept in the same bed," he once told Disney associates. "I used to wet the bed, and I've been pissing up Roy's leg ever since."

Walt got one of the worst beatings of his life when Elias came home early one afternoon and discovered his son in the master bedroom he shared with Flora. Walt had put on his mother's clothes and made up his face. He was mincing in front of the mirror, pretending to be a girl.

That night Elias beat Walt "to within an inch of his

Walt Disney may have been marred for life by his brutal childhood. He not only inherited many of his father's prejudices, but had to endure this strict fundamentalist parent who believed in corporal punishment and forced child labor.

Throughout his life, Disney was plagued with what one biographer called "sexual inadequacies," which may explain, if the rumors are true, why he turned to virile young men to provide him with the sexual pleasure he could not provide, except in rare instances, to women.

Although his psychosexual conflicts may have driven him to the depths of despair, he brought love and laughter to children everywhere, an intriguing contradiction.

Walt Disney (*left*) and his brother, **Roy Disney**, pose with their star attraction, **Mickey Mouse**, which won a special Academy Award in 1928. The brothers were partners but also had serious sibling rivalry issues. The studio, in fact, was divided into "Walt's Men" or "Roy's Men." Like Walt himself, as a child, the older Roy had to endure long days working the Disney farm to earn his keep. Almost nightly their father marched them to the woodshed where he dispensed his brutal, almost sadistic punishments. The screams of the boys pierced the night.

life," shouting at his son, "I'm not raising a queer under this roof."

As he grew into manhood and served in the Red Cross in Europe during World War II, his attitude toward women did not change. The young males working in the corps had been warned about the venereal diseases "loose" French girls might be carrying.

To enforce the Red Cross warnings, the young men of the Corps were shown a horrible documentary, showing the genitals of both males and females infected with various venereal diseases. Walt later told his comrades, "After seeing that disgusting film, I decided I really hate women."

In the summer of 1923, after the war ended, and after several false starts in Kansas, Walt stuffed his meager belongings into a suitcase and headed for Hollywood. Arriving on the doorstep of Robert Disney, brother of Elias, he told his uncle he needed a place to stay. The uncle agreed, in exchange for five dollars a week in rent.

Walt, who was later joined by his brother Roy, set up a cartoon studio in Hollywood. In 1925, Walt hired a young woman named Lillian Bounds to ink and paint celluloid.

Idaho-born Lillian was then 24 years old. Walt began to take an interest in her. Roy was pleased to see him attracted to a female. Walt paid her $15 a week and, within a relatively short time, he proposed to her. They were married on July 25, 1925.

Lillian didn't really know Walt when she married him, and in her opinion, he had many strange habits. One involved removing the lid from a stinking garbage can to watch maggots devour meat waste. The honeymoon was cut short, and the marriage may not have been consummated by the time they returned to Hollywood.

As the Silent Screen of the late 20s drifted into the Talkies of the early 1930s, Walt created a character based on a mouse he'd had as a pet back in Kansas City. He called it Mortimer Mouse, until Lillian suggested "Mickey Mouse" as punchier and easier to remember. Mortimer later became the name of Mickey's rival for Minnie.

One of Walt's early attempts at filmmaking resulted in a silent film, *Plane Crazy,* featuring a cartoon version of Mickey, which failed. Learning from his mistakes, Walt then crafted an animated talkie entitled *Steamboat Willie.* It was an instant success. From this mouse an empire would be created. The voice associated with Mickie until 1946 was that of Walt himself; after that, Mickie's voice was dubbed over the animation by professional actors.

From all reports, Walt was plagued with sexual impotency, a condition whose symptoms became embarrassingly obvious during his honeymoon, and which returned at various stages until the end of his life. Approaching the ripe age of 29, Lillian practically begged Walt to impregnate her, even though he seemed horrified at the idea. Finally, it worked: Lillian announced that she was pregnant.

A daughter, Diane Marie, was born on December 19, 1933. Some employees of Walt—behind his back, of course—suggested that her birth represented the only time Walt ever had sex with Lillian.

It is believed that most of Walt's employees resented the boss man. The victim of an abusive father, he also treated his employees with disdain. He enforced a stringent dress code—"no facial hair, no cussing." Only he could wear a mustache. He also developed a policy of firing his employees and then rehiring them after "they sweated it out for two or three weeks—it keeps the overpaid bastards on their toes."

Lillian wanted another child, but after her third miscarriage, she and Walt decided to adopt. The result of that decision was a six-week-old daughter, Sharon Mae, who arrived on their doorstep on December 31, 1936.

The years between 1937 and the debut of America's entry into World War II, represented

Hollywood's "Golden Age of Animation." Disney's big entry in those sweepstakes was *Snow White and the Seven Dwarfs*, a big, complicated film which was in production from 1934 to mid-1937. It was the first full-length cel-animated feature in motion picture history, the first ever produced in full color, and the first to be produced by Walt Disney.

At its premiere on December 21, 1937, Snow White received a standing ovation. It was the first animated feature in America and was in Technicolor. It became the most successful motion picture of 1938 and earned more than $8 million, a staggering figure back then.

For *Snow White*, Walt received an Oscar—one of them full size, plus seven miniature Oscar statuettes. In 1940, he followed with such animated features as *Pinocchio* and *Fantasia*. Both of them were failures. Greater glory, however, was on the way.

But en route to that glory, there were serious problems to overcome, as Hollywood insiders learned about Walt's "dark side." In 1941, when the Screen Cartoonists Guild went on strike, Walt hired thugs to break up their gangs. He also publicly defined their strike as a communist plot.

Reportedly, he also joined the America First Movement, opposing U.S. entry into World War II. It was said he attended meetings of the American Nazi Party.

Of course, many of those pro-German sentiments evaporated on December 7, 1941, after the Japanese attack on Pearl Harbor.

By the late 1940s, Disney had survived financial disappointments and setbacks and launched full-length features like *Alice in Wonderland* and *Peter Pan*, projects whose completion had been postponed during the war. Work on *Cinderella* began, and this would become Walt's biggest hit since Snow White.

It was around this time that Walt seemed to launch a one-man war, ranting against communists in Hollywood. He became a founding member of the anti-communist Motion Picture Alliance for the Preservation of American Ideals. In 1947, just as the Cold War was heating up, he testified before the House Un-American Activities Committee.

He named names, and in an outrageous claim, charged that the Screen Actors Guild was part of the communist front. Privately he supplied names of some of his own employees whom he claimed were communists, whether they were or not.

He also became an informant for the FBI. J. Edgar Hoover expressed admiration for what he was doing to clean up Hollywood.

By the early 1960s, the Disney studio was the world's leading producer of family entertainment. Theme parks were on their way, and the Disney studio turned out the blockbuster feature film *Mary Poppins*, released in 1964. The future of the studio, by now a major American empire and to some extent a symbol of the country itself, seemed secure.

Regrettably, Walt died of lung cancer on December 15, 1966, and never saw the opening of Walt Disney World Resort in Orlando. Today what had started out as Walt's little cartoon studio is taking in more than $35 billion a year.

Walt had become a legend, a folk hero of the 20th century. His films touched the hearts and emotions of millions of people around the world, bringing joy and happiness to kids of all ages across the planet.

***

That was and is the public Walt Disney. But with the release of controversial biographies, a very different perception of Walt Disney has emerged. Famed biographer Marc Eliot even entitled his biography of Walt *Hollywood's Dark Prince*.

Walt Disney's Most Devoted Fan:
Adolf Hitler

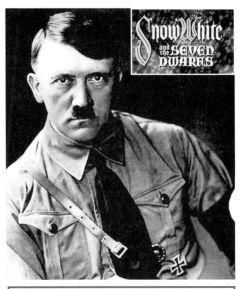

Greta Keller, a *chanteuse* and cabaret singer who entertained supper club crowds in Berlin during the 1930s, claimed that she attended a showing of Disney's *Snow White*, a classic animation adapted from a German fairytale which had been recorded into literary format by the Brothers Grimm. Here's how she described its showcasing at the time:

After the film was released by Disney in December of 1937, Hitler obtained a copy, and ordered that it be shown at his own premiere, to which he invited only a select few members of the Nazi hierarchy. His guests included Josef Goebbels, the Nazi propagandist, his wife, and children. [Almost eight years later, on May 1, 1945, Goebbels and his wife Magda arranged for an SS doctor to kill each of their six children by crushing ampules of cyanide into each of their mouths. A few minutes thereafter, he and Magda committed suicide jointly, immediately prior to the collapse of the Third Reich.)

During the course of the film party, Keller, to her astonishment, learned that *Snow White and the Seven Dwarfs* was Hitler's favorite film, and that he'd privately viewed it three dozen times before this small public showing.

In 2008, William Hakvaag, the director of a Norwegian war museum, claimed that he had purchased a painting by "A. Hitler" at an auction in Germany. The painting, according to Hakvaag, contained Disney characters sketched by Hitler himself during the darkest days of WWII.

It was as if Hitler were retreating into the fantasy world of Disney cartoons, an escape from the bad news emerging from battlefields on both the Eastern and Western fronts.

Who could imagine that a world class butcher like **Adolf Hitler** would delight in such harmless entertainment as Walt Disney's *Snow White and the Seven Dwarfs?* But he loved fairytales, especially if they were of Germanic origin. One major biographer has suggested that Hitler himself was a "fairy."

Entirely dressed in white, **Magda and Josef Goebbels** in a happier day in 1937 when the family, at Hitler's invitation, got to see *Snow White and the Seven Dwarfs*. The children (left to right) are **Helga, Helmut, and Hildegard**. They were years away—1945 to be exact—when an SS doctor fed them cyanide in Hitler's bunker at the request of their parents.

WAS
WALT DISNEY
A HOMOSEXUAL?

"Oh, Walt, say it isn't so!"
—Mickey Mouse

William Kern, a journalist who wrote under the pseudonym of "Bill Dakota," was the editor of *The Hollywood Star*, a gossip tabloid that was a hot seller during the 1970s. Dakota seemed to have the inside scoop on anything transpiring within gay Hollywood.

His most notorious edition appeared in 1976, and was identified as Volume 1, no. 4. It carried the red-letter, front-page headline: WALT DISNEY WAS HOMOSEXUAL—EDITOR REVEALS FACTS!

When that paper hit the newsstands along Hollywood Boulevard, it outsold *Playboy* and every other publication. It is reasonable to say that the first major outing of Walt was the talk of the town at every dinner party and in every bar that night.

The editor even went to a notary public and signed in a sworn statement, placed on that edition's front page, that the events he revealed about Walt were true. The article revealed that he had been paid to have sex with Walt. Dakota's experience with the creator of Mickey Mouse was given further credence by other men who testified to having had the same experience.

Even though the term "outed" had not been coined at that time, Walt Disney, creator of Mickey Mouse, was officially "outed," becoming one of the first of many stars—both male and female—who would be outed in the years to come. In the immediate aftermath of Walt's death, the underground press in Hollywood—much of which was produced on old-fashioned mimeograph machines without a lot of design savvy—went into overdrive. Hustlers came forth and described the details of their paid encounters with Walt.

Although the various sources derived from widely varied backgrounds, a pattern emerged. According to several of these allegations, Walt rarely, if ever, requested that the young man remove his clothes. "I was subjected to a quick blow-job, paid a hundred dollar bill, and shown to the door as quickly as possible," said hustler Ralph Ferguson. "For me, it was easy money. Walt was known in the hustler world as a good mark."

Over the years, insights into the marriage of Walt and Lillian have remained largely a closely guarded secret. What she knew of her husband's nocturnal activities, if anything, is not known. Obviously she might have been suspicious. Walt often didn't come home at night. He used the excuse that he was working late at the studio and was sleeping over.

He was rumored to have maintained different apartments in the Greater Los Angeles area, which he rented under assumed names. It was alleged that he entertained paid hustlers there. One of the many "male madams" of Hollywood supplied him with a discreet group of young men, often out-of-work actors.

One question that remained a puzzle for years was how Walt was introduced to some of the reigning "male madams" of Hollywood.

The missing link was supplied by Jay Garon, who later became a leading literary agent in New York City. Among many other achievements, he launched the career of best-selling author John Grisham.

During the early 1940s, Garon lived with director George Cukor, more or less as his "boy." As has been documented in other biographies, Cukor himself was a frequent patron of Hollywood hustlers. One of his best friends was the bisexual actor Spencer Tracy. Almost from the beginning, Cukor and Tracy bonded, and Cukor often arranged for paid sexual liaisons between various young men and Tracy.

Disney's close bond with Tracy began at least in 1933, just prior to the birth of his daughter, Diane Marie.

As Walt's biographer, Marc Eliot, wrote:

"As Lillian's delivery date neared, Disney increased his already considerable drinking, his chronic cough worsened, and his smoking increased to three packs of cigarettes a day. In addition, his bouts with insomnia extended to weeks at a time, the facial tics and eye twitches from which he periodically suffered returned with renewed intensity, and he obsessively washed his hands several times an hour, every hour."

In that latter regard, he shared the same obsession as Howard Hughes.

It is not at all clear why the birth of a child caused such anguish in Walt. The man who might have answered that question, assuming he would, was Tracy himself.

As Eliot noted in his biography, Walt turned to Tracy for comfort, understanding, and sympathy. The *maitre d'* at the Polo Lounge of the swank Beverly Hills Hotel claimed that on many a night, he spotted Tracy and Walt holding onto each other for support as these two drunks practically carried each other on unsteady feet out of the bar.

At some point during these drunken nights, the two repressed homosexuals unburdened themselves to each other and discovered each of their deepest, darkest secrets—mainly that each of them desired sex with virile young men.

Sometimes Tracy and Walt in their drinking binges were joined by Tracy's pal, Cukor. Cukor was known as the most reliable and regular employer of male hookers in Los Angeles County. He was the person who hooked Tracy up with some of the "male madams" operating in the area.

Jay Garon claimed that even after Walt broke with Tracy, Cukor continued to see Walt privately and continued to link him to the hustler scene. More than anything, Walt was terrified of the possible exposure of his homosexuality, telling Cukor that if word ever got out, his burgeoning empire would crumble. Reportedly, he also told Cukor, "Mothers wouldn't even let their kids go see a Disney picture if word got out that I was a homo."

Although Walt's relationship with Cukor continued for years, he abruptly ended his friendship with Tracy when he learned that the actor was involved in some sort of a relationship with Katharine Hepburn. Why Walt would take some sort of moral position about Tracy being an adulterer is not known. Perhaps Walt was a friend of Tracy's long-suffering wife, Louise.

According to Garon, Cukor urged Walt to change his position, but Walt remained adamant.

One night, Cukor staged one of his famous dinner parties, inviting both Tracy and Walt without informing the other of who was coming.

When Walt arrived and found Tracy nursing a drink in Cukor's living room, he turned and walked out of the dinner party. As far as it is known, Walt never spoke to Tracy again.

Garon speculated that Walt's break with Tracy might have been "all for show—after all, he was attacking communist-inspired immorality in Hollywood. He couldn't be seen hanging out getting drunk every night with Tracy. Even though the public hadn't heard, news of the Tracy/Hepburn link was known all over Hollywood at the time."

Another reason has emerged: According to Garon, Cukor felt that Walt somehow blamed Tracy for introducing him to the hustler world, to which he had become addicted. "It's like blaming the dealer who turns you on to drugs. You get hooked. It ruins your life."

Fess Parker was a friend of Walt's. When Walt went looking for an actor to play Davy Crockett, he turned down James Arness and selected Parker, who'd begun his show business career in 1951 in a $32-a-week job as an extra in *Mister Roberts*.

The Davy Crockett TV series was a tremendous hit, launching a merchandising frenzy for coonskin caps and all things Crockett. Parker became a contract star for Disney.

Walt would never lend him out, even when he was wanted for the choice role of the cowboy appearing opposite Marilyn Monroe in *Bus Stop*.

"I later confronted him and accused him of blowing my chance to fuck Marilyn," Parker said.

"Who would want to fuck *her*?" Walt responded. "She's nothing but a slut."

"But, oh, what a slut!" Parker said to Walt.

Parker never wanted to be drawn into the controversy over Walt's alleged homosexuality, at least as long as he was under contract. Later in life, when he no longer maintained any ties to Disney, he was more outspoken.

"I'd heard all the stories about Walt being gay, and I don't know what to think," Parker said. "I knew him for a long time. During all our times together, he never expressed the slightest interest in women. Of course, he was married. But in Hollywood that doesn't mean a damn thing. I can't tell you how many married actors have come on to me, especially during that Davy Crockett craze. Bottom line: What do I think? I think he was gay, but couldn't accept it in himself. I think that was his tragedy. It darkened his life. It's sad that the man who brought so much joy to others never knew any real happiness himself."

"**Davy Crockett** was my kind of hero," said Walt Disney. "The type of buckskin frontiersman who created America. Did you know he was one of the defenders of the Alamo?"

When "The Ballad of Davy Crockett" was released, it shot to the top of the pop music charts, nesting there at Number One for thirteen weeks. "I should have gotten a hell of a lot more money for parading around in that fucking coonskin cap and wearing buckskin," said **Fess Parker** (above). "One drunken night I had a buddy photograph me jaybird naked with an erection and mail a picture to Walt. I never heard from him about my picture. I bet he kept it to jerk off to. I'm what is known as 'hung.'"

The Short, Tragic Life of

Bobby Driscoll

Tinseltown's Most Chilling Casualty of Child Stardom

Walt Disney told his studio chiefs that he found **Bobby Driscoll** "irresistible," and he suspected movie audiences would too. Of course, in lieu of Driscoll's later allegations, Disney's declaration could have had another meaning.

The sad decline of one of Disney's biggest money makers is one of Hollywood's most tragic tales.

At the age of six, Bobby was a *bona fide* movie star, appearing with some of the biggest names in Hollywood. At the age of eleven, an Academy Award was sitting on a chest of drawers in his bedroom. At the age when most privileged young men like Driscoll were entering college, he was a junkie. Not only that, Hollywood insiders, especially the chiefs at Disney, referred to him by that dreaded name of "has-been."

Born on March 3, 1937, child actor Bobby Driscoll died tragically on March 30, 1968 at the age of 31. He was active in films between 1943 and 1960.

The son of an insulation salesman and a former schoolteacher, Bobby was born in Cedar Rapids, Iowa. When Cletus Driscoll, his father, was advised to relocate to California because of pulmonary ailments he was suffering, the family packed up their belongings and headed for Los Angeles. Cletus was suffering from his work-related handling of asbestos.

Settled into Altadena, California, the cute, curly-haired Bobby went to get a haircut. The barber said, "You should be in pictures." His son, an actor, had a connection at MGM and arranged for Bobby to get a two-minute part in a 1943 family drama, *Lost Angel*. The film's star was a young girl, Margaret O'Brien, who at the time was successfully replacing Shirley Temple as America's leading child star.

Other roles for Bobby soon followed, including an appearance with Anne Baxter and Thomas Mitchell in the 1944 WWII drama, *The Sullivans*, released by Fox. Baxter recalled working with Bobby. "I think I was the first to nickname him Wonder Child. He was a natural in front of the camera. Even though he was just a kid, he could memorize lines faster than any actor in Hollywood. I thought he was going places."

In that same year, Bobby was cast in *Sunday Dinner for a Soldier* (1944). In that picture, he had to blow his whistle while standing on his head. Also in 1944, he played the "child brother" of Richard Arlen in *The Big Bonanza*.

In *So Goes My Love* (1946), he appeared as young Percy Maxim with Don Ameche and Myrna Loy. "Bobby stole every scene from us, and practically chewed up the props," Loy said. "He was adorable."

All these child performances brought Bobby to the attention of Walt Disney, who became aware of his charm and emerging talent. Brought to the Disney Studio in a limousine for the occasion, Bobby had his first meeting with "Uncle Walt," the producer who would change his life.

From all reports, Disney was "mesmerized" by the seductive boy. That very afternoon, Bobby was seen sitting on Disney's knee. Bobby was the first actor he put under contract. Disney cast him in the lead in the 1946 *Song of the South*.

Bobby appeared with Luana Patten in this film based on the Uncle Remus cycle of stories by Joel Chandler Harris. Disney publicist Vern Caldwell wrote to producer Perce Pearce: "The Negro situation is a dangerous one. Between the Negro haters and the Negro lovers, there are many chances to run afoul of situations that could run the gamut all the way from the nasty to the controversial." Even during filming, Disney honchos feared that parts of the film would be viewed as "racially insensitive toward black people."

When it was released, though praising the artistic merit of the film, the NAACP decried "the impression it gives of an idyllic master-slave relationship."

Both Bobby and Luana became overnight sensations, and there was talk of granting special Oscars to them as child actors. The idea was later abandoned. However, the hit song from the movie, "Zip-a-Dee-Doo-Dah" won the 1947 Oscar as Best Song of the Year.

During filming of *Song of the South*, on March 4, 1946, Walt Disney came to the set with a big cake to celebrate Bobby's ninth birthday. Ruth Warrick, one of the co-stars, attended the party. "Walt gave Bobby a kiss. It wasn't on the cheek. It was a big wet one, real sloppy, that lingered far too long. It seemed inappropriate. Later I started hearing stories, but I don't want to go into that. You see, I want to continue to work in Tinseltown."

Bobby and Luana were billed as "Walt Disney's Sweetheart Team" when they co-starred in *So Dear to My Heart*. The film was not released until 1948 because its distributor, RKO Radio Pictures, wanted Disney to include some animated content in it.

In the film, Bobby appeared opposite the balladeer Burl Ives and the veteran actress Beulah

Walt Disney (on the right) came down from his ivory tower to help **Bobby Driscoll** celebrate his ninth birthday.

"He's the apple of my eye," he told his brother Roy Disney. "We're going to make millions off him, but we've got to do it now. Little boys grow up. I want Bobby to remain a boy as long as possible." The birthday cake ceremony took place on the set of *Song of the South*.

In 1949, **Bobby Driscoll** (left) reached the pinnacle of his career when veteran show business performer **Donald O'Connor** presented him with an Oscar as outstanding juvenile of the year.

Backstage that night, O'Connor warned him about the pitfalls of child stardom. "I literally was in vaudeville when I was still in my diapers," O'Connor said. "My parents were circus performers. The worst years are your late teens. Most child stars don't make the transition. Watch out! There are pitfalls along the way."

Bondi.

During the shoot, Bondi, a majestic old actress born in 1888, befriended Bobby and had long talks with him. She too had begun her acting career as a child. She later told Ives that she felt "Disney's attention to Driscoll is excessive." Ives, who the following year would appear on the notorious *Red Channels* list of Hollywood "communists," told Bondi that he didn't think Disney's attention "excessive—I have another word for it."

After the wrap of the film, he confided to Bondi, "Little Bobby is a tragedy waiting to happen."

There were a lot of rumors in Hollywood about Bobby and his Uncle Walt. In time, some of these would see cold print—for example, when Kenneth Anger published *Hollywood Babylon II*, he wrote, "Studio personnel have been quoted to the effect that Bobby's charm worked wonders on 'Grumpy' old Disney—some animators stated that the boss seemed to have fallen in love with the boy. There may be truth in this—if so, it was a love which deepened with the successive hefty box office returns of the films Driscoll made for Uncle Walt—all five of them were big buck hits."

Disney lent Bobby to movie mogul Howard Hughes for a starring role in the film noir, *The Window*, based on Cornell Woolrich's *The Boy Who Cried Murder*. The movie starred Barbara Hale, who is best known today for her role as Della Street on *The Perry Mason Show* which ran from 1957 to 1966.

When director Ted Tetzlaff showed Hughes a cut of the film, the billionaire producer hated it. "It's a lousy picture," Hughes claimed. "No one will want to see this piece of shit. Why don't you send this no-talent Driscoll kid back to Disney so he can resume pounding the kid's ass." Hughes, who had spies "everywhere," had heard the rumors about the close bond between Bobby and his Uncle Walt.

Hughes wanted to bury *The Window* in his film vault, but was persuaded to release it in 1949. He had completely misjudged the appeal of *The Window*, which became a sleeper hit. It remains today Bobby's best movie. *The New York Times* called his child acting "brilliant."

It was *The Window*, along with *So Dear to My Heart*, that earned Bobby a special Oscar as outstanding juvenile actor of 1949. Presenting him the award

A triumph when it was released, *Song of the South* won an Oscar for best original song. Disney was even applauded for casting a black actor, **James Baskett** (see above), in a lead role.

Later, Baskett couldn't attend the movie's premiere in Atlanta because he couldn't find a hotel that would agree to put him up for the night.

In its day, *Song of the South* was viewed as a warm-hearted salute to the "coloreds" of the Deep South. Today it is somewhat of a shameful embarrassment for the company and is viewed as racist. As one critic put it, "It implies that African-Americans stuck below the Mason-Dixon line were a cheerful bunch, who liked nothing better than going fishing, spinning tall tales, and looking after white folks' kids."

was a drunken Donald O'Connor, who managed to conceal his intoxication.

In the summer of 1949, Bobby was back with Uncle Walt filming Robert Louis Stevenson's *Treasure Island* with British actor Robert Newton starring as Long John Silver. Shot in England, this was the studio's first all-live action picture. However, British authorities discovered that Bobby did not have a valid British work permit. His family and Disney were ordered to leave the country.

The British judge, however, granted them six weeks for an appeal. Hastily, the film's director, Byron Haskin, filmed all of Bobby's close-ups before his deportation. Distance scenes were shot later, using a stand-in.

Upon the release of *Treasure Island*, Bobby received his star at 1560 Vine Street on the Hollywood Walk of Fame.

Still mesmerized by Bobby, Disney signed a second long-term contract with him.

Marc Eliot, the author of *Walt Disney: Hollywood's Dark Prince*, claimed that Disney "referred to Driscoll with great affection as the living embodiment of his own youth and believed that the role in *Treasure Island* would make the 14-year-old a star."

Treasure Island was a big success worldwide. Disney wanted to rush Bobby into Mark Twain's *Tom Sawyer*, until he encountered story rights ownership, which pitted him against another Hollywood producer, David O. Selznick, who had issued his own version of the literary property in 1938.

Disney then turned to a screenplay where he wanted to cast Bobby as Robin Hood's youngest follower, with Robert Newton playing Friar Tuck. The film was to be shot in England, but Bobby's previous run-in with British immigration sabotaged the project.

As he matured into a teenager, Bobby painfully learned that his greatest roles were behind him, even though Uncle Walt still offered him work such as lending his voice to Goofy Jr. in Disney cartoon shorts, *Fathers Are People* (1951) and *Father's Lion* (1952).

The former child star's last big success was *Peter Pan*, which was launched in May of 1949, when he was 12, the project extending to the summer of 1951, when he was 14. Bobby appeared in that film opposite Kathryn Beaumont in the role of Wendy. She was publicized as Disney's "Little British Lady."

Bobby Driscoll loved working with **Burl Ives** pictured in his bathtub with a cigar. "He was the first actor who treated me like an adult. He gave me advice. He told me that, 'I can't see my dick unless I stand in front of a full length mirror. Don't ever get fat.'"

Ives was hefty, bearded, and with a quiver to his voice that made him perfect as Big Daddy in Tennessee Williams' *Cat on a Hot Tin Roof*, a performance for which he won raves. He was nominated for an Oscar when he sang "Lavender Blue" to Beulah Bondi in the Driscoll film, *So Dear to My Heart*.

"I adored Bobby," said the Chicago-born actress **Beulah Bondi**, "but for some reason I felt that Disney was exploiting him, robbing him of his youth."

She shared her memories with Bobby of starting out in show business as a child cast into the title role of *Little Lord Fauntleroy*. "But by the time I was only 40, I was being cast as the ultimate hair-in-a-bun archetype of motherhood. I've been dear old mum to everybody from Helen Hayes—what a sweet gal—to Bette Davis—what a bitch!"

"I dreamed one day I'd grow up to marry Kathryn," Bobby said. "I loved her voice of Alice in *Alice in Wonderland* and Wendy in *Peter Pan*. But I learned that most dreams in Hollywood are only to be dreamed."

After 1952, when he was 15, few jobs turned up, even though Bobby was pulling in $1,750 a week. Walt could have signed him for a two-year extension of his contract, but he decided to let him go. When Bobby came to Disney's office to see what had gone wrong between them, he was refused admittance.

Just weeks before *Peter Pan* was released theatrically, Bobby developed what he called "history's worst case of acne." Puberty had set in.

For the TV shows that followed in the immediate aftermath of his termination from Disney, Bobby had to wear heavy make-up. Unable to get movie work, Bobby turned to TV, where he got to appear with such fabled stars as Gloria Swanson and Loretta Young. He met Jane Wyman, the former Mrs. Ronald Reagan, when he appeared in *Dirty Faces* as part of her *Jane Wyman Presents the Fireside Theatre*.

She told her friend, June Allyson, "I had several long talks with Bobby. He's emotionally troubled and needs help. There was something going on between Walt and Bobby, something that's been hushed up, something that should be investigated. I abhor child abuse."

June related the incident with Wyman to her husband, Dick Powell, who indiscreetly spread the word.

When Bobby attended Westwood University High School, the other kids ridiculed him for his roles in Disney films. Feeling depressed and alienated, he experimented with drugs. He began to take heroin—"because I had the money to pay for it." In 1956, he was arrested for possession of marijuana, although the charge was dismissed.

When he was 19, in 1956, Bobby and his girlfriend, Marilyn

Anne Baxter's signature performance as Eve Harrington in the 1950 *All About Eve* lay far in her future when she appeared with a very young Bobby Driscoll in *The Sullivans*. She told Bobby that she too got an early start at the age of 13 when she made her Broadway debut in the short-lived *Seen But Not Heard* in 1936.

"I'd never met a child who talked like Bobby," Baxter said. "One day he told me he couldn't wait to grow up so he could fuck gals. I gave him my phone number and told him to call me in ten years. I promised not to change my number so he could get in touch with me a decade later."

Bounding out of St. Louis, **Ruth Warrick** appeared opposite **Orson Welles** in *Citizen Kane* (1941), still hailed as the greatest film of all time. Welles hired her to play Charles Foster Kane's very proper first wife, Emily, the President's niece.

She was cast as Bobby Driscoll's disapproving mom in the notorious Disney film, *Song of the South*. "I started at the top and drifted downward," she later recalled. However, she found her niche later in life when she was cast as Phoebe Tyler in *All My Children*. She held onto that soap opera role until way past retirement. In fact, she called her 1980 autobiography *The Confessions of Phoebe Tyler*.

Jean Rush, eloped to Mexico. Their union would produce three children before their eventual separation in 1960.

His last feature film, with Connie Stevens and Frances Farmer, was called *The Party Crashers* and released in 1958.

Bernard Girard, who directed *The Party Crashers*, later claimed that Bobby and Farmer had an affair during the production of this ill-fated film. "Bobby looked in such bad condition I'm surprised he could get it up at that point. Connie Stevens was also cast in the film. Poor Connie. She must have wondered, 'What am I doing here?'"

By the time the once-beautiful Frances Farmer (1913-1970) appeared with Bobby, he was almost as tormented, confused, and emotionally troubled as she was. Farmer had suffered an involuntary commitment to a mental hospital.

As in the case of Bobby, the turbulent life of Farmer became the subject of lurid speculation after her death. Various writers have claimed that during her brutal incarceration, she was forced to eat her own feces and act as a sex slave for male doctors and orderlies. It was also alleged that the hospital had performed a lobotomy on her.

One day, Bobby was in the driveway of his front yard washing his car when two teenage boy hecklers recognized him. "Faggot!" one of the boys shouted at him, another calling out "Suck my dick, you Disney queer."

Bobby carried a pistol with him. Quickly removing it from the car, he ran after the boys, striking one of them over the head with the pistol as the other boy fled. Arrested by a policeman, he was charged with "assault with a deadly weapon," but the charges were subsequently dropped.

When Bobby Driscoll was cast with **Frances Farmer** (above) in *The Party Crashers,* they both were two performers on the road to hell.

Her descent into hell was even worse than Driscoll's. On the first page of her notorious autobiography, *Will There Really Be a Morning?,* she got right into the mess of her life. She wrote: "For eight years I was an inmate in a state asylum for the insane. I was raped by orderlies, gnawed by rats, and poisoned by tainted food."

As his drug intake continued, more arrests were on the way, and judges were getting less tolerant of his status as a movie star. He was arrested in 1961 and charged with drug addiction. Complicating matters, he and some unknown French woman broke into an animal clinic and made off with $450.

Three months later he was arrested for forging a $45 check, and this from an actor who had made $50,000 a year when working for Walt. Bobby was sentenced to six months in prison and sent to the Narcotic Rehabilitation Center of the California Institution for Men in Chino, California.

Drugs had changed Bobby, making him an embittered young man. He didn't care about his appearance and rarely bathed. His teeth became loose. Even though he had a high IQ, narcotics had affected his brain and he often spoke as if in a coma.

When he was sent to Chino, his mother, Mrs. Isabella Kratz Driscoll, complained of the way her son was treated. "They handcuffed him and dragged him away to that place, which was crawling with rats and homosexuals."

In prison, Bobby learned about gay life, suffering a brutal introduction. He later claimed that he was held down and raped by five of the prison's bullies. No charges were ever filed against the rapists.

Released from Chino in 1962, Bobby made several attempts to get in touch with Disney, but the producer would neither return his calls nor answer his urgent letters. "I was dropped like garbage when I was no longer a cute little kid, and I didn't appeal to him anymore. He didn't think I could make any more millions for him."

"Bobby didn't even get a Christmas card from Disney," Mrs. Driscoll claimed.

Arriving in New York in 1965, Bobby tried to find work on the stage. For a few brief months, he kept showing up at Andy Warhol's The Factory in Greenwich Village, with some vague hope that the pop artist might star him in one of his films.

Nothing came of that, but Bobby was reported to have had a number of homosexual liaisons.

He did appear in an experimental underground film aptly entitled *Dirt*. This was his last appearance in any movie. The film was shown for the first time in 1965.

Desperate for money to support his drug addiction, Bobby set up a meeting with Donald Fine, who became known as the founder of Arbor House, a publishing firm. Bobby pitched a proposed memoir to this battle-sharpened editor.

The former child star's charges were sensational. The major accusation against his once beloved Uncle Walt was that he had been sexually molested. Fine listened patiently to Bobby's pitch, including a request for some freelance writer to draft a coherent written version of his story.

After Bobby left his office, Fine told his editorial assistant, "I wouldn't touch that story with a ten-foot pole. I don't even know if it's true. Maybe he's just making up the whole thing for a quick buck."

In December of 1967, at the age of 30, Bobby disappeared from The Factory, wandering the streets penniless. Reportedly, he came up to people on the streets, begging for money. "Remember me? I used to be Bobby Driscoll in the movies."

In the early months of 1968, he had virtually disappeared and was no longer seen begging. Manhattan's underground had enveloped him.

On March 30, 1968, two teenage boys broke into an abandoned tenement at 371 East 10th Street. They discovered the dead body of a young man. An ambulance carried the corpse to the local hospital, where a doctor determined that he had died of heart failure brought on by an advanced hardening of the arteries—the direct result of longtime drug abuse.

There was no identification on Bobby's body. The staff at the morgue hardly recognized the former child star of Disney's *Treasure Island*. Physically, he had changed almost beyond recognition. The corpse was fingerprinted and then buried in a pauper's grave in Potter's Field on Hart Island. Maintained by the New York City Department of Corrections as a 101-acre burial site positioned off the western coastline of The Bronx, it's the largest tax-funded

As **Bobby Driscoll** went from puberty into manhood, he became more embittered. In 1959 when sheriff's officers spotted needle marks on his arms, he was strip searched. A "stash" of heroin was found on him. He was arrested, tried, and found guilty. He was sentenced to jail on a narcotics charge. On his second night in prison, the still handsome young man was entrapped in the shower and raped by five other convicts. Found bleeding, he was sent to the infirmary to be sewed up. More arrests—in 1960 and 1961—followed.

"When a cute kid is thrown into prison," he later said. "Rape is inevitable. I think the jailers view it as part of the punishment."

cemetery in the world.

It wasn't until around November of 1969 that Bobby's mother, in a search for her son, found his fingerprint match at the New York Police Department branch on Hart Island.

His death was not widely publicized until late in 1971 or early 1972 when reporters went searching for him to discover "Whatever Happened to Bobby Driscoll?" Interest in the child star had been rekindled because of Disney's heavily edited and heavily censored re-release of the film, *Song of the South*.

Forgotten at the time of his death, Bobby has found a new generation of young fans with the re-release of his Disney films. Children born in the 21st century are happily watching this once-charming, curly haired boy.

In a final interview, Mrs. Driscoll said, "Bobby had a great deal of love for Walt Disney. And he always did whatever Disney told him to do."

A question remains. Just what *did* Uncle Walt tell him to do?

AUTHORS ALLEGE DISNEY WORLD ATTRACTS PEDOPHILES

The most violent attack on the World of Disney came from **Peter and Rochelle Schweizer** who wrote *Disney the Mouse Betrayed: Greed, Corruption, and Children at Risk*. In their controversial book, they leveled a mass of charges, including the most notorious—"rampant pedophile and sexual abuse problems." The italicized words in both of the boxes on this page are quoted directly from their book:

"Of all Disney's secrets, none is perhaps as dark and troubling as the growing number of active pedophiles in and around the Magic Kingdom.

"'Disney is having more problems than anyone else' said Detective Matt Irwin, who has cracked down on several pedophile cases for the Sheriff's Department. 'The sheer size of the place means pedophiles can operate in relative anonymity.'

"'Pedophiles are attracted to children, and they go where children are,' says Sergeant Mark Thompson of the Osceola County Sheriff's Department. 'They're going to search for them, somewhere where they can reach that child. They're attracted to Disney because it's so big, their chances of getting caught are close to none.'

"Thompson should know. He's both worked the sex crime beat and done security work at Disney."

—Peter Schweizer and Rochelle Schweizer

"SATAN, PORNO, AND RAMPANT VOYEURISM"

Schweizer and Schweizer also charged that Disney-owned **Hollywood Records** produces *"some of the raunchiest, violent, pro-suicide, and pro-Satan music in the industry."* They further revealed how Disney became a partner with "the nation's largest pay-per-view pornography distributor."

The authors alleged that *"sometimes the walls have eyes in the Magic Kingdom."* Dancers have reported that they felt they were being spied on as they undressed and changed into costumes. *"There is a subculture of voyeurs so large and open that even new employees can get involved fast, if they want to,"* the Schweizers claimed. *"Oddball voyeurs have a network. They pass along information that things are tolerated."*

The Schweizers also alleged that Disney sends a *"weird message"* when employees are caught peeping on--even filming—co-workers and guests in their dressing rooms.

Disney The Mouse Betrayed

Greed, Corruption, and Children at Risk

Peter Schweizer and Rochelle Schweizer

In Memoriam
BOBBY DRISCOLL
CHILD STAR

RJP

SOUTHERN BAPTISTS
CALL FOR THE DESTRUCTION
OF DISNEY "PERVERTS"

DISNEY IS EVIL!

SAYS WHO?

The Southern Baptist Convention, the largest Protestant Church in America, with 16 million members and more than 42,000 churches, has viciously attacked the Disney Empire for allegedly promoting "unchristian and immoral material, which they are pumping into American homes under the guise of family entertainment."

In 1996, as a reaction against Disney World's promotion of "Gay Days" at their theme park in Orlando, 12,000 Baptist delegates, meeting in Dallas, Texas, voted overwhelmingly for a boycott of all Disney-owned companies, a boycott that would continue for eight years.

The redneck Baptists also formally objected to Disney's extension of employee benefits to the partners of gay men or lesbians working within their organizations. The Bible thumpers specifically asserted that forty percent of all Disney employees are homosexual. The church leaders never specified what percentage of gay employees would represent an "acceptable" percentage—perhaps zero. In later proclamations, they also blasted ABC-TV's Ellen DeGeneres and her talk show, deliberately misspelling her name "DeGenerate."

Richard Lamb of the Southern Baptist Convention's Morals and Ethics panel, said: "You can't walk the family side of the street and the gay side of the street in the Magic Kingdom at the same time—there's a sense of betrayal and outrage."

Not the brightest bulb in the church, the Rev. Roy Fisher of the First Baptist Church of Nashville, said, "I know of hundreds of people who have dropped the Disney Cable Channel. Disney has abandoned traditional family values to promote the homosexual agenda. The time has come to stop patronizing any company that promotes immoral ideologies and practices."

Lisa Kinney, a Southern Baptist Convention delegate based at the time in Largo, Florida, near Tampa, weighed in with enlightenment of her own. "The boycott affirms to the world that we love Jesus more than we love entertainment. If we must turn off our TVs, so be it. It's no great loss. We can't participate in Disney's godlessness."

Wiley Drake of Buena Park, California, said that he took his three children to Disney and "was shocked to see men in drag French kissing each other in front of our children."

In other charges, church officials claim that at Gay Day at Disney World, studio executives allowed homosexual organizers of the event to portray Donald Duck and Mickey Mouse as lovers, with Minnie Mouse and Daisy Duck as lesbians.

[Editor's note: Personally, we've always believed that Minnie Mouse was a lesbian, terrorist sponsoring and child molesting anti-Semite, Negrophobe, serial killer, rapist, and card-carrying communist.]

Despite millions of fans around the world, Walt Disney never enjoyed a squeaky clean image with EVERY member of the public. But the most notorious attack, shotgun-blasted at both Walt and the organizations bearing his name, was posted on the web under "The Walt Disney Illuminati Pedophile Agenda."

The site alleged that Walt was part of the Illuminati family, claiming "His initial interest was not in kids in the way you might think, but he was in fact a sexual pervert and pedophile which was displayed in everything he did."

Shortly after Walt's death, J. Edgar Hoover, Director of the FBI, himself a homosexual, had a very different interpretation of Disney from what the church alleged. He sent a telegram to Lillian. In it, he wrote:

IT IS MY HOPE THAT YOU WILL DERIVE CONSOLATION FROM KNOWING THAT HIS OUTSTANDING CONTRIBUTIONS WILL BE A LASTING MEMORIAL TO HIM. HIS DEDICATION TO THE HIGHEST STANDARDS OF MORAL VALUES AND HIS ACHIEVEMENTS WILL ALWAYS STAND AS AN INSPIRATION TO THOSE WHO WERE PRIVILEGED TO KNOW HIM.

Both **J. Edgar Hoover** (above) and Walt Disney were reported to be homosexuals. They became friends and shared many secrets with each other.

Disney became an official Hollywood informant for the FBI. He had a "special relationship" with the Bureau that stretched over a 25-year period. Ultimately he was designated by Hoover as "Special Agent in Charge." Hoover reportedly told Disney, "even if it's not communist activities, I want to know all the dirt on the stars. Under certain circumstances, we might arrange entrapment and even pictures if a star is homosexual."

In 1947, the House Un-American Activities Committee launched its purge. The hearings became a circus. Witnesses who were friendly to the prosecution included Gary Cooper, Robert Taylor, and Walt Disney, who testified that Communists at his studio were trying to use Mickey Mouse to spread Communist propaganda.

FBI DIRECTOR J. EDGAR HOOVER AND HIS WAR AGAINST GAYS AS QUOTED BY HISTORIAN ANTHONY SUMMERS

"J. Edgar Hoover's sexual torment had effects far beyond his personal life. In his day, as is still often the case today, anything other than evident heterosexuality could destroy a public official. Acutely aware of the danger, Hoover overcompensated. Like several other public figures with a secret homosexual life, Hoover often behaved viciously toward homosexuals. On several documented occasions, Hoover attempted to smear other public men--including Adlai Stevenson, Martin Luther King Jr., and three aides to President Nixon--as homosexuals. This occurred at a time when rumors of Edgar's own homosexuality were circulating among high government officials."

from <u>Official and Confidential: The Secret Life of J. Edgar Hoover,</u> by **Anthony Summers**

Tales from the Deep Freeze

Walt: "I'll Be Back."
Hibernating Like Sleeping Beauty

The death of Walt Disney, caused by circulatory failure related to complications from lung cancer, spawned at least two urban legends. One is that he had his body cryogenically frozen. The second legend is that Walt's body rests in the deep freeze below Sleeping Beauty's Castle in Disneyland in Anaheim, California.

There is yet another legend which claims that after his death at 9:30am on December 15, 1966, his body was decapitated and only his head was frozen. Presumably, that head could be thawed out decades from now and attached to a healthy body.

The theory of a head placed on another body was first promulgated in a rather gruesome seven-minute Mickey Mouse cartoon made in 1933. In that scenario, a mad scientist cuts off Pluto's head and then tries to attach it to the body of a chicken.

One publicist for Disney, speaking anonymously, claimed that Disney Studio animators with a "bizarre sense of humor"

Does **Disney's frozen corpse** rest under Sleeping Beauty's Castle? This urban legend won't go away. The charge is so prevalent that almost everyone has heard of it. So much misinformation about Disney's death has gone out, including a mysterious "burial," that it has only contributed to promote the legend. The legend has various versions, including one accusation that only his head was frozen. Others claim that his entire body was frozen, to be resurrected when a cure for lung cancer is eventually discovered.

deliberately started the rumors as a final prank on their boss, who had been abusive to them. Although Disney employees tended as a whole to be a fairly satisfied group, many who worked closely with Walt actually hated him, denouncing his behavior behind his back.

Walt's official death certificate asserts that his body was cremated.

But in contrast, critics of this storyline claim that death certificates have been erroneous or faked since the invention of such a document. As one fan put it, "There may be some ashes in Disney's crypt, but I seriously doubt if they belonged to Walt. Perhaps from some fireplace in California."

The "official" version remains that Walt was cremated and his ashes interred at Forest Lawn Cemetery in Los Angeles. But because of so many cover-ups associated with his death, the true story may be known only to his heirs.

A mysterious delay in the announcement of Walt's death helped promote the freeze legend. News of his death was suppressed for several hours. That delay, before reporters learned of his death, according to such authors as Leonard Mosley, allowed Disney aides to whisk his body from the hospital into a secret cryogenic chamber.

News of the precarious nature of Walt's health was also suppressed from, or at least aggressively downplayed, for public consumption. On November 6, 1966, after a diagnosis that one of his lungs "was riddled with tumors the size of walnuts," it was removed. Prior to his death five weeks later, when he checked into a hospital for the final time, the press was told that he was undergoing "a routine post-operative checkup." The media had not been alerted to a Disney "death watch," and as such, only some of them had prepared, in advance, the obligatory tributes and obituaries.

Walt's funeral was conducted at the Little Church of the Flowers at Los Angeles' Forest Lawn Cemetery at 5pm Friday, December 16, the day after his death. No announcement of the funeral was made until after it had already taken place. Executives from Disney were not invited; only family members attended.

According to reports and available documentation, Walt's preferences regarding the disposal of his body are, mysteriously, not part of the public record. Instructions for his funeral and burial were not included in his will, which the law requires to be made public. These startling omissions gave rise to the frozen body theory.

Associates of Walt have maintained that he had a fascination with death, perhaps an obsession. When he was in his 20s, a fortune teller reportedly told him that he would die when he was only thirty-five years old.

Throughout his life, Walt was known for extended periods of depression, and was said to brood frequently about his "untimely" death.

Disney's daughter, Diane, wrote in 1972: "There is absolutely no truth to the rumor that my father wished to be frozen. I doubt that my father had ever heard of cryonics."

Others dispute her statement, claiming that Disney was fascinated by cryonics and studied every piece of literature that he could find.

Another source claimed that Walt could well have been aware of life extension through cryogenics. In scientific and medical reports in the 1950s and early 60s, there were numerous articles, even books, on the subject of hypothermia and the preservation of animal tissue through freezing.

In Walt's office was found a copy of *The Prospect of Immortality* written in 1964 by Robert C.W. Ettinger. That was two years before Disney's death. Ettinger maintained that "at very low temperatures, it is possible to preserve dead people with essentially no deterioration indefinitely."

In Leonard Mosley's 1986 book, *Disney's World*, appeared this statement:

"The chief problem that troubled Walt was the length of time it might take for doctors to perfect the process. How long would it be before the surgical experts could bring a treated cadaver back to working life? To be brutally practical, could it be guaranteed, in fact, that he could be brought back in time to rectify the mistakes his successors would almost certainly start making at EPCOT the moment he was dead?"

A writer for *The Mickey Mouse Club* TV show claimed that Walt had once inquired about cryogenics and that he asked him to have the Disney Studio library research the subject in great detail.

Ward Kimball, an animator at Disney, also went public with the claim that just weeks after Walt died, studio department heads were invited into a screening room. Once there, they were shown a film of Walt sitting at his desk, talking about future plans. He announced on screen that he would be seeing them soon.

Such a statement would eerily evoke Arnold Schwarzenegger's famous line, "I'll be back," in the *Terminator* series.

Staff members at Disney, who would never go on record for fear of losing their jobs, claimed that "The boss man was fascinated by the subject of the cryonic storage of human beings and talked frequently of it in the last months of his life."

In Marc Elliot's biography, *Hollywood's Dark Prince*, he writes:

"Disney's growing preoccupation with his own mortality also led him to explore the science of cryogenics, the freezing of an aging or ill person until such time as the human body can be revived and restored to health. Disney often mused to Roy about the notion of perhaps having himself frozen, an idea which received indulgent nods from his brother."

Walt's death occurred in the wake of the 1950s and 1960s craze over sci-fi when cryogenic freezing fascinated the general population. On film, studios created monsters rising from the dead. Why not real people?

One of the most famous movies regarding a cryonics-like process was the 1992 *Forever Young*, starring Mel Gibson.

The Disney frozen body rumor first appeared in print in 1969 in a magazine called *Ici Paris*.

Picking up on the story, *The National Tattler*, a tabloid scandal sheet, claimed that Disney had instructed his doctors to thaw him out in 1975.

The *Tattler* article appeared to be very far-fetched, optimistically suggesting that between 1966—the year of Walt's death—and 1975, science could have advanced to the point where a frozen cadaver could be brought back to life.

Midnight, another supermarket tabloid, made a charge claiming, "Walt Disney is being kept alive in the deep freeze." In this publication, a Disney studio librarian claimed that a vast file of filmed material on cryogenics was viewed by Walt.

Another tabloid, *National Spotlite*, claimed that one of its correspondents sneaked into St. Joseph's Hospital, where Walt had died. Disguised as an orderly, the newspaperman picked the lock on a storage room and spotted Walt's body suspended in a metal cylinder.

If Disney wanted to be preserved for rejuvenation at a future time, he was not the most famous person ever to express that interest. In 1773, Benjamin Franklin wrote a letter, expressing regret that he lived "in a century too little advanced, and too near the infancy of science" that he could not be preserved and revived to fulfill his "very ardent desire to see and observe the state of America a hundred years hence."

Other famous people who have publicly expressed an interest in cryogenic preservation include TV talk show host Larry King, boxing legend Muhammed Ali, and author Gore Vidal.

The first known case—the emphasis here is on known—of a body being frozen for future resurrection was that of Dr. James Bedford, a 73-year-old psychologist from Glendale, California. He was frozen on January 12, 1967, which, of course, was after the death of Walt.

According to the Alcor Life Extension Institute—a non-profit organization established in 1972 in Scottsdale, Arizona, which bills itself as the world's leading authority on cryonics and cryonic research—more than 100 bodies, as of 2002, have been frozen since Bedford's. At least 1,000 people worldwide have made financial and legal arrangements to be preserved with Alcor, which charges $80,000 to preserve a person's brain and $150,000 to preserve a whole body—in addition to annual dues and maintenance fees.

BASEBALL LEGEND TED WILLIAMS

A Bizarre Post-Mortem for a Hall of Famer

"They c an talk about Babe Ruth and Ty Cobb and Roger Hornsby and Lou Gehrig and Joe DiMaggio and Stan Musial and all the best, but I'm sure not one of them could hold cards and spades to Ted Williams in his sheer knowledge of hitting. He studied hitting the way a broker studies the stock market, and could spot at a glance mistakes that others couldn't see in a week."

—Baseball legend Carl "Yaz" Yastrzemski

Baseball great **Ted Williams** (above) is seen in 1939 after he joined the Boston Red Sox. Below in 1951 he's pictured with **Joe DiMaggio,** another great.

DiMaggio and Williams, although friendly on the surface, were rivals. DiMaggio's achievements, such as a 56-game hitting streak in 1941, often overshadowed that of Williams.

"Joe also beat me to Marilyn Monroe," Williams later recalled. In 2002 it was reported that Hall of Famer Williams had been placed in "cryonic suspension" after being declared legally dead. His body was cooled to temperatures where physical decay essentially stops.

An entire Hollywood motion picture could be made about the death and after-death dramas of baseball great Ted Williams.

The subject of whether Walt Disney is frozen—or not—continues to be debated today. As for Williams, however, there is no debate. He was frozen. As far as it is known, he is the most famous person ever to undergo cryogenic suspension.

Ted Williams, born August 30, 1918, died on July 5, 2002. He was a leftfielder in Major League Baseball and played 21 seasons with the Boston Red Sox. He is widely hailed as the greatest hitter in baseball history, and was a two-time American League Most Valuable Player winner. He was inducted into the Baseball Hall of Fame in 1966.

Upon his death, his body was immediately flown by private jet to the Alcor Institute in Scottsdale, Arizona. There, according to reports, his body was separated from his head in a procedure known as neuroseparation.

Sports Illustrated, in an article, claimed that his head is

stored in a steel can filled with liquid nitrogen and that it has been shaved, drilled with holes, and accidentally cracked 10 times.

Apparently, the holes were drilled into the head so that lab workers could monitor the condition of Ted's brain, determining any deterioration.

The magazine also alleged that Ted's decapitated body stands upright in a 9-foot tall cylindrical steel tank also filled with liquid nitrogen. But according to urban legend, his body is suspended intact and upside down.

It has been alleged that employees of the Alcor facility had their pictures taken while posing with the body of the baseball hero, both before and after the decapitation. Talk about souvenirs.

Larry Johnson, a veteran paramedic and former employee of Alcor, wrote a memoir, published in 2009, entitled *Frozen: My Journey Into the World of Cryonics, Deception and Death*. In that sizzler, he maintained that he personally witnessed Ted's severed head being abused. He stated that an Alcor official "swung a monkey wrench at Williams' frozen severed head to try to remove a tuna can stuck to it. The first swing accidentally struck the head, and the second knocked the tuna can loose."

Why the tuna can? According to Johnson, the tuna can came from food given to a cat that lived on the premises. These discarded tuna cans were used as pedestals to prop up Ted's head. When the head was being transferred from one container to another, the monkey wrench "batting" incident allegedly occurred, according to Johnson.

"The disembodied face set in that awful, frozen scream looked nothing like any picture of Ted Williams I've ever seen," wrote Johnson.

In one of his most explosive charges, Johnson asserted that he saw "tiny pieces of the frozen head sprayed around the room," after the clubbing from the monkey wrench."

Johnson, or so it is believed, was the primary source for the exposé published in *Sports Illustrated*.

When Johnson's book was published, Alcor denied all allegations and threatened legal action. Johnson has claimed that his family was terrorized and that his life was repeatedly threatened as a result of his whistleblowing.

In 2003, *The New York Daily News* reported that Buzz Hamon, Ted's best pal and the former director of the Ted Williams Museum in Hernando, Florida, sneaked into Alcor with the help of a mortician friend.

Hamon later told the press that he was "appalled" by the conditions he found there. He reported that his friend's body, along with about 50 other cadavers, were stored in steel tanks alongside cardboard boxes and plain junk. A year later, Hamon died. Allegedly, he committed suicide, although there were rumors he was murdered.

Ted Williams' son, John Henry Williams, died in 2004. He was only thirty-five years old. He'd been engaged in a legal battle with his sister, Bobby-Jo Williams Ferrell, who claimed that her father had wanted to be cremated and his ashes scattered at sea off the Florida Keys. In time, because of a lack of funds, she abandoned the legal battle.

Pictured above is one of **Alcor's cryogenic chambers**. Alcor in Arizona is the world's leading cryonics facility. Many critics said that cryonics is only for the rich. An official at Alcor claimed that, "Far from being expensive, cryonics is one of the most affordable healthcare options available."

Facing death and dreaming of immortality, a person under certain circumstances can take out a life insurance policy, entitling him or her to cryonic suspension after death. If a person is in moderate good health and only in middle age, some of these policies might be arranged for only ten dollars a month.

THE MAN WHO TURNED AMERICA ON

DR. TIMOTHY LEARY'S DECAPITATED HEAD ON ICE

Walt Disney and Timothy Leary, from reports, had something in common: their fascination with cryonics. Leary went so far as to sign a document expressing his desire that his body be frozen for future rejuvenation. Shortly before his death on May 31, 1996, he changed his mind, opting instead not to have his body cryo-preserved.

Leary, of course, is the American writer, psychologist, futurist, and advocate of psychedelic drug research. This icon of the 1960s counterculture virtually immortalized himself with the catch phrase, TURN ON! TUNE IN! DROP OUT!

He once publicly stated, "LSD is an extremely powerful, mind-opening agent. We are now in the psycho-chemical age. In the future it's not going to be what book you read, but what chemical do you use to open your mind to accelerate learning."

This son of a dentist, who was born in Beverly Hills, was known for other utterances as well. He once said, "I declare that The Beatles are mutants. Prototypes of evolutionary agents sent by God, endowed with a mysterious power to create a new human species, a young race of laughing freemen."

After being arrested for possession of two marijuana joints, Leary was sentenced to 10 years in the California Men's Colony at San Luis Obispo. However, he escaped in 1970, the bust-out aided by the radical left Weather Underground Organization and his third wife, Rosemary Woodruff Leary.

He fled from country to country, showing up in Algeria, where they were the guests of Eldridge Cleaver, a once-prominent member of the radical

In 1959 drug guru **Timothy Leary** joined the faculty of Harvard University where he hooked up with another professor, Richard Alpert, in a series of controlled experiments with psychedelic drugs. For four years the men used undergraduate students, each a willing volunteer in their experiments.

When the administration at Harvard found out, they fired both Leary and Alpert. They moved to Millbrook Estate, a 63-room mansion in New York State. Here they continued their experiments and were visited by some of the greatest cultural figures of the era, including Abbie Hoffman, Jack Kerouac, Aldous Huxley, William Burroughs, and, of course, Allen Ginsberg.

Black Panther Party. After a political argument, Cleaver kidnapped Leary and his wife, but they escaped, fleeing to Zurich. In 1973, Leary was arrested in Kabul and deported from Afghanistan to the United States. Sent to Folsom Prison near Sacramento, he was paroled in 1976.

In 1982, he went on the lecture circuit with G. Gordon Liddy, the Watergate bad man. The press called them "The Odd Couple," writing satirical pieces about their tour.

Even though the druggie withdrew his deep freeze plans, the movie, *Timothy Leary's Head* (1996), has a simulated sequence in which the psychologist allows his head to be decapitated and placed on ice. At the end of the movie is another sequence, showing the creation of the artificial head used in the film.

After his death, instead of being stored in a freezer, Leary's body was actually cremated. Seven grams of his ashes were "buried" aboard a space rocket which also carried the remains of Gene Roddenberry, creator of *Star Trek*. A Pegasus rocket with these ashes, and those of others, was launched on April 21, 1997. The vessel remained in orbit for six years until it burned up in outer space.

Talk about a mind-blowing ending for one of the icons of the psychedelic revolution.

SPACED-OUT HOLLYWOOD?

Gene Roddenberry got his wish. Upon his death, some of his remains were shot into Outer Space for "burial."

His ashes, along with those of Timothy Leary and 19 other persons, were launched into orbit around a Pegasus XL rocket fired from near the Canary Islands.

Roddenberry was a screenwriter and futurist. He created the science fiction TV series, *Star Trek*, which earned him the nickname of "Great Bird of the Galaxy." The original *Star Trek* made its debut in 1966 and ran for three seasons. Viewers followed the intersteller adventures of Captain James T. Kirk and the crew of the Federation Starship *Enterprise*. The *Star Trek* media franchise in time became a multi-billion dollar industry. When selling to the networks, Roddenberry pitched the show as "Wagon Train to the Stars" or "Horatio Hornblower in Space."

The Ballad of Pinup Queen
Bettie Page

THE TRAGIC, SHOCKING LIFE OF THE CHEESECAKE HOTTIE

"To be naked is to be oneself. To be nude is to be seen naked by others and yet not recognized for oneself."

—Art Critic John Berger

Bettie Page, Queen of the Pinups in the 1950s, died on December 11, 2008. After a turbulent life, she managed to reach the age of 85.

She was one of the earliest "Playmates of the Month" for *Playboy* magazine. After aging in seclusion, no one would recognize Bettie Page in later life as the former "Empress of Kink."

She enjoyed a renaissance during the 1980s and 90s that continues to this day. "I'm more famous now than I was fifty years ago," she said in 1993.

Her bust was 36", her waist 23", and those measurements became known around the world. Her jet black hair—all bangs and bob 'do—became an iconic trademark during the rockabilly subculture of the Eisenhower years.

The Tease from Tennessee

Her Father's "Love Child"

On one frosty morn, deep in the heart of springtime Dixie (April 22, 1923), a girl was born to redneck white trash in Nashville, Tennessee. She was the second child of Water Roy Page, an auto mechanic, and a hillbilly woman named Edna Mae Pirtle.

On her birth certificate, she was named "Betty" Mae Page. Later in life she changed it to "Bettie." Four more children would follow, and Bettie found herself changing the diapers of her siblings. She learned early that little boys are not like little girls.

Edna had married Roy only to escape the horrors of an orphanage. Bettie's earliest memories were of her mother having to fight off the sexual demands of her father—"he wanted it all the time." Edna was thrown out of the house one night during a thunderstorm. She was pregnant at the time and didn't want to have sex. Roy had demanded she perform fellatio on him, and she'd refused.

From Tennessee to Texas to Oklahoma, Roy drifted from job to job, taking his family with him. Work was hard to come by in the Depression. Evicted from their home in Tulsa, the Pages had no money. Roy stole a car and drove his family back to Tennessee where he was arrested. He was jailed for two years for car theft.

Paroled from a prison in Atlanta, Roy returned home to find his family in dire financial conditions, Bettie going to school with no shoes.

The nine-year-old Bettie developed an interest in boys, notably the good-looking Clarence Daubenspeck, who was nearing his sixteenth birthday and was fully developed. "It was his cowlick that I fell for," she later said. "We played doctor even though I didn't know why."

When Roy knocked up a 15-year-old farm girl, Edna almost tried to kill him. She left him, thumbing a ride to Nashville without her children.

Bettie, along with her two sisters, Joyce and Goldie,

"I think she was a remarkable lady, an iconic figure in pop culture who influenced sexuality, taste in fashion, someone who had a tremendous impact on our society," said Playboy's founder Hugh Hefner, who years previously had provided Bettie with her greatest "exposure."

In 1995, Bettie was referred to as "Miss Pinup Girl of the World," "The Dark Angel," and "The Queen of Curves."

Bettie Page images have spawned picture books, biographies, fan clubs, dozens of websites, comics, beach towels, and even lunch boxes.

Look-alike contests in the 1980s and 90s brought out "kitten-with-a-whip Betties," all in leather and lace.

Celebrities took note. Uma Thurman in bangs reincarnated Bettie's image in Quentin Tarantino's *Pulp Fiction*. Madonna ordered that her own bondage photographs, some of them inspired by Bettie, be widely distributed.

When someone showed Bettie a copy of Madonna's *Sex* book, the former pinup beauty wasn't impressed.

"She's not much of a looker," Bettie said. "If I was Madonna, I'd keep my clothes on."

How did Bettie Page, idolized by the world, climb such a rickety ladder to fame only to fall off and tumble on the way down into a dangerous cesspool? It all began in an unlikely setting.

eventually ended up in a church orphanage.

When Bettie turned twelve, Edna rescued her from the orphanage, but life was still one of extreme poverty.

In 1936 Roy came back, renting a room in the basement of his former wife's house. It was during this period of Bettie's life that her father repeatedly raped her, muffling her cries with his hand as he penetrated her, often causing bleeding. He gave her a dime and warned her to keep her mouth shut.

With that dime, she lost herself in the world of the movies, dreaming that she too one day would become a movie star.

Bettie did well at Nashville's Hume-Fogg High School and was voted "Most Likely to Succeed" by her fellow classmates.

While still in school, Bettie met a star athlete, Billy Neal. He was more than six feet tall, a bit on the thin side, and had beautiful raven-black hair. Both teenagers were attracted to each other.

Her mother wouldn't let her date, but she secretly saw Billy behind Edna's back. He told her fascinating tales of how he'd traveled around the country, taking odd jobs where he could find them. He told her that one afternoon, while hitching from Los Angeles to Palm Springs, he'd been picked up on the road by Clark Gable, who'd made a pass at him. Bettie didn't know if these stories were true or Billy's fantasies.

At one point, Edna's new 24-year-old boyfriend tried to pull Bettie into his car and rape her. When Edna found out, she kicked Bettie out of the house, blaming her for dressing so seductively.

Bettie enrolled in Nashville's George Peabody College to study for a career in teaching, but still dreamed of becoming another Bette Davis.

When the United States entered the war against the Japanese Empire on December 7, 1941, Billy, age 21, was drafted.

Fearing that he'd be shipped overseas, Billy talked Bettie into marrying him in 1943, although she suspected, beginning with their honeymoon night, she'd made a big mistake.

Bettie's teaching career at a college preparatory school didn't last long. As a new teacher entering a classroom in high heels, she was greeted with wolf-whistles and catcalls.

"On my third day of teaching," Bettie recalled, "one of the older students, a burly 17-year-old, said he had a problem with his homework and wanted to talk to me when class let out. While I was leaning over his desk to study a paper, he put his hand up my dress and grabbed my vagina. That was it for me. I decided the teaching profession wasn't for me."

"I still held onto my dream of being a movie star, especially when I heard about the emergence of Ava Gardner," Bettie said. "I thought if that little Tarheel gal from North Carolina could make it in Hollywood, I could too."

Bettie joined Billy in San Francisco. Soon after, he was shipped off for military action in the Pacific in 1945 as the war slowly ground to an end.

After Billy left, Bettie met Art Grayson, who had directed silent pictures, and he arranged for a screen test for her in Los Angeles at 20th Century Fox. Makeup artists made her up to look like a whorish version of Joan Crawford. Her screen test with the handsome actor John Russell was also a disaster. Her Southern accent was even thicker than Ava Gardner's during a similar screen test for MGM.

Like Bettie's husband, Billy, Russell was a WWII veteran. He'd also been an athlete at the University of California. At 6'4", he towered over her. "I met this talent agent who told me I was tall, dark and handsome," he told her. "That's what movie stars are supposed to be. So I came to Hollywood."

When Bettie met him, he was drifting between bit parts in minor pictures, many of them Westerns. "He didn't tell me about his private life, and I didn't ask," Bettie said. "To me, he was a big movie star. After my test, we had this brief fling and promised to keep in touch when I left."

Perhaps unknown to Bettie, Russell was married at the time to Renata Titus, the couple living together from 1943 to 1965 and bringing up three children.

She claimed she was "happy for John" when he hit it big playing Marshal Dan Troop in the hit TV series, ABC's *Lawman*, which ran from 1958 to 1962.

During the prolonged absence of her husband, Billy, Bettie admitted she played the field—"one handsome sailor after another. San Francisco was full of them in those days."

An emaciated Billy, his weight less than 110 pounds, returned from the Pacific and immediately accused his wife of having affairs. When he boarded a Greyhound bus back to Nashville, Bettie told him to go travel cross country by himself.

Bettie had also become pregnant by some man, but she had a miscarriage. She turned down another screen test, this time at Warner's, and she regretted it for the rest of her life. She decided to start life anew in Miami.

One day on a Florida beachfront, she encountered a furniture importer who was closing his small operation in Port-au-Prince because of tensions between the U.S. and Haiti. President Harry S Truman was cutting off aid, which was causing riots in the streets.

Even though it was a dangerous assignment, Bettie agreed to accept a four-month job with him as a secretary and stenographer.

Arriving in Haiti, Bettie fell in love with the exotic island and its mysterious voodoo. She also fell in love with a Haitian.

Handsome **John Russell**, who made a screen test with Bettie, was her first movie star seduction. "I would have married him if he'd asked me," Bettie recalled years later. "I wrote him several letters, begging him to marry me. But he never answered me. Not even when I told him I was pregnant. There was a miscarriage. I also read in a movie magazine the John was already married."

"I do not have a photograph left over from my first screen test with John Russell, " Bettie said. "But if you saw **Joan Crawford** portraying the whore, Sadie Thompson, in *Rain,* you know exactly how I was made up. My makeup man that day, a real queen, more girl than I was, told me that the only roles I could get was as a cracker whore. The studio makes a lot of redneck movies, and you'll probably get cast in a few roles. I can see you on the screen as a gun moll and maneater."

Bettie's husband, Billy Neal, told everyone that while he was hitchhiking in California, matinee idol **Clark Gable** picked him up along a desert road and made a pass at him. The charge was dismissed as "one of Billy's fantasies." However, when he died and his relatives went through his things, they discovered a picture of Billy posing with Gable at a garage somewhere on the road to Palm Springs. Could his accusation have been true? That was in the days before Photoshop.

BETTIE INVADES
(AND ESCAPES FROM)
THE ISLAND OF VOODOO

On Miami Beach, Bettie had made it clear to the furniture employer that she'd accept a job as his secretary, but not as his mistress. He agreed to those terms. "He seemed such a gentleman," she said, "and I trusted him. One afternoon he drove me to this country place he owned. He said he was selling it and had to close out the deal. But that night he tried to rape me. My job ended right then and there. I ran away into the arms of another man I'd fallen in love with."

"I had overcome my Southern prejudice against Negroes and had really fallen for this guy. He referred to himself only as 'Mandingo.' He was about six feet four inches, and he was built like some Mayan God. I'd never encountered such a man before or since. He walked naked around the small house we shared. Always naked every chance he got. He was such an exhibitionist. He had plenty to show. I never knew that men came in that size. He was the greatest lover I'd ever had."

"I knew a lot of men in my life," Bettie confessed, "but never anyone like **Mandingo**, whom I lived with in Port-au-Prince. He once told me there wasn't a white man on the planet who could measure up to him. No wonder he was hired as a sexual performer on stage. I found out later he was known as 'Superman' in Port-au-Prince. During the heyday of Batista in Havana, there were fourteen Superman shows with live sex acts. After I left Port-au-Prince, I heard that Mandingo got an offer for a lot more money to perform in Havana."

"He'd hired a young gal—they called her a 'High Yaller' because of her skin tones—to work for us," Bettie said. "She did the shopping, cleaning, and cooking. She was jealous of me because I think she was in love with Mandingo too. I think they'd been lovers before I arrived on the scene."

"Mandingo said he worked the night shift at the Hotel Olaffson, so I was left with her at night," Bettie said. "We didn't get along. That's why I was surprised when she invited me to go with her to this club. She said Katherine Dunham's dancers were putting on a show."

"A taxi took us down this dark alley to a part of town I'd never visited before," Bettie recalled. "Inside it was filled mostly with American tourists who were slumming. The show opened. A beautiful blonde white gal appeared on stage and stripped off her clothes. There was loud applause. Then, to my shock, Mandingo appeared before the audience. He was completely nude and fully erect. The audience, especially the women, screamed their approval."

"That night I saw my lover make love right on stage with this blonde," Bettie said. "Not only that, but he invited three women in the audience to volunteer to come on stage and also be seduced. I couldn't believe what was happening. Several women volunteered, and Mandingo made his selection. He actually penetrated each of the women on stage in full view of everybody."

"Tears were rolling down my cheeks, and I wanted out of the club," she said. "I asked the gal I was with to leave, but she wanted to stay. She pointed to a group of men on the other side of the club. She said they were homos who'd flown in from Miami. For the second show, she told me that Mandingo would perform the same act but with men. I just couldn't stand any more, so I ran out of the club."

In the dark alley, she saw about six taxis lined up, waiting for the American tourists after the show. She got into the first one and asked him to take her back to her apartment. The route didn't seem right. The cab driver was taking her to another part of town, a place up in the hills overlooking Port-au-Prince. She objected to the route.

He paid no attention to her and told her to shut up. He continued to drive on for about a mile, coming to an abrupt stop. Four other Haitian men piled into the cab. One of them held a gun to her temple. The driver, who spoke a bit of English, told her that his friend would shoot her if she screamed.

A blindfold was placed on her and her hands bound. She was driven to a secluded house where she was carried inside and down some stairs. When the blindfold was removed, she found herself in a cell-like basement with five men standing over her. She was ordered at gunpoint to remove all her clothing. When she refused, one of the men struck her and was aided by another in stripping off her clothing. She was tied to the bed and repeatedly raped by the men until morning came.

"I was held there in bondage for 18 nights," she claimed. "Later I would pose for bondage photographs in America, but this was the real thing. I don't know why my captors finally freed me but all of them raped me for a final time. Then, they blindfolded me and drove me outside of the town where they dumped me beside the road. I was rescued by a family who had a rickety old truck. They drove me back to town. The next morning I was on a plane to Miami."

Bettie Page was intrigued by the sights, sounds, and smells of **Haiti.** "From my first day, I knew I wasn't in Nashville anymore," she said. At least three times a week she wandered through Port-au-Prince's famous "Iron Market," a showcase for the crafts of Haiti. "I bought an entire collection of stuffed voodoo dolls," she said. "To get my attention, the vendors put their hands on me and tried to pull me to their stand. A lot of Haitian men felt my titties in those days. Every time I went to the Iron Market, I got felt up, but I didn't really mind."

One night in Port-au-Prince, when Mandingo was secretly performing in sex shows, Bettie dressed up and went to the famous **Hotel Olaffson,** where her lover claimed he'd been working the night shift. "No one had ever heard of him, so I knew he was a liar," she said. "Still, I was afraid to confront him to find out the truth. But I fell in love with the hotel itself. Even movie stars like Anne Bancroft went there in those days. I slipped away and on several nights went to the bar there. I was very popular. All the international tourists tried to pick me up. One night I met a British actor there and was so turned on by his voice, I said yes. Imagine my surprise when I learned he was the famous **Richard Burton."**

[In 1967 Burton along with Elizabeth Taylor, made *The Comedians*, based on a Graham Greene novel about political intrigue in Haiti.]

"The Most Photographed Model in History"

After a brief stint in Miami, and a job with a standup comic, Bettie saved enough money for the airfare to New York. With fifty dollars in her pocket, she started life anew in October of 1947, hired as a secretary for the American Bread Company.

Even though she'd been raped repeatedly in Haiti, Bettie still retained her country girl naïveté in the big city. Strolling alone, window shopping on Broadway, Bettie was approached by a tall, handsome young man who asked her to go dancing with him. He said they would be joined by his best friend and his wife. Although a bit leery, Bettie agreed and joined the couple in their car, where it was parked beside 8th Avenue.

The big black sedan stopped ten blocks later and picked up another two young men, who had obviously been waiting on a street corner. After another two blocks or so, the driver picked up two more young men. These guys looked like hoodlums. Bettie became alarmed and begged to be let out of the car.

Like that driver in Haiti, this driver paid no attention to her. She was driven to a deserted schoolyard somewhere in Queens. When the car came to a stop, the driver and his girlfriend fled the scene, leaving Bettie trapped with the other hoods.

"In that strange world of girly pictures, I was the superstar," **Bettie Page** rightly claimed. "I was not only Queen of the Pinups, but the superstar of bondage pictures. I appeared in a series called 'Battling Babes.'

"I also learned how to use a whip. I learned that men really got turned on watching one scantily clad woman spank another woman. Sometimes I was on the receiving end. My ass was red a lot in those days. I got offers but never wanted to appear in live burlesque. Other strippers told me about it. Middle aged men cover themselves with their hats, coats, or newspapers and masturbate while they watch gals perform."

She was told they planned to rape her. If she put up a fight, she'd be beaten—maybe even disfigured. To save herself from a gang-rape, she told the men she was having her period.

Their leader then demanded oral sex from her, providing "you'll swallow." With great fear, she agreed and performed fellatio on each of them. She was driven back to Manhattan and let off on a corner near 44th Street and 10th Avenue. She stumbled home in tears.

Ashamed and humiliated, she didn't go to the police but called Billy in Nashville, begging him to take her back. He wired her the bus fare for Greyhound transit back to Tennessee.

The first three nights back in Tennessee went smoothly enough. "It was a constant round of sex," she later recalled.

But she soon learned that Billy was as jealous as ever. "It almost bordered on insanity. He kept me a prisoner. I knew it wouldn't work the second time around. I saved up some money working in a shop. I decided to divorce Billy once and for all and return to New York in spite of the horror I'd faced there. I was a bit smarter this time."

Back in New York, Bettie found work again as a secretary in an insurance firm. She later claimed she'd had an affair with a Peruvian engineer that lasted for several months before she learned that he was married and broke off the relationship. In 1959, when she was interviewed in Key West by Darwin Porter, she didn't want to reveal the details of this adulterous affair. "It was a sin," and that was all she said.

She didn't recall the exact series of events in her life that transpired after her affair. She went back to Tennessee again, sharing an address with her former husband, Billy Neal, whom she found as "explosive and jealous as ever." After that, she returned once again to New York.

There were occasional acting gigs in summer stock performances. Bettie was cast in a small part in *Gentlemen Prefer Blondes*. The director later said, "She was a Betty Grable type who wanted to be another Bette—Miss Bette Davis. Gals can dream, can't they?"

At the end of the summer, Bettie decided to give New York "one final try before calling it quits." By the time of this visit to the big city, her streak of bad luck finally changed.

One day she opted for a visit to Coney Island for a stroll along the beach, donning a bathing suit under her dress. At Coney Island, she encountered an amateur photographer, a black police officer who lived in Harlem. "You'd think that I would be afraid of black men for life after what happened to me in Haiti," she said. "But he seemed like a decent person. He asked me to pose for him. Feeling reckless on an otherwise boring day, I said yes. His name was Jerry Tibbs, and he ended up shooting my first pinup portfolio."

At his studio in Brooklyn, she didn't like it when Tibbs stuffed her bra with Kleenex, but she did go for his suggestion about her hair. He felt that she parted her hair in the wrong way, which made her face look long, rather unattractively so. It was this Harlem policeman who created the famous Bettie Page "bangs" that would become her hairdo for life. After checking her out in his camera's viewfinder, he informed her that, "Now you look like you

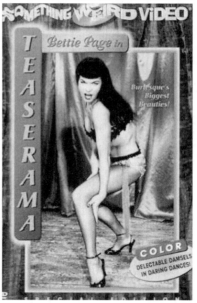

Bettie Page appeared with a famous stripper of her day, **Lili St. Cyr**, in *Striporama*. The highlight of the B-movie burlesque show is when Bettie disrobes for a short, sudsy bathtub scene.

Striporama was a great success, generating almost $100,000 at the box office. (That was bigtime in those days). Today, it's available on the Internet.

Bettie also appeared with an even more famous stripper, **Tempest Storm**, in *Teaserama*, Bettie is shown on screen in her trademark black silk underwear and stockings.

could stop an eight-day clock."

She later said that the policeman never came on to her. "He was married at the time to a white Jewish woman. That was a big social taboo back then."

Bettie flitted from assignment to assignment, modeling for camera buffs, amateur camera clubs, or entering swimsuit competitions and beauty pageants. She came in second place in the 1951 Miss New York pageant.

At first reluctant to do so, Bettie agreed to pose nude for cameramen. That made her extremely popular.

Some models at the time called Bettie names. Connie Mills said, "Page was a real Southern tramp. She was staying out all night and sleeping with every Tom, Dick, and Harry who asked her to."

Second only to Tibbs, Bettie's favorite photographer was another black man from Harlem, Cass Carr, who had come to New York from Jamaica. He was also a band leader. He claimed that Bettie was "completely uninhibited" in front of the camera. Soon her half-naked pictures were seen in such men's magazines as *Eyeful* and *Titter*.

Right before Christmas of 1951, Billy Neal unexpectedly showed up in New York to "reclaim" Bettie. His visit was a disaster. In just a few days he was arrested three times for assault and battery of men he tangled with, including a male friend of Bettie's that Billy cut with a pocket knife. Bettie put Billy on the Greyhound back to Nashville.

Bettie's life changed once again when one of her camera club amateur photographers showed a provocative picture of her to Irving Klaw, "America's King of Pinups." He operated a mail order service for clients across the United States.

Irving immediately recognized Bettie's potential as a model and hired her right away. At his 14th Street studio, Bettie became "a big fish in a brackish pond," in the words of one commentator.

Some sources claim that Bettie married the rather ugly Irving, but this appears never to have happened. Along with his sister, Paula Klaw, he ran a seedy Manhattan emporium called *Movie Star News*, peddling cheesecake shots of movie stars like Jane Russell or Lana Turner.

Both of the Klaws were the first to lure Bettie into her "bondage" photographs, which became one of the most enduring aspects of her legend. "No model looked more comfortable when trussed up with a rope than Bettie Page," said Irving. He often posed her tied to a chair or with a whip in her hand. There was a heavy demand for pictures of Bettie wrestling with other women.

She was clad in black lingerie and elaborate leather cos-

Bettie Page (*pictured on the left in both photos above*) plays a sort of wardrobe assistant to the notorious **Tempest Storm**, who at one time was almost a household name in America. Here they appear in the burlesque film *Teaserama*.

Married four times, Tempest was a friend of Marilyn Monroe. Born in the cotton fields of Georgia, she rose from that lowly beginning into international stardom.

She had begun to "develop" when she was in the seventh grade. The boys teased her about that but by the time she'd turned 12 they raped her. To escape from Georgia, she married when she was 14. "The marriage lasted one night," she said. She once married the "Bronze Buckeroo," a singing cowboy for Duke Ellington. One magazine carried the headline: TEMPEST STORM: "WHY I MARRIED A NEGRO."

tumes, often impersonating a stern dominatrix punishing a helpless man tied hand and foot. Many men requested that she pose in bondage pictures with women.

"I was introduced to lesbianism for the first time during this period of my life," Bettie said. "Personally, I think homosexuality is a sin, but I indulged in it. Later when I found God, I realized how wrong it was."

Bettie also posed for "special request" photos whenever a client requested one. One fan was willing to pay one hundred dollars for a picture of Bettie's feet.

"I was always asked to do porn, but I turned down all offers," Bettie said. "There was one exception. It was a setup. It was at a party. Normally, I don't drink but that night I got really drunk on May wine. A camera had been set up in the bedroom. I was taken in there where two girls about my age—lesbians, probably bisexual—held me down and did all sorts of things to me. I tried to resist but the cameraman said he'd 'ruin my face,' if I did. I hope, I pray to God that film doesn't exist. I hope it was destroyed."

Irving himself never made porno. He'd previously shot informal 8mm and 16mm cheesecake loops of Bettie, but he didn't opt for a launch into feature films until the mid-50s. Then he cast Bettie into a soft core porn film opposite Lili St. Cyr, a famous stripper of her day.

Bettie made two soft-core films with Lili—*Striporama* (1952) and *Varietease* (1954). A bisexual, St. Cyr had previously sustained an affair with Marilyn Monroe during their early days in Hollywood. Bettie also teamed up for an appearance in a girlie film named *Teaserama* [shot in color and released in 1955] with the most famous stripper of her day, Tempest Storm. Also appearing in that film was a campy cameo from Vikie Lynn, a well-known female impersonator of her day. Tempest eventually moved on to have affairs with both Elvis Presley and John F. Kennedy.

On a visit to Miami, Bettie met photographer Bunny Yeager who shot a long series of candid shots of Bettie—lounging with leopards, frolicking in the ocean waves, donning a devil's costume—in all a "Vargas girl come to life," as Yeager put it.

The photographer also shot Bettie's most famous picture. Wearing a Santa Claus cap, she's winking as she places a bulb on a Christmas tree. In January of 1955, this picture appeared as the centerfold in *Playboy*. Bettie earned only $20 for the shot, but among collectors it became the second most valuable issue of *Playboy*, topped only by the magazine's first edition wherein a nude depiction of Marilyn Monroe is featured as its centerfold.

During a brief vacation in Key West, Bettie met a teenage boy thirteen years her junior. In his bathing trunks, he appeared handsome and well developed. As it happened, Armond Walterson was still a virgin. Bettie taught him not only how to make love but to "French kiss."

Kissing Armond goodbye, Bettie returned to New York but trouble lay ahead for her.

In 1956, Senator Estes Kefauver, the coonskin-cap-wearing Tennessee Democrat, had beaten John F. Kennedy for the vice presidential nomination, although in the general election he lost to Richard Nixon under Dwight Eisenhower's banner.

The coonskin-cap wearing senator from Tennessee, **Estes Kefauver** (1903-1963), twice sought the Democratic Party's nomination for President of the United states. While serving in Washington, he was dubbed "the most hated man in Congress."

A moral crusader, he launched hearings, targeting what he called "indecent" publications and pornography. Bettie Page was among his targets. Upon his death, a large stash of her cheesecake photographs was found in his office. Were they for his pleasure or a tool in his investigation?

As part of an attempt to curry favor in the upcoming general election, Kefauver decided to launch an anti-pornography campaign with his Senate subcommittee. Ostensibly it was inaugurated as a means of cutting off income for organized crime, and as such, "pornography" and "the pornography industry" received even more of a spotlight than "organized crime." Kefauver wanted to return America to its original puritanical soul.

Irving Klaw and his "girl-in-peril" pictures of an eroticized Bettie aroused the ire of Kefauver's hound dogs. The FBI had ruled that Irving's photographs weren't pornographic, but both Bettie and Irving remained at the top of the senator's "shit list," as he called it. Although she was hauled into the Senate chambers as part of the proceedings, Bettie never had to testify.

Both Bettie and Irving narrowly escaped being slapped with obscenity charges, but their careers seemed destroyed. A broken, defeated man, Irving died in New York in 1966 at the age of 59.

In the wake of the hearings, Bettie reportedly tried to jump from the upper windows of a tall building in New York, but was restrained by her boyfriend at the time. Just before Christmas of 1957, Bettie left New York forever, turning her back on her modeling career at the peak of her fame.

Many sources report that she just disappeared, and, to some extent, that is true. What isn't widely known is that she made one final stab at a career in acting before a return to oblivion.

Much of **Bettie Page's** 1950s cheesecake work, especially the bondage shots taken by Irving Klaw, outraged the puritans trying to "protect" innocent America in the 1950s. Her critics, especially Senator Estes Kefauver, made so many threats against Bettie that they drove her into hiding.

At one point Kefauver told his aides, "Bettie Page is a pervert—no doubt a lesbian. Only a card-carrying lesbian would pose for some of those sordid pictures. I vomited looking at them."

STAR SEDUCTIONS

THE PINUP GIRL & JFK

THE BONDAGE QUEEN

MEETS KATE HEPBURN & THE RAT PACK

"Lined up all in a row were card-carrying members of **the Rat Pack** (left to right)—**Peter Lawford, Dean Martin, Sammy Davis Jr.,** and **Frank Sinatra,** the "chairman" of all the Rat Packers. Not pictured is Joey Bishop, fellow member.

"I had all of them," Bettie later confessed. "All of them had big dicks, all except Lawford. In Las Vegas they were cool cats but had a dark reputation. Pity their shamefully neglected wives and children. They discarded women like a used razor blade. They had talent; they brought joy to millions; and they were great in bed, except for Peter."

At this lonely, desperate time in Bettie's life, a call came in from Johnny Meyer, who identified himself as the publicist for Howard Hughes. Throughout the entertainment industry, Meyer was known as Hughes' pimp.

Hughes regularly, even systematically, flipped through girlie magazines and selected the model of his choice whom he then lured to Hollywood with the promise of an RKO contract. He had taken over the studio, and was using it as a vast casting couch. Hughes was a notorious bisexual, seducing as many good-looking young actors as he did young actresses.

Thrilled at the prospect of a movie contract, Bettie accepted the offer. The next day a thousand dollars in spending money, plus an airline ticket on TWA, arrived at her hotel.

Wanting to leave the pinup world behind her, and fearing that time was running out for her, she was eager to make it as a legitimate actress. Upon her arrival in Los Angeles, she was not met by Meyer, but by one of Hughes' chauffeurs. He drove her to a fairly luxurious house in Beverly Hills, where she was installed.

The next day Meyer called and warned her not to leave the house. "Mr. Hughes' schedule is never certain because the boss man is very busy," Meyer told her. "But he wants you there in case he drops in unexpectedly. Try to have yourself camera ready day and night because he keeps some strange hours."

Bettie later recalled that she was a virtual prisoner in that house until one night Hughes arrived on her doorstep.

"He was a man of few words and had a hearing problem," she said. "He must have found me appealing. We retired to the bedroom where he pulled off his jacket but none of his other clothes. He performed oral sex on me and then left. I tried to ask him about the screen test, but he told me that Meyer would make those arrangements."

Meyer called the next day and said "the boss man has talked to Frank Sinatra in Las Vegas. Frankie is very interested in using you in his next picture. I'm arranging for you to be picked up in a limo and driven to Las Vegas to attend Frankie's opening night at The Sands."

"It all sounded so glamorous at the time," Bettie recalled. "I was thrilled. All the way across the desert to Vegas, I dreamed that stardom for me was just around the corner."

She not only attended Frank's star-studded opening night but accepted an invitation to dinner in his suite.

"It was the most thrilling night of my life. I adored Frankie. He was romantic and sensitive to my feelings. By morning I think I wanted to marry him."

"He made arrangements for me to stay at another suite at The Sands for a whole week, with all expenses paid," Bettie said. "But the next morning I realized that Frankie had other plans and other gals. I'm afraid he treated me like a whore."

"During that week, my suite was visited by Dean Martin, Peter Lawford, and, much to my horror, Sammy Davis Jr.," Bettie said. "All three of them treated me well. Although I was initially afraid of Sammy, he turned out to be the nicest of them all. I kept waiting for a call from the fifth member of the Rat Pack, Joey Bishop, but he never showed up."

"At the end of my stay, a bellhop delivered a note from Frankie," she said. "It contained two thousand dollars. He wrote, 'You showed me and my boys a great time. Let's do it again sometime.'"

Bettie Page was aptly named. She formed only a "page" in the life of billionaire **Howard Hughes**, one of the 20th Century's greatest Lotharios. He seduced an all-star cast of lovers—male and female—and even managed, for a while at least, to become an American hero.

"He was an equal opportunity seducer," said Johnny Meyer, his pimp. "The gender of the victim didn't matter. He had just one requirement. Beauty."

"Except for Frankie, I never heard from the other Rat Packers again," Bettie said. "If I did, I guess I would have come running. After all, they were stars, weren't they?"

"There was a screen test at RKO and some still pictures, but nothing came of it. Hughes never showed up at the studio while I was there. Personally, I think he decided I was too old for him."

A month later, Sinatra called her again. She mistakenly thought that he was arranging another date or a trip to Las Vegas for her. He told her that he had a friend—"a very important friend"—who wanted to meet her, as he was one of her biggest fans. "He refused to divulge the name of his friend, however, but told me was charming, rich, and handsome. Trusting Frankie's judgment, I agreed to meet this mysterious stranger."

The meeting was to be not in Las Vegas, but at a place Sinatra either owned or rented in Palm Springs. "I don't know which," Bettie said. "At the last minute, Frankie called again. The plans had been switched. Instead of having a limousine take me to Palm Springs, a chauffeur would drive me to a mansion in Beverly Hills. I still didn't know the name of this man, but I was mighty intrigued."

The rendezvous was set for four o'clock the following afternoon, Bettie claimed. "I must have changed clothes two or three times before deciding on the right outfit. I figured this was a man of culture who had taste, so I decided to go for the demure, girl-next-door look instead of arriving with whips and chains. I figured that if this guy was into S&M, Frankie would have warned me."

A manservant ushered Bettie through the living room and out toward the pool area where she saw a young man swimming. He called out to her. "Bettie, why not take off your clothes and jump in? It's a hot day."

"I told him I didn't have a bathing suit with me."

"You of all women aren't ashamed to show the human body, are you?"

"Not at all," I said. "Right before him, I pulled off all my clothes and jumped completely jaybird naked into the pool with him. I swam to him. He didn't swim to me. When I got close to him, he pulled me to him and gave me a long, lingering kiss. 'I've waited a long time for this,' he said, hugging me close. 'I collect your pictures.' It was all too obvious that he was naked and aroused. Our kissing continued until he wanted it consummated under a cabana."

When pressed for details, she hesitated. "It was nothing out of the ordinary. He lay on his back. He wanted me on top. After he finished with me, he showered by the pool but didn't invite me to join him. He didn't kiss me goodbye but thanked me."

"By the way," he said, "I'm Jack Kennedy."

"I know it seems unbelievable, now that he became the most famous man on earth in the 1960s," Bettie said. "But you have to believe me. I only knew Ike in the White House. I had never heard of the Kennedy family. Millions of Americans in the 1950s didn't know who the Kennedys were, even though Jack had once sought the nomination for Vice President on the Democratic ticket. He didn't get it. I didn't even know that about him at the time. I never listened to those nominating conventions."

Bettie said that when she dressed and headed for the door and the waiting limousine, she expected to be handed a thousand dollar bill. "The man at the door offered me nothing," Bettie said. "I was a bit pissed off. Frankie had told me he was rich. However, the very next day, Frankie sent over ten one-hundred dollar bills and two dozen red roses. He also enclosed a note: 'JACK LIKED YOU A LOT AND WANTS TO SEE YOU AGAIN THE NEXT TIME HE'S IN LOS ANGELES.'"

"One night months later I was watching television, and I heard that Jack Kennedy had been nominated to run against Richard Nixon," Bettie said. "That night on the TV news I saw his beaming face. I couldn't believe it. It was the man who seduced me. He was running for president of the United States. Frankly, I didn't think he would beat Nixon. Everybody knew who Nixon was. But who was this Jack Kennedy with the funny accent? They would make fun of an accent like that in Tennessee where I grew up."

"He never called me again," Bettie said. "I would have

"Would you believe that when I first went to bed with **John F. Kennedy**, I didn't have a clue as to who he was," said Bettie Page. "Of course, that was before he became the President of the United States. Then the whole world knew who he was. I've known better lovers, of course, but never one that famous."

In a rare moment of self-confession, Kennedy told his male friends, "I'm not interested in carrying on for the most part. I like the conquest."

"I may not have known who John F. Kennedy was the afternoon I met him, but I sure as hell knew who **Katharine Hepburn** was," Bettie said.

"At the time it never occurred to me that she might be a lesbian. Those stories about her came out much later. That woman knew how to guard her privacy. I could have sold the story of my night with Hepburn to *Confidential* magazine, but I decided not to. I didn't want my male fans to think I, too, was a lesbian."

gone to meet him in the White House when Jackie wasn't around. I regretted not seeing him again, although the sex was hardly special. But he was the president. I heard stories that he was seeing Marilyn Monroe, but I didn't know if they were true or not. I was real sad that day he was shot in Dallas. He was far too young to die."

It was during her stay in Hollywood that Bettie also received a mysterious call from a woman who claimed she worked for a photographer who wanted to hire Bettie to pose in lingerie at an address in Hollywood. "I was far too trusting in those days, even though I'd been sexually assaulted," Bettie said. "I was offered a thousand dollars a night for the gig."

Arriving by taxi, Bettie was greeted at the door of a Hollywood home. The door was opened by an older woman, probably in her 60s, who did not identify herself.

"After getting me a glass of orange juice, she ushered me into a downstairs bedroom," Bettie said. "On the bed was some lingerie. She asked me to slip into whatever lingerie fitted me and wait for the photographer. It was the most expensive lingerie I'd ever seen. There was no bondage stuff, nothing like that. I slipped into a bra and a pair of pink panties, but kept on my high heels. Guys liked that."

Bettie waited about fifteen minutes until there was a knock on the door. She went to open it and discovered, to her total surprise, Katharine Hepburn dressed in a pair of slacks and a man's white shirt.

"At first I was so astonished I couldn't speak," Bettie claimed. "She was one of my favorite actresses. I had loved her in *The African Queen*. She wore only some bright red lipstick and no other makeup. She looked sort of regal, but not particularly young."

Like an old movie, Bettie drew the curtain at this point, refusing to divulge exactly what transpired between Hepburn and herself. "I did nothing except lay back and close my eyes. She did all the work."

Bettie claimed that "it was all over very soon. Miss Hepburn got up, thanked me, excused herself, and left the room. She told me her friend would pay me and see me out."

"When I got dressed and headed toward the foyer, that same older woman was waiting for me," Bettie said. "A taxi was also waiting. The woman handed me ten one-hundred bills. I thanked her and left. More money was on the way. Johnny Meyer arrived one afternoon and told me the contract with RKO wasn't coming through. He gave me an envelope with five one-thousand dollar bills and a one-way TWA ticket back East—and that was that."

Katharine Hepburn
Her Other Side

Spencer Tracy and **Katharine Hepburn** appear together in a scene from the film, *Pat and Mike* (1952). "They were great friends—not great lovers," George Cukor told the gay star of the Silents, William Haines. During the filming of *Pat and Mike*, Tracy had the "hots" for the leading male players, Aldo Ray and Chuck Connors.

Hepburn pursued her own game. She had a reputation for being fearlessly honest, yet concealed affairs with the likes of everybody from Laura Harding, the American Express heiress, to Irene Mayer Selznick, Louis B. Mayer's daughter. Tracy was an alcoholic and an abusive bisexual that spent his later years buying male hustlers, some of whom were arranged by his best friend Cukor.

Of all the stars of Golden Age Hollywood, four-time Oscar winner Katharine Hepburn kept the door to her lesbian closet more tightly bolted even than Greta Garbo.

In contrast, Hepburn wrote a scenario for herself and got the world to believe it. Except for insiders in Hollywood, the public never learned her true story until her death at the age of 96 in 2003.

Darwin Porter, in his landmark book on Hepburn, was the first author to reveal details of her life as a bisexual woman. Published in 2004, it was called *Katharine The Great, Secrets of a Lifetime Revealed*. The public response to this international favorite was for the most part favorable, but some of Hepburn's diehard fans were outraged, attacking Porter's insolent examination of an American icon.

Weeks and even months later you could walk into a supermarket and read stories in *The National Examiner* about KATHARINE HEPBURN'S GAY LIFE. In the wake of the tabloids, other biographies followed, outlining a bisexual Hepburn. One of them was *Katharine Hepburn: The Untold Story* by James Robert Parrish.

Another well-respected Hepburn biographer, Anne Edwards, had previously published *Katharine Hepburn, A Remarkable Woman* in 1985. After Hepburn's death, she publicly admitted that she was forced to conceal the truth since Hepburn was still alive at the time Edwards published her biography.

On national TV, Edwards asserted, "Katharine romanticized and fictionalized her relationship with Spencer Tracy, a bisexual, abusive alcoholic. She and Spencer were great beards for each other throughout their lives. I can understand why she would have to keep her sexuality a secret."

Hepburn married only once, even though she'd proclaimed, "I'm not mad about the male sex—perfectly independent as I am." Her husband was Ludlow Ogden Smith, who had a male lover, Jack Clark, at the time. Hepburn herself was deep into her decades-long affair with Laura Harding, the American Express heiress.

Over the years Hepburn, whom her father had called "a raging bull," enjoyed affairs with many famous men and women, not only Garbo, but director John Ford, Claudette Colbert, Charles Boyer, and Jimmy Stewart.

Her "romance" with Howard Hughes as falsely depicted in the Martin Scorsese film, *The Aviator*, starring Leonardo DiCaprio as the billionaire, lasted longer on screen than it did in real life. For Hepburn, the affair evolved into a publicity stunt, as she hoped to revive a stalled film career after having been been defined as "box office poison."

Director George Cukor, a best friends of both Hepburn and Tracy, once admitted, "Kate's love affair with Spence—widely touted as one of the great romances of Hollywood—wasn't quite the way the public perceived it. They were great, supportive friends, their so-called love affair platonic."

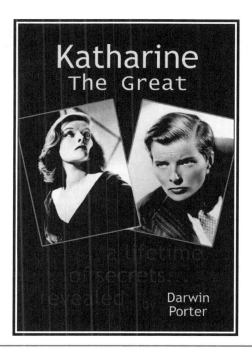

Within a few days of **Katharine Hepburn**'s death in June of 2003, a tastefully whitewashed memoir of the screen goddess, *Kate Remembered*, was rushed with "unseemly haste" into print.

In September of 2003, in a review "Kate Selectively Remembered" by David Ehrenstein, *The Advocate* referred to that biography as a "mixture of cautious disclosure and obsequious deference" and asked why that biography "does nothing to question that public persona that Hepburn had carefully constructed over the years."

In the same review, *The Advocate* issued a challenge to the writers and publishers of America: "One can only hope that there's someone out there who remembers Kate a bit better than A. Scott Berg and has a manuscript ready."

Darwin Porter had such a manuscript, and it had taken him years of gathering data to publish. ***Katharine the Great***, ***A Lifetime of Secrets Revealed*** (ISBN 978-0-9748118-0-2), published by Blood Moon Productions, remains to this date the only detailed and revelatory biography of Hepburn's early affairs with both men and women.

STRANGERS IN THE NIGHT

VS.

JESUS

After the collapse of her last attempt at becoming a Hollywood star, Bettie resettled in the little seaport of Key West, Florida. Here she became a teacher again of fifth graders at Harris Elementary School.

She should have brought out that whip used in bondage pictures. Once again she couldn't control the rowdy boys in her class, many of them coming on to her and asking to date her.

Obtaining work as a secretary within Key West's burgeoning naval base, Bettie took up once again with Armond Walterson, who also worked on the base.

She married Walterson a few weeks later. She was thirty years old, and he had just turned 18. "All he cared about was sex, sex, sex—morning, noon, and all night long—movies, hamburgers, and going out drinking with his brothers," Bettie said.

After she'd settled into Key West, the co-author of this book, Darwin Porter, then the bureau chief of the Florida Keys division of *The Miami Herald*, heard of her arrival. His friend, Monroe County sheriff, John S. Spottswood, knew where Bettie was living and arranged for Porter to meet her.

Not knowing what to expect, Porter arrived at her house to meet a somewhat shy and reserved woman with a soft, lilting Southern accent. They bonded by talking of their mutual childhoods, his growing up in North Carolina and hers "next door" in Tennessee.

"She didn't really want to be interviewed, but mainly wanted to talk," Porter said. "Although she had a man in her life—who was never around—she seemed lonely. Our talks stretched out over a period of a month. It seemed she didn't want an interview published that would tell her public that she was hiding out in Key West. She seemed to want to unburden herself of her past, as if that would free her from the 'sins' she felt she had committed."

She asked Porter if he'd write the story of her life, sharing secrets she'd never told anyone before. Some of the incidents related were rather shocking, indicating that as a famous model she'd had far more scandalous experiences than she'd previously admitted.

That memoir was never written. Her jealous husband heard that some young man had been visiting her during the afternoons and beat Bettie severely. After that, she wouldn't return Porter's calls or answer the door.

The only way Porter could contact her was when she went to church. Encountering her there one Sunday morning, Bettie told Porter that she couldn't see him again. She'd told Walterson about the book project, but he had forbidden her to cooperate. He claimed that once such a book was published, "all of Key West would know I'm living with a whore." She shook Porter's hand and wished him well, but asked him not to "invade my privacy again."

Bettie "had found Jesus," in her words. The sound of church music had drawn her inside the Key West Temple Baptist Church. "The Lord took me by the hand and I went inside. I was crying in the back row, repenting my sins. That night, I turned my life over to the Lord."

Her first visit to the church had occurred on New Year's Eve—December 31, 1958. She'd been wandering the streets of Key West alone. Where was her husband? Certainly not celebrating New Year's with Bettie. As it turned out, he was in the arms of a fourteen-year-old girl, who became pregnant. While Bettie was in church, Walterson was busy bringing an unwanted child into the world.

A fire-and-brimstone preacher, Morris Wright, was cajoling his flock. The son of a share-cropper, he'd just been released from the Key West jail. He would become the primary spiritual force in Bettie's life during her remaining months in Key West. Bettie stuck it out with her young husband for a few months but abandoned him in the summer of 1959.

On a Greyhound bus, she returned to Nashville. Walterson followed her there but Bettie's door was closed to him. He'd never again see the sexy model who'd stolen his virginity.

In Tennessee, Bettie filed for divorce. Walterson returned to Key West, where, after going through a series of women and leaving a few of them pregnant, he died from unexplained causes at an early age in the 1970s.

In a "fit of madness" [Bettie's words], she contacted Billy Neal again and asked him to remarry her.

Very reluctantly he did so. Unlike before, however, he refused to consummate the marriage, believing falsely that she'd contacted syphilis "while whoring around New York."

She also urged him to become a Christian missionary and travel to Angola with her. He refused.

One night after a violent argument, Billy allegedly attacked her, strangling her but letting go when she screamed out that he'd burn in hell.

Fleeing the next day, Bettie was on the Greyhound bus to her "refuge," the city of Miami. There, she would divorce Billy for the second time.

As the years went by in Florida, Bettie wandered in and out of churches, and in and out of the beds of "strangers in the night." She told her acquaintances she wanted to be a "good girl," but found herself being bad. "I can't help myself," she said in desperation. "I feel I'm split into two different personalities."

One night in 1966, she wandered into an old-fashioned dance hall in Miami, the Palace Ballroom on Biscayne Boulevard. Here she met her final husband, Harry Lear, who was her same age, forty-three years. She still looked gorgeous, and Lear thought she was not even thirty at the time. A lineman by day with Florida Bell, he moonlighted as a chauffeur at night, driving a large black hearse around Miami, hauling dead bodies from place to place.

After meeting him, she saw him every day, marrying him on St. Valentine's Day in 1967. She moved into his home in Hialeah where she found a "ready-made family," as he had three children from his previous marriage.

After only a year or so of peace, her mental condition began to deteriorate rapidly. She'd often become violent with the children, beating them for the smallest infraction of her Draconian house rules. She had spotlights placed in the backyard and would work throughout the night, often until dawn, in her garden, "planting vegetables for Jesus."

With the return of October in 1971, Lear knew that by now, Bettie was perhaps psychotic. It was time to end the marriage. He arranged for her to find a bed in Boca Raton's Bible Town, where she need pay only $25 a month for room and board.

On January 17, 1972, Bettie was notified at the Bible School that Lear's divorce from her had come through. She went berserk.

The religious zealots at the Bible School started screaming and running for cover. Somehow Bettie had obtained a .22 caliber pistol and was running through the motel complex threatening her fellow residents "with the retribution of God." The police were summoned and managed to subdue her.

Lear was called and came for Bettie, managing to convince the police to let her go. He took her back to his home in Hialeah. There, her behavior became increasingly erratic.

She barely kept herself under control, punctuating her days with frequent outbursts of anger against both Lear and his children.

When Lear came home from work on April 13, 1972, Bettie raced into the living room brandishing a large butcher knife from the kitchen. She demanded that each of them, including her former husband, stand before a picture of Jesus on the wall and pray to him. "Or else I'll de-gut each of you like my mama used to do with a chicken."

After three hours, Lear begged to go to the bathroom. She granted him permission. He sneaked out the back door and asked a neighbor to call the police before returning to the living room where his children were still being held hostage.

When Bettie Page "found **Jesus**" [her words], it didn't bring the peace of mind she had hoped. Instead, her obsession with religion seemed to bring out the slasher in her, and she threatened human life and later indulged in murderous knife attacks—in one case slashing an elderly woman's throat.

In her pinups, she was known for her "girl-next-door" quality. That may be true if the girl next door was a psychotic killer in a rage against the world.

Doctors at Jackson Memorial, a mental hospital in Miami, said, "religion, and Jesus in particular, has turned into a violent obsession with this patient."

With dome lights flashing, Tom Fitzpatrick, a Hialeah policeman, came through the open door and wrestled the butcher knife from Bettie as she screamed "God's hell and damnation upon your soul."

He forced her into the back of his squad car while he took a statement from Lear.

Back in the car, he found Bettie masturbating, with her panties down to her knees. He drove her to the police station in Boca Raton where he filed a report, asserting that she was definitely psycho. Eventually, assault and battery charges were dropped, and she was delivered to the psycho ward at Jackson Memorial Hospital where she remained for six months under a suicide watch.

Amazingly Lear accepted her back into his household, despite the fact that she still might have been a threat to his children. He'd built a separate room for her. To pay for her room and board, she did the housework and cooked for the family, still gardening from midnight to dawn.

During this time she remained "locked in her own world and I didn't have the key to it," Lear said. "There were no more violent outbursts."

With his children grown up and gone, Lear retired in 1978, telling her he was moving to South Carolina. He did not invite her to go along.

Psychotic Stabbings & *Attempted Murder*

In the aftermath of Lear's departure, Bettie was rescued by her brother, Jimmie Page, who invited her to live with him in Santa Monica, California, doing housework and cooking for him. "Each day," she later said, "I looked in the mirror and seemed to have aged more and more."

Lear still sent her money at the rate of $50 a month, the amount that the court had ordered in alimony. Even after the period of court-mandated alimony payments ended, he continued to send the $50.

Bettie came and went from her brother's house in California. For reasons not known, she also lived at other addresses, including with strange men she picked up, men who seemed to want to have an affair with the famous Bettie Page, even though she had long ago lost her fabled beauty.

When her latest boyfriend kicked Bettie out in favor of a younger woman, she rented a trailer in Lawndale, California, from her landlords, Esther Trevin, age 67, and Esther's husband, James Hunter Trevin, age 77.

On the night of April 19, 1979, Bettie attacked Esther with a butcher knife, stabbing her several times. Her elderly husband hit Bettie over the head with a wrench.

The old lady survived, and policemen were called to haul Bettie away. She was booked on two accounts of assault with a deadly weapon "by reason of insanity."

The judge sentenced her to five years' confinement in the Patton State Hospital in Highland, California. She was released in February 1981, although the court mandated that she participate in a program of outpatient mental treatment.

Bettie found lodgings within the home of Leonie Haddad in Santa Monica. At four o'clock on the morning of June 12, 1982, Bettie entered the elderly woman's room and straddled her, brandishing a foot-long serrated bread knife.

She screamed at the woman: "God told me to kill you." With the knife she sliced the woman's face from the corner of her mouth to her right ear. She then stabbed the woman four times in the chest, narrowly missing a direct wound to her heart. She also stabbed the woman's left hand eight times, slicing off the ends of her fingers.

On September 26, 1983, at the age of 62, Bettie went on trial for attempted murder. A judge had ruled her mentally competent to stand trial.

A policeman guarding the door later said, "I'd seen those pinup and bondage pictures. I couldn't believe this haggard old lady was once the Bettie Page pinup queen of the 1950s."

After doctors testified that Bettie was "criminally insane," another judge agreed, rescinding the mandate of a former judge who thought she was aware of her actions. She was dragged kicking, screaming, and shouting obscenities from the courtroom to face a decade-long sentence, again at Patton State Hospital.

Bettie would remain at the mental facility until 1992. Upon her release, there were no more violent attacks. She would spend the rest of her life in seclusion, except for occasional forays.

THE REBIRTH OF A
Cult Goddess

Upon her release, she discovered that the Bettie Page of the 1950s had become famous all over again. A new generation of horny young men had rediscovered her pinups anew. Regrettably, she would not financially benefit from these provocative poses, or the bondage pictures, because she had signed away her rights.

The press wanted to interview her and photograph her, but she refused. "I want to be remembered for what I used to look like, not the fat old lady I am today," she said.

She did grant an interview with Hugh Hefner's *Playboy*, her *alma mater*. "I never thought what I did was shameful," she said. "I felt it was normal. What I did was so much better than pounding a typewriter eight hours a day, which gets monotonous."

"After all, when God created Adam and Eve, they were stark naked," Bettie said. "And in the Garden of Eden, God was probably naked as a jaybird too!"

On reflecting on the impact of Bettie on America, Hefner claimed that "she helped usher in the sexual revolution of the 60s."

Her greatest regret was that "I did not become a movie star. My fantasy was to be the leading lady to Burt Lancaster or Errol Flynn in some swashbuckler film."

"I guess I did better than other American icons," Bettie said. "Elvis Presley, Marilyn Monroe, James Dean. I walked away from my career as a model while still alive. They didn't."

Gretchen is lookin' fetchin' in *The Notorious Bettie Page*, playing the 1950s pinup and sex icon. **Gretchen Mol** brings Bettie to life again in this film of the model's tumultuous life. "Even when she's lashed to a chair, chains around her ankles, and a gag over her mouth, there's something innocent and practically perky about pin-up Bettie Page," wrote one critic.

Mol herself said, "The idea of fetish was sort of underground—now we see it on every street corner. Bettie had a lack of shame before the camera." Before appearing as "Queen of Kink," Mol made two Woody Allen movies, *Sweet and Lowdown* and *Celebrity*.

For nearly four decades, the life of **Bettie Page** was a complete mystery. Along came Richard Foster's shocking tale, *The Real Bettie Page*, and the seventh veil was dropped, exposing Bettie as never before.

Bettie had lived in the memories of her fans who were eager to learn more about her life. **Foster** (whose photo is inset into the cover of the book he wrote), tells of her modest beginnings as a young girl in Nashville and follows Bettie through her stormy marriages, even her trial for attempted murder and her decade-long isolation behind the walls of a mental institution.

In 2005 Gretchen Mol re-created the life of the pinup star from the mid-30s to the late 1950s in *The Notorious Bettie Page*.

"Why did they have to call it notorious?" Bettie asked after viewing the film.

Bettie Page's legacy is heading for the movie screens once again in Mark Mori's docu, *Bettie Page Reveals All*. Appearing as themselves are such key players in Bettie's life as *Playboy's* Hefner and stripper Tempest Storm.

In Los Angeles, after pneumonia and a heart attack, and after lapsing into a coma, Bettie died at 6:41pm PST on December 11, 2008. She was buried at Westwood Village Memorial Park Cemetery.

Today only Marilyn Monroe rivals Bettie in terms of Internet traffic. In five years alone, Bettie's website scored some 600 million hits.

Bettie Page was exploited by photographers who had taken pictures of her in the 1950s and were making a living by hawking those long-ago images. In the last few years of her life, when she was living in near poverty, she hired a law firm to help her recoup some of the profits being made from her likeness. It seems that everybody has profited from Bettie Page except the model herself. There are tribute songs, countless web sites, and more than a thousand products for sale on e-Bay. At first her loops were sold under the counter or mailed in plain brown wrappers. Yet decades later she was elevated to the status of pulp goddess. The "Bondage Babe" has gone mainstream.

According to her business agent and long time friend, Mark Roesler, Bettie was hospitalized in critical condition on December 6, 2008. She had suffered a heart attack, which led to her falling into a coma. When her funeral was conducted at California's Westwood Village Cemetery, there was a large blowup of Bettie in all her cheesecake glory resting among the tribute flowers. Displaying soft core porn at a funeral may have been a first.

Three Graces, Three Playmates

For years **Bettie Page** refused to be photographed, not wanting her fans to see her as she was above, in her 80s, but as she used to be when she donned those leopard-skin outfits—or nothing at all—to romp along Florida beaches. Suddenly, for reasons known only to herself, she decided to change her mind. Not only that, but she agreed to pose between two modern-day pinup queens, **Anna Nicole Smith** (left) and **Pamela Anderson** (right).

Bettie had been a brunette bombshell of the 50s. The late Anna Nicole Smith was a bombshell. Pamela Anderson remains so today, still generating headlines.

Like Bettie, Anna Nicole was a model and sex symbol who also gained popularity in *Playboy*, becoming 1993's *Playmate of the Year*. Following in Bettie's footsteps, Anna Nicole was a teenager when she married. She was also a high school dropout in Texas. She became famous for her second marriage to oil tycoon Howard Marshall, who was 63 years her senior. She denied that she married the octogenarian for his money. Of course she didn't. "It was for the sex, silly."

When Marshall died, she carried the battle over his estate to the Supreme Court, but ultimately lost. She died at the age of 39, apparently as a result of an overdose of prescription drugs.

The Canadian actress, Pamela Anderson, born in 1967, became known in such TV roles as *Baywatch*. Like Anna Nicole and Bettie, she too became *Playboy's Playmate of the Month* in February, 1990. In early 2004, Pamela appeared naked on the cover of *Playboy*, the first time she'd appeared naked on any magazine cover.

Her private life has made her notorious. Her most tumultuous relationship was with super hung Tommy Lee, drummer for Mötley Crüe, whom she married on February 19, 1995 after knowing him for only 96 hours. The couple eventually had two sons together. Tommy Lee certainly possesses the weapon to become a baby maker.

Pamela filed for divorce from Lee twice and reconciled with him twice before eventually breaking up with him for good. An amateur sex video of Pamela with Tommy Lee on their honeymoon was stolen from their home and became the best-selling celebrity porn tape of all time. Eventually, after a lawsuit, Pamela was awarded $1.5 million plus attorney fees for her share of the profits.

After Kid Rock, Pamela hooked up with Rick Salomon, who also made a notorious sex tape starring Paris Hilton. To judge from both of these sex tapes, Pamela believes that SIZE DOES MATTER. She married Salomon on October 6, 2007. But on February 22, 2008, she requested that the court annul her marriage, based on "fraud." To judge from his sex tape, Salomon will have no trouble finding future partners. If he ever turns gay (highly unlikely), he'll be a size queen's delight.

Although aging, the blond bombshell still remains in the news. Pamela wrote an open letter to President Barack Obama, urging the legalization of cannabis. It has also been suggested—that if Obama wants to try a blonde for a change, Pamela is available. But Scarlett Johansson saw prexy first.

In the Arena With Bad Boy
Charlton Heston

WHAT HE DID WHEN HE WASN'T PAINTING THE CEILING OF THE SISTINE CHAPEL

"He has a bad memory. He still thinks he's parting the Red Sea."
—Barbara Stanwyck

Charlton Heston made some 75 films over half a century, but his celebrity far exceeded his limited talent. A hero of big screen historical dramas, the wooden actor starred in such films as *The Ten Commandments* and *Ben-Hur*.

In later life he became what one newspaper called "the white man's last stand against becoming a second class citizen in a world dominated by effeminate white liberals, black gangstas, militant fags, and assorted multiculturalists who make decent white people feel ashamed of their heritage. "

As president of the NRA, he was known for his advocacy of guns in every home. When he died, one commentator said, "I guess we can finally pry Charlton Heston's guns from his cold, dead hands," mocking references which Heston had used during a speech he had given at an NRA. rally.

Heston spent his final days stricken with Alzheimer's and growing increasingly demented. But there was another side to him, a dark sinister personality, that he managed to suppress during his lifetime. Charlton Heston was a far more complicated man than most of the world ever knew.

WHAT'S IT ALL ABOUT, CHARLIE?

In 2000, when Mart Martin published his *Didn't He Or Didn't He?* book, outlining the lovers, flings, or "just friends" of various male movie stars, he awarded a special prize to Charlton Heston. According to Martin, Heston is the "Grand Prix winner of the right half of the tightly upraised Zipper Award, since his name has never been connected 'romantically' with anyone outside his marriage."

Whereas it's true that his name has never been linked romantically with anyone, he was long ago outed in the underground press for his behind-the-scenes sexual indiscretions. And although Heston's nocturnal activities escaped the scrutiny of the mainstream press during his lifetime, his "outing" continues today.

In 2002, Heston's name began appearing on Mark Winburn's Weblog, the most notorious over-the-top collection of Hollywood gossip in history. An entry about Heston from 2002 contains this brief description. "Right Wing gun kook. Reportedly likes young girls—and, if rumors are to be believed, young boys, too. Abuser of women. Alcoholic."

Indeed, Heston maintained a long and successful marriage to former drama student Lydia Clarke, but he was not always faithful. "He has an ego the size of Texas and a talent the size of South Dakota," said actor Sal Mineo.

"In spite of all his right-wing stances, including his belief that every household should have a gun, he liked to pound young ass on the side," Mineo charged. "That is, young ass of both genders. It didn't matter to him. A hole was a hole, providing it was a young hole. I should know."

Mineo, a fairly out gay actor, was only seventeen when he encountered Heston on the set of *The Private War of Major Benson,* released in 1955.

At its inception, the film was tailored for Cary Grant. Hollywood insiders were shocked when Heston was cast after Grant bowed out. Heston in a light comedy inspired by Cary Grant was a stretch for the imagination. Cast opposite Heston was Julie Adams, with Mineo in a supporting role.

"At first I thought Heston would hate me," Mineo said. "He probably

He was described by casting agents as **"Handsome Heston,"** In his own words, he said, "I have a face that belongs in another century."

At the end of WWII, Heston spent the last two years guarding the Aleutian Islands against a Japanese invasion that never came. Returning to mainland America with 13 million other young Americans, who'd been trained only to kill, he faced the same dilemma as to what to do next. Nude modeling led to acting, which led to Hollywood. Suddenly, Charlton Heston woke up one morning and announced to the world, "I'm a fucking movie star."

As far as it is known, young **Sal Mineo** was the first boy that Charlton Heston ever sexually pursued. If Heston thought he was getting a boy virgin, he was too late. Yul Brynner had already been there, done that. Heston had nothing to say about Sal in his autobiography, *In the Arena.* How could he? There was nothing fit to print.

knew I was gay and liberal, and he was as conservative as Attila the Hun on most of his political positions."

In a chat in a Chelsea, New York, apartment years after the making of this movie, Mineo claimed, "I was dumbfounded. At first I thought he was just being friendly. He even invited me out for a drink, although I was too young to drink. That drink turned out to be not beer or liquor but a smoothie. We drove up into the Hollywood Hills and watched the sunset."

Later, according to Mineo, Heston drove him to a fairly luxurious house—it wasn't his—and there was no one at home, not even a servant. "Gradually, he lured me to one of the upstairs bedrooms where he was all over me. The man was hungry. I think he didn't get much. Once he mounted me, I didn't think he would ever get off me. I think he wanted to stay in the saddle all night. But eventually he was satisfied. On the way home, he asked me if I'd be his steady piece. I found him a very good-looking man, but dull. He was nicely equipped, though, and he showed me a good time. I wanted more. We carried on like this for about two years. Eventually, he got tired of me. I was growing up, and he didn't like that."

"We made one more picture together," Mineo said. "*The Greatest Story Ever Told*, which came out in 1965. We were directed by George Stevens, and the picture was released by United Artists. By that time I hadn't seen him in a number of years, and he'd moved on. When I ran into him, we chatted very briefly—there was nothing much to say. He seemed like he hardly knew me, although his most intimate part knew one of my most intimate parts very, very well."

Susan Hayward, while staying in Fort Lauderdale, told her "Boy Friday," Peter Pell, that she'd had a fling with Heston when she'd made *The President's Lady* with him for Fox in 1952. Based on a novel by Irving Stone, the movie starred Heston as the future U.S. president, Andrew Jackson. According to Hayward, "Frankly, I was the one who seduced Chuck. He didn't come on to me. I came on to him. Call me aggressive. He was okay in the sack, but I later learned he liked much younger women than me. The grapevine even claimed he liked a

"**John Derek** had about as much acting talent as Heston," said Anne Baxter. "But he looked great. Back in those days if a woman was gorgeous, or a man really handsome, the first thing people said to you was, 'You should be in the movies.'" Derek had a notorious past as the highest paid male hustler in Hollywood before becoming known for marrying some of the most beautiful women in show business. Like Heston, he liked his female flesh young and tender on the bone.

Charlton Heston faced a lot of ridicule when he played Moses parting the Red Sea in *The Ten Commandments* (1956), a picture the actor made for Cecil B. DeMille. When Moses comes down from Mt. Sinai, he explodes in anger at the people "writhing in orgiastic worship of the Golden Calf."

The scene took two days to shoot. As Heston recalled, "At first, the pretty extra girls and brawny muscle men DeMille cast as the principal orgiasts threw themselves into their task. But on the fourth day, their energies began to flag. The lion skins they were rolling around on began to rub raw places, and they had honey in their navels and grape juice in their hair. As one of the extra girls said, 'Who do I have to fuck to get off this picture?'"

boy on occasion, but I don't know that for a fact."

Heston once said, "Nudity is never erotic, except in the bedroom." That was a strange statement coming from a man who became the first major American film star to show his ass in a movie. That occurred onscreen when the apes stripped his tattered rags away in *Planet of the Apes* (1968). But his statement contained a second, more subtle, irony as well.

When he was a struggling actor in New York, living with Lydia Clarke, he was hired by the Art Students League to pose nude for life studies classes. He was paid a dollar and a half an hour, plus all the tea he wanted to drink and all the sugar biscuits he wanted to eat.

"In those days, male models for life studies got to wear little jockstraps. My wife was doing very well as an actress by that time but I had not yet begun, and she made me a little grey velour jockstrap."

Some teachers wanted their students to paint the male genitalia—"after all, Michelangelo did that." In those cases and in those days, however, only male students were allowed to sketch a live model nude.

For those all-male classes, Heston showed the full monty. Most of the young would-be artists were gay. It is said that many nude sketches of Heston still exist and are valuable collectors' items. As far as it is known, none of these sketches has ever been offered for public sale.

There were rumors that to earn much-needed cash in New York and during his early days in Hollywood, Heston peddled his meat for a buck. That appears not to be true, although it's hard to trace a man's private life which was spent almost exclusively in shadows.

By the time he became famous, most of the general public had readily accepted Heston's assessment of his own private life. "I'm too dull, square, and protestant—in the philosophical, not the religious, sense—to

In 1981, then-President **Ronald Reagan** bestowed the Medal of Freedom on his friend **Charlton Heston**. The actor liked Reagan more than Bush, perhaps because as thespians, they had a lot more in common. Both of them had been presidents of the Screen Actors Guild.

Actually it was Lyndon Johnson, not Reagan, who appointed Heston to the executive body controlling the National Endowment for the Arts. That turned out not to be one of Johnson's smart moves. Heston had his own ideas about what was art—and what was not.

Heston was even invited by Reagan to watch the election returns on that night in 1980 when he swept into the presidency. "From that time on, Ron became 'Sir' to me," Heston said. He later claimed he "saved" Reagan's inauguration by preventing a "smashed" Dean Martin from performing and embarrassing the president.

Charlton Heston liked President **George W. Bush** from the day they first met.

In 1992 Bush invited Heston and his wife Lydia to a state dinner at the White House for the president of Chile. Heston was seated next to the Chilean president "where I had to squeak by in Spanish." Lydia ended up next to Jim Baker, Secretary of State.

In the picture above both Heston and Bubba Bush look very solemn as one right-winger bestows the Medal of Freedom on another right-winger.

be a big, popular figure, a beloved figure. I'm not a drunk. I've had only one wife. My kids aren't runaways. It's not what people expect."

He lied about not being an alcoholic—in fact, in 2002 he checked himself into an alcohol rehab program.

Actor Richard Harris, a world-class "hell raiser," more or less, went along with Heston's own assessment of himself. "The guy's so square he came out of a cubic womb."

But other Hollywood insiders disagreed with these appraisals, notably Orson Welles, who cast Heston in *Touch of Evil*, a Universal International Picture released in 1958.

Other members of the cast included Janet Leigh, Welles himself, Marlene Dietrich, Zsa Zsa Gabor, and Joseph Cotten. In that movie, Heston agreed to play, of all roles, a Mexican detective.

Welles later told his associates that, "It's a well-known fact that I'm a connoisseur of the world's finest whorehouses from Singapore to Shanghai. A concubine of Thami el-Glaoui, the Moroccan pasha of Marrakesh, taught me more about lovemaking with a woman than any Hollywood goddess I ever fucked. His highness lent the concubine to me for the night."

"I've always seduced actors," Welles claimed. "I make them fall in love with me. When I was young and pretty back in my early days in Hollywood, I was the Lillie Langtry of the older homosexual set. I tried to seduce Heston one night. But that didn't get me anywhere. He agreed, though, to go with me to a whorehouse. He let it be known that he liked very young stuff—'but not children,' he cautioned. The night we went out together, he requested that both a boy and a girl be sent to his room at the same time. To show that I was a man of the world, I showed no surprise whatsoever at the request for the boy. I told him that in Italy, one of my favorite countries, men believe that any young boy is meat for a quick seduction, and that it will have no effect on him or on his masculinity when he grows up. Heston more or less agreed."

In 1969, *Planet of the Apes* was released, starring the one and only **Charlton Heston**. The actor later referred to it as, "the first of the space operas and dangerously expensive."

Evocative of his nude modeling days, Heston appeared virtually naked in the film. "Full male frontal nudity was out, of course, although I had the equipment for it," he later said. "The director wanted me naked for the trial scene, but it was shot from the rear. Rear is the word. One of the girls supplying coffee on the set said archly, 'Mmmm, nice buns.' I suppose I could nail her for sexual harassment for that today."

"At the whorehouse, the madam had arranged a beautiful Mexican boy and girl for Heston," Welles said. "They had olive skin and large dark eyes. Actually I wanted them for myself, but it had been arranged for me to seduce two Mexican women. I requested they look like a Latina version of Eartha Kitt and Lena Horne, two black actresses I had also seduced."

"She didn't really come up with anyone who looked like Lena or Eartha, but I happily settled for what I got," Welles said. "I had finished in two hours, but Heston took five hours in the room with that boy and girl. I wish there had been a peephole, but there wasn't. Whatever Heston did to that beautiful boy and girl will remain a secret of those old brothel walls. Too bad. I wish I could have filmed it for my private collection of porn, which I used to show to Lucille Ball. It turned her on."

Welles was not the only actor who provided sex for Heston. When he made *Three Violent People*, released in 1956, Anne Baxter was his co-star, and both Tom Tryon and Forrest Tucker were cast as a supporting player. Tryon later became a successful novelist.

Almost from the first, Tryon and Heston became fast friends, even though politically they were miles apart. It was already known at the time that Tryon liked handsome young men and rather masculine ones at that. As a dashing man about Hollywood, he had no trouble collecting quite a harem. Apparently, Heston heard of that and invited Tryon out for drinks one night.

"Before the rooster crowed, they obviously had confessed their mutual interest in teenage boys," Baxter claimed. "Tryon, of course, collected these guys like the Pied Piper lured children in Hameln, and I guess Heston wanted in on some of the action."

Later Forrest Tucker claimed that Tryon began to "hook up Heston with young boy meat. From what I heard from my buddy Nick Adams, he kept Heston well supplied with dick. These liaisons—I'd call them fuck fests—went on for many years. From what I saw of the guys Tryon hung out with, he had good taste, and I'm sure on many a night he supplied Heston with a lot of good tastes."

Heston seemed to like young girls far more than he liked young boys.

The same year (1956) that *Three Violent People* was made for Paramount, Cecil B. DeMille hired both Heston and Anne Baxter for an appearance in the all-star cast of *The Ten Commandments*. It was pointed out to DeMille that the face of Heston and the face of Michelangelo's Moses in the Church of *San Pietro in Vincoli* (St. Peter in Chains) in Rome bore a startling resemblance to each other. When a reproduction of Michelangelo's art was shown to DeMille, he agreed, and consequently, Heston was cast into the film's leading role.

"Water seeks its levels," Baxter said. "Soon Heston was bonding with John Derek, who had a supporting role in *The Ten Commandments*. I'm sure that Derek and Heston soon discovered that each of them thanked God every day for little girls, to borrow a line from Maurice Chevalier."

Although he'd been a male hustler, servicing such

In *Planet of the Apes*, **Charlton Heston** taught us that it was all right to French kiss an ape. In the lower of the two photos above, he appeared off set in what he called "a pouch bikini. I have quite a bit to hold in place, so I need a strong fabric."

Recalling his experiences during the shoot, he said, "Barefoot and all but naked in most of the scenes, I was ridden down by gorillas, whipped, chained, gagged, stoned (even rubber rocked), fire-hosed, and finally trapped in a net and jerked upside down."

At lunch on set, he noted the actors portraying simians segregated themselves by species—ape actors at one table, gorillas at one table, chimps at another, and orangutans at still another.

Hollywood notables as Spencer Tracy when he was a young man, Derek was a certified womanizer. He is remembered today for being the husband of such beautiful actresses as Linda Evans, Ursula Andress, and Bo Derek.

Derek, like Heston, liked them young. In addition to the beautiful women he married, he also collected a string of teenage beauties, many of whom had high school crushes on him. It was Baxter's observation that "Derek shared the wealth with Heston. After all, Derek had far more than he could handle. From what I saw and heard from working with Heston on both pictures, Heston was like a drug addict who had found two pushers who would keep him supplied for many a year—Tom Tryon and John Derek. And it was handled so discreetly. A lot of people in Hollywood knew what was going on with Heston, but no one ratted him out, to borrow a phrase from Edward G. Robinson, who was also in *The Ten Commandments*."

"Eddie also made another picture with Heston, a sci-fi/police thriller flick called *Soylent Green*," Baxter said. "It came out in 1973. When I ran into Eddie in a restaurant one night—I was with my best friend Tamara Geva, the ex-wife of George Balanchine, and Darwin Porter that evening—he told me that Heston was still playing his dirty little games. Eddie said that Heston should have been a Roman emperor. 'That way,' Eddie said, 'he could have a whole harem of young boys and young girls awaiting his pleasure.'"

Robinson had a parting quip for the two actresses. "Those horny bastards DeMille cast into *The Ten Commandments*—Heston, Derek, Judith Anderson, Vincent Price, Yvonne De Carlo, and Yul Brynner—violated each of the Ten Commandments again and again. What a crew, what a film!"

When actor/novelist **Tom Tryon** made *Three Violent People* (1956) with Heston, both of them bonded and came to realize that each had a taste for young male flesh, Tryon exclusively so, Heston "on occasion."

During his early days in Hollywood, the handsome Tryon had almost a male harem flocking around him, and he shared his wealth with Heston. "I never knew Chuck had a gay streak in him," Tryon later told his lover, the gay porn star Cal Culver. "At first I couldn't believe it when he revealed that fact to me. After I hooked him up with this cute kid, and he told me what Chuck did to him, I believed it. Some of these right-wingers like Chuck appear to be anti-gay, but they're just covering up their secret desires."

Anne Baxter in a rare cheesecake photograph immortalized herself when she was cast as Eve Harrington opposite Bette Davis in the 1950 *All About Eve*.

Years later, she did "lesser fare" when she appeared with Charlton Heston and Tom Tryon in *Three Violent People*. "I knew what was going on," she said later. "Everybody on set knew but no one really cared. All of us were aware that Tom was gay, but we had no idea that Chuck did anything but go home to his wife after the studio shut down for the night. Frankly, I was glad that Heston was sexually adventurous. Before that, I thought he must have had the dullest sex life in Hollywood—far from it. He was getting more than I was at the time."

MERV GRIFFIN'S
AMOROUS PURSUIT OF
CHARLTON HESTON

Money was tight and a struggling young actor and boy singer, Merv Griffin, found a modest rental at the Commodore Garden Apartments behind Grauman's Chinese Theater off Hollywood Boulevard.

Two days after moving in, Merv had seen most of his fellow tenants. "There's not an ugly among them," he told his gay pal and sometimes lover Roddy McDowall. "The most gorgeous guys and dolls I've ever seen in Hollywood, or seen anywhere in one bunch for that matter."

Roddy was familiar with the Commodore. "No wonder they're so hot: That building contains the most high-priced hookers in town and the most expensive hustlers. Movie stars go there to fuck them all the time."

With that in mind, Merv began to evaluate his fellow tenants, keeping an eye on two particularly handsome young men who lived next door to him. He'd never seen them during the day. Perhaps they slept all day. He agreed with Roddy that the male tenants at the Commodore were the most well built in town. He suspected that all of them had come to Hollywood dreaming of becoming the next Rock Hudson, but had to hustle gay men as a means of supporting themselves.

Fans who remember **Merv Griffin** as a fat, jolly TV host are surprised to learn that he was once young, horny, and reasonably handsome.

He pursued some of the big beef in Hollywood, and often got his man, beginning with his uncle's close friend, Errol Flynn, Merv's teenage idol. Even in his autobiography, he praised Flynn's equipment, although he didn't admit to having sex with him. Merv's best friend was Liberace, and often they "traded" boyfriends.

When he met Charlton Heston at a Hollywood hot bed hotel, Merv reasonably assumed he was a male hustler. But Heston remained one of the few men who escaped Merv's net. James Dean, living in the same building, succumbed—but for a price.

When Merv got his next paycheck, he introduced himself to those two studs next door. They turned out to be two other struggling actors named James Dean and Nick Adams. At night they sold their meat along Santa Monica Boulevard. Merv was an eager buyer of their wares, and they gladly accommodated him. But he really had staked out another object of his desire within the building—a handsome, lantern-jawed young man with a sculpted physique.

No doubt he was an actor, at least in Merv's mind, and probably hustled on the side to earn a living. Early every afternoon, he appeared on the roof, lying on a chaise longue. A lot of the hustlers did that to keep their bodies tanned and ready for the next customer. Every actor wore a bathing suit except the young man who intrigued Merv. He wore the skimpiest of posing straps crafted from gray velour that clearly outlined his genitalia.

On his first payday, Merv, in baggy swimming trunks got up enough courage to make his move. The only problem was, he didn't know how much money to offer the actor. He finally decided that a twenty-dollar bill would do just fine.

"Hi," he said moving in as close as he could to the posing strap. "I'm Merv Griffin."

"Hi, yourself," said the young man, shading his eyes from the sun to get a good look at Merv. "I'm Charlton Heston."

Merv didn't feel comfortable initiating a dialogue, and felt nervous coming on to this athletic-looking man. Rather awkwardly, he said, "That swimming suit you're wearing is a bit brief. I would never be seen in that even in the privacy of my bedroom."

Charlton laughed. "It's not a swimming suit. In New York I posed for art classes for $1.50 an hour. They didn't want me to show my dick, so I had to wear this strap. During all the days I spent posing nude, I got an erection only once. And I had this problem. It gets pretty crowded down there."

After that remark, Merv's suspicion was confirmed. Charlton Heston was definitely a hustler.

"My wife made the strap," Charlton said.

"Oh, I didn't know you were married," Merv said.

"My wife, Lydia, is an actress. She's out of town on a job."

Even after hearing this, Merv did not immediately abandon pursuing Charlton. He'd been in Hollywood long enough to conclude that all actors were at least bisexual.

Charlton did confirm that he was an actor and was appearing in a movie that was presently being screened at a nearby theater. He invited Merv to come and see it with him. "I've seen it ten times already. Each time by myself. It'd be good to get another opinion. Are you an actor too?"

"Yes," Merv said rather proudly. "Jack Warner is grooming me to become Doris Day's next leading man."

After both men had dressed separately within their respective apartments, they met in front of the Commodore to stroll down Hollywood Boulevard together. At the movie house, Merv learned that the film was *Dark City*, and he was startled to see that Charlton was the actual star.

Noting his surprise, Charlton said, "I didn't get all that much money for it. That's why I'm still living at the Commodore Garden Apartments."

During the screening of *Dark City*, which was first released in 1950, Merv was impressed with Charlton's performance. He'd been cast as a war veteran opposite the sultry blonde, Lizabeth Scott, who was hailed in the press as a combination of Lauren Bacall and Veronica Lake. The press

Audiences became aware of Heston and his startlingly good looks when he made the film, *Dark City*, released in 1950. His brooding voice, no-nonsense countenance, and sculpted physique won him male and female admirers. His co-star, the sultry blonde **Lizabeth Scott**, didn't fall for his manly charms. Scott became known for her hair and husky voice. *Confidential*, the scandal magazine, repeatedly described her as one of the "baritone babes of Hollywood"—code word for lesbian.

Reportedly, the police found her name and phone number in a call girls' little black book. The secret gay underground alleged that she'd had affairs with both Tallulah Bankhead and Barbara Stanwyck.

often referred to Lizabeth as "one of the baritone babes of Hollywood," hoping the reading public would draw their own conclusions from that.

In *Dark City*, Lizabeth played a nightclub singer, and Merv sat through five of her songs, later claiming that the movie was the only musical *film noir* he'd ever seen. "If this keeps up," he whispered to Charlton, "Humphrey Bogart will be singing in his next film."

At one tense moment in the film, Merv decided to go for it. He slowly placed his hand on Charlton's left knee and let it gradually move upward to his target, which had been so recently encased in a posing strap.

With his own firm hand, Charlton took Merv's hand and slowly placed it back in Merv's lap. The actor leaned over and whispered into Merv's ear, "I'm not that kind of actor."

When the movie was over, Merv complimented Charlton on his performance. On the walk back to the Commodore, no mention was made of the groping.

At the door to Charlton's apartment, Merv shook his hand and congratulated him one more time. "Let's be friends."

"Sure thing," Charlton said, "providing we carry on that friendship outside of a dark movie house."

As Merv later sighed over the phone to Roddy, "Let's call him the man who got away. That package in the posing strap looked most promising."

In the trade papers, Merv was startled to read that Cecil B. DeMille had cast Charlton as one of the leads in his next big epic, *The Greatest Show on Earth*. The film would go on to win an Oscar as Best Picture of 1952 and gross $40 million, the equivalent of $300 million at today's prices. Very quietly Charlton moved out of the Commodore, without telling Merv good-bye.

Charlton did not mention Merv in his autobiography, *In the Arena*, published in 1995. He maintained throughout his later years that when he'd moved into the Commodore, he didn't know "it was the hottest whorehouse in Hollywood. You never knew what movie star you'd run into there. Clark Gable slipping down the hallway to knock on the door of a high-priced hooker. Even Gary Cooper and Robert Taylor came to call. With all that money exchanging hands, I found the tenants, both men and women, a little sad. They'd come to Hollywood to become stars and ended up working the oldest profession in history."

In his own autobiography, Merv summed up his experiences at the Commodore this way, "So we had god in the front apartment, the boy singer upstairs, and hookers and con men everywhere else."

Charlton Heston published his autobiography, *In the Arena*, in 1995, but he hardly emerged from the closet in its pages. As the picture he selected for its cover revealed, he stayed close-lipped about his personal involvements.

As president of the National Rifle Association, perhaps his greatest acting role, Heston, in the words of Dennis Perrin, "made a big fuss about fascist gun control laws, pretending that the countless millions of American gun owners are somehow a besieged minority, like Jews in Nazi Germany. It was an asinine stance, but played big with his white male core audience."

CHARLTON HESTON &
THE QUEERING OF
BEN-HUR

It was altogether appropriate that director William Wyler either auditioned or interviewed a wide spectrum actors for the title role of Ben-Hur, Wyler's 1959 remake of the 1925 silent film that had starred gay actor Ramon Novarro, the lover of Rudolph Valentino. Much more than just a sword-and-sandal epic, it was the big-budget third film interpretation of Lew Wallace's fictional 1880 novel, *Ben-Hur: A Tale of the Christ*.

For the male lead of Ben-Hur, Metro-Goldwyn-Mayer's producer Sam Zimbalist had originally wanted Paul Newman. His preference was revealed during a well-documented script conference with gay author and the film's scriptwriter, Gore Vidal, Newman's best friend at the time. Vidal promptly informed Zimbalist that Newman would never accept such a role.

"Why not?" Zimbalist asked. "It's the most coveted role in town."

"After his disastrous debut in *The Silver Chalice*, Paul swore he'd never appear again on screen in a cocktail dress," Vidal said. "Besides, he always claims his legs are too skinny."

In the wake of that meeting, Zimbalist conferred with Wyler, then jointly decided that Rock Hudson would be ideal as Ben-Hur. "He's certainly got the physique for it," Zimbalist said. But when he called Universal to pop the question, studio executives there refused to release Hudson from his pre-existing contract.

Next on the list was Marlon Brando. He'd hated himself on the screen in the 1953 version of *Julius Caesar* and wasn't anxious to return to Rome for the filming of another "swords and sandals" epic ever again.

Then Burt Lancaster, another actor with a great physique, was pitched the script as the studio's choice for Ben-Hur. Lancaster, to his regret, had already contracted for another picture, and couldn't resolve their conflicting schedules.

By coincidence, in one of the great gay ironies asso-

The pressure was on. **Charlton Heston** (photo above) not only had to win that famous chariot race, but he had to save MGM too. If *Ben-Hur* failed at the box office, the nearly bankrupt Metro-Goldwyn-Mayer, once the most famous studio in the world, would have closed its doors.

Although the studio was losing $5 million a year, in a nail-biting gamble, it agreed to bankroll *Ben-Hur* at a then-staggering cost of $10 million.

William Wyler turned down the role of director six times before finally accepting. He'd worked as an assistant on the original production of *Ben-Hur* in 1926. His first recommendation involved hiring Charlton Heston to play the villain, Messala.

"But who, then, will play *Ben-Hur?*" asked producer Sam Zimbalist.

"There's only one man who can pull it off," Wyler said. "Rock Hudson. He's got a great body, and Ben-Hur is going to be naked throughout most of the film. Hudson's a fag, but he's good at butching it up in front of the camera."

ciated with casting issues in Hollywood, each of the actors noted above were either homosexual or bisexual.

Finally, however, Charlton Heston was offered and accepted the role. He signed his contract despite the stated objections of Gore Vidal, who remarked at the time, "He has all the charm of a wooden Indian."

Casting the role of Messala, the film's Roman officer, was almost as convoluted. Victor Mature, who'd scored a big hit with the 1949 release of *Samson and Delilah*, was the first choice. Soon after, that proposed deal collapsed, as did a similar pitch to Steve Cochran. (VOYEURISTIC NOTE TO SIZE QUEENS: Cochran and Mature were known at the time for swinging the two biggest clubs in Hollywood.)

In the end, Stephen Boyd (1928-1977), the ruggedly handsome Northern Irish Protestant actor, accepted the choice role of Messala. In yet another (parallel) coincidence, Mature, Cochran, and Boyd were each also bisexuals.

By now, on-set wags had noted how appropriate it was that a film script about repressed homosexuality was being cast with mostly repressed homosexual actors—a literal gay houseparty whose offscreen permissiveness might have vaguely reflected the sexual mores of ancient Rome at the time.

Regrettably, Sam Zimbalist died in 1958 and never got to see "my dream film" or any of the various awards it generated.

During his compilation of the film script, Vidal faced many perplexing challenges. Ben-Hur and Messala had been intimate childhood friends. Years later, they meet as strong-willed, testosterone-permeated adults whose personalities and political allegiances have by now been clearly defined: Heston is a land-owning, fervently patriotic Zionist Jew, Messala is an aristocratic Roman officer [i.e., a ruthless and hostile foreign conquerer.]

Initially, their reunion is affectionate, but soon, Ben-Hur and Messala quarrel bitterly over sovereignty and the politics of the day.

A mutual loathing follows, with rivalry that leads to Messala's death in that famous chariot race.

Early in the filming, as scriptwriter, Vidal protested to Wyler that there was "no motivation for all this fury," but subsequently he came up with a motivation.

He reckoned that Ben-Hur and Messala had been boyhood lovers. Meeting again as adults, the more

Charlton Heston (left, in photo above) and **Stephen Boyd** take time out for a sightseeing tour of Rome, in a style inspired, perhaps, by what Gregory Peck and Audrey Hepburn had done in *Roman Holiday* (1953), six years before.

When Boyd saw this candid shot of themselves on a motorcycle, he told Wyler, "My legs are more shapely than Chuck's. Mine look like they were sculpted by Michelangelo. Chuck's look a little too toothpickey. And before this shoot is over, I plan to find out if, under the tunic, he's as much of a man as he says he is."

In one of the most controversial scenes in *Ben-Hur*, **Boyd** (left) and **Heston** (right) share a communal bond in memory of their boyhood when they were best friends. "Chuck is trying to look macho throughout our bonding," Boyd later said, "but I was playing Messala like Gore Vidal intended. According to Vidal's version, we had been boyhood lovers, and I'm looking at Chuck with lust in my eyes. Any fool can see that. But Chuck missed the point of the scene."

decadent and more permissive of the two, Messala, is still in love with Ben-Hur and wants to resume pounding his ass.

Ben-Hur, as a virtuous Old Testament-thumping Zionist, righteously rebuffs Messala's come-on. As for Messala, hell hath no fury like a horny Roman officer rejected in love, "from a Jew, no less."

A very reluctant Wyler agreed to go along with this homosexually motivated plot device, providing that it was so understated and so subtle that relatively naïve mainstream audiences of 1959 wouldn't get it, but gay men would.

Wyler, Vidal, and their collaborators decided to bring the sexually sophisticated Boyd into the loop. Wyler knew that the Irish homosexual had deflowered a lot of boy-ass in his day. Wyler, however, insisted that Heston should not be informed that the scenes he'd be filming with Boyd contained a homoerotic undercurrent, subliminal or not.

In his literary memoirs, Vidal noted: "Chuck (i.e., Heston) was now imitating Francis X. Bushman in the 1925 silent screen version, tossing his head, chin held high, oblivious of what was going on. Boyd at one point winked at me. He was in character."

In countless newspaper and magazine articles, Heston has been made the butt of jokes. "How dumb can an actor be?" Wyler once asked. "How can an actor play a gay love scene and not even know it? When Heston saw the rushes, couldn't he see the gleam in Boyd's eyes?"

As the years went by, Heston gave the impression of having been more enlightened. During his lifetime, at least, his own sexual decadence had never been revealed in any lurid *Confidential* magazine way. Only the underground press ever got a whiff of what was really going with Heston when the cameras weren't rolling.

In a 1977 interview, he got the message. Perhaps he had assessed the gay undercurrent at the time of its filming, yet never reached out to inform Wyler, Boyd or Vidal that he understood.

"The story behind *Ben-Hur* isn't really about Christ," Heston recalled. "It's certainly not a story about Ben-Hur and Esther, either. It's a love story between Ben-Hur and Messala, and the destruction of that love and the world they had known. In the wake of that destruction, there remained only hatred and revenge—it's a vendetta story."

Incidentally, the 1959 remake of *Ben-Hur* saved MGM from bankruptcy and won a record 11 Oscars out of a dozen nominations. When it was re-released in 2010 on Warner Home Video, it was viewed by consumers who were infinitely more sophisticated, sexually speaking, than those white-

WILLIAM WYLER
CHARLTON HESTON · JACK HAWKINS
HAYA HARAREET · STEPHEN BOYD
HUGH GRIFFITH · MARTHA SCOTT · CATHY O'DONNELL · SAM JAFFE
KARL TUNBERG · SAM ZIMBALIST

**THE GREATEST STORY
THE SCREEN HAS EVER TOLD!**

Charlton Heston (left), **Stephen Boyd** (center) and director **William Wyler** (right) were all smiles and cooperation during the early weeks of film production on *Ben-Hur,* although the inevitable tensions arose as production dragged on.

At first, Heston had applauded Wyler's choice of the Irish actor, Boyd. Soon he was calling him "Steve."

"I'm glad you cast a manly man like myself in the role—not one of those homosexual boys you were considering," Heston told Wyler. "Between us, Steve and I can produce enough testosterone to give birth to *Ben-Hur.* The 'baby' that Stevie boy and I can produce will grow into a giant at the box office. MGM will be rescued—take my word for it."

bread-with-vanilla viewers of 1959. Hip modern-day critics immediately noted the "homoerotic relationship" simmering between Ben-Hur and Messala.

Years later, in a bar in Dublin, near the end of his short life, and after too many drinks, the still-very-handsome Boyd swaggeringly but only half-jokingly told his hangers-on: "I never got around to plugging Chuck Heston during the filming of Ben-Hur, but I have no doubt he would have bottomed for me."

Not since D.W. Griffith's *Intolerance* (1916) had such a gigantic film set ever been constructed. The scene involved the bitter chariot race between the characters of Messala and Judah Ben-Hur. An army of Italian craftsmen had constructed the largest set in the history of cinema as an evocation, sprawling over 18 acres, of the ancient arena at Antioch.

The night before the shoot, a drunken Boyd, in the bar of a hotel on the Via Veneto, had come on strong to **Heston** (charioteer in the photo above), who had scornfully rejected him, thereby ending their friendship in a way that eerily paralleled the scenario of the movie itself.

Whoever said pictures don't lie? This candid snapshot of *Ben-Hur's* (left to right) director **William Wyler,** screenwriter **Christopher Fry**, **Gore Vidal**, and **Charlton Heston** does not reveal the seething rage transpiring behind the scenes among this unholy quartet of egos and frustrations.

Pressured by the studio, Wyler had brought in Christopher Fry, the English poet and playwright, to rework much of the script Vidal had previously written. Wyler had objected to the homosexual dynamics that Vidal was establishing between Ben-Hur and Messala.

Although in the picture, Heston is amicably placing his ringed hand on Vidal's shoulder, he actually despised him. In his memoirs, *In the Arena,* Heston had nothing but praise for Fry, but referred to Vidal as "a tart, embittered man, an odd choice" for the screenplay of *Ben-Hur.*

Vidal, Heston claimed, was sent packing, with Fry taking control of the script. In years to come, Heston repeatedly downplayed Vidal's contribution, although Vidal claimed "I rewrote the script from the first page through the chariot race. Fry wrote the rest."

The debate continues to this day. At any rate, Vidal never got the credit he deserved. In fact, at MGM the false legend persisted for years—at least until many of the participants in the affair died—that Vidal had tried to turn *Ben-Hur* into "a fag picture."

On the night **Susan Hayward** presented **Charlton Heston** with his Best Actor Oscar for his portrayal of Ben-Hur, they posed for cameramen backstage after the show. Here, Hayward looks approvingly at Heston, although she could be quite candid about him in private.

Six years before, she'd co-starred with him in *The President's Lady,* a costume drama about former U.S. president Andrew Jackson. Heston, of course, had been cast as Old Hickory.

"We had a brief fling at the time," Hayward confided to her assistant, Peter Pell, in Fort Lauderdale. "I had a mirrored wall in my dressing room. All during the fuck, Heston kept staring at himself in action and didn't once look into my eyes, even though he was right on top of me. Later, I learned that he much preferred very young women—or young boys, as the Hollywood grapevine had it at the time."

Susan Hayward wasn't the only leading lady Heston bedded. During the shoot of *Lucy Gallant,* released in 1955, he had a brief fling with **Jane Wyman**, the ex-Mrs. Ronald Reagan.

Later, he went to great pains to conceal the tryst, fearing word would get back to Reagan. Although Wyman had already divorced Reagan, he still would have exploded if he'd known that Heston had bedded her.

Heston later expressed his disappointment with the film, feeling the role would have been better suited for Rock Hudson. He urged his friends not to see it.

IN MEMORY OF

RAMON NOVARRO, *BEN-HUR'S* ORIGINAL CINEMATIC STAR

MGM's 1959 release of **Ben-Hur** was not Hollywood's first attempt to get some cinematic mileage out of Lew Wallace's 1880 novel. MGM had produced an earlier, silent version in 1925 with just as many queer subliminal behind-the-scenes dramas. Shamelessly promoted at the time as "The Picture Every Christian Ought to See," it was the most expensive silent film ever made.

In 1997, it was selected for preservation in the United States National Film Registry by the Library of Congress as being "culturally, historically, and aesthetically significant."

At the time, Metro claimed that their budding star, **Ramon Sameniagos** (later **Ramon Novarro**; two photos above) was "Michelangelo's David with the face of an El Greco Don." The "too-beautiful" Ramon loved to be topped, especially by his arch-rival, Valentino, and by Latin heartthrob Antonio Moreno.

Before his tragic death in 1968, the result of a psychotic hustler who stuffed Valentino's Art Deco dildo down his throat, Ramon was a sweet, adorable youth and a nude model.

With its S&M implications, *Ben-Hur* was the role of a lifetime for **Ramon** as Ben-Hur (right in photo above) and the cinematic comeback for horse-hung but faded matinee idol **Francis X. Bushman** as Messala (left). Here, they glare at each other, perhaps re-activating the sexual role-playing they'd enjoyed together during their romantic heyday six years before.

"The noblest Roman of them all," **Ramon Novarro** as Judah Ben-Hur was both a romantic lover and a swash-buckling hero. Billed as "a second Valentino," in the photo (left) he plays golf in Rome wearing a stripped-down version of gladiator fetish during a break in the filming.

Ramon as a naked galley slave in a publicity still for MGM's 1925 version of *Ben-Hur*. Even his pubic hair was showing, a first ever for a male film star.

The caption read, "This photograph proves rather conclusively that he has no intention of ever joining a monastery."

EDITOR'S NOTE: For more about what was being swept under the carpets during the bad old days of early Hollywood, refer to Darwin Porter's bawdy info-novel, **Hollywood's Silent Closet (ISBN 978-0-9668030-2-0)**. Based on eyewitness accounts of the debauched excesses of the Silent Era's closeted and very lavender past, it was reviewed by critics as "The most intimate and realistic account of sex, murder, degradation, and blackmail in early Hollywood ever written...a brilliant primer for **Who Was Queer and Who Was Who**."

CHARLTON HESTON
AN ICON OF CONTRADICTIONS

Film icon Charlton Heston of the chiseled granite jaw died at the age of 84 after a career that spanned five decades.

Suffering from Alzheimer's disease and prostate cancer, Heston passed away at his Beverly Hills home with his faithful wife, Lydia, by his side. He'd married her in 1944. He also left behind two children and three grandchildren.

Janet Leigh, pictured above with **Heston**, almost lost out on *Touch of Evil*. She broke her arm before filming began. **Orson Welles** retained her in the role with her arm in a cast, but hidden from the camera. In the more revealing motel scenes, the cast was removed for the shot, then reapplied afterword. For Janet, the pay was so low her agent turned it down. When she found out, she was furious, claiming that "to be directed by Orson Welles, I'll even go without a paycheck." The bizarre casting of Heston as a Mexican, which was widely ridiculed, was not the studio's idea. It was Welles himself who wanted to make Heston a Mexican.

Leading a nationwide tribute, Nancy Reagan remembered Heston as "a hero in life and Ronnie's best friend." Like her husband, Heston was a Democrat early in life, embracing liberal causes as an advocate in the civil rights marches of the 1950s and 60s. "Martin Luther King, not me, should have played Moses," he once said.

Later in life he became archly conservative and was president of the N. R. A. from 1998 to 2003. During his tenure, he loudly, passionately, and frequently proclaimed that the only way his gun would be taken from him was "from my cold, dead hands."

Throughout his life, his fellow actors weighed in with their opinions about him. Frank Sinatra told him, "If you're not careful, you're going to give actors a good name."

Filming *Touch of Evil* with him in 1958, Marlene Dietrich propositioned him. He rejected her advances. She told her director, Orson Welles, that she suspected that he was a homosexual. "What red-blooded American male would turn down Marlene Dietrich?" she asked.

America doesn't produce movie stars like Clark Gable, John Wayne, Cary Grant, James Stewart, Henry Fonda, Gary Cooper, or Charlton Heston any more. *The New York Times* called Heston "one of the last American movie stars."

We'll let Heston himself have the last words on himself. "Audiences adore stars like Judy Garland who suffer, who are disappointed in love, always on the brink of some personal disaster. Well, I'm not like that."

In a 1978 interview, Heston said, "my goal in life is to live to be 105. If you need a ceiling painted, a chariot race run, a city besieged, or the Red Sea parted, call on me."

Future generations of movie-goers will be doing just that.

Considered by many movie goers as the last classic "film noir" ever made, *Touch of Evil*, released in 1958, was **Orson Welles**' baby.

It was his last masterwork. He was fired as director during post-production, and the film was recut contrary to his wishes.

Originally Welles was contracted only to act in the film, but it was Heston who demanded that the studio allow him to direct the picture as well. The studio caved in but only if Welles would agree to be paid as an actor, not for writing or directing.

"**Charlton Heston** never looked uglier," said James Cameron, most recently famous as the much-respected director of both *Titanic* (1997) and *Avatar* (2009).

Cameron also directed *True Lies* (1994), starring Arnold Scharzenegger in the most expensive movie ever made at that time, costing $120 million. In it, Heston appeared in a cameo, playing the head of the CIA. Cameron told Heston, "I need you in the part because you're the only actor in Hollywood who can intimidate Arnold. A patch over your eye will do the trick."

When the film was released, the American-Arab Anti-Discrimination Committee called for a boycott of *True Lies* in 54 Arab and Muslim countries, because the film "depicted Middle Easterners as homicidal, religious zealots."

When Heston heard of this, his response was, "But aren't they?—fuck the bastards!"

Orson Welles cast his longtime friend, **Marlene Dietrich**, as a very spooky gypsy, wearing an old black wig from her film, *Golden Earrings*.

When the studio honchos saw Dietrich in the film, playing Tanya, they were shocked. They had no idea that she'd even been cast. The fabled star had agreed to play Tanya only as a personal favor to Welles, and she'd agreed to appear at minimum union wage.

When the studio wanted to give her star billing, they had to pay her more.

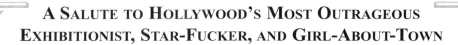

A Salute to Hollywood's Most Outrageous Exhibitionist, Star-Fucker, and Girl-About-Town

Liz Renay

"I Seduced 200 Movie Stars"

(But It Took Her 30 Years)

"I'd rather be a star than chase one," or so wrote **Liz Renay** in her highly unreliable memoirs, *My First 2,000 Men*.

"In the private world I've created for myself, I am a star, the super star of my domain. Star of the Bedroom! Queen of Sheba. Queen of the Nile, Cleopatra, Helen of Troy, Princess of the Night, Goddess of Love. Queen of the House—MY house. I'm whatever I want to be! Being a star is largely an illusion anyway."

When her friend, Sammy Davis Jr., read those words, he said, "I was somewhat truthful in my memoirs, but my dear friend Liz lied. She was the ultimate star-fucker. All of us had her. She tried to be candid, but that was just a pretense. If you had a walk-on in a film made in 1933, she'd fuck you. A great gal, though. Just great!"

Was She Really the World's Most Beautiful Woman?

"IF THEY COULDN'T GET MARILYN MONROE, THEY CALLED ME.
I WAS THE NEXT BEST THING, WITH BETTER HYGIENE."
—LIZ RENAY

Married eight times, **Liz Renay** was also famous for appearing before grand juries. She was after all, gangster Mickey Cohen's gun moll. "I was also the swinger of my generation," she claimed.

Liz Renay (1926-2007), love goddess and cult film star, used to be written up in the press as "the most beautiful woman on the planet." She had another reputation as well: she was the most notorious and promiscuous actress ever to step off the train in Los Angeles.

Escaping her parents, both of whom were religious fanatics, in the little town of Mesa, Arizona, Liz fled to New York, where she found work as a stripper on 52nd Street when she wasn't modeling high-fashion clothes. As a WWII "V Girl," she became a one-woman USO, entertaining love-starved military men returning, horny but victoriously, on battleships from Europe.

From New York, Liz traveled to Hollywood, winning a Marilyn Monroe look-alike contest, which transformed her overnight into a national celebrity. In 1950, *Life* magazine did a five-page spread on her.

In Hollywood, she took up with the mobster Mickey Cohen, who used his influence to land her bit parts in movies. As *confidante* and gun moll to Cohen, she was eventually indicted and later sentenced to three years probation for her unwillingness to testify against the mob boss, for whom she'd laundered money. A violation of that probation landed her in a Los Angeles prison for three years, where she was gang raped by lesbians.

In jail she wrote her first memoir, *My Face for the World to See* (1971), which was in time followed by a second memoir, modestly entitled *My First 2,000 Men* (1992). Both confessionals hit certain bestseller lists.

These memoirs were more curious than revelatory. She wrote, "I've never been known around Hollywood's inner circles as a star-chaser." *Hold on here a minute, Liz.* You were infamous in Hollywood for being the ultimate star-chaser. In fact, she once confided to Darwin Porter that her goal from the day she first set foot in Hollywood was to seduce 200 male movie stars.

Liz preferred to date from the A-list, and did so many times. Frank Sinatra, George Raft, and Marlon Brando come to mind. Her greatest love was Glenn Ford, who went from seducing Bette Davis, Joan Crawford, and Barbara Stanwyck to making passionate love to Liz. Even though she fell madly in love with him—and agreed to "perform every sex act imaginable"—he eventually dumped her.

But for Liz, it wasn't essential that each of her actors had his name displayed above the title of new movies hitting the billboards. If a man ranked third or even fourth in the supporting cast, he qualified as a movie star in Liz's book. It took years, but Liz apparently achieved her goal.

And throughout her campaign, she rated each of her conquests on a scale of one to ten within a secret diary. Burt Lancaster earned an impressive rating of "10," Jerry Lewis a meager rating of "1."

At the back of her diary, she kept a short list of names labeled "The Men Who Got Away." Ronald Reagan and Paul Newman were both on that list.

Liz claimed that 80% of the male stars she pursued succumbed to her charms and her impressive measurements (40"-26"-36"). As for the 20% who rejected her "come hithers," Liz dismissed them as either gay or "taken," or "uptight," or "priggish," or "terrified of public exposure," or lacking in some important psychological or testosterone-derived way. One or another of those factors might have explained her strike-outs with Reagan and Newman.

"Some of my lovers couldn't get Marilyn, so they settled for me," she said. "In almost every case they were glad they did. I dressed like Marilyn and made my face up like hers. I did my hair like Marilyn. And when the lights were low, I even imitated her voice."

Her method of seduction was simple: She sent a fan letter attached to a nude photograph of herself. Since in those days she was a dead ringer for Monroe, with the body to match, and in an era prior to the present epidemics of sexually transmitted diseases, very few red-blooded males ever turned her down.

"I had the greatest breasts in Hollywood," Liz Renay claimed. "Larger and more beautiful than those of Marilyn Monroe. She was only 34 although she claimed to be 38. I was a 40, probably more. I can't tell you the penises I've got off between my breasts. I was famous for that. Just ask the Rat Pack. When this publicity shot was taken, I was almost 50 and a grandmother."

Sometimes Liz didn't even have to spend any money on postage. Since she was well known among the Hollywood colony of horny males as a good-time girl, many actors simply called her. "Her name was passed around a lot in men's locker room," said her jealous rival Veronica Lake.

Before he started making all those millions from *Hairspray*, director John Waters cast Liz as Muffy St. Jacques in the cult classic, *Dangerous Living* (1977). One of her many claims to fame derived from a notorious scene from that movie in which she kills her drug-tripping babysitter by smothering her in a bowl of dog food.

As her life and career progressed, Liz stayed abreast (no pun intended) of current fads. In 1974, at the height of the streaking craze, Liz stripped off her clothes and ran buck naked down Hollywood Boulevard in full-frontal view of 5,000 male paparazzi and Peeping Toms. A California jury later found her not legally guilty of any wrongdoing. After the trial, some male jurors asked her to autograph nude pictures of herself.

"Like Mother, Like Daughter. **Brenda** (*right figure in photo above*) wanted to be a stripper like me, and I not only encouraged her, but joined her act. I told her, if anyone asks, I'm the pretty one and the younger one."

As a stripper, Liz was known for a unique act where she appeared with her daughter, Brenda. This mother-daughter act was wildly popular, even though Liz later asserted that "most of the guys in the audience thought we were sisters."

Throughout the course of all those lovers—famous, infamous, or unknown—Liz managed to marry eight husbands. Upon her death in Las Vegas at the age of 80, on January 22, 2007, she left behind a son, Johnny McLain. Her daughter, Brenda, had died in 1987. She is also survived by five grandchildren, 12 great-grandchildren, and two great-great grandchildren.

Her last appearance was in Las Vegas in June of 2006 at the 49th annual Striptease Reunion sponsored by the Exotic World Burlesque Museum. She was held aloft by four scantily clad Adonis-like young men, who carried her out on a royal pillow—"just like Cleopatra." Although surrounded by some of the world's most beautiful showgals, Liz stole the show. Regardless of what you think of her morality (or lack thereof), you have to hand it to an octogenarian granny who could pull off a stunt like that only months before her ride to the grave.

"Baby," Liz said in Las Vegas, "I discovered women's lib before the term was invented."

"If you've got it, flaunt it," **Liz Renay** said, during her infamous streak along Hollywood Boulevard in 1974. "The papers later claimed there wasn't one red-blooded man on that boulevard who didn't get a hard-on. The papers also claimed there were 5,000 men out to see me, each one with a camera. It was more like 10,000. You know how the press lies."

Ask Liz:

LIZ RENAY ON THE SUBJECT OF COCKS AND THEIR SIZE

"The talk about the huge cock being practically a necessity is just poppycock. You may be interested to know that I've known men with enormous cocks who'd had trouble finding a sex partner. The reason? It was so big that it hurt their sex partners. Now, I don't want to leave the impression that oversized penises don't have their admirers. They do. About 20% of the female population, by my rough estimate, dote on oversized cocks while the majority, the other 80%, prefer average-size cocks. What counts is a lover achieving and sustaining an erection throughout the love session."

Ask Liz:

HOW DID HER MOVIE STARS PERFORM IN THE SACK?

The names of Liz Renay's lovers, many of whom died as recently as 2002, read like a *Who's Who* of movie stars buried at Forest Lawn.

During one long-ago summer in the late 1960s, Liz shared a house at Laguna Beach in California with the author, Darwin Porter. The owner of the house, their host, was the late real estate developer and philanthropist Gordon R. Howard, patron of a museum of antique cars bearing his name in Burbank, California.

During their time together, Liz showed Darwin her little black book, where she'd inscribed her appraisals of the stars she'd seduced.

Some of her "reviews," even those appraising the sexual talents of a big-name star, were rather brief. She had a lot to say about some of her conquests, but was less inspired by others.

If we ran pictures of all of these guys, it would fill a book. Within the pages that follow, we've included only a sampling of her conquests, particularly those that generated pithy comments. As Liz herself asserted, "Some of these men took me to the top of the mountain, making me feel like I was up in the clouds 10,000 feet above the earth. Other guys didn't even give me a two-foot liftoff."

For reasons of her own, Liz might have remained a lady because of the way she *didn't* describe most of her conquests within her two volumes of published memoirs. At the time of their publication in 1992 and 2002, many among her armada of lovers were "happily married" men—and still very much alive.

Those whose names and sexual prowess are described within the pages that follow derive from Liz's conversations with Darwin Porter during the dialogues within the house they shared during that long-ago summer in the late 60s.

A STREAK OF VENUS   "On my tombstone, I want it writ—LIZ RENAY, CONNOISSEUR OF MEN. Guys have called me everything—whore, slut, Princess, Queen, Mona Lisa, Goddess, Aphrodite. A lot of newspaper guys wrote I had 'the most beautiful face in America,' I called those guys up. 'Whoever wrote that? It's not just my face,' I told them. 'It's the whole fucking package.' If they didn't believe me, I told them to come over for a little love in the afternoon, and I'm sure they'd leave convinced."

"The girl with the polka dot eyes"—that's what columnist Walter Winchell dubbed **Liz Renay** when he noted the gold flecks in her hazel-green eyes. During World War II, at the age of 15, she married a soldier. "He struggled for two weeks to bring me to my first climax—but failed miserably. I filed for divorce. If a husband can't satisfy his wife, why marry him? In the future with all my other husbands, I held extended auditions before walking to the altar."

Liz Evaluates
DANA ANDREWS

"If you've seen some of his movies, you may have noticed that he shows a big basket on screen. Trust me, that was not padding—it was the real thing. I should know. He fucked me on five different occasions. When he wasn't too drunk, he was good at it. When I first met him, he was still battling the bottle—and losing. He was known for drunk driving, which got him into big trouble.

"*Laura* was one of my favorite movies, and that's when I fell in love with the big lug. I really stalked him long before he gave me a tumble. It was worth waiting for.

"The guy started out as a gas jockey, the son of nine children born to a Baptist minister, who obviously didn't take a vow of celibacy. One of his brothers grew up to be the actor Steve Forrest, who was hotter and handsomer than Dana. I never got around to him. Dana's drinking got so bad and the arrests so frequent that one day he had to stand before AA and say, 'I'm Dana Andrews, and I'm an alcoholic.'

"After a series of strokes in the early 1990s, he was sent to the John Douglas French Center for Alzheimer's Disease in Los Alamitos. I went to see him, but he didn't remember me. But when I told him I was Gene Tierney, he remembered."

Dana Andrews (1902-1992) was the star of Samuel Goldwyn's *The Best Years of Our Lives*, one of the great triumphs of the 1940s, both artistically and financially. It won an Oscar for Best Picture in 1946.

Wooden as an actor, he nonetheless conveyed a solid virility both on and off the screen.

116

Liz Evaluates
DEZI ARNAZ

"Hot nights in old Havana with an uncut Cuban salami. He preferred well-stacked blondes. 'After all,' he told me, 'I have a redhead at home with no tits.'

"Desi loved sex. He couldn't get enough. He even fucked men like Cesar Romero, who had a life-long crush on him.

"The first time he took me on a date at the race track at Bel Mar, he told me that he possessed something in common with the horses. Even a blonde bimbo could figure that one out.

"He came to the states at a young age and worked his way up. He began by cleaning bird shit from cages, but soon went into show biz. The girls loved him. I heard he was a real stud in his day, taking on all the whores at Polly Adler's bordello in New York, even Adler herself. But when I met him, he'd seen better days. He was drinking a lot. I'd play with it and do and use every trick in the book but often we couldn't get a rise out of the floppy thing."

Desi Arnaz (1917-1986) will always be known as Ricky Ricardo, the man who loved Lucy—that is, he loved Lucille Ball sometimes.

He lost his virginity to the family cook in Cuba when he was 12 years old, and he learned about sex in the brothels of Santiago.

Liz Evaluates
SCOTT BRADY

"He was bisexual and bragged a lot about his equipment. He was very proud of the size of it, and he didn't exaggerate one inch the night he picked me up in Las Vegas. He told me I looked like Marilyn Monroe. 'Tell me something I don't know,' I said back to him. His idea of foreplay was to talk about other gals he'd screwed. He told me he had Anne Bancroft three ways before he was finished with her. He was the younger brother of Lawrence Tierney, and one night he arrived with his brother for a three-way. Joan Crawford had already had a three-way with these boys.

"Scott had been a lumberjack and a prize fighter, and both of these professions turned me on. Not only was he a boxing champ in the Navy, but a boxing champ in bed. He fucked around in the military in WWII. He told me when he couldn't get a gal, a hot young boy ass would do just fine. He also told me he screwed Yul Brenner when they made *Port of New York* [1949]. I told him when I got around to seducing Yul, I'd bring him a dildo. My final opinion of Brady? I think he could give a woman multiple orgasms even if he were raping her."

Scott Brady (1924-1985) was a movie tough guy in various action films, westerns, and war movies.

He appeared as the Dancin' Kid in that camp classic, *Johnny Guitar* (1954) with what he called "a very butch pair of ladies," Joan Crawford and Mercedes McCambridge.

Liz Evaluates
MARLON BRANDO

"He was very proud of his 'noble tool,' perhaps prouder than he should have been. I heard that when he wasn't screwing Tallulah Bankhead or Marilyn Monroe—my rival—he liked to plug the boys, especially James Dean.

"Shelley Winters was crazy about him, and she slapped my face one night in a club when she saw me. She'd obviously heard that Marlon was banging me, too.

"With me, Marlon was just great, and had I known him in his heyday, back in the late 40s and early 50s, I bet he was fantastic. He was exciting, warm, and earthy, and I can almost understand why Rita Moreno practically committed suicide over him. When making *A Streetcar Named Desire,* he told me he fucked both Vivien Leigh and even her husband, his Highness (he had some title) Laurence Olivier.

"There was nothing phony about Marlon. He knew what most bastards in Hollywood were like. Phonies, the whole lot of them. He told me I should have been a bigger star than Marilyn. I know I could have been if it weren't for the phonies. He also told me I was better in bed than Marilyn."

Marlon Brando (1924-2004) was called the greatest actor of his generation. Even Laurence Olivier said he was better than he was on stage and on screen. Brando won an Oscar for the 1954, *On the Waterfront*, but accepted no more prizes from the Academy. He turned down the Oscar the second time around for his defining role in *The Godfather* (1972), his comeback picture.

Liz Evaluates
YUL BRYNNER

"He was a bit of a shit, a pig really, but he knew how to turn a woman on. He wanted me three ways. He told me that in addition to Marlene Dietrich, Joan Crawford, Marilyn Monroe, and Tallulah Bankhead, he once banged Nancy Davis. She was the one who married that president. I went after Ronnie myself, but he got away. I was too much woman for that nerd.

"Even though Scott Brady had warned me, I didn't get a request to use a dildo on Yul. He had an uncut cock and used to pose for nudes. I understand that Andy Warhol bought an original nude of him for a lot of money. When aroused, Yul rose to an impressive eight inches. Something like that. I didn't actually take measurements.

"He told me he lost his virginity to a woman when he was only ten years old. Perhaps he exaggerated, but things like that happen. I found out he was addicted to opium. Deborah Kerr, of all people, has gone on record claiming he was 'very, very sensual.' He was. He liked to eat half a grape then kiss me while I shared the other half. I guess that's what is known as sensual."

Yul Brynner (1915-1985) was born in Russia and will forever be identified for the role of the Siamese king in *The King and I*. He opened on Broadway in the role in 1951 and brought it to the screen in 1956. For that, he received a much deserved Oscar. He brought the Rodgers and Hammerstein musical back to New York in 1977, opening to raves once again. In 1984, he carted out the role once again, shortly before he died of cancer.

Liz Evaluates
RICHARD BURTON

"I've known guys with bigger equipment, but he was okay in the sack—that is, when he didn't show up drunk. He once told me, 'If there's a dame in Hollywood I can't screw, my name's not Richard.' Like Brynner, I found him a bit of a shit. I could never understand why another Liz—Liz Taylor that is—had the hots for him.

"Richard told me that 'God put me on this earth to raise sheer hell, and that's what I've been doing ever since.' He also told me that the next best thing to fucking Marilyn herself was going to bed with me. He loved the way I impersonated Marilyn's voice and whispered vulgar things in his ear as he plowed into me.

"On a few nights of pillow talk, he spoke of his father. He said the man was a 'fearsome boozer,' consuming at least twelve pints a night at some country pub. Somehow he managed to get up and head for the coal mines the next morning.

"My turnoff with Richard was that he was badly pockmocked. On my final night, he asked me to press some black heads out of those pockmarks. Talk about a man spoiling his sexy image. He called me one more time, but I had another engagement. I actually did. I went back home to one of my husbands. I forgot which one."

Richard Burton (1925-1984) will be long remembered as the actor who married Elizabeth Taylor, divorced her, married her again, and divorced her again. In spite his string of bad films, including *Cleopatra* (1963), he was one of the world's most brilliant actors. But mostly he squandered a great talent.

Liz Evaluates
RORY CALHOUN

"He was Guy Madison's longtime lover, and those two gorgeous boys enjoyed banging each other more than they enjoyed banging me. But I had both of them on several occasions, and once we tried a three-way similar to the one I had with those brothers, Lawrence Tierney and Scott Brady. One night Rory fucked Guy in the ass, while Guy pounded me. Quite a night.

"Rory came up the hard way and even served time in prison. But then who hasn't? He climbed the lavender ladder to success with handsome Alan Ladd and with that voracious, cocksucking faggot, Henry Willson, agent from hell. When he wasn't plugging Guy, Rory nailed Betty Grable, Marilyn Monroe, and Susan Hayward.

"He told me he broke into movies fucking Ladd, who suggested he give acting a try. I told him Ladd had also fucked me. Rory agreed with me that most actors are bi. Every man makes requests for what turns him on. Instead of a blow-job, Rory liked his armpits licked as a means of getting really hard. He told me that both Guy and Marilyn (Monroe) would do that for him. I saw two of his last movies. He ended up white haired and campy in such pieces of shit as *Motel Hell* (1980) and *Hell Comes to Frogtown* (1988). He really fell on bad days toward the end of his life—death came in 1999--and once I had to lend him money."

Rory Calhoun (1922-1999) once said, "I never made it really big, and will probably always be remembered as the hunk who appeared in two movies with Marilyn Monroe." He was referring to *How to Marry a Millionaire* (1953) and *River of No Return* (1954). "Mostly the studios put me in crap except for *With a Song in My Heart* (1952) with Susan Hayward."

Liz Evaluates
JOHNNY CARSON

"He was okay, I guess, but a rather selfish lover. He had me in Las Vegas, where he had any number of other women. I think he was over-sexed. Outside of his home, he wasn't particularly interested in just one woman. He played the numbers game. He must have had many leather belts with many notches on them. He was real proud of his body, but, believe me, I've seen better.

"He kept comparing me to that Marilyn Monroe clone from the 50s, Mamie Van Doren. I told him I was most often compared to Marilyn. He said he couldn't compare me to her because he never balled her.

"The funniest story I ever heard about Johnny was when he sued a company that marketed portable toilets. These crappers were advertised as HERE'S JOHNNY!

"He was always promising to make me a regular on his *Tonight Show*. But his promises didn't amount to shit. In that respect, he was like every other asshole in Hollywood and New York. He liked to stage orgies in some penthouse in Las Vegas. He invited me to join in the fun, but I turned him down. The way I figured it, if a man had Liz Renay, what in the hell did he need with a lot of bimbos?'"

Johnny Carson (1925-2005) was "King of the Night," the most successful performer in the history of television as host of *The Tonight Show* for 30 years, beginning in 1962.

He was an immensely talented comedian when the cameras were on him, but there was a dark side to his fame. For two decades he joked on air about his ex-wives and how they exploited him.

Liz Evaluates
DANE CLARK

"I liked to fuck these *film noir* kind of guys. Dane was born in New York as Bernard Zanville, and he wanted me to call him Bernie. He hated his stage name (Dane Clark), a name given him by Warner Brothers. He'd studied law at Cornell University, but didn't go far with it. Instead he made his living as a tough street kid boxer and later a nude model, where he developed quite a following among 'the boys.'

"He told me that most guys, when stripped in front of an art class, with all eyes watching, shrank to the size of a peanut. 'Not me,' he said. 'I often got a full erection. Maybe I'm an exhibitionist at heart. No one ever complained about drawing me with a hard-on. I was proud of it.'

"He danced with Joan Crawford in *Hollywood Canteen*, and she reminded him that he looked too much like John Garfield to go far in Tinseltown. 'Not that I needed reminding of that,' Clark said. 'You've been to bed with Garfield, I'm sure. Who's the better man in bed? Garfield or me?'

"'You've got him beat by a country mile,' I told him. I lied, of course. Poor Dane suffered all his life because of unfavorable comparisons to Garfield. When we went out, many fans came up and asked, 'May I have your autograph Mr. Garfield?' That really pissed him off."

Dane Clark (1912-1998), born in Brooklyn, called himself "Joe Average," and so he was in film after film with such stars as Humphrey Bogart in *Action in the North Atlantic* (1943) and *Destination Tokyo* (1943) with Cary Grant.

Bogie suggested he change his name from Bernard Zanville, and Grant made a pass at him.

Liz Evaluates
STEVE COCHRAN

"He had one of the biggest cocks in Hollywood and his nickname was '*Mr. King Size*.' In some circles, he was known as 'The *Shvantz*.' Although he gave a lot of 'mercy fucks' [his words] to the likes of Joan Crawford or Mae West, most of the time he fucked strictly for fun. Such was the case with me—I couldn't advance his career like some of those other old dames.

"I got to know Steve pretty well. He was one of my all-time great lays. He was not a pretty boy but had a tough demeanor. He was the same way off screen. He was perfect when cast as a hood or a cut-throat. This son of a lumberman from Eureka, California, had a lot of run-ins with the police. He was a bad boy both on and off the screen.

"He told me he plugged Danny Kaye when they used to work together. He also had an affair with Virginia Mayo. When he made *Storm Warning* with Ronald Reagan, 'we once pissed together,' Steve claimed. 'I had three times as much as he did.'

"He was always making headlines. One-23-year-old girl singer claimed he tied her hands and feet with neckties and beat her. I can believe that. He liked his sex rough. He claimed that slapping a woman and spitting in her mouth during rough sex made her hotter."

Steve Cochran (1917-1965) was ideal for *film noir*. He zoomed to fame playing Virginia Mayo's immoral lover in *The Best Years of Our Lives* (1946) and *White Heat* (1949). On three occasions, he gave Danny Kaye a hard time in *Wonder Man* (1945), *The Kid from Brooklyn* (1946), and *A Song is Born* (1948). "I gave the faggot something hard off screen as well," Cochran said. "He choked on it."

Liz Evaluates
CHUCK CONNORS

"Don't get me wrong. Among the 2,000 or so men I've bedded, most of them had average-size dicks, but some of them had no more than three inches. I'm not inspired by those, and therefore I choose to discuss only my highlights instead of the pitfalls.

"And among those highlights was Chuck. *Mr. Rifleman himself.* He was once a baseball player and carried a big bat between his legs. I saw a gay porno film he'd made when he was young, and wanted to get in on some of the action. He really pounded that gay guy in the film and I wanted to try him on for size myself. It was two years later when I got my wish. He was everything—and more—than he was in that piece of porn.

"My greatest disappointment with Chuck came not in bed but during the follow-up. I gave him my phone number and begged him to call me. He never did. I'd practically killed myself making it good for him, and he really enjoyed it. But with that equipment he carried around, his phone was probably ringing off the wall. Men went after him too."

Chuck Connors (1921-1992) was a star athlete who made his 1952 film debut starring in *Pat and Mike* with Tracy and Hepburn. Tracy fell for him bigtime. The next year Burt Lancaster starred with him in *South Sea Woman* and came on strong to Connors. But by 1958 he was too big a star to "drop trou" for famously bisexual stars. He began a five-year run as TV legend Lucas McCain in *The Rifleman.*

Liz Evaluates
RICHARD CONTE

"Richard Conte is linked in my mind with beddy-bed time with Dane Clark, Stephen McNally, and John Garfield, so in recalling what each of them was like in bed, my memory gets blurred. I mean, each man was different, but somehow alike. On the screen, each one of them could easily have played the other's roles.

"Conte wasn't the prettiest kid to land in Hollywood, but he could play those tough guys. He was an Italian from Jersey City. His father wanted him to be a piano player but he ended up a truck driver, where he got a lot of blow-jobs on the road. He certainly wanted me to perform that same act on him, claiming he'd become addicted to fellatio at all those truck stops. He was well hung—not extraordinarily so, but way beyond adequate. Susan Hayward, Anne Baxter, and Gene Tierney were just some of the bitches who got to feel his inches.

"Right before he died, Richard called me and wanted to get together. I thought it was because he wanted to bang me again, even though he must have been 60 years old at the time. Not that. He was writing a bio of John Garfield, and he wanted me to give him all the dirt. But because he died in April of 1975, he never kept that date."

Richard Conte (1910-1975), an Italian-American, was at home in *film noir* dramas, gangster films, and war movies. He had granite features and a gritty delivery. Starring roles included *Guadalcanal Diary* (1943) and *The Purple Heart* (1944) in which he played a captive flier brutally interrogated by the Japanese. His first romantic lead was with the lesbian actress, Barbara Stanwyck, in *The Other Love* (1947).

Liz Evaluates
SAMMY DAVIS JR.

In her memoirs Renay claimed that Sammy was a "good platonic friend of mine" for some three decades. She said he came on strong to her one night in Las Vegas but she turned him down, because she was marrying actor Read Morgan that night. When queried about this "platonic" relationship years later, she said she deliberately lied because her lover and patron, mobster Mickey Cohen, did not "want me to sleep black. Also Sammy had been threatened by the mob when news broke of his affair with Kim Novak. Some mobsters threatened to put out his other eye. We kept our nocturnal activities a deep secret.

"He had the stamina of the bull, and was very well hung. He was ugly as a pile of crap, but good in bed. I don't usually date black, but I figured he was a star.

"He told me that one night in Las Vegas, he let Liberace give him a blow-job, but he much preferred getting it from Linda Lovelace. She was the bitch who starred in *Deep Throat*."

Sammy Davis Jr. (1925-1990) never became a true movie star, although he was one of the most talented and dynamic performers of the last half of the 20th century, a certified member of Frank Sinatra's "Rat Pack." He met Liz Renay when she was working as a stripper in New York.

Liz Evaluates
BRAD DEXTER

"The first language of that handsome hunk of manhood was Serbo-Croatian. Whenever we fucked, he'd switch from English to his native tongue.

"He was once married to Peggy Lee, but he told me I was much more uninhibited in bed than that canary.

"He met Karl Malden while serving in the Army Air Force during World War II. He said that Malden made the rounds at night, going from bunk to bunk, sucking off any guy who wanted it. He also told me that during the making of *The Magnificent Seven*, both Yul Brynner and Steve McQueen were hot to fuck Horst Buchholz, who acted very gay off camera.

"During the making of *None But the Brave* (1965), Brad saved Frank Sinatra from drowning. As a means of thanking him, Sinatra put him on his payroll. When he wasn't licking Sinatra's ass as his golf caddy, Brad often slipped away and made love to me. Sinatra broke with him, however, when Brad advised him not to marry 'that boy,' Mia Farrow."

Brad Dexter (1917-2002), square-jawed, broad shouldered, and menacingly handsome—became known in the early 50s in *film noir*. His appearance in *The Asphalt Jungle* (1950) is remembered chiefly today because of its casting of then-rising starlet Marilyn Monroe, who shared her charms with Dexter. He frequently starred with Yul Brynner and often had romantic trysts with him. Both men were bisexuals.

Liz Evaluates
HOWARD DUFF

"A Wisconsin-born boy, Howard Duff had this torrid affair with Ava Gardner. He met her on the set of *Brute Force* (1947) in which he was co-starring with Yvonne De Carlo and Burt Lancaster. Even though he was having a torrid affair with De Carlo at the time, he was mesmerized by Gardner when she arrived on the set to see Lancaster. Duff claimed, 'I told myself I had to have her if it kills me.'

"He also married Ida Lupino, but he told me she wore the pants in that relationship. He was tough and virile in bed, just like he was on the screen. I found him ruggedly handsome, and I liked to run my fingers through his wavy hair as he plowed into me. He liked to make love to a certain kind of music—he'd been a former disc jockey. Johnny Mathis or Peggy Lee put him in the mood.

"To his ever-lasting regret, he wanted to be up there in the same league as Burt Lancaster, Robert Mitchum, and Kirk Douglas, but he never got there. He was always worried that he didn't look matinee handsome. I told him not to fret about that. John Derek and Montgomery Clift were fantasies on the screen. 'But you look like a regular guy, the kind most housewives in America eventually marry,' I told him. 'That will assure you of roles for years to come.'"

Howard Duff (1913-1990) derailed a promising career by appearing in too many run-of-the-mill films.

Although married to Ida Lupino from 1951 to 1968, he was never faithful to her.

After playing Dustin Hoffman's intimidating lawyer in *Kramer vs. Kramer*, he ended up on a trio of nighttime TV soaps—*Flamingo Road*, *Knots Landing*, and *Dallas*.

Liz Evaluates
DAN DURYEA

"Dan had a talent for villainy on the screen. Off-screen he was married to the same woman for years and was a rather nice guy—painting in oil, planting vegetables, and building sailboats in his back yard. But every now and then he liked to stray from hearth and home."

"He told me why he decided to become an actor. 'I looked at my nude body in a full-length mirror. Ugly puss. So-so dick. A 155-pound weakling. No leading man. So I decided right there and then to become the meanest SOB in the movies.'

"From our first night together, he made it clear he wanted to enter through the back door. 'I can go into the front door at home. But when I cheat on my wife, I want a different kind of sex, something I can't get at home, and we're not ruling out blow-jobs either.'"

Dan Duryea (1907-1968) always had a sarcastic look on his face. "That made me ideal when cast as a cynic, even a creep or a villain. I was the guy the hero of the film always slapped around." His stage success on Broadway in the 1939 hit, *The Little Foxes*, brought him to the attention of Hollywood. He repeated the part in the 1941 film version with Bette Davis.

In *Scarlet Street* (1945), with Edward G. Robinson, he was so loathsome the audience cheered when he went to the electric chair for a murder he didn't commit.

Liz Evaluates
ERROL FLYNN

"He was quite a cocksman, and I learned the secret of his success with women or young boys. He was completely bisexual. Before mounting me, he put cocaine on the tip of his penis. Before getting into the saddle, he liked to be fellated, and he sure filled up a girl's mouth. He told me he'd had sex 12,000 to 14,000 times in his life—the gender didn't matter—sometimes at the rate of four a day.

"I was honored to be included in his list of lovers—some really big names like Howard Hughes, Laurence Olivier, Eva Peron, Tyrone Power, Doris Duke, Rock Hudson, Barbara Hutton, and Truman Capote. 'I'm just a goddamn phallic symbol to the world,' he told me.

"I wanted my thing with Errol to continue, but he had too many other holes in Hollywood to service to make me one of his regulars. Frankly, I think he preferred 14-year-old boy ass and 15-year-old girl virgins, and I didn't fit into either category.

"I later read that he was the Gestapo's most glamorous agent. That really startled me. I found that hard to believe. Instead of spying for the Nazis, I think he preferred rape—statutory or otherwise, personal brawls, drinking bouts, voyeurism, and old-fashioned screwing at the front or back door."

Errol Flynn (1909-1959) was *Robin Hood;* he was *Captain Blood*. On screen, he was the personification of a handsome devil on horseback.

His private life was more scandalous than anything he played on screen. With his sly smile, he was a lady-killer and deflowered young boys. He excelled at "swordplay," both on and off the screen. "He was the screen's most glorious pirate," or so said Olivia de Havilland, his frequent co-star. Ironically, he was cast as the deteriorating John Barrymore in *Too Much, Too Soon* (1958). The title of that movie could have been his epitaph.

"I pursued Clark Gable for years before I finally got him to agree to penetrate my love nest. I wanted the night to be really special for the 'King of Hollywood.' He still carried that moniker, but it had been a long time since he'd really ruled over Tinseltown. Other than Jerry Lewis, Gable was the major disappointment of my life. Although he'd screwed everybody—Joan Crawford, Nancy Reagan, Ava Gardner, Jean Harlow and Grace Kelly; he even fucked Lionel Barrymore—he had less than five inches. His wife Carole Lombard called him the Queen of Hollywood.

"I learned medical terms after bedding him. He suffered from phimosis. What in hell is that? It's when the foreskin doesn't retract properly. That left a real bad smell on his uncut dick. After he died, Joan Crawford admitted he wasn't a satisfying lover. I heard that in the late 20s he was a male hustler using both men and women to get ahead, everyone from Marion Davies to Billy Haines.

"After bedding me, he never came back, and I never wanted him to."

Clark Gable (1901-1960) immortalized himself in the role of Rhett Butler, in *Gone With the Wind*. He made many films, mostly for MGM, but most of them are unknown to the modern generation. Relentlessly virile, and noted for a winning smile that showed his false teeth, Gable had his heyday in the 1930s when he was the number one leading man in Hollywood. His 23-year career at Metro came to an end with his final teaming with Lana Turner (his lover in the early 40s) in a forgettable film called *Betrayed*, released in 1954.

"This New York kind of guy was the rebellious sort, a real bad boy, tough and cynical, just like I wanted. I went for him big time. He was hot tempered, and you didn't dare cross him. Before intercourse, he preferred me to go around the world on his body. He really, really liked that. I fell in love with him when I saw him with Lana Turner in *The Postman Always Rings Twice*. He screwed her during the shoot and also made it with Joan Crawford when they filmed *Humoresque*. He told me that when he met Crawford, she extended her hand to shake but he grabbed her right breast and fondled it. He claimed, 'She smiled back at me and said that she thought we were going to get on just fine. We hit the sack again and again all throughout the shoot.'

"He claimed that he had been in Hollywood a whole week 'before I got laid—some sort of world's record.' The gossip columnist Sheilah Graham accurately summed up John's technique in bed. 'He made love like a sexy puppy,' she said. 'In and out, huffing and puffing in quick gasps.' In fact, John was fucking some gal at the moment he died. Talk about dying in the saddle. He was only 39 when he had a heart attack. A lot of women missed out on a good thing when he passed away."

John Garfield (1913-1952) preceded such rebellious actors of the 1950s as Marlon Brando and James Dean. The tough New Yorker virtually invented the Hollywood term "bad boy." He was noted for his intensity on the screen. As illicit lovers/murderers with Lana Turner, he immortalized himself with the 1946 release of *The Postman Always Rings Twice*.

"He had a penchant for picking up girls, sometimes two at a time," said Lana. "He also had a reputation as a demon lover. He died young and in bed with a woman. How fitting!"

STERLING HAYDEN

"I think he was a commie, but I didn't care a damn about his politics. He was once labeled 'The Beautiful Blond Viking God.' That was the part of him that intrigued me. The first time he stripped down to go to bed with me, I thought I'd been delivered to Valhalla. Sometimes I've been to bed with big men with a peanut between their legs. But Sterling had a club, and he knew how to use it.

"He ran away to sea at 17, first as a ship's boy. He told me that he thought every sailor was gay. He was stalked day and night and sometimes had to beat off his admirers. He was going to play Quint in *Jaws* but couldn't come back into the country because he'd be arrested for tax evasion. After Lex Barker left the Tarzan role, it was offered to Sterling but he turned it down. He would have looked great in the jungle swinging from tree to tree with all those goodies dangling in the wind."

Sterling Hayden (1916-1986) won a studio contract for his good looks and sculpted physique. He shot to fame in the early 40s in two Technicolor productions with the equally beautiful Madeleine Carroll, who became his wife. He was in the Marines during World War II, coming back with a divorce and a new career.

He was known for seducing female stars in his pictures—Anne Baxter in *Blaze of Noon,* (1947), Dorothy Lamour in *Manhandled* (1949), Marilyn Monroe in *The Asphalt Jungle* (1950), and Jane Wyman in *So Big* (1953). He seemed to have passed on Bette Davis when they made *The Star* together in 1952.

JOHN HODIAK

"John and David Niven had the same kind of penis . . . a beer can. That Anne Baxter, who married John, was one lucky gal. Remember her as Eve Harrington in *All About Eve*? John came back to see me on at least four occasions and talked freely about himself. He started off in Hollywood billed as 'the new Gable,' but didn't go far with that moniker. He fucked Lucille Ball off the set in *Two Smart People (*1946) and Judy Garland off the set in *The Harvey Girls* (1946), and he had the rod to pump it to those lucky bitches. He was Ukranian. If he's typical of the men from that region, book me a ticket. The St. Louis Cardinals offered him a contract but he turned it down. Instead of playing baseball professionally, he became a golf caddy.

"He told me that some of his male stars came on to him sexually—Van Johnson in *Command Decision* (1948) and Robert Taylor in *Ambush* (1949). But I'm sure that happens to many actors once gays or bisexuals learn they've got Budweiser between their legs. Hedy Lamarr, he told me, wanted to marry him when they made *A Lady Without a Passport* (1950).

"I felt very sad when I read in the papers that he'd died of a heart attack. He was only 41. He was a very sensitive lover and a sensitive man. Some of those *film noir* guys were brutes—but not John."

John Hodiak (1914-1955). The world came to notice this actor when he played opposite Tallulah Bankhead in *Lifeboat* (1944) and opposite Lana Turner in *Marriage Is a Private Affair* (1944). "I fucked both of them," he later confessed to Liz Renay. He fell in love with Anne Baxter, 21 years old, when they made *Sunday Dinner for a Soldier* in 1944. His favorite role was that of an American soldier in the WWII story, *A Bell for Adano* (1945).

Liz Evaluates
WILLIAM HOLDEN

"I've gone to bed with men who had a hygiene problem. Not so William Holden, who became my on-again, off-again lover for three years. This Golden Boy was a compulsive bather. He told me he took as many as four showers a day. He took a bath before sex and after sex. He fucked from the A-list but somehow managed to fit me in. Did he ever have the classy broads—Nancy Reagan, Dorothy Lamour, Jackie Onassis, Barbara Stanwyck, Audrey Hepburn, Susan Hayward, Grace Kelly, you name them.

"One night during pillow talk, I asked Bill if he'd fucked Gloria Swanson during the making of *Sunset Blvd.*, because as he'd admitted on many occasions, he serviced older actresses. He told me that he did not. 'Swanson's mother, Adelaide, had a crush on me. She came to the set every day to watch me, not her daughter. She was so infatuated with me that she bought stock in Billy Wilder's *Stalag 17*. The picture not only brought me an Oscar in '53, but it turned out to be a tidy investment for the old bat.'"

William Holden (1918-1981) became Barbara Stanwyck's *Golden Boy* (1938) both on and off the screen. His career limped along until the forties came to an end. Then a miracle happened in 1950. He appeared opposite Gloria Swanson in *Sunset Blvd.* that year, after Montgomery Clift turned it down. Both Holden and Swanson were Oscar nominated for their role in that film. Then, ironically, whereas Swanson lost the Oscar to Judy Holliday that year for her role *Born Yesterday*, Holden had actually starred with dim bulb Holliday that same year, playing her bespectacled tutor. Thanks to his starring roles in two Oscar-winning films in the same year, Holden's career was made. In time he gave the world such other noteworthy films as *The Country Girl* (1954) and *The Bridge on the River Kwai* (1957).

Liz Evaluates
JOHN IRELAND

"I went to bed with both Clark Gable and John Ireland. Gable was called the 'King of Hollywood,' but the title should have belonged to John. He was the ultimate size queen's delight. Seeing was believing in his case. I felt a tree trunk was going up in me.

"When I saw *Red River* (1948), there was a scene between Princess Tiny Meat, Montgomery Clift himself, and John. They were ostensibly comparing the size of their guns, but it was a secret Hollywood wink to John's infamous physical endowment. When John made *Queen Bee* (1955) with Joan Crawford, she later insisted that he had the biggest cock in Hollywood— 'and I should know,' she said. 'I was married to Franchot Tone.'

"John confided in me about his private life, and I was all ears. He fell in love with the actress, Joanne Dru, when they made *All the King's Men* and married her. At one point, he beat the shit out of her, and she was rushed to the hospital. He showed up and swallowed sleeping pills in a suicide attempt to get her to come back. She divorced him in 1957. John, at the age of 45, took up with 16-year-old Tuesday Weld. She wanted to see for herself if the legend about John was actually true."

John Ireland (1914-1992) came out of Vancouver, bringing his angst-ridden features to Hollywood. He made a few good pictures, including *My Darling Clementine* (1946) before shooting to fame with Broderick Crawford in *All the King's Men* (1949). It won the Academy Award as Best Picture of the year, and Ireland was Oscar nominated for Best Supporting Actor. It was a long, slow descent after that, as he appeared in a series of B-list westerns and foreign films. In the late 80s he took out an ad in a newspaper seeking work in the movies. After placing that ad, Ireland said, "The phone didn't stop ringing."

Liz Evaluates
ALAN LADD

"He was a switch hitter with an understanding wife. He picked up another of my lovers, Rory Calhoun, during a horseback ride in Griffith Park. Rory told me he took good care of Alan. But Alan liked women on occasion, especially June Allyson.

"Alan was still pining for her when I met him. He described himself as having 'the face of an aging choirboy and the build of an undernourished featherweight.' He was about 5 feet four. Measured in inches, his dick would be about 5.4 inches.

"Alan came out of Arizona (I think), and was very, very short. He was good looking and a dirty blond. He was tight-lipped and had absolutely no humor about him, but I sorta fell for him in spite of his flaws. On a few nights we went swimming together in the Pacific...in the nude, of course. As a teenager, he'd been a diving champion.

"I was driving down the coastal highway in late January when I heard over the radio that Alan had died. Some people, especially his son, called it an accident, but I knew in my heart that Alan had killed himself. He'd come to the end of the line. He couldn't go on. He was the unhappiest man I've ever known."

Alan Ladd (1913-1964) appeared with Virginia Mayo in *The Iron Mistress* (1952). "The whole problem with his psyche," she said, "was his inability to recognize that he was a big star." That's what he was, at least for a time. He shot to fame as the gunman in *This Gun for Hire* (1942) with Veronica Lake. Paramount recognized them as a screen team, and they continued their *film noir* in other roles like *The Glass Key* (1942) and *The Blue Dahlia* (1946). *Shane* (1953) remains his greatest film, and it's the most watched today.

Liz Evaluates
FERNANDO LAMAS

"Arlene Dahl, Esther Williams, and Lana Turner were tough acts to follow. He said I was great at giving head, which he liked. He claimed Lana didn't like to do that and that is what really broke them up. 'I am a handsome Latin and a wonderful lover,' he told me, and he lived up to his billing. He never wore underwear because he wanted people to look at his crotch. He said he was 'hung very high—that is, his dick was placed high on his pubic bone. It makes my thing look like it goes on forever.'

"He admitted to me that he got into movies because 'it was a great way to meet broads.' He also liked the money that went with stardom. He told me stories about his life, which I found fascinating. He had to kiss Ethel Merman when he appeared on Broadway with her in the show, *Happy Hunting* (1956). After kissing her, he walked to the edge of the stage and wiped his mouth. This infuriated Merman. He told me that Merman was mostly dyke anyway."

"Fernando Lamas (1915-1982) was a Latin lover both on and off the screen. He told me that in Buenos Aires he once fucked Evita Peron, and I believe that. He talked a lot about Lana Turner whom he'd co-starred with in *The Merry Widow* (1952).

"After seducing every woman in Hollywood, he settled down with that swimmer, Esther Williams. He'd known her years before he married her. He claimed that she told him, 'Come back in ten years. You've got a lot of fucking to do!'"

Liz Evaluates
BURT LANCASTER

"Like so many of my lovers, he was a switch hitter. He had a great physique which was obvious whenever he took off his clothes. It was probably best displayed in *The Crimson Pirate* (1952). He told me he was Cecil B. DeMille's first choice to play Samson in *Samson and Delilah*. When he first took off his pants, I was disappointed at my first view of his uncut piece of meat. But he turned out to be a grower, not a show-er.

"He 'deflowered me' in his dressing room at Columbia overlooking the beach at Santa Monica. He was there shooting some picture—I forgot which one. He asked me to strip down and lie on a leopard skin rug. I'll never forget that sight of him screwing me on that rug. He was fantastic, everything a great lover should be. He was sensual, tender, passionate, just what a gal needs. After that, we began to date. He laughed a lot. He liked me to jiggle his balls—stuff like that. On some nights he couldn't get it up but we had a big laugh about that. Most of the time he came on like gangbusters. When I couldn't get a rise out of him, I brought him off oral-ly—or else gave him a hand job. That usually worked."

Burt Lancaster (1913-1994) smiled with a beaming self-assurance rarely seen on screen. A tower of physical strength, he was proud of his circus-trained body, best displayed in *Trapeze* (1956). He was the star of that 1953 blockbuster *From Here to Eternity,* and electrified audiences with his 1960 *Elmer Gantry*. The film was a huge hit and brought Lancaster a much deserved Oscar. "On the screen he was larger than life, and isn't that what being a movie star is all about?" asked Liz Renay.

Liz Evaluates
MARIO LANZA

"The first night I went out with Mario, he kept eating and drinking so much, I thought he'd be no good when I got him into bed. But he turned out to be great in bed. Toscanini, he told me, called him 'the greatest voice of the 20th century.' I'd rate him the actor with the most stamina. The guy was a satyr. He had the wettest tongue in history, which he kept ramming down my throat. I must have drunk a quart of spit. He told me that, 'The more women I lay, the better husband I am.'

"I figured that going to bed with Mario was like going to bed with Caruso himself. At one time in his career, he was about the biggest thing in Hollywood. He hated it when fans mobbed him, practically tearing his clothes off. Young girls climbed up the fire escape and hid out in his bedroom waiting for him to come in. 'They wanted more than my photograph,' he once told me. 'They wanted me to take their virginity.' One night he got really mad at me over some simple little thing. He was fueled by liquor and he became violent, breaking the vases, the lamps, and even a window or two. The manager was pounding on the door. Mario promised to pay for all the damages, and we spent the rest of the night pounding home."

Mario Lanza (1921-1959) had a brief but brilliant career with a voice not heard in the world since Enrico Caruso died. Trained as a boy to become an opera singer, he also became a notorious bad boy in Hollywood and pursued his leading ladies and any other attractive woman available (or not). "He was a terror to work with," said his frequent co-star Kathryn Grayson. "The first day he met me, he told me that he'd heard that I had the biggest breasts in Hollywood. 'In just a few days, my erect cock will be resting between those breasts,' he said. "I told him to 'dream on.'"

Liz Evaluates
LASH LA RUE

"Only die-hard cowboy movie fans remember whip-tossing Lash La Rue. He was, in a certain light, a dead-ringer for Humphrey Bogart—in fact, he was nicknamed 'Bogey With a Whip.' He always dressed in black. His 'Lonesome Trail' ended in Miami in the mid-50s where I heard he was arrested for vagrancy after his Hollywood days had more or less come to an end. The last I heard of him, he was helping drunks and derelicts find God and salvation.

"When I knew him, rescuing lost souls was the last thing on the guy's mind. He was ready for action. He even taught me how to use that damn whip, and I got so good at it that I even incorporated a whip into one of my striptease acts in Las Vegas. The guy had a real drinking problem. I tried to end our bedtime maneuvers early in the evening because by two o'clock in the morning he was completely zonked out. One night when I was hard up for cash, and when he was sprawled nude across my bed, I took some photos of him and tried to sell them to *Confidential*. Back in those days, they didn't run frontal nudes of men, so I got turned down, although I was later able to peddle them to a gay guy who was a big fan of Lash's. He gave me a hundred dollars.

"Lash was real proud of the fact that Lash La Rue comic books had sold 12 million copies in 1952."

Lash La Rue (1921-1996) took the whip to many a bad guy in Western films shot between 1947 and 1956. "The studio fired me when I demanded more pay, and no other studio wanted me. I was washed up. That's when I turned to the bottle." His first film was *Song of Old Wyoming* (1945), and some of his hits were *Mark of the Lash* (1949) and *King of the Bullwhip* (1950).

Liz Evaluates
GUY MADISON

"In 1944, when I saw Guy in his screen debut in *Since You Went Away*, I nearly fell out of my seat. He was the most gorgeous man I'd ever seen. Henry Willson, Hollywood's most infamous cocksucker, had discovered him, and after endless 'auditions' in his lavender bed, launched the kid in movies.

"Guy had been a sailor in tight pants when Willson first met him. Guy was into women, but when I got to know him he claimed he much preferred getting fucked by Rory Calhoun. *Touché*. I never told this to Guy, but I too much preferred getting fucked by his best friend, Mr. Calhoun.

"Howard Hughes once hired struggling 'starlets' Guy and Marilyn Monroe—or Norma Jean back then—to make a porno film for him. He couldn't have chosen two better stars, although Guy and me might have been better at it than him and Marilyn.

"Guy had been married to the actress Gail Russell, who was a total bitch and an alcoholic. She fucked around on him—with John Wayne, for example. But her husband was getting plowed by any number of Hollywood hunks like himself."

Guy Madison (1922-1996). "Stiff of jaw and hard of cock," was agent Henry Willson's appraisal of his dazzlingly handsome new discovery, a member of the Coast Guard during WWII. Madison couldn't act but he looked great. Directors eventually concluded he came off best in the saddle, and he ended up on TV as the star of *The Adventures of Wild Bill Hickok* (1951-58). His last film was *Won Ton Ton, the Dog Who Saved Hollywood* (1976).

Liz Evaluates
FREDRIC MARCH

"He was a bit long in the tooth when I hooked up with him, but was still proficient in bed. Actually, he'd been quite a womanizer, taking on Clara Bow to Tallulah, although I heard he struck out with Hepburn.

"He liked to put his hand up a girl's dress. Sometimes the situation was reversed. March was known for wearing no underwear. He said that Charles Laughton, during the filming of *The Sign of the Cross* (1932), kept trying to look up his toga to get a glimpse of his cock and balls.

"When Fredric talked to the press, he sounded like a Presbyterian deacon. He once said, 'I do not believe in matrimonial vacations. I am conservative, old-fashioned, domestically speaking. I like being married. Maybe he liked being married but he was known as the most lecherous fanny-grabber in town.

"Shelley Winters, not my favorite blonde, once told the press, 'March was able to do a very emotional scene with tears in his eyes and pinch my fanny at the same time.'"

Fredric March (1875-1975) was an actor who loved to act. From the stage, he broke into Talkies when sound arrived, mainly because of his rich stage voice. Beginning with *The Studio Murder Mystery* (1929), he appeared several times on screen with Florence Eldridge, whom he'd married in 1927. She had to put up with his numerous infidelities. He starred in many classics, some of which brought him an Oscar nomination, including the time he appeared as Norman Maine in *A Star Is Born* (1937). His career peak came in 1946 when he starred in *The Best Years of Our Lives* for Samuel Goldwyn. He won one final Oscar nomination for starring in Arthur Miller's masterpiece, *Death of a Salesman* (1951).

Liz Evaluates
DEAN MARTIN

"A lot of women could sing the praise of Dean Martin—Marilyn Monroe, Lana Turner, even Catherine Deneuve (or so I heard). He was very romantic, all wine, kisses, roses, and candlelight. In bed he was a stud, a good, thick eight inches, I'd estimate.

"But he wasn't much for conversation, just action. He told his broads, 'You wanna talk, see a priest.' He took a lot of Percodan, which is supposed to be very addictive. Come morning, Romeo had fled the scene. All a gal ever got was a pat on the ass and 'a thank you, ma'am.'

"One night in Las Vegas, Dean introduced me to Elvis Presley. Dean told me that at first he and Frankie never liked Elvis. They found his gyrations distasteful. Dean also said he didn't like the sexual innuendo in Elvis's voice. Can you believe that Dean talked like a prude, although I saw him bring a certain leer to his lyrics too. 'Frankie thinks Presley's lip-curlings border on the epicene,' Dean told me. 'Too sensual for a real man. A lot of people don't know this, but Presley is a fag.' I don't think that's true. When I met Elvis, he asked me if he could autograph my breasts. Would a fag do that?"

Dean Martin (1917-1995) later claimed he had to "get rid of Jerry Lewis" to prove what a real star he was in his own right. Fans by the millions took to his persona of a smarmy crooner with too much liquor in his gut and a roving eye for fast ladies of the night. Martin managed to push aside Tony Randall and take over his role in *The Young Lions*, which put his acting style up against that of Montgomery Clift and Marlon Brando, two heavyweights. At the time he was known as "the monkey's ex-partner." But this film proved he could also do drama.

Liz Evaluates
VICTOR MATURE

"When you mix the gene pools of France, Switzerland, Germany, Italy, and Greece, you come up with a macho like Victor. Although he liked to suck young boy cock on occasion, he was a man for the ladies. Just ask Rita Hayworth, Betty Grable, Veronica Lake, Lana Turner, or Elizabeth Taylor."

When he was in the Coast Guard, lying naked on his bunk, a nude picture of him was snapped. "If the Nazis had seen that picture," said Gore Vidal, "they would have surrendered much sooner."

According to Liz, "Victor was very thick and measured 6 and a half inches soft, rising up to 10½ when aroused. And that's what I did to this magnificent hunk of beefcake. Aroused him time and time again. He hit the spot. What a man!

"He told me he was a mean kid growing up. On the first day of school, he bit his teacher. He arrived in Hollywood with a stash of candy which he sold to pay the $8 rent on a burned-out garage.

"When he left Hollywood, Victor said, 'Let them call me what they want—Technicolor Tarzan, Lush Lothario, Overripe Romeo. Fuck it all, I made money and had a blast and screwed anything I wanted.'"

Victor Mature (1913-1999) once said, "I can't help it if I've got a good set of muscles. I want to prove I've got something more. I'm tired of being a male striptease." He once placed an imprint of his bare buttocks on a slab of concrete outside his dressing room door. "I was pissed off that I had not been invited to place my hands and feet in Graumann's Theatre. I should have left an imprint of my cock." Mature is still remembered today for his appearance in Cecil B. DeMille's blockbuster epic, the 1949 *Samson and Delilah*, in which he co-starred with hot-to-trot Hedy Lamarr.

Liz Evaluates
LEE MARVIN

"Lee Marvin was one of the wildest men I'd ever met. He may have been prematurely gray upstairs, but he hadn't begun to atrophy down below. He was one of the most masculine men I've ever bedded. He preferred hanging with the guys and wanted women for only one thing.

"I met him in Honolulu. Only the night before I heard he'd pulled off all his clothes and danced the hula on top of the bar at the Kawaii Hotel. He dared show his face—but not his ass—the following night at the same hotel, where he met me in the bar. Amazingly, they still let him in. He told me, as he'd told so many other women, 'I hear you've got the prettiest little pink clittie in all of Hawaii.' Later that night he found out how true that was.

"When Lee plowed me, he broke a rule of his. He used to say, 'There's an old adage in show business—never shack up with anyone with lower billing than you.' Lee made a lot of enemies but I found him fascinating. Marlon Brando told me he hated his guts. Josh Logan, who directed Lee in *Paint Your Wagon* (1969), expressed it more eloquently. 'Not since Attila the Hun swept across Europe, leaving five-hundred years of total blackness, has there been a man like Lee Marvin.'"

Lee Marvin (1924-1987) is famous for late night re-runs of *The Wild One* , a picture he made in 1953 with Marlon Brando. As an actor he could be either heroic or menacing. A tough former marine, he entered the pantheon of all-time screen sadists when he tossed scalding coffee in poor Gloria Grahame's face in *The Big Heat* (1953).

Liz Evaluates
STEPHEN McNALLY

"I could never get my fill of those tough guys in *film noir*. I would love to have played the gun moll with each of them. It would have been typecasting of course, what with me being Mickey Cohen's girlfriend and all.

"Of all the bad boys, Stephen was the smartest. He was born in New York right before World War I and studied hard and became a lawyer. He gave up the profession to become an actor. His real name was Horace McNally, but it sounded too close to that character actor Horace McMahon, so the studio assigned him a new name.

"He's still remembered as the vile brute who raped Jane Wyman, the deaf-mute in *Johnny Belinda*. Stephen told me he tried to fuck Jane offscreen even though she was married to Ronald Reagan at the time. 'The major star of the picture, Lew Ayres, beat me to Jane's pussy and locked it up for himself.'

"He told me that Burt Lancaster gave him blow-jobs all during the shoot of *Criss Cross* (1949). Burt was AC/DC but I adored him.

"Stephen was a fairly intense lover with a seven-inch dick that he knew how to use proficiently. He was a breast man with a few kinks. He liked to pour chocolate syrup on my breasts and then lick it off. Very kinky, and very messy, but fun."

Stephen McNally (1913-1994) said, "If it's an action picture or a western, I'll get a call," he said. "One of my most remembered parts was James Stewart's brother who steals the rifle in *Winchester '73* (1950). For most of the 50s, Universal assigned me programmers. Could I do camp? Did you see me in *The Black Castle* (1952)? I played an eyepatch-wearing count with Boris Karloff and Lon Chaney Jr. I guess you didn't. Let's face it; the only one who ever really thought I was a big Hollywood star was Liz Renay."

Liz Evaluates
RALPH MEEKER

"Meeker once claimed he was a 'rough kid who became an actor.' I thought he had a real menacing sex appeal."

The Broadway producers of *A Streetcar Named Desire* decided, after Brando moved on to film roles, that Meeker was the only guy around who could bring a sexual menace onstage to equal Brando's portrayal of Stanley Kowalski. And before that, when gay playwright William Inge wanted a stud for the lead in *Picnic*, he picked Meeker.

During the run of *Picnic*, Meeker learned that Paul Newman was bisexual and offered the actor a chance to suck him off. According to Liz, "That foolish Newman declined. I did not. I slurped on that big lollipop for an hour or so before he mounted me for the rest of the night. He had the stamina of a bull. He was a bad guy on the screen and an even badder boy in bed. When he crawled off a woman's body, she was satisfied for a week."

Ralph Meeker (1920-1988) was brazenly macho and had a great screen presence, but never made it big like his rival Marlon Brando. When he appeared on Broadway in *Mister Roberts* (1948), directors took notice.

"I was an also ran, suitable for features. I hit it big on Broadway when I did William Inge's *Picnic* (1953). William Holden did the movie role—and he can go fuck himself. My career came to an inglorious end. I got eaten by rats in *The Food of the Gods* (1976) and knocked off by aliens in *Without Warning* (1980)."

Liz Evaluates
RAY MILLAND

"Grace Kelly didn't seem to mind, but Marlene Dietrich did. When she starred with Milland in *Golden Earrings* (1947), and went to bed with him, she told everybody on the set, 'Milland doesn't practice personal hygiene. His thing stank.'

"He often got revenge on people who annoyed him. He told me that when he shot *Beau Geste* back in '39 with co-star Brian Donlevy, he nicked Donlevy's unpadded penis in a fencing sequence, bloodying his pants.

"He also enjoyed water sports—but not with me. When he made *Jungle Princess* in 1936, during a scene in the pool with Dorothy Lamour, he had to pee in the worst way. While tonguing her mouth, he pissed in his trunks right in the pool water.

"All during dinner, Milland told me how much he hated Hollywood gays—he seemed obsessed with them. What was his problem?

"Bette Davis thought he was 'a shit!' But Grace Kelly, who was screwing as many stars as I was—well, almost—fell for him bigtime when they starred in *Dial M for Murder* (1954). It almost broke up Milland's marriage. He moved out for a while and took an apartment with Grace."

Ray Milland (1905-1986) emerged from Wales to enjoy a long career that lasted from 1929 (when he was known as Spike Milland) to just months before his death. His bull's eye came playing an alcoholic writer for Billy Wilder in *The Lost Weekend* (1945). The movie was a smash, voted Best Picture of the Year with Milland walking off with an Oscar as Best Actor. After that it seemed there was no place to go but down.

Liz Evaluates
ROBERT MITCHUM

"He was a *I-don't-give-a-damn* kind of guy. When he propositioned me one night, he was blunt: 'Do you want to fuck or don't you?'

"I answered, 'If Robert Mitchum is asking, the answer is yes, yes, and double yes!' Back at my apartment, he flipped through my records and wanted to hear only Elvis Presley. He even sang for me that night: Calypso, Trinidad style.

"He was married to long-suffering Dorothy Spence for nearly 60 years, but he fucked around a lot—Lucille Ball, Ava Gardner, Rita Hayworth, Shirley MacLaine, and maybe Jane Russell too. Monroe thought he was a lousy kisser with bad breath. I thought he was all right. But he got me drunk just by smelling his breath. He was fairly well hung and had hustled guys during his early days in Hollywood, and had plowed Clifton Webb.

"Bob told me that he used to regularly fuck Marilyn Monroe, who was called Norma Jean Baker back in the early 40s when he was a sheetmetal worker at Lockheed. He was a good buddy of James Dougherty, her boyfriend. What piqued his interest, Bob claimed, was when Dougherty showed him pinup pictures of this fifteen-year-old beauty."

Robert Mitchum (1917-1997) was a star for half a century, from 1943 to the year he died. This was amazing, considering that he arguably made more undistinguished films than any A-list star of his day. With his ultra-cool demeanor and his droopy eyelids, he walked through many a picture such as *His Kind of Woman* (1951) and *Macao* (1952). Both of these lackluster pictures were attempts by Howard Hughes to promote Mitchum and Jane Russell as a hot screen team.

Liz Evaluates
DAVID NIVEN

"When I first met him, he needed a boost to his male ego. Ian Fleming had wanted him to play James Bond in *Dr. No*, but producer Albert Broccoli nixed that idea. He told Niven he was too old.

"He wasn't too old for my bed. What was he like? Ever had a beer can shoved into you? Ever since losing his virginity at the age of 14 to a whore who was trawling Piccadilly Circus, David made the rounds—Doris Duke, Ava Gardner, Barbara Hutton, Hedy Lamarr, Ginger Rogers—even Mae West. He claimed that Princess Grace was his most satisfying lay—that is, until he met the one-and-only Liz Renay.

"David told amusing stories of his life, even one about Princess Grace. While visiting Grace and Prince Rainier in Monaco, the prince asked him what was his hottest piece. 'Grace,' he blurted out, belatedly realizing what he'd said. 'Er…Gracie…I mean, Gracie Fields.' The prince's warm welcome grew chilly after that.

"I think I was the only star on the B-list he ever fucked. All the rest seemed to be legends. Other than the ones I named, he also plowed into Alice Faye, Paulette Goddard, Rita Hayworth, Deborah Kerr, Ida Lupino, Carole Lombard, Norma Shearer, Ann Sheridan, and Loretta Young."

David Niven (1909-1983), born in London, was sophisticated, urbane, and upper class, with a dry British wit. His accent was part of his characterization whether he was appearing in comedy, costume dramas, or war films. Sometimes he was in hits he didn't like: *Wuthering Heights* (1939) for example. His most controversial film (for its era) was *The Moon Is Blue*, (1953) in which he tried to seduce virgin Maggie McNamara.

Liz Evaluates
JOHN PAYNE

"His beefcake photos from the early 40s really turned me on. I was not alone. Howard Hughes went after John and got him.

"There was one scene of him in boxing trunks shot by lensman George Hurrell. It revealed his massive thighs and a promising mound between his legs. Whenever sexy John swung into action, that mound swelled into a mountain. He was one of the handsomest men who ever bedded me. Today they'd call such a man a hunk. He had a slightly devilish smile, and I really dug tonguing that cleft in his chin. He'd fucked Alice Faye, Betty Grable, Sonja Henie, and lots of beautiful women. But he told me that none of them could really give him great rim jobs like I did. That seemed to be his favorite thing. I nicknamed him *Rosebud*.

"He never reached the big ranks of stardom that he deserved—what a pity. Before Hollywood, he'd been a boxer and a wrestler, so he was one tough guy. That handsome, six-foot, four-inch stud was a natural for both frothy musicals and lightweight comedies with Betty Grable. He knew all the Hollywood secrets, like bisexual Carmen Miranda falling big for Grable."

John Payne (1912-1989) once said, "I could never quite take working in movies seriously—it was all kind of fun. It was a lucrative job. I certainly couldn't have earned that kind of dough anywhere else. Providence was very kind."

What would 20th Century Fox in the 1940s have been without Payne? He was the perfect foil for Alice Faye or her replacement, Betty Grable, in those silly wartime musicals. Occasionally he went real A-list as in *The Razor's Edge* (1946) but his enduring fame came in *Miracle on 34th Street* (1947) as the lawyer who ends up defending Santa Claus in court.

Liz Evaluates
GEORGE RAFT

"That Hell's Kitchen gangster—a crook in both *real* and *reel* life—was a sharp dresser and had good looks. When he dropped his pants, I learned why all the gals at Polly Adler's bordello in New York called him Blacksnake. He had the blackest dick I'd ever seen on a white man.

"Having plowed everybody from Mae West to Rudolph Valentino, he knew what to do with his heavy equipment. Close friend Mack Grey said, 'Screwing was his only game. He could get up in the morning and put in a whole day at it. For year after year after year, George averaged two different women a day.' That was not true in my case. When I finished with him, he didn't need another woman for a month.

"Since I was a sweet sixteen, I fell for George and his dark, smoldering eyes on the screen. His way of talking made my girlish flesh tingle. That guy really turned me on. I started dating him when I came to Hollywood. He surpassed my fantasies. We went everywhere—Chasen's The Brown Derby, and the Cocoanut Grove. We were in all the columns. He had a recirculating fountain in his apartment. We made love night after night by that fountain, listening to the sound of the cascading water."

George Raft (1895-1980). Often compared to both James Cagney and Edward G. Robinson, he was one of the bigtime movie gangsters in the 1930s. On his rise to stardom, he'd been a gangster himself, hanging in with the notorious Owney Madden. *Scarface* (1932) made him a name in Hollywood, and Mae West stole *Night After Night* (1932), from him, but he endured. Ray Danton, one of Liz Renay's many lovers, played Raft on the screen in *The George Raft Story* (1961).

Liz Evaluates
ALDO RAY

"This gargle-voiced guy, who grew up in California, was a good time Charlie. He was the perfect kind of actor to get cast as a sergeant leading a platoon. He'd been a Navy frogman and had played football in college, so he was a rugged guy, especially when it came to making love to a woman. He had a sizable endowment. There's a famous nude photo of him circulating about, and that's his cock all right. When it was hard, it shot up to about nine inches and was rather thick. He was bait for gals who liked their men with hairy chests.

"He dropped trou for that gay director, George Cukor, who helped him in his career, and also climbed the lavender ladder with Spencer Tracy when he made *Pat and Mike* (1952) with that dyke, Katharine Hepburn. Rita Hayworth went for him big time when they did the Sadie Thompson movie together.

"It's sad that Aldo ended up on the skids. Someone told me that one of his last films was in porn. This jarhead became so famous for his voice, that I was sad to learn that he died of throat cancer."

Aldo Ray (1926-1991) In movies of the 1950s, he was frequently cast as the ideal soldier, as in the box office hit *Battle Cry* (1955). His biggest part was playing opposite Rita Hayworth in *Miss Sadie Thompson* (1953). He was cast in John Wayne's controversial *The Green Berets* (1968) about the Vietnam War, but by the end of the 60s his once promising career had stalled. His final roles were in a string of fly-by-night cheapies, including *Won Ton Ton, the Dog Who Saved Hollywood* (1976), wherein he tried to rape Madeline Kahn.

Liz Evaluates
ROBERT RYAN

"He was one of the screen's biggest heavies. When he stripped down for action, I learned why he'd been cast in *The Battle of the Bulge*. The guy had been a boxer in the Marines, and he kept his body in shape. I saw him hard and thought he had the usual six inches, but once he got excited it grew at least two inches more. When it came to women, he had a take-no-prisoners approach. He was out to get his satisfaction, and he didn't care too much what the woman had to go through to bring him off. But I loved it. He told me that he fucked my look-alike, Marilyn Monroe, on the set of *Clash by Night* (1952), 'that is, when she wasn't letting Barbara Stanwyck go muff-diving.'

"Most people think he always played villains, but he told me that he appeared in more hero roles. 'My mother wanted me to play the violin, my father wanted me to be a boxer,' he once told me. Before stardom, he had various kinds of jobs—digging sewer tunnels, rounding up horses in Montana, or working the engine room on a giant ocean liner. At one time he was a bill collector, but couldn't stomach that job. 'I spent seven years of my life as a vagabond,' he said."

> **Robert Ryan** (1903-1973) was the quintessential film noir actor, although most of the movies he made are forgotten today. Movie buffs still remember him, however, as a cold-hearted hood, a tough gangster, or a psychotic spouse. Liz Renay got turned on by him when she saw *Crossfire* (1947) in which Ryan appeared with two other Roberts-- Mitchum and Young. Ryan was nominated for Best Supporting Actor in his role. After a final struggle that lasted three years, he lost his bout with cancer.

Liz Evaluates
FRANK SINATRA

"I'd heard all the stories and was very excited when Sinatra took me to bed. When he pulled off his pants, I was expecting something really big. After all, Ava Gardner had said, 'There's only 10 pounds of Frank but there's 110 pounds of cock.'

"Although he was well-endowed, his advance press was a bit exaggerated. I used to know Marilyn Monroe. She and I talked about Frank. Marilyn told me, 'He was no DiMaggio.' Opinions of other women varied. '*Mais oui*...the Mercedes-Benz of men!' said Marlene Dietrich. 'A complete shit,' recalled Lauren Bacall.

"My first encounter with Sinatra led to no action at all. I was dating Joe DiMaggio, who took me and my fifteen-year-old daughter, Brenda, to Sinatra's opening night at Skinny Ennis's place in Atlantic City. A party followed later in Sinatra's suite. DiMaggio had to leave but Brenda and I stayed on.

"Since we had several hours to go before our 10:30am flight, Sinatra asked us to sleep in his bed. Nothing happened, but I kept one eye open in case the Chairman of the Board went for my daughter. He was the perfect gentleman. Ol' Blue Eyes certainly got in the saddle when I met up with him a few months later in Las Vegas. That time I didn't have Brenda with me."

> **Frank Sinatra** (1915-1998) was the most controversial crooner in America. He was loved or hated, depending on who you talked to. Today, long after his death, he's still an international icon.
>
> Notoriously linked to the underworld, he was also known for his tempestuous romances with both Jackie Kennedy and Marilyn Monroe. He also showed the world he was a hell of a good actor, as when he played the doomed Private Maggio in *From Here to Eternity* (1953).

Liz Evaluates
ROBERT STACK

"Of all the actors I bedded, none was quite as sophisticated as Robert Stack. He was Hollywood royalty and spoke fluent Italian and French and was charming in the nicest sense.

"When he was very young, he'd become the toy boy of Howard Hughes. He became one of the swinging bachelors of Hollywood and made the usual rounds—Judy Garland, Betty Grable, Lana Turner.

"In the summer of 1940, he shared his bachelor apartment in the Hollywood Hills with a young, handsome, and horny John Fitzgerald Kennedy. 'I've known many of the great Hollywood stars and only a very few of them seemed to hold the attention for women that Jack did,' Robert said.

"Like so many stars of the day, Robert was a switch-hitter. He had a very closeted affair with Paul Newman, that bastard who turned me down. I later heard that Newman had a small dick, so I didn't miss out on much. Stack was very generously endowed, not the biggest in Hollywood, but certainly not the smallest. I should have taken measurements, but I didn't."

Robert Stack (1919-2003) burst on the screen giving Deanna Durbin her first on-screen smooch in *First Love* (1939). Although at first he appeared no more than a good-looking somewhat stoic guy of the type who arrived by the trainload in Hollywood every day, he was a durable and reliable performer through picture after picture, some 40 in all. Finally, he really became a household word when he appeared as Eliot Ness in the hit series, *The Untouchables* (1959-63), which won him an Emmy award. The *Untouchables* became one of the most famous crime dramas in TV history.

Liz Evaluates
LAWRENCE TIERNEY

"After I enjoyed a three-way with Lawrence and his brother, Scott Brady, Lawrence came back for second helpings by himself. Amazingly, he had virtually the same large package as his brother. It was like getting the same fuck twice. I enjoyed both of them, but somehow I think Scott had the edge. At least Scott was handsomer, but both were very proficient when it came to satisfying a woman.

"Tierney was a total wild boy, much more than Scott. He liked barroom brawls, and in 1973 got himself stabbed. If you want to know what he was like, it's all up there on the screen when he played the consummately brutal lover of Claire Trevor in *Born to Kill* (1947). He was the same two-fisted, tough guy off screen.

"He had a strange quirk, though. He liked to bring me to the point of orgasm and drive me wild, but wanted me to beg him to finish me off. He liked having that power over a woman. After we did the bloody act, he could finish off an entire quart of whisky.

"One night when he was sprawled nude across my bed, I went to sleep with his penis in my mouth."

Lawrence Tierney (1919-2002) became a cult favorite in *film noir*. Eventually his career was cut short by his off-screen behavior and numerous arrests. A newspaper columnist likened him to the fictional character of Dr. Jekyll/Mr. Hyde. "When he's sober, he's serious, thoughtful ambition. When drunk, he's close to crazy." One of the best examples of his *noir* work was in *The Devil Thumbs a Ride* (1947). It was panned at first—"it's pictures like this that gave movies a bad eye," according to *The New York Times*. In later years, it found a cult following.

Liz Evaluates
FRANCHOT TONE

"I hit it lucky with Joan Crawford's former husband. He was known as Jawbreaker, and he lived up to his name. Once, I practically choked on it before we got down to some serious man-on-woman action.

"He was charming, sophisticated, and well educated, unlike Steve McQueen. He told me that I reminded him of Barbara Payton, the blonde starlet who became a $10-a-night whore in Las Vegas.

"On one of our dates, Franchot told me that when he was making *Dangerous* in 1935 with Bette Davis, she fell in love with him. They screwed throughout the entire shoot. He was also involved with Crawford at the time. Do you think that was the beginning of the famous feud between those two old broads? When he walked away from Davis after the shoot, she never forgave him. 'Too bad for my career,' he told me. He claimed he was up for the male leads in both *The Sisters* and *Old Acquaintance*, but Davis nixed appearing with him.

"Whenever he entered a woman, she felt well stuffed, like a Christmas turkey. He said he was born in Niagara Falls, and that he'd take me there one day, perhaps on our honeymoon. It was just bullshit. He never called me again."

Franchot Tone (1905-1968) may have longed for meatier fare, but he was often cast as a devil-may-care kind of guy, strutting around in a tux while obviously inebriated. Trained as a stage actor, he broke into films in 1932, appearing in *The Wiser Sex* as the doomed cousin of attorney Melvyn Douglas. In *Today We Live* (also 1932), he played Joan Crawford's brother and later became her husband in real life. On screen, Crawford and Tone teamed up again and again. He achieved notoriety during his marriage to blonde floozy Barbara Payton (1951-52), and hit the front pages after a brawl with her other lover, Tom Neal. "I should have known better than to marry this whore," he later said.

Liz Evaluates
FORREST TUCKER

"I told a gal pal of mine—yes, I have such creatures—that getting fucked by Forrest Tucker felt like giving birth to a big baby boy. He was one big guy, and I mean big. This Indiana boy liked to be called Tuck, and he was a hard-drinking, hard-living man. Most men who brag about the size of their equipment exaggerate, or so I've found. Tuck bragged a lot about his endowment, but he lived up to every inch of it. He once drunkenly suggested that his penis be immortalized along Hollywood's 'Walk of Fame.' Once word of his physicality spread, his phone kept ringing off the wall. Both the gay boys and women wanted him.

"He and John Wayne used to hang out together. Tuck had so many inches he could have spared some for a penile transplant with Wayne so The Duke could live up to his name when he took off his cowboy drag. The gals all told me that Wayne was a disappointment in bed, just like Clark Gable. Sometimes big names on the screen in Hollywood aren't big in the boudoir."

Forrest Tucker (1919-1986) arrived in Hollywood in the early 40s, telling friends, "I may not be the prettiest face in town, but I've got the biggest dick. That should stand me well with some queer directors." And so it did, especially when Tucker landed a role in *Keeper of the Flame* (1942), opposite Hepburn and Tracy. Tucker went over "big" with both Tracy and gay director George Cukor. Tucker is still remembered today by "camp" followers because of his appearance with Rosalind Russell in *Auntie Mame* (1958).

ROBERT WALKER

"He was my most mixed-up lover, but he was extremely talented. Off the screen he was a troubled alcoholic in deep despair. During the time he was screwing around with me, he was also balling Peter Lawford and Nancy Reagan. That bitch was known as Nancy Davis back then, and she was a nothing starlet.

"Robert also made it with Ava Gardner and Judy Garland, but he wasn't that great in bed. He had average size equipment, but enough to entice Jennifer Jones to marry him. David Selznick stole Jennifer away and Robert later married Barbara Ford, the daughter of John Ford. One drunken night Robert asked me to marry him, but I wisely turned him down. My life was screwed up enough all on my own without taking on baggage like Robert.

Robert Walker (1918-1951) led a short, tragic life. He is remembered mainly today for his "role of a lifetime," that of a homicidal homosexual who ensnares Farley Granger in a deadly web of vengeance, murder, and psychosis in Hitchcock's *Strangers on a Train* (1951).

"In 1951, he met an early death. Unstable even during the best of times, he became loud and suicidal after a drinking binge. By mistake, his doctor gave him an injection of sodium amytal, something that had been intended as a sedative. He turned blue and died a few minutes later of respiratory failure.

"The final time he visited me, he was too drunk to get it up. I remember his last words. He told me, 'I'm always trying to make my escape from life.'"

JOHNNY WEISSMULLER

"He was Tarzan and I was his Jane for the night. And what a night. The guy had one of Hollywood's largest appendages, and the longest foreskin I'd ever seen on a man. He told me he liked starlets and chorus gals. I think he viewed me as a blonde bimbo starlet. It really didn't matter. This is one guy who knew how to handle a woman. After all, he'd had everybody in Hollywood, including that wild enchilada, Lupe Velez, as well as Joan Crawford and Tallulah Bankhead. True to form, when he came, he gave the Tarzan yell.

Johnny Weissmuller (1904-1984) emerged from the Austro-Hungarian empire to become the greatest screen Tarzan of them all. A swimmer since childhood, he was equally at home among elephants and chimps.

"Johnny was a real athlete and had a lot of stamina. The weekend after our first encounter, he invited me to a party at his house, where he staged an exhibition. He masturbated himself in front of his select guests, both men and women. He sure knew how to put on a show, but I told the gal standing next to me that all this solo performance was a waste of talent. Jungle Man belonged in bed on top of a woman, because that's where his true talent came out.

"After that, he called me for a final date, but warned that I was not to wear panties. While eating his meal with one hand, or so he claimed, he liked to explore a gal under the table.

"He lived up to his word. He gave me an orgasm while I was devouring a steak."

Liz Evaluates
GLENN FORD
"My Greatest Love"

"Who is that son of a bitch that should say he helped me have a comeback? That shithead wouldn't have helped me out of a sewer!"

—**Bette Davis** comments on her former lover having helped her stage a comeback in *A Pocketful of Miracles (1961).*

Glenn Ford
(1916-2006)

"He was the man for me, although he obviously didn't agree. I took up with him after his marriage to Kathryn Hayes, an actress, came to an end, and before his marriage to Cynthia Hayward, another actress. Those two were nothings on the radar screen. Glenn's first wife was the famous tap dancer/actress Eleanor Powell.

"He was one of my most exciting lovers, a guy I really fell for. I first encountered him when we were both guests on some TV talk show—not Johnny Carson. He came to my rescue when I was having a fight with wardrobe. Some asshole claimed I was showing too much cleavage. I told the bitch I can't help the way I was born. She stuffed a scarf between my breasts, but Glenn came over and yanked it out. He threatened to walk off the show if I wasn't allowed to show a little décolletage. I fell in love with him at first sight. He was so very handsome.

"Nothing happened that first day, but I bumped into him a year later when I showed up at some affair honoring Liza Minnelli. On the dais sat Glenn sandwiched between two old whores, Zsa Zsa Gabor and Lucille Ball. I'm sure he'd had both of them. During the ceremony, his eyes devoured me in my dark red satin dress cut obscenely low. I didn't wear a bra.

"Glenn started throwing kisses at me and got Ball and Gabor to throw kisses as well. Everybody was straining their neck to see who the hot bitch in the audience was.

"Edith Head was also honored. You know, the lesbian costume designer. She told how she'd had to stuff many a bra or many a male jock strap 'long before Tom Jones got the idea.' The dyke bitch sure didn't have to stuff my bra.

"After the show, and right in front of twenty people, Glenn said, 'You're beautiful. Why don't you marry me?' He asked for my phone number, and I gave it to him.

"Thus, began our courtship. We rolled in the hay on the first date. How did I know at the time he was a hit-and-run lover? I should have asked Judy Garland, Rita Hayworth, or Barbara Stanwyck. They could have told me. I became his 'Angel,' he became my Prince Charming. I got to know every inch of his dick. He inserted it in every orifice I had or between my breasts. I must say of all the men I've seduced, he had the sweetest tasting cum.

"The man knew how to make wild, passionate love. Kisses, sweet nothings in my ear for *après-sex* pillow talk. But while that boy mounted me, he was a hard driving pounder. He left me screaming at orgasm time. After sex, we talked over drinks for hours at a time. He had big plans for the both of us, or so he said.

"After Robert Taylor walked out on Stanwyck, Glenn was the first man she called. She met him at the door in a pinkish 'baby-doll' *négligée* with a glass of bubbly. 'Come in, Glenn,' she told him. 'Take me into the bedroom and make me a woman again.'

"After three months of love making, it occurred to me that Glenn wanted to see me only in the bedroom. He never took me to the hotspots like George Raft did. He was very secretive. We were never photographed together. Glenn was so hot for my body he interrupted the shooting of *Midway*—or so he said—to come and pound the hell out of me. Then he put on his pants and rushed back to the set.

"Later, at the same studio, I went for a job interview. I asked to be given a pass to the *Midway* set to watch Charlton Heston and Glenn in action. The security guard told me that Midway had finished shooting at least three weeks ago. Glenn had obviously lied to me.

"When a reporter from *The National Insider* called Glenn to check on rumors of a romance with me, he told the guy, 'I don't even know Liz Renay!'

"I finally concluded that he was playing our romance like a non-paying trick. Even with all his faults, I still wanted this exciting lover. I was a prisoner of love.

"After a gig in Canada, I returned to Hollywood to find that a gal named Cynthia Howard had become Glenn's live-in love. She also became his third wife. He took that one out to dinner.

"I left town and headed for Vegas where new loves awaited me, including one hunk, a cross between Joseph Cotten and Paul Newman. For me, he even gave up the stripper, bit-tit Tempest Storm, who had every man from Elvis Presley to JFK. He became husband number seven, Jerry Heidebrink.

"I tried to wipe Glenn right out of my hair, but he wrote me from all over the world. I put an autographed picture he sent of himself up on my trophy wall. I added him to my ever-growing collection of men.

"I even helped the bastard get over his divorce from that Howard gal. I know it would come to that. Glenn never could be faithful to one woman. He begged me until I gave him the key to my honeypot once again. Between wives, he invited me to come to his home in Beverly Hills for trysts. I still think of him with love.

"Soon I heard he was going to marry Karen Johnson, but he got a divorce from her, too. He took up with another gal, Jeanne Baus, and married her too.

"One night while watching the Johnny Carson show, I heard that he was dating the former Mrs. Carson. Johnny made so many cracks about Glenn that he threatened to sue, but nothing came of it.

"Much of an actor's life is just make-believe. Glenn believed in carrying that make believe crap off-screen as well. I didn't really lose. At least I got to enjoy the best sex I've ever had and that's something, isn't it?"

Liz Renay Evaluates
JERRY LEWIS
"My Worst Lay"

Jerry Lewis
(born 1926)

"Although he is serious about his flirting, from a woman's point of view, it is funnier than his pratfalls."
Judith Campbell, JFK's mistress

"Through the years I've seen him turn into this arrogant, sour, ceremonial, piously chauvinistic egomaniac."
Actor Elliot Gould

"Some of the handsomest and best hung men in Hollywood have made love to me. Then there was Jerry Lewis. He was definitely not my type. I like blond Viking gods like Sterling Hayden, but long ago agreed to go to bed with any man so long as he's a movie star. Fortunately, Boris Karloff or Charles Laughton never pursued me, and I truly don't think I could have made it with Edward G. Robinson either.

"Along came Jerry Lewis. He wasn't a member of Sinatra's Rat Pack. Sammy Davis Jr., Sinatra, Dean Martin, Joey Bishop—all of them knew Jerry, but didn't have a good opinion of him. When Dean heard Jerry wanted to direct, he told me, 'Jerry can't direct traffic!'

"Jerry's particular type of comedy didn't grab me, although I heard the French adored him. I got to experience his love-making, if that's what it's called.

"Unlike Glenn Ford, Jerry wasn't stingy. Glenn never picked up the tab for anything. He even drank my liquor. He could have at least brought over a bottle from time to time. One day Brenda, my daughter, and I visited Jerry on the set. He wanted to be alone with me, so he suggested that Brenda go out and buy herself a sandwich. He reached into this pocket and gave Brenda nearly a hundred dollars back in the days when most sandwiches cost less than a buck.

"Jerry could be cute and boyish at times, but was subject to rapid mood swings. Like many comedians, he seemed to suffer bouts of depression.

"One day he asked me to visit him in his portable dressing room after his cast had left for the day. I wasn't really looking forward to getting plowed by him, if plowed is the right word, but he was *the* Jerry Lewis. He's still around, but he was very, very famous at one time.

"I went along with his plan of seduction. To me, he looked the type who'd jump on and off a girl in about five seconds.

"In his dressing room, he told me that he had agreed to be faithful to his wife. I thought at the time, 'What in hell am I doing here then?'"

"He explained that he didn't plan to touch me sexually but wanted me to perform for him. He told me to go into the dressing room and remove all my clothes—all except my high heels, a pair of black silk stockings, and a garter belt. He wanted me to parade around in front of him 'until you drive me crazy.'"

"I wasn't wearing a garter belt or black silk stockings, but Jerry told me they were waiting for me in the other room. I went inside and stripped down, putting on this fetish gear for the man. I wondered at the time how in hell he expected me to get off doing this. Did he want me to masturbate in front of him?

"I came out looking like the cheapest whore who ever walked Santa Monica Boulevard. Jerry was standing on the other side of the room. He'd loosened his tie and unbuttoned his shirt. He was ready and waiting for me with his little erect cock. On the floor he'd placed a small white shag rug. I got the point right away. As I performed my act for him, he was going to jerk-off, shooting on that God damn rug.

"As he started jerking, he called out to me like a director. 'Play with your breasts. Finger yourself!' I could tell he was working himself into a feverish pitch. It was all over before it had really begun. He was quick on the draw.

"When he shot on the floor, he told me that shag rug was 'the world's most honored rug.'

"I went into the back and emerged later in my street clothes. Jerry was at the sink washing the slime off his dick. He then rolled up that carpet and put it away. 'Until next time,' he promised the rug. 'You see,' he said, turning to me. 'I can have my fun but still be faithful to my wife.'

"As I made my way out the door, I reminded him that he wasn't exactly 'the perfect lay.'"

Deitch Projects and the Burlesque Hall of Fame present

I LOVE ME !

A tribute show to the beautiful artist Liz Renay

produced by Julie Atlas Muz and the World Famous *BOB*
Hosted by the World Famous *BOB*

starring

Dirty Martini, Jo Boobs, Paula the Swedish Housewife, Bambi, Bunny Love,
Dr. Lukki, Little Brooklyn and Julie Atlas Muz,

with an installation by Sequinette

musical selections by Scott Ewalt

Santos Party House

100 Lafayette & Walker

Sunday Jan 11th doors 8pm, show 9pm

Liz Look-A-Like contest at 10pm

Five dollars to enter

Liz Renay Discusses

"When Joltin' Joe Used Me to Replace Marilyn"

Joe DiMaggio and Marilyn Monroe, pictured above on the cover of *Newsweek,* were hailed as "America's Sweethearts" when they married in 1954. Meeting on a blind date, the baseball star and the blonde Hollywood bombshell made love on their first date in the back seat of her car.

Joe DiMaggio
(1914-1999) *au naturel*

"Frank Sinatra introduced me to Joe DiMaggio after his break up with Marilyn Monroe. I'd heard that Joe was anxious to meet me, especially since I'd won that MM Look-Alike Contest. I wanted to meet him too. I figured if he turned on Marilyn, according to all reports, he must be pretty good in the hay. I wanted a sample.

"There were a lot of Marilyn Monroe acts in those days, and I heard Joe got around to seducing most of them. There were even rumors he took on a few drag queens look-alikes on a few drunken nights. But that could be libel spread by Sinatra after Joe fell out of favor with him.

"Joe seemed very lonely the night he invited me out for a date. I don't know why. He could have almost any gal he wanted. I guess he wanted Marilyn. Well, I decided to make him forget her. I pulled out all the stops in bed with him and let myself go. I figured if I did that, he'd come back for more—and he did.

"He was not only a good lover 'but a nice, likable guy—a real gentleman.' I wrote that in my memoirs and I meant it. He screwed me more than a dozen times, and he really knew how to do it, too. But he was good for only once a night. He warned me, 'I come once, but I last a long time.'

"In bed with me Joe did not want to talk about Marilyn. He never did. I guess the memories were too painful.

"I always liked Italian lovers, and Joe was one of the best. He told me that his father, Zio Pepe, had been a fisherman. The family moved to San Francisco from Sicily.

"One night, and only for one night, I thought Joe was going to propose marriage to me. He was not only a great lover, but rich and retired. He knew virtually everybody and was an American hero. I thought he would be the most desirable catch I could ever snare. But the subject never came up again.

"Every morning after he'd seduced me the night before, he sent me three dozen red roses. He said he always did that for Marilyn back when they were dating.

"I met one of Marilyn's lovers in Las Vegas. He was a security guard in a hotel. I was feeling lonely that night, and I invited him up to my room, where I turned on my Marilyn voice. He told me he seduced Marilyn one night. I feared a comparison sexually, but I shouldn't have. 'She was a beautiful gal,' he told me, 'but a lousy lay.' I was stunned, shocked, and surprised—

and also delighted.

"From that night on, I was determined to make it extra special for Joe. If Marilyn was lousy in bed, I was going to be the best ever for him, so he'd marry me or at least become my steady boyfriend. He never told me I was better in bed than Marilyn. I just knew that I was. I played every trick in the book with Joe and sent him to heavenly delights.

"I got the impression that Joe and Marilyn had serious ego problems. Before meeting her, he was idolized by millions. But after meeting her, a whole new generation of writers had come along. Some of the press was identifying him as 'Marilyn's mate' during their marriage. He couldn't stand that.

"He knew that I'd been to bed with friends of his, notably Sinatra. One night he asked me, 'Am I a better lover than Sinatra?' I assured him that he was. I've lied to many men about their love-making, but in this case I told the truth. Joe was a better lover than Sinatra.

"Things were going terrific the last time Joe came to my bed. Our sex life was really thrilling at that point, because we had learned what the other partner liked best. I was almost certain that, unlike Glenn Ford, Joe was going to start taking me out in public. I planned to dress up like Marilyn on those occasions.

"I expected the red roses and the late morning call the next day. I waited and waited by the phone. But not a word, nothing came from Joe. Tired of waiting, I dialed his private number. The operator came on and told me that the number was unlisted and had been changed. That was that! I'd been dumped.

"I was heartbroken and I cried for three nights, but then I picked up the pieces and was determined to start all over again. I missed Joe terribly. If he ever wants to swing that bat in my direction, I'm sure he'd hit a home run. He always did."

"If Joe ever reads this, and he's old and gray, he's always welcome to put his shoes under my bed any night he wants."

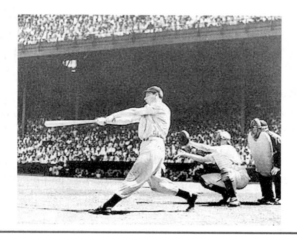

Joe DiMaggio, the pride of New York in 1941 (left) and in 1949 (right). For a brief time, the press called DiMaggio and Monroe "Mr. and Mrs. America," but the two legendary figures were soon dethroned. Their searing drama, the clash of two powerful egos, was played out in public. It was one of the world's most dazzling romances, but shadows lay in their path—her need for love, her affairs, his temper, his jealousy. The hawk-faced baseball hero and the sex goddess ended their marriage because, as he claimed, "I tired of sharing my wife, *naked* at that—with the world."

Liz Renay Evaluates Her Status As Gun Moll to
MICKEY COHEN

Dreaded Mobster
Meyer Harris ("Mickie") Cohen
(1913-1976)

"I never killed a guy who didn't deserve it."
— **Mickey Cohen** (1913-1976)

"I don't have to tell most people who Mickey Cohen is. He was a Jewish gangster from Brooklyn who made it big with the Mafia—and in Hollywood.

"Mickey even mentioned me in his memoirs, which he called *In My Own Words*. But he didn't tell the story of our life together.

"Mickey was my friend. I liked him. I loved him. I trusted him. My last visit was to his death bed.

"My friendship with him lasted nearly two decades. I recalled my first date with him in a bulletproof Cadillac Eldorado limousine, driving through Hollywood, Palm Springs, and Beverly Hills with him in the back seat with me. Someone was always trailing him, maybe another mobster who wanted him dead.

"I met everybody through Mickey: Red Skelton. Mike Wallace. Red Foxx. Don Rickles. Lena Horne. Even his pal, Johnny Stompanato. He became Lana Turner's boyfriend. Lana claimed her daughter stabbed Stompanato to death with a kitchen knife. But Mickey told me it was Lana herself who plunged the knife into Stompanato. Mickey seriously considered having one of his boys toss acid in Lana's beautiful face.

"Like Al Capone, Mickey was eventually trapped by the IRS. He was tried for income tax evasion and sentenced to fifteen years behind bars.

"When Mickey got out of jail, he came to the Santa Monica Hospital when I was in for major surgery.

"He held my hand and assured me I'd pull through. He visited me every day. One of my husbands, Tom Freeman, dropped in on occasion. But Mickey was steadfast.

"One afternoon, he confessed to me that I was the love of his life. 'There is only one Liz Renay,' he said. 'They don't make dames like you no more.'

"When Mickey was in UCLA Medical Center with The Big C, I came to visit him every day as he lay dying. Every day I watched as his life slowly slipped away. I cried a lot.

"Regrettably, it was because of Mickey that I spent three years in a federal prison when I refused to rat him out. Those years cost me dearly and destroyed my chance to become a big-time star like Marilyn. Prison smashed my life, but I did it for Mickey."

Homage to Movie Star
Liz Renay

(1926-2007)
QUEEN OF SHEBA, QUEEN OF THE NILE, PRINCESS OF THE NIGHT, GODDESS OF LOVE
REST IN PEACE

At death's door, **Liz Renay** tried to maintain the illusion of her once-fabled beauty. Under a blonde wig and hidden behind fire engine red lipstick and layer upon layer of pancake makeup, Liz at the age of 80 tried to hold onto a look that had once been celebrated. That relentless enemy, time, was about to engulf her.

"I could have been a star," she said, "if I hadn't taken a bullet for Mickey Cohen and gone to prison. When I first arrived in Hollywood way back when, Cecil B. DeMille spotted me in the Paramount commissary. 'Yours is the most exciting face I've seen in twenty years,' he told me. He planned to cast me in one of his big productions. I was to play Esther from the biblical story. Agents clamored to sign me up. I was going to be Paramount's next big star.

The DeMille picture never materialized. "Gloria Swanson got her closeup," Liz said. "I didn't. Instead, my closeup came when Federal agents hustled me out of the Plaza Hotel in New York for questioning about Mickey before a grand jury. Walter Winchell, a true judge of talent, told me that I could have been a bigger star than Marilyn. DeMille also told me that my toes were the most suckable in Hollywood. He had this foot fetish thing."

Murdered by the Mob
Mario Lanza

America's Caruso

"It's all sex when I'm singing. That's me. It comes right out of my balls. And the more I lay other women, the better I am as a husband."

Mario Lanza

His career was brief, and his output of films very limited, but **Mario Lanza** had one of the greatest voices of the 20th century. He was a trouble-maker as a young boy, and even more of a trouble-maker when he became a star, but no one could deny his talent.

His concerts were sold out, as were his box office smash movies. His albums topped the charts. As his professional life soared, his private life collapsed into shambles.

His ego knew no bounds. In Hollywood, he said, "I'm a movie star, and I should live like one. Nobody wants movie stars to be like the guy next door."

LANZA!

HIS GIGANTIC APPETITE FOR FOOD, DRINK, MUSIC, AND SEX

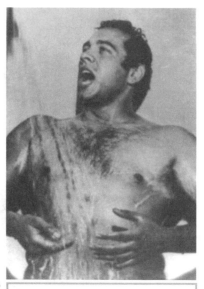

An American tenor and Hollywood movie star, Mario Lanza (1921-1959) enjoyed wildly popular success in the late 40s and 50s. He was naturally chosen to play *The Great Caruso* in the 1951 film. Professionally, this Philadelphia native could sing like no other American. Privately, he was a mess addicted to food, wine, and women.

In 1942 he studied for six weeks with Leonard Bernstein. "Having his mouth on me week after week sickened me," Lanza later told pals in the Army. "I closed my eyes and pretended it was Betty Grable giving me all those blow-jobs."

Lanza made his operatic debut in Otto Nicolai's *Die lustigen Weiber von Windsor* at Tanglewood in the summer of 1942. But his operatic career was interrupted by World War II when he joined the U.S. Army Air Corps.

It was while still in the Army that Lanza began his life-long career as a womanizer.

Lanza was sent to a small dusty town in Texas. It was Marfa, where in 1956 Elizabeth Taylor, Rock Hudson, and James Dean would converge to shoot *Giant*. "It was pussy heaven," Lanza later wrote Bernstein in a letter.

Dozens of hookers—many from Mexico across the border—had converged on Marfa to peddle their wares at five dollars a throw, or, on a slow night, three bucks. Lanza liked to boast to his new pals in the Army that he could have sex with a dozen women all at once. No one believed him.

The opera singer fought a life-long battle with his weight. He hated to diet. He constantly attacked the press. "That's all they ever think about—Lanza's fat!" His wife, the former Betty Hicks, assured him that he didn't have to diet and make himself nervous. "Your voice," she told him, "that's all your public wants from you."

When he wasn't attacking the press, he ranted about "all those fuckers out to get me," without ever exactly explaining what he meant.

Betty Grable *(left)*, the pin-up girl of WWII, was Mario Lanza's dream girl. He told male friends that he used to masturbate while holding her famous WWII pin-up picture in his other hand. In Hollywood he got to meet Betty herself when he signed to do a TV special, *The Shower of Stars,* with her then-husband, bandleader Harry James. For his appearance, he was given $40,000 and two new Chrysler automobiles.

"I didn't get to screw Betty because Harry was hanging around, but she did slip away to my dressing room to give me a blow-job."

But the singer was willing to put up five-hundred dollars to prove that he could pull off the stunt.

A lieutenant from North Carolina hired twelve *putas* only too willing to sample Lanza when the officer showed them pictures of the handsome singer. One prostitute said, "I'd do this wop for free!"

What Lanza would later call "My greatest performance" was staged on the cement floor of a garage. A spotlight was assembled to shine on the center, and the nude girls were arranged with their heads touching, their bodies branching out like a flower petal.

As the cheers echoed through the garage, Lanza proved a man of his boast. One by one, he penetrated each of the women, pumping them for five minutes before moving on to the next. By the time he reached the twelfth woman, he rode her for only two minutes since he could no longer hold back his climax.

A traveling show, *On the Beam*, came into town to entertain the soldiers. One of its stars was Major Frederick Brisson, the gay husband of Rosalind Russell and former lover of Cary Grant.

Brisson heard of "The Singing M.P." and asked him to audition. Instead of that, Lanza played a recording he'd made. Brisson fell for the voice and the tenor soldier himself. After giving Lanza a series of blow-jobs, Brisson arranged for Lanza to be transferred to Special Services, where he joined the cast of *On the Beam*.

Lanza was such a success in the show, he became known as "Caruso of the Air Force." In New York at the end of a nationwide tour, Lanza joined the cast of *Winged Victory*, a big Moss Hart production with many stars, including Karl Malden, Edmond O'Brien, and Red Buttons. One day, after Hart heard Lanza sing "Celeste Aïda" backstage, he came to him with a promise that he

It is not know what **Rosalind Russell** (left) knew of the gay affairs of husband **Frederick Brisson**. She married the Danish-American producer in 1941, the marriage lasting 35 years. Ironically, Rosalind appeared with her husband's lover, Cary Grant, in *His Girl Friday* (1940).

From the moment he met Mario Lanza, and heard him sing, Brisson was mesmerized by the singer and his blatant sexuality. "To break into show business, Mario had to get a lot of blow-jobs in those days," Brisson said. "He didn't give them; he received them."

Moss Hart (left) invited Mario Lanza to join the New York cast of a big production called *Winged Victory*. A member of the chorus, Lanza worked with 342 men and women in the show, including Edmond O'Brien, Karl Malden, and Red Buttons.

Hart had heard Lanza singing "Celeste Aida" and was intrigued by him. "I had no idea such a voice was hidden in the chorus." When Hart invited Lanza into his office, the opera singer said. "I guess you want what Freddy Brisson and Leonard Bernstein wanted." Moss replied, "I guess in their case, you're right."

Kitty Carlisle, singer, actress, and spokeswoman for the arts, spent a lifetime denying that her husband, Moss Hart, was gay. No one on Broadway believed her. Hart's proclivities were too well known.

She became a household name as a regular panelist on *To Tell the Truth* from 1957 to 1978. She never remarried after Hart died in 1961.

In the 1940s, she dated Thomas Dewey, former New York governor and presidential candidate. Dewey ran against FDR in 1944 and again against Harry S Truman in 1948. Carlisle told her pals "Roosevelt is not going to survive the campaign, and Thomas is going to become president. I will be his First Lady."

could make him into a big-time stage star.

Although he was a closeted homosexual, Moss Hart would go on to marry Kitty Carlisle. Hart, like Brisson, had also had an affair with Cary Grant. Lanza became involved with Hart, but later asked actor O'Brien, "Is everyone in show business a cocksucker?"

"It's called the casting couch," O'Brien told him. "All a good-looking actor like you has to do is lie on it for a few minutes from time and time—and you can end up making millions."

"I want women," Lanza said, "and I resent having to give my seed to all these men. But I was born poor and I want to be rich, so I guess I'll go along with it, but these guys disgust me."

At a Hollywood party in the autumn of 1944, Walter Pidgeon heard Lanza sing in another room and thought it was a recording of Enrico Caruso. Later, Pidgeon introduced Lanza to Frank Sinatra. Lanza sang an aria from *Tosca*, and Sinatra, a devotee of opera, later claimed, "The kid knocked a hole through me."

Lanza quickly discovered that Sinatra was a straight-shooter, even though he admitted to "swooning" when he heard Lanza's voice. "When I first met Sinatra, I thought he'd be another cocksucker like all the rest, but he wasn't," Lanza told Pidgeon. "We became great pals."

Lanza and Sinatra began to chase women together. To hell with the wives. Stories still persist that Sinatra asked Lanza to join him on a secret date with Judy Garland at a private hideaway in the San Fernando Valley. The hotel manager later claimed that the trio shared a large bed together. "I wasn't in bed, writing every-

Two womanizers, **Frank Sinatra** (above) and Mario Lanza, used to get together and compare fan letters, but only when they contained pictures of females in the nude, some posing in pornographic acts. Lanza told Sinatra, "I need to put on asbestos gloves to open some of these letters, every gal from bobbysoxers to grannies."

Sinatra did him one better, claiming that he had to wear asbestos padding over his genitals, not his hands. "The gals really go for Long John," he said. "I remember one bitch—she must have been eighty if a day—who practically yanked it off me. She wanted a souvenir."

Walter Pidgeon, Canadian actor, was one of the first Hollywood stars to discover the power of Lanza's voice. Unlike other show business personalities, he wasn't interested in seducing Lanza, but appreciated his artistry.

With the arrival of Talkies, Pidgeon became a huge star in the 1930s until his career faltered. Teamed with Greer Garson in a series of movies such as *Blossoms in the Dust* (1941) and *Mrs. Miniver,* (1942), he bounced back, and they became a hot screen team until their allure faded in the 1953 *Scandal at Scourie*. Pidgeon was nominated twice for Best Actor, both for *Mrs. Miniver* and *Madame Curie* (1944).

Producer Joe Pasternak told **Judy Garland**, "I heard a guy whose voice sounds like Caruso coming back to life."

"What else can he do?" Garland quipped. Lanza was assigned a dressing room across the hall from Garland. Louis B. Mayer wanted to keep sexes on opposite sides of the hall, but Lanza was seen frequently crossing that hall to seduce Garland.

thing down," Howard Wiess later said, "but when two men and one gal check into a hotel room, and there's only one bed, I can assume only one thing."

Word reached Louis B. Mayer at MGM of the new singing sensation, and the mogul contacted Lanza, signing him to a seven-year contract in 1948. Mayer cast Lanza in *That Midnight Kiss*, starring Kathryn Grayson, who reportedly had the largest bust measurements in Hollywood. In their first love scene together, Lanza instructed Grayson: "You've got to be more sexy. Push up to me. Let me feel your pussy next to my cock." He then stuck his tongue down her throat.

Grayson was horrified. The next day in a huddle with costume designer Helen Rose, Grayson asked that brass knuckles be sewed into her gown. Later, on set, when Lanza plunged his tongue down her throat again, she fisted him in the balls with the brass knuckles. Screaming in pain, he backed away. Future kisses from the tenor were more demure.

Toward the end of the film, Lanza's weight began to balloon. Too much pasta. It was a problem he'd have for the rest of his life. Mayer hired Terry Robinson, a physical therapist and "trainer of the stars," to keep his new star in shape. In time, Robinson became Lanza's closest friend.

Years later Robinson recalled how Lanza and he had encountered a drunken Judy Garland leaving a screening room late one night on the nearly deserted MGM lot. Of course, Lanza already "knew" Garland as David had "known" Bathsheba.

With Robinson driving, Lanza offered to give Garland a lift, but first they stopped at a liquor store to purchase a bottle of Chivas Regal. Drinking from paper cups in the backseat, Lanza asked Robinson to drive the star into the Hollywood Hills.

Coming to a scenic spot an hour later, Robinson got out and left Lanza and Garland in the backseat. After waiting what he thought was a reasonable time, Robinson came back to the car. Though the windows were foggy, he

In the 1950s, **Mario Lanza** and the beautiful MGM songbird, **Kathryn Grayson**, were the most successful musical team at MGM. Lanza was always coming on to Grayson, but she detested him and complained to Howard Hughes, who threatened to have Lanza wiped out. In their film together, *The Midnight Kiss* (1949), Lanza was billed as "the singing Clark Gable."

By the time the singing duo filmed *The Toast of New Orleans* together in 1950, they had made up and often worked out at a gym together, with her lifting rather heavy barbells. In later life, Lanza claimed he repeatedly seduced Grayson, although she denied it. "Her breasts were the greatest in Hollywood to masturbate between," he claimed. On several occasions, she continued to deny a sexual involvement with the singer. Who do you believe?

A ROYAL LINE-UP. As part of a "Royal Variety Performance," a young and rather beautiful **Queen Elizabeth II** greets show business stars, including singer **Frankie Vaughan** *(left)*; **Joan Regan** *(center)*, a pop music singer in the UK in the 1950s, and **Mario Lanza** *(right)*. Lanza referred to Vaughan as "A cheap vaudeville performer. I was the only real singer there that night to entertain the Queen."

could still see in. Lanza was mounting Garland, and her legs were up in the air. She was screaming encouragement for him to go to it.

Robinson disappeared for another thirty minutes. Upon his return Lanza and Garland, still half dressed, had resumed their drinking. "Get in!" Lanza commanded Robinson. "Drive Judy home. After all, we promised to give her a lift."

"That he did!" Garland yelled from the backseat.

Later in the 1950s, Lanza's body wasn't the only thing that had swollen. So had his debts, especially unpaid back taxes. One day the heavyweight champion, Rocky Marciano , came to call at Lanza's Hollywood home. With him was Mafia boss Thomas Lucchese, who offered to settle Lanza's debts in exchange for some singing appearances.

Lanza hated the idea. He shouted at Lucchese, "No cheap lousy hood can buy me. I'm no fucking puppet. I wasn't made with a finger, you assholes. I was made with a prick! You think I don't know your kind." He kicked them out of his house.

At the door, Lucchese called back to him, "Listen, you fat slob. You don't talk to me that way. Keep your big mouth shut or you've sung your last note, sweetheart."

In 1957, the Lanza family decamped to Italy, where he filmed *Seven Hills of Rome*, introducing the classic, "Arrivederci, Roma." Suffering from phlebitis and high blood pressure, Lanza settled into the deluxe residence, Villa Badoglio.

It was here, two years later, that an even bigger Mafia boss, Lucky Luciano, came to call on Lanza. He demanded that Lanza appear at a charity concert in Naples in September of 1959.

Lanza refused and ordered Luciano out of his house. At the door, Luciano turned and in a quiet voice said, "You'll never sing again!"

A few weeks later, on October 7, Lanza was rushed to the Valle Giulia Clinic. There were rumors that he'd suffered a heart attack. While recuperating in the hospital, and to cut down on his weight, he agreed to undergo a radical new weight reduction therapy, involving the intravaneous injection of urine from a pregnant woman.

Lanza's chauffeur had accompanied him to the hospital, sleeping in an adjoining room.

Late one afternoon, the nurse on duty told Lanza that she was sending in a substitute because she felt ill. A red-haired woman in a nurse's uniform came into Lanza's private room to give him the intravenous feeding.

Two hours later, when the chauffeur went to check on Lanza, he found his boss dead. The intravenous needle was still plugged

Mario Lanza was "Lucky Pierre," with his wife **Betty Hicks** kissing him on the left, and **Zsa Zsa Gabor** doing the honors on the right. He shot his last film, titled *For the First Time*, with co-star Gabor. They were rumored to have had an affair. For a party at the completion of the film, Gabor went to a beauty parlor to have her hair bleached. Upon her arrival at the party, it had turned green.

Rocky Marciano was an Italian-American boxer and the heavyweight champion of the world from 1952 to 1956. When he quit the ring, he was the only boxer in history to retire having won every fight of his professional career.

Lanza and Marciano joined a mutual fan club of each other. Until their friendship turned sour, these two burly Italians, in the words of Lanza's biographer, Raymond Strait, "fell into each other's arms, hugging and kissing like brothers." When Marciano arrived at Lanza's house, a "stalking horse" for Mafia kingpin Lucky Luciano, Lanza turned against his former friend. Then, after Marciano pitched a "deal" to Lanza, the singer kicked him out of his house.

into his arm but there was no fluid in the jar. Only air bubbles were entering Lanza's bloodstream. The chauffeur yelled for the nurse.

It was all too late. One of the world's greatest singers had been murdered. An investigation failed to reveal the identity of the mysterious "nurse" who had administered the needle. The hospital later issued a report that Lanza had died from the new weight reduction therapy, which had not been sanctioned by the FDA in Washington but was legal in Italy.

In the wake of Lanza's death, the chauffeur disappeared and was never found. Grief stricken, Lanza's wife, the former Betty Hicks, died six months later at the age of 36. Her family claimed she died of a broken heart.

Shortly after he died, she made a terrible decision. Giving in to demands from his relatives, she agreed to have the body of her late husband displayed in Philadelphia, his hometown. But at the time of his death, embalming was not in vogue in Italy. The funeral parlor where his body was sent found a small coffin made of oak. The massive bulk of Lanza wouldn't fit in it. The undertakers broke his shoulders as a means of fitting his massive chest inside the coffin. They even broke his ankles so that his feet could be turned sideways to fit into the closed confines. Why a larger coffin wasn't ordered is not known.

Without embalming, his already bloated stomach became abnormally large, and his skin became badly discolored, a greenish purple with black splotches. For three days, Lanza's body lay rotting in his villa. Reportedly, the stench was unbearable.

The corpse was then transferred to Philadelphia for an open-coffin funeral attended by thousands of fans. "He looked like a movie monster," said one of the rubberneckers, Marion Hatfield. "His flesh had rotted, his face contorted into a lurid goodbye smile. I'd never seen anything this horrible in my life. I would never have allowed my hus-

Lucky Luciano, a Sicilian-born American mobster, was boss of the Genovese family crime syndicate and the father of modern organized crime in America, taking control of the nation's heroin trafficking.

In Rome, after his deportation from the U.S., Luciano called on Lanza. Lanza hated the mob and didn't want any deal Luciano proposed to him--even that of a singing engagement. In retaliation, the gangster sent a threat that he was going to have mobsters kidnap Lanza's children. Luciano eventually ordered the death of the singer.

When a funeral service was conducted for Mario Lanza's unembalmed body at the Church of San Bellermino in Rome's Parioli district, the stench of putrefication permeated the chapel. The casket was carried through the streets of Rome by a horse-drawn carriage, as thousands of onlookers lined the streets. By the time the body was finally buried in Los Angeles, the corpse had deteriorated so horribly that a member of the family was called down to the funeral parlor to identify what remained of "The Great Caruso"—the name of Lanza's biggest hit.

band to be exhibited in such a way."

When one woman, a former friend of the family, stepped up to view the corpse, she fainted. En route to the hospital in an ambulance, its red dome lights flashing, the woman suffered a fatal heart attack.

Leonard Bernstein was a great American conductor and composer, of course. *The New York Times* called him "one of the most prodigally talented and successful musicians in American history."

He told his gay pals in 1942 that while he was teaching music to Mario Lanza, "I always devoured his Italian salami—very tasty."

In the 50s when asked about Bernstein, Lanza said, "He had a great passion for life. He devoured people."

The statement was enigmatic.

Lanza often invited guests to his dressing room (really apartment) to show them his dirty pictures—Joan Crawford from her porno flicks, a nude shot of Joan Blondell sunbathing, and that notorious photograph of Carmen Miranda swinging through the air without her panties.

In Palm Springs he wanted nude pictures taken of himself by a woman photographer, and posed with a proud erection. Whether these pictures exist today or were destroyed isn't known.

Lanza did not often bare his chest, because he had a tendency to "put on blubber," and he was leary of ending up on the front page of the tabloids with a big belly.

Barechested or fully clothed, he liked to seduce young actresses. On a beach, he picked up Inger Stevens, who became a TV and film star—also a suicide—and invited her to his house to show her porn. She asked him to sing for her. He propped her up on a piano and pulled down her bikini bottom. "This is the first time a Lanza high note will come from a woman's body." Then he put his mouth on her vagina and sang "Be My Love."

On August 6, 1951, *Time* magazine put **Mario Lanza** on its cover with the great Enrico Caruso, wearing a hat, looking on. *Time* reporters described Lanza as a young tenor with "the spry nonsensical air of a chipmunk."

The magazine article made the singer a household word, and "I could never escape my fans who stalked me." Sometimes he wore a disguise— horn-rimmed glasses, a false nose, and a green felt hat. Whenever he wanted to run away from the world, he hid out at his Palm Springs retreat with a "bimbo du jour."

(left) **Lanza** appears as Pepe Duval in *The Toast of New Orleans* (1950) in which he co-starred with David Niven and Kathryn Grayson. In the film, he played a robust Cajun fisherman in Louisiana's Bayou Country. Grayson later turned against him because of his temper and his abuse of liquor. Too bad. The romantic-appearing screen duo still creates magic on the screen. Lanza's Oscar-nominated theme song from that film, "Be My Love," lost that year to "Mona Lisa."

Grayson frequently criticized Lanza for his weight, noting that in some scenes he appeared about to burst out of his too-tight jacket. She later recalled, "If Lanza had quit gorging himself and learned anger management, he might have stayed on in Hollywood a bit longer. He was self-destructive. His idea of romance involved reaching up a woman's dress and grabbing her vagina."

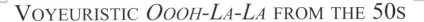

Stag Nights at the Finlandia Baths

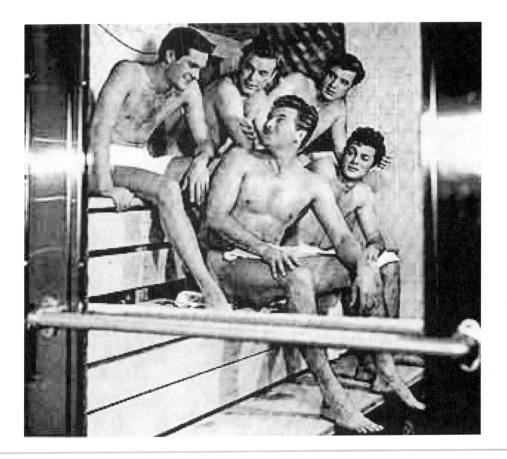

An undercover reporter for the notorious magazine *Confidential* frequented Hollywood's **Finlandia Baths** on and off for a month, hoping to catch the town's "Golden Boy," Tab Hunter in a compromising position with **John Bromfield** (front left with **Tony Curtis** sharing the same wooden bench). Tab never showed up with John. He was too busy involved in a torrid love affair with "Mr. Psycho," the handsome, sexy actor, Anthony Perkins. *Confidential*, however, in a ludicrous homophobic article, "outed" Tab in its September, 1955 issue, when a gay party in Walnut Park, a suburb of Los Angeles, was raided. In those days, the police often broke up all-male gatherings in private homes.

Incidentally, that lineup of hunks on the top row included (left to right) **Hugh O'Brian, Scott Brady,** and **Rock Hudson.**

SOME LIKE IT HOT

THE STEAM ROOM JUST GOT STEAMIER

In the early 1950s, California-based Sam Amundsen opened Finlandia, a Finnish bathhouse for men only, in the basement of the Bing Crosby Building in Hollywood. In more ways that one, it soon became the "hottest" address in Los Angeles County.

Any gay man who wanted could drop into the baths, take some steam, cool off under a shower, enjoy a luncheon spread, and see the hunks of Hollywood in various states of undress. It was a voyeur's paradise. Among many others, Rock Hudson, one of the bath's regular devotees, didn't mind exhibiting himself in front of some of his more adoring fans.

The Finlandia Baths attracted some of the biggest names in Hollywood at the time, including Kirk Douglas

Rock Hudson (standing) takes a close shave as **Tony Curtis** (seated on the left) and **John Bromfield** (right) oversee the action. Tony wrote three separate memoirs, but he was less than candid in each of them. As he himself noted, if he had really recorded what he'd been an eyewitness to in Hollywood, the pages would have steamed up. Before he reached Tinseltown, he lost his virginity in a Panama City whorehouse. He was 17 years old at the time, serving in the US Navy.

Scott Brady (seated on the left) gets the shit beaten out of him by the gin rummy king, **Tony Curtis** (seated on the right). **Hugh O'Brian** oversees the game, making sarcastic comments. In the background **Rock Hudson** gets a salt rubdown before returning to the steam room. Finlandia's ace masseur, **"Richard,"** works over Rock, preparing him for a hot date that night. Unknown to Richard, that date was with young Sal Mineo. Rock later confessed that sometimes he got a full erection during those rubdowns. "I can't help myself," he confessed. "Call it Ever Ready."

Chowtime at the Finlandia, as the hungry mob digs in. **Sam Amundsen** (standing), the owner, sent out for a special spread for his movie star guests, and the hungry boys wasted no time digging in to the treats. Later the boys would "drop towel" and head for another quick bake to sweat off the food they'd just devoured. "We were selling our buffed bodies to the general public back then, and we had to keep in shape," said **Rock Hudson**. "The boys tried hard in those days to have a physique like mine. But in one department all those workouts couldn't give them the 'muscle' I possessed between my legs. Okay, I know it's not a muscle, and it doesn't grow bigger by constant workouts."

and Humphrey Bogart. Forrest Tucker was a frequent visitor. He liked to lie on a massage table and get an alcohol rubdown before downing a pint of whiskey. He would then lie there drunk throughout most of the afternoon, exhibiting one of Hollywood's largest endowments. Seeing Tucker completely nude practically became one of the attractions of Hollywood.

Gays, straights, and bisexuals mingled freely and unselfconsciously in this steamy atmosphere. On any given day you might encounter Hugh O'Brian, who was straight, alongside Zachary Scott, who was not.

Perhaps Paul Douglas would drop in, reciting tales of lesbian love between Barbara Stanwyck and Marilyn Monroe when the three of them made *Clash by Night* together in 1951-1952. His other co-star in that film, Keith Andes, arrived on the scene with Douglas one afternoon, but he went home afterward with that handsome hunk, Scott Brady.

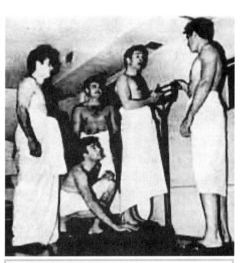

Each of the towel-clad young men faced the moment of truth at the end of their workouts at the Finlandia. **Hugh O'Brian** expresses his disappointment that in spite of the steam room, "I've actually gained weight." What he doesn't know is that **Scott Brady** is pressing down hard on the scales.

Nick Adams, a former hustler who'd been one of the best friends of both James Dean and Elvis Presley, appeared for a steaming at least twice a week. He never bothered to wear a towel. "If you've got it, flaunt it!" he always said.

John Agar, an ex-Army sergeant who married Shirley Temple and appeared on screen with her, occasionally showed up. He showed the boys what had delighted Shirley, at least temporarily.

Dana Andrews, who had been ideally cast in a film, *Battle of the Bulge*, also turned up to prove that what he showed on screen wasn't a sock stuffed into his pants.

The impossibly handsome Lex Barker, who'd played Tarzan in the movies and who had once been married to Lana Turner, always attracted the most attention." The gay actor, Roddy McDowall told his friends, "Lex is the sexiest man I've ever seen in my life, with or without clothes, but especially without clothes."

Solid he-man Bruce Cabot, who had rescued Fay Wray from the clutches of King Kong atop the Empire State Building, even allowed himself to be photographed under a shower in the nude.

Lovers Rory Calhoun and Guy Madison thrilled the boys whenever they came in together. Each would give the other a rubdown that produced an erection which neither of them concealed.

Jeff Chandler or Steve Cochran could always be

Emerging from the steam room, **Tony Curtis** *(left)* gets an icy shower. As he tries to flee, **Scott Brady** *(right)* holds him down under the Arctic water. The ice shower was Scott's way of paying Tony back for beating him at gin rummy.

Scott slapped Tony on the ass. Was it a playful slap or an invitation? With Scott, you never knew. As the two men were drying off, Tony confided in Scott that the gay costume designer Orry-Kelly, former lover of Cary Grant, told him that Tony's ass was better looking than that of Marilyn Monroe's.

counted on for a reliably good show, as could Gary Cooper, "The Montana Mule."

Obscure today, remembered primarily to nostalgia buffs, John Bromfield was the most popular member. He'd been rejected by Cecil B. DeMille during the casting of Samson in *Samson and Delilah*, the role going instead to Victor Mature. Bromfield, however, could still be seen working out with the club's body-building equipment, showing off his sculpted physique. Whenever possible, he also appeared in public in a skimpy swim suit, revealing the rounded outlines of his package. "Do you stuff an orange in there?" fellow actor Burt Lancaster once asked him.

The question was entirely rhetorical. Lancaster was already fully aware that it was no orange Bromfield carried in his bathing trunks. He and Lancaster had tangled in a romantic way when they'd made *Sorry, Wrong Number* with the lesbian actress, Barbara Stanwyck, in 1948.

It was around this time that Bromfield married the sexy French actress Corinne Calvet. But the marriage was not successful. Her husband spent more time with the boys than with her. The marriage dragged on until 1954, when they divorced, long after they'd stopped sleeping with each other.

"John was a sort of Steve Cochran and Rory Calhoun blended together," said his friend, Roddy McDowall. "If a gay man wanted sex, John never minded dropping his bikini. He was generous and very accommodating, with absolutely no hang-ups."

Although Bromfield retired from films in 1960, many older homosexual men still visit his gravesite, sometimes depositing flowers beside it at Forest Lawn Cemetery in Glendale, California.

When a writer, researching an article, came across an old copy of *Modern Screen* in 1950, he was shocked and amazed when he saw a picture of Hugh O'Brian, Tony Curtis, Rock Hudson, John Bromfield, and Scott Brady, each of them sweating and only partially dressed, at the Finlandia Baths.

The photo bore the caption, "Stag Night in the Steam Room." But the writer saw this communal portrait as one of the gayest ever photographed in 1950s Hollywood, especially "considering that there were three known *mos* in this spread." By *mos*, of course, he meant known homosexuals.

He asked this provocative question: "*Who'd have thunk it*? The best hiding place in the world, it turned out, was a national fan magazine."

Of course, today's audiences would interpret the cluster's body positions and body language differently.

Just imagine what would be said if a modern-day national tabloid ran group pictures of Brad Pitt, Tom Cruise, Colin Farrell, Toby Maquire, James Franco, Channing Tatum, Orlando Bloom, and Johnny Depp, each of them partially naked in a communal steam room?

John Bromfield, in spite of his marriages (to women), was said to have seduced more of the male patrons at Finlandia than any other member. "Pussy, I can get at home," he once told Rock Hudson.

During his brief film career, he appeared in a number of *film noirs* and westerns, including fright films such as the 1955 3D horror, *Revenge of the Creature*. He hit it big in the syndicated western TV series *Sheriff of Cochise* (1956), which later was retitled *U.S. Marshal*. He always liked to exhibit his body to gay guys, and even told them how he had developed such a grand physique. "I eat soupfin shark liver; it's rich in Vitamin A." In 1960, he retired from acting to become a commercial fisherman and died at age 83 on September 19, 2005.

160

Vampira

GLAMOUR GHOUL OF TELEVISION

"Nicolas Ray, the director, told me that James Dean was 'intensely determined not to be loved—or to love.' Jimmy himself told me that the only success is immortality. In that he succeeded brilliantly. In spite of his small oeuvre of only three pictures, the world remembers him and not dozens of guys who made more than fifty movies."

Vampira

During her brief reign in the 1950s, **Vampira** ruled the night, terrorizing audiences with her just-risen-from-the-coffin appearances where she introduced blood-sucking horror movies on television.

Of the many gay boys who surrounded her, James Dean was her favorite. All her homosexual friends wanted Dean, and many of them won the prize. Others who were rejected had to take extreme measures, as Vampira later learned to her horror.

Three years after Dean's tragic death at the age of twenty-four, Vampira met with director Elia Kazan to discuss the actor's growing legend. "I don't like it," Kazan said. "His fans are glorifying a Dean that never existed. They see him as a little waif brutalized by Hollywood. He was a sicko with talent. He hated everybody, mostly himself. I'd call him a half-baked pudding of hatred.   If you actually tasted that pudding, it was poison."

And What Her Groupies
Did to James Dean's Body
in the Morgue

Maila Nurmi

If you were alive and living in Los Ange les in 1954, you knew who Vampira was. Looking like a more sexually alluring version of Morticia Addams, she came on the then-new medium of television like an exotic voodoo priestess.

Born Maila Elizabeth Syrjäniemi in Finland in 1922 (some sources say 1921), she came to the United States and adopted the last name of her famous uncle, Olympic runner Paavo Nurmi, emerging as Maila Nurmi.

She failed as an actress, although in 1944 she'd been cast on Broadway with Mae West in a play Mae had written, *Catherine Was Great*. It was produced, incidentally, by Elizabeth Taylor's future husband, Mike Todd. West, fearing that the younger girl was upstaging her, booted her out of the play.

Migrating to Hollywood, Maila supported herself by posing for pinup photographs in men's magazines such as *Gala*.

After several more failed attempts at acting, she hit it lucky. Attending a masquerade ball, she dressed as a female vampire, complete with ghoulish white make-up, evoking a Charles Addams cartoon. She won first place in costume design.

A TV producer at station KABC spotted her and offered her the role of television hostess for a series of horror films they were going to run. She gladly agreed and officially changed her stage name to "Vampira."

The series ran for 16 episodes in 1954, with frequent reruns throughout the rest of the decade. For each of them, Vampira made a spectacular entrance amid dusty spider webs and dry ice fog. As the camera

In her way, **Vampira** loved James Dean but was aware of his dark side, "which was darker than the black nail polish and black gown I wore to introduce those horror movies," she said. "I agreed with Elia Kazan, who claimed that Dean 'was a punk but a helluva talent.' He also said that 'Dean liked cars, waitresses—and waiters.' Sometimes, though, he dated high on the hog—Barbara Hutton, for example, one of the richest women in the world."

The bisexual actor also managed to seduce Marlon Brando, Paul Newman, Steve McQueen, Merv Griffin and Liberace. Even Howard Hughes found out what his underwear was hiding, but had to pay for it.

"He often took me as his date," Vampira said. "One night we showed up at a party in Malibu—September of 1955, I think—and Jimmy encountered a former lover, who denounced Jimmy in front of everybody, claiming he dated women only for publicity. 'Nobody in his right mind thinks you're straight,' the queen shouted to Jimmy."

zoomed in on her vampire-deadly face, she'd let out a piercing scream before introducing the movie of the night. Usually, she reclined seductively on a skull-encrusted Victorian sofa.

Like a Zombie-mate of Bela Lugosi, she accessorized herself with all the trappings of Fright Night. Her drag included long, heavily painted fingernails in midnight black, with a mane of raven-colored hair, and a big-busted, slim-waisted, black-as-night outfit set off with fishnet hosiery.

Her eyes were heavily mascara-ed which contrasted with her blood-red lipstick. In character as a vampire-inspired sex kitten driven by a powerful thirst for fresh blood, she introduced such films as *Devil Bat's Daughter* and *Revenge of the Zombies*.

[In 1989, she lost a $10 million lawsuit that charged that Cassandra Peterson's late-night hostess "Elvira" had pirated her character.]

She was an overnight sensation and developed a campy cult following thanks partly to a ghastly appearance that made her look like she'd just emerged from a haunted coffin.

When she wasn't emoting in front of a TV camera, Vampira became a kind of "Mother Confessor" to the Bad Boys of Hollywood, notably and most famously James Dean, her on-again, off-again lover. She also hovered over Paul Newman and Anthony Perkins, and was privy to their off-the-record romance with each other.

In those days, these secretly bisexual men found it difficult to talk to a woman and make her privy to their affairs. Vampira, or so it is said, gave birth to the term "fag hag."

Years later, Vampira claimed that she and Dean often ended their nights together at an all night diner/coffee shop on Sunset Boulevard called Googie's. "Paul and Tony (a reference to Newman and Perkins) were beginning their day," she said. "We would be wasted, and Paul and Tony would come in all bright-eyed and bushy-tailed. Even though I knew they were bed-hopping like rabbits in

"The first time Jimmy invited me back to his apartment, I was shocked to see a noose hanging from the ceiling," Vampira said.

"He told me he kept it there in case he wanted to commit suicide in the middle of the night. Of course, who was I to be surprised? At the time, I was driving around in a funeral hearse. I also noted that he kept a lot of books on black magic scattered around the room. One night he threw a party. What a motley crew of friends he had. A lot of bongo players and dope smokers. A lot of actors who had never acted in anything. Dope, dope, and more dope—that's all that crowd was interested in. Jimmy could have any beautiful woman in Hollywood, but was sleeping with guys.

"He was also going through his amputee period, dating this ugly woman who had only one leg. Jimmy told me that she was the leader of a gang of beatnik thieves who made their living robbing the homes of rich movie stars. That night, Jimmy stripped down to his underwear and rubbed her stump. To judge from the rising bulge in his underwear, that turned him on big time."

those days, they seemed totally in love, totally devoted to each other, at least when they were together."

Dean held court almost nightly at Googie's, sometimes lingering till long after the sun came up. Vampira was always there among his devoted listeners.

Almost nightly at some point Dean would speak about the possibility of his upcoming death. "Live fast, die young," was his motto.

In Donald Spoto's biography of Dean called *Rebel*, he quotes Vampira as asking Dean why he was so obsessed with death. "That's the only way I'll have any peace," he told her.

Both Dean and Vampira shared the same ghoulish humor. For a publicity photo, Vampira once wandered through a local cemetery, announcing to the press that "I'm attending my own funeral."

One afternoon in Fairmount, Indiana, Dean visited Wilber Hunt's General Store, which also did double duty as the town's funeral parlor. As a sick joke, he crawled into one of the coffins and had his picture taken.

Life magazine turned down the photo, but after Dean's death it was published in periodicals and newspapers around the world.

Vampira cultivated a devoted following of campy gay men in the 50s, and many of them often performed free favors for her just for the privilege of being in her company. One man did her hair; another designed outfits for her, and one, Freddie Brandell, even drove her around Hollywood, without charge, in his car, a luxurious Cadillac, a gift from his rich father.

At the peak of her fame, Vampira had at least eight gay boys on call. Each of them was introduced to James Dean, and each developed a crush on the sexily handsome young actor.

Dean referred to the boys as "flamers," and rejected each of their invitations for sex.

Freddie Brandell, who himself would die in a car crash in 1966, developed the most overwhelming crush of them all on Dean. He told Vampira, "I'm gonna have him if it's the last thing I do on this earth. I'm mad about the boy."

Dean would abuse Freddie, send him on stupid errands, or even give him his dirty underwear to wash. Vampira protested the abuse. "Girly boy loves it," Dean told her. "He'd even eat my shit if I asked him to."

In some respects, Vampira agreed with that.

Freddie wanted to be a studio publicist, but his career was going nowhere. When Vampira's TV show was cancelled, she set up several appointments with other stations who might desire a similar show.

Freddie remembered the two graveyard or funeral home photos that Vampira and Dean had posed for, and he suggested that they appear in a similar publicity stunt shot.

"We'll have Dean lying in a coffin, pretending to be dead, and you hovering over him, looking like the most glamorous vampire who ever invaded a cemetery."

At first Dean was reluctant, but one night, after a liberal consumption of drink and drugs, he agreed to it. Freddie drove them and a photographer to a funeral home owned by the uncle of one of his friends. There were no dead bodies there the night this ghoulish party arrived.

Before Dean agreed to crawl into the casket and lie down, pretending to be dead, Freddie offered him a final drink. The young actor made a big mistake in downing the drink in one gulp.

Inside the coffin, Dean jokingly sat up pretending to rise from the dead, but finally drifted off into a coma. Vampira just assumed he had fallen asleep on the satin-cushioned upholstery of the casket and wouldn't wake up for some time.

She had another appointment, and asked Freddie if he'd hang around and drive Dean home. Planting a kiss on Dean's lips, she left the funeral parlor accompanied by the photographer.

The next afternoon Freddie told Vampira what he'd done the night before. Before Dean got inside that casket, Freddie had slipped him a vodka-based Mickey Finn. Not knowing the drink was drugged, Dean drank all of it, fast.

"After you and that guy left, I went and opened the back door and let in four of our friends," Freddie confessed. "Jimmy was knocked out, and we were sure that he'd remain that way for a long time. We lifted him from the coffin and placed him on a mortuary slab where we stripped off every piece of his clothing."

As Vampira listened in horror, Freddie told her more. "As you know, Jimmy has denied us any sex for a hell of a long time, even though all the guys have been panting for him. Unconscious on that marble slab, he could deny us nothing. We did everything we could think of, sexually speaking, before the rooster crowed. We left him lying on that slab to be discovered by the mortician in the morning. I hope he realized that Jimmy was still alive and didn't embalm him."

Vampire let out one of her famous screams and slapped Freddie's face. "You little fool! Don't you know each of you guys could get ten years or more for a stunt like that? Get out! I never want to see you or any of your so-called friends again. All of you are sick. Sick!"

She immediately called the photographer and told him to destroy all the negatives. She didn't want a picture with her in it to be used in evidence in case a trial was later held and the boys' rape of Dean exposed in open court.

In one of Hollywood's tragic ironies, a few weeks later, on September 30, 1955, Dean suffered a broken neck, and subsequent death, during a car accident while recklessly driving his Porsche near Salinas, California. His ruined body was placed in an equivalent coffin at the Kuehl Funeral Home on Spring Street in Paso Robles, California, and the news flashed to mil-

Vampira always claimed that she was surprised that **Paul Newman** (*left*) bonded with **Tony Perkins** (*center*) and **James Dean** (*right*). "Tony and Jimmy were wild boys," she claimed. "They should have been put away somewhere. They were such tormented souls. Paul seemed only mildly disturbed. He drank a lot. It was a difficult time for him. He couldn't make up his mind if he wanted to be straight or gay. I think Paul was basically straight, and had a great love for women. But back in those days, a good-looking gay guy could get him into bed.

"I dated Tony but he always took me home at nine o'clock, and I had to settle for kiss on the cheek. With Jimmy, I saw some action, but I don't think his prick was really up for it most of the time. Oh, did I tell you? I was married at the time. To a guy named Dean Reisner. At least I think that's what his name was."

lions around the world. Amid wailing and weeping, and something approaching mass hysteria, his body was transported for burial to the Park Cemetery in Fairmount, Indiana, a site of pilgrimage for cultish fans ever since.

Four years later, in 1959, Vampira made one last attempt at stardom when director Ed Wood, who made the most ridiculous movies ever filmed, cast her alongside Bela Lugosi in the schlocky, not-even-funny-enough-to-be-camp *Plan 9 from Outer Space*. Critics have, since then, defined it as "the worst film of all time." It was the last film Lugosi ("Count Dracula") ever made, an inglorious end to a fabulous career that had made Lugosi a legend.

In 1994, when the historic reality of Vampira had evolved into a cultish and very campy icon brought back to the screen, she was too old to play herself in *Ed Wood*, Tim Burton's tribute to the F-movie director, starring Johnny Depp. Vampira was portrayed by the Goth-inspired Lisa Marie Smith, a model and actress from New Jersey who billed herself simply as "Lisa Marie." (No, not that one.)

In 2006, two years before her death, Vampira's life story, or at least a heavily edited version of it, would be related in a documentary by Kevin Sean Michaels, *Vampira: The Movie*.

Vampira never benefited financially from her fame, and in later life—almost destitute—she sold handmade jewelry. At her lowest point, she lived in a garage and became a cleaning woman in a restaurant.

Unlike her friend, James Dean, who died young, Vampira would not meet the Grim Reaper until January 10, 2008, in Los Angeles. She'd lived a turbulent, unhappy life before finally—at the age of 85—releasing her last breath.

In her later years, she proclaimed, "The world doesn't have much use for a broken-down old fag hag. Where are all my golden boys of the 50s? Of course, they were sleeping with each other and rarely gave me a tumble, but I loved them all the same."

The crash scene where James Dean lost his life, September 30, 1955

Superman & The Porno Star

CAL CULVER AND THE
SEXUAL LIBERATION OF CHRISTOPHER REEVE

"Either you decide to stay in the shallow end of the pool or you go out in the ocean."
—Christopher Reeve

In 2006, when the gorgeously humpy **Brandon Routh** appeared in blue tights and a bulging red bikini in *Superman Returns,* gay newspapers proclaimed that this film, along with *The Devil Wears Prada,* were the two must-see homo movies of the summer. Some film critics claimed that Routh had impersonated Superman as a "feminized icon," others asserted that the young actor had played up Superman's "soft side."

Newspapers ranging from *The Advocate* to *The New York Times* asked: "Is Superman gay or just sensitive?"

All that media speculation about Superman also outed two other gay comic strip characters, as interpreted by Joel Schumacher and George Clooney in *Batman and Robin* (1997). Clooney was described as a "rubber-nippled, impressively cod-pieced bondage queen."

Turn the page to learn a deep, dark secret about an even more iconic verson of Superman, **Mr. Christopher Reeve**, who joins an impressive list of an estimated 75% of actors who have had, during the course of their lifetimes, at least one or two gay experiences —and sometimes a hell of a lot more.

Just How Gay Was
The Man of Steel?

Christopher Reeve

Except for a chance encounter occurring in 1975, it was probably unlikely that "Superman" Christopher Reeve would ever have met Cal Culver, the actor who evolved into the notorious "Casey Donovan," star of the celebrated porn flick, *Boys in the Sand*. Their encounter changed both of their lives.

In the autumn of that year, Katharine Hepburn was holding auditions for the Broadway comedy, *A Matter of Gravity,* authored by the then-86-year-old Enid Bagnold, whose earlier works had included the 1946 play upon which the Elizabeth Taylor movie *National Velvet* had been based. In *A Matter of Gravity*, Hepburn would play a rich, aristocratic, and aging Englishwoman living alone in a grand country house. Up for grabs was the role of her grandson in that play.

In his career as an actor, Cal had garnered a few good notices in 1972 when he was cast in a short-lived Broadway revival of George Bernard Shaw's *Captain Brassbound's Conversion*. It starred Ingrid Bergman, who described Cal as "having the same kind and as much charisma as Robert Redford." Cal thought that on the basis of that recommendation, Hepburn might be interested in casting him.

Christopher wanted the role and so did Cal. Cal was born in 1943 during the war years, and Christopher was born in 1952, so although Cal did not look his age, Christopher was nine years closer to the age of the character Miss Hepburn was casting.

Christopher got the role, and Hepburn turned down Cal. She did not exactly keep up with gay porno, so apparently her objection to him was not based on his previous performances with an erection. Right to Cal's face, she bluntly told him, "You lack a certain masculinity."

"No one could ever say that about you," Cal said, insulting her as he walked off the stage.

Cal's landmark film, *Boys in the Sand*, had been released in 1971. Christopher knew nothing about this.

Born in East Bloomfield, New York, Cal was well built and educated, a former actor and model. He'd had a stint as a high school teacher in an upscale private school on Central Park West in New York, and had previously played romantic leads in general summer stock productions. Unknown to Christopher and to Miss Hepburn at the time, Cal moonlighted as a male hustler.

In Key West years later, Cal recalled, "I thought Chris was the handsomest, most charming male animal I'd ever met when we both vied for the role in the Hepburn play. I didn't think he was gay—and I still don't—but I think he was curious. I definitely came on to him without doing anything overt. He seemed interested but a little timid."

"He was a very liberal kind of guy, and seemed willing to try anything once," Cal said. "As soon as I met him, I knew Hepburn would give him the role. I wasn't jealous. I agreed to meet him at Joe Allen's for a bite. That was a joint on 46th Street very popular with actors in those days. He agreed and showed up at exactly seven o'clock."

"I noticed that he turned heads when he walked in, but when I walked in I also turned a few heads," Cal said. "I think half the guys in the restaurant knew who I was."

"Christopher was a great lover, and I think I liberated him sexually," Cal claimed. "But he didn't stick around long enough for me to have benefitted from that."

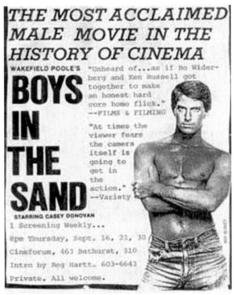

Cal Culver

At Manhattan's Broadhurst Theater, Cal showed up to watch the first performance of *A Matter of Gravity*. "It was the play's first night, and I was eager to see Chris perform. He walked out on stage, delivered his first line, and then promptly fainted."

Hepburn walked to stage center and faced the audience. "This boy's a goddamn fool. He doesn't eat enough red meat." Christopher's understudy finished the play for him.

Hepburn called a doctor for Christopher when the curtain went down. He was put on a healthier diet and regained his strength and finished the run of the play with the aging star. In fact, they became very close friends. There were even rumors in the gossip columns about an affair. "She was sixty-seven, and I was twenty-two," Christopher later said. "But I thought it was quite an honor to be linked romantically with her."

He dropped out of the play when it moved to Los Angeles in 1976, after he and Hepburn had performed in the play together for six months. But he stayed in touch with her for another five years until he stopped answering her notes.

"My own love affair with Christopher lasted for only two glorious months," Cal claimed. "He was the man of my dreams. In my life I've had literally hundreds of sexual involvements with men of all colors, but he was definitely *the* man. If I had been upfront with him from the beginning, it might have worked. He might have accepted my past and kept coming back to me. No, it never could have worked. But I'm allowed to dream, am I not?"

"One night when I met him again at Joe Allen's, he confronted me with my lies," Cal said. "He didn't think we could go on together, because he feared that everything I'd told him about myself was untrue. I pleaded for him to understand that I was trying to be a legit actor and wanted to hide my past."

"He told me that I'd become too notorious and might have to settle for a life in porn, because he suspected that porn was the only role I would ever be offered," Cal said. "And as it turned out, he was more or less correct."

"Christopher left me that night, moving on to become Superman," Cal recalled. "I think I'd fallen in love with him, and he broke my heart. On looking back, I guess it was my fault. But I felt he could have been more understanding of my past indiscretions. He didn't have to leave me because of what I'd done in the past."

"My final conclusion was that Christopher wasn't really gay," Cal said. "His thing with me was just a fling. In his career he'd play gay characters. I think he wanted to experiment briefly with the lifestyle and see if it was for him. He obviously decided it wasn't. After me, and I'm only guessing here, he didn't have any more experiences with gay lovers."

Cal was actually duplicitous in his relationship with Christopher. Two years previously, he'd launched a torrid affair with actor-turned-writer Tom Tryon. And during the time he was "dating" Christopher, he continued his affair with Tryon. That relationship ended in Key West in 1977 when Tryon, too, became disturbed by Cal's infidelity and his growing notoriety.

By 1985, Cal's health had begun to deteriorate after contracting HIV, probably through his working as a rent boy for so many years. Ironically, he was the author of an "Ask Casey" advice column for gay men, in which he urged them to limit the frequency of their sexual encounters as a means of preserving their health. Perhaps because he assumed he'd already been infected, he didn't follow his own advice

Cal made his final erotic film for director Christopher Rage. The golden boy of porn was no longer golden. The film was called *Fucked Up*, which accurately described Cal's condition. As one of his friends, Rob Richards, said, "Cal was sitting in the corner of a room as faceless people arrived and pushed toys and fists up into him. He was holding what appeared to be a big mayonnaise jar full of poppers or ethyl chloride—I'm sure there were other drugs in him at the time as well. He was drooling and was completely wiped out. He should never have been filmed."

Manshots, an international film review specializing in gay pornography that published bi-monthly editions between 1988 and 2001, referred to *Fucked Up* as "a haunting study in self-destruct, a pathetic footnote to a glittering career, an unsettling record of the Golden Boy on a collision course with his own mortality."

Slowly losing his mind, Cal died of an AIDS-related pulmonary infection in Inverness, Florida on August 10, 1987. He was forty-three years old.

Superman Christopher also ended his life tragically. He'd learned how to ride a horse in 1985 while training for his role as the dashing and romantic Vronsky that year in the made-for-TV version of *Anna Karenina*. He then continued riding as a personal hobby for ten years after that. On May 27, 1995, during a jumping exercise, his horse had a "refusal," and he fell off the animal, causing a cervical spinal injury that paralyzed him from the neck down. He had no memory of the incident after regaining consciousness.

He struggled for years to rehabilitate, becoming a highly visible and highly vocal advocate for disabled people throughout his latter life. He was elected Chairman of the American Paralysis Association and Vice Chairman of the National Organization on Disability.

In 1998 he produced and starred in *Rear Window*, a remake of Alfred Hitchcock's 1954 film with Grace Kelly and James Stewart. He also campaigned for stem cell research, rallying broad-based support in the face of then-President George W. Bush's opposition.

At the age of 52, after a valiant struggle that lasted for years, he died of heart failure on October 10, 2004. In 2005, his brave wife, Dana Reeve, head of the Christopher Reeve Foundation, was diagnosed with lung cancer, dying in March of the following year, at age 44.

"Christopher Reeve and Cal Culver were two of America's golden boys," said another porn star, Jack Wrangler. "Sometimes God, if there is such a thing, punishes those to whom he gives everything."

Mark Frechette

Movie Star / Sex Slave

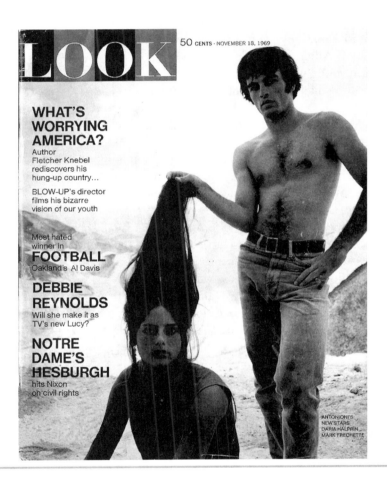

With absolutely no experience, **Mark Frechette** became a star overnight when director Michelangelo Antonioni cast him in the controversial 1970 *Zabriskie Point*. Frechette, along with co-star **Daria Halprin**, made the cover of *Look* magazine in March of 1970. That same month, *Rolling Stone* also ran the young actor on its cover.

"I'm young, handsome, and hung," he told some members of the underground press, who came to interview him. That great film career that had been predicted for him never materialized, of course. What awaited him was a prison cell for robbing a bank. His early death on September 27, 1975, is still the subject of lurid speculation.

ZABRISKIE POINT

ONE OF THE GREAT DISASTERS OF CINEMATIC HISTORY

ANTONIONI's **ZABRISKIE POINT**

In 1970, the late Miche langelo Antonioni (1912-2007) showed he had more *cojones* than any other filmmaker of his day when he released *Zabriskie Point*. It was one of the most damning portraits of American society ever filmed until Michael Moore came along nearly 40 years later.

The original ending included a shot of an airplane sky-writing the phrase FUCK YOU, AMERICA. The film's producer, MGM president Louis F. Polk, ordered that the scene be cut before general release.

The film is told through the eyes of two young people—Mark (played by Mark Frechette), who is sought by the police for killing a fellow officer during a student riot, and Daria (Daria Halprin), who is an assistant to a realtor who's constructing a village in the desert. Also cut from the film's final release were scenes of a then-unknown Harrison Ford, except for a brief glimpse of him during a jail scene.

Because of Antonioni's leftist politics, various right-wing groups, including FBI agents tailing cast and crew, and the sheriff of Oakland, California, tried to shut down the filming. The U.S. Attorney's office in Sacramento opened a grand jury investigation, citing possible violations of the Mann Act, a 1910 law prohibiting the transport of women across state lines "for immoral conduct, prostitution, and debauchery" during scenes shot in the scalding heat of Death Valley. The witch-hunters called off that particular tactic when they learned that *Zabriskie Point* was 13 miles west of the California-Nevada border, and that no state lines had actually been crossed.

As background, the music of Pink Floyd was used, since Antonioni had earlier rejected "L'America," provided to him by Jim Morrison and The Doors.

In spite of massive publicity, the film bombed and quickly faded into oblivion, as did its handsome, masculine star, the tortured Mark Frechette, who had emerged from nowhere, bursting onto the front pages of entertainment news from the world press. In spite of the film's failure, he became a household

Hailed as the new screen team for the 70s, **Mark Frechette** and his co-star **Daria Halprin** were photographed by paparazzi across the country even before the release of *Zabriskie Point*. The film cost $7 million, but earned only $900,000 in domestic release.

It was the only film Antonioni ever directed in the United States. Vincent Canby of *The New York Times* called it "a noble artistic impulse short-circuited in a foreign land."

word—if only temporarily.

A bearded Frechette had been discovered in 1968 standing on a street corner in Boston repeatedly shouting "MOTHERFUCK-ER." A talent scout for Antonioni, on a search for a young unknown American to star in the epic, wired Antonioni: "We've got our young man. He's twenty and he hates!"

There were predictions that Frechette would become the next Marlon Brando, or at least the next James Dean. When the film failed, Frechette's career was all but over, even though he made two other films in Italy—*Uomini Contro* in 1970 and *La Grande Scrofa Nera* in 1971.

Frechette donated the $60,000 he earned for *Zabriskie Point* to a commune in New England. The commune was little more than a hippie drug-culture crash pad, an offshoot of the disillusioned, Vietnam-era flower children.

After his brief but famous career, Frechette escaped with his costar, Daria Halprin, to the commune, where the Lyman Cult ruled with severity. After a few months, Halprin fled, later to marry actor Dennis Hopper.

Even before the release of *Zabriskie Point,* seemingly in anticipation of the next big star of the 70s, fan clubs for **Frechette** formed across the country.

The beautiful actor faded from the public's mind after the dismal release of the film. With its DVD release, however, the long dead Frechette is gathering new fans and critical praise. The stark beauty of both its star and the film itself is being re-evaluated.

Frechette stayed on, and then made a fatal mistake. In 1973, along with three members of his commune, he agreed to rob a Boston bank.

He entered the Brigham Circle branch of the New England Merchants Bank with a Smith and Wesson revolver. But he had no bullets in it. When the police stormed in, he dropped the revolver and flung his arms upward before the police even knew that he was one of the hold-up men. They had initially walked past him, thinking he was an innocent bank customer.

On August 29, 1973, in the shootout that followed, one of his accomplices, Chris (Hercules) Thien, was shot and killed by the police. "There was no way to stop what was going to happen," Frechette later said. "We just reached the point where all that the three of us really wanted was to hold up a bank. And, besides, standing there with a gun, cleaning out a teller's cage—that's about as fuckin' honest as you can get, man!"

Arrested and tried, the failed actor was sentenced to fifteen years at the Massachusetts Correctional Institution. It would turn out to be a death sentence.

Very few of his fellow inmates had seen any of his movies, but they were familiar with his delicate features and brooding, haunt-

Michelangelo Antonioni (1912-2007) was an Italian modernist film director, who pioneered a radical new style, presenting a series of apparently disconnected events into sometimes lyrical cinematic wholes.

He achieved international fame upon the release of *L'avventura* in 1960. He completed his "trilogy" with *La note* in 1961, starring Jeanne Moreau and Marcello Mastroianni, and *L'eclipsse* in 1962, featuring Monica Vitti and Alain Delon. *Blowup* (1962), set in Swinging London, was his greatest commercial success.

ing eyes, which had made the covers of both *Look* and *Rolling Stone* Magazines. Word quickly spread among the fellow inmates, 600 in all, that the prison was providing them "with a beautiful movie star with a tight boy ass to fuck."

The horny inmates lived up to their potential. Before Frechette had spent twenty hours behind bars, it was rumored that the emotionally troubled but "disturbingly beautiful young man" had been held down and repeatedly sodomized by both blacks and whites. One rape from an exceptionally well-endowed inmate was so severe and damaging to the actor's anal canal that he had to be sent to the hospital ward "to be sewed up."

After recovering, Frechette was sent back into the prison among the same inmates for more sexual assaults. Depressed and refusing to eat, his weight fell at one point to 150 pounds.

As his sentence dragged on, Frechette almost gave up trying to defend himself, giving in to months and months of repeated sexual assaults.

A possible way out arrived when a tough, 275-pound bruiser was admitted to the ward. He took a real liking to Frechette but the feelings weren't mutual. The bruiser wanted the handsome young actor to become his "bitch"—that way, he wouldn't be repeatedly raped nightly. The still rebellious Frechette bitterly rejected the offer. According to two inmates, Frechette made fun of the bruiser's small penis.

On the morning of September 27, 1975 in Norfolk, Massachusetts, Frechette's body was discovered by a fellow inmate. It was pinned beneath a 150-pound set of weights, with the bar resting on his throat. An autopsy, announced the following day, revealed that the prisoner had died of asphyxiation. It was suggested that the weights might have slipped from his hands as he tried to bench press them. Death, or so it was believed, was instant.

The county DA's office in Norfolk investigated the death. Although no charges were ever filed, a member of the DA's office claimed the death "a little strange—the bar left no mark on Frechette's neck, which it would have if that was how he was killed."

Several inmates over the years have told reporters that it was their belief that Frechette was murdered for his refusal to become a "sex slave" in prison.

In his last known remarks, Frechette said, "I just do what I have to do. Because if you fall asleep like most people in this society, you're a fuckin' dead man."

And so he became.

(Left photo above) **Antonioni** (left) directed **Halprin** (center) and **Frechette** (right) in Death Valley, presenting Frechette as a "postreligious Marxist and existentialist intellectual." Halprin, a young San Francisco-based dancer and actress was linked romantically with Frechette, but in time broke from him to chart her own course and career, later becoming a psychologist.

As her creativity burgeoned, her former lover endured prison bars and "unspeakable acts" upon on his lean, lithe, sculpted, and very famous body.

Natalie Wood

"This is Splendour. We think we may have someone missing in an eleven-foot rubber dinghy."
—Robert Wagner

"Let Me Entertain You," or so the song went when **Natalie Wood** played stripper Gypsy Rose Lee in the Hollywood version of *Gypsy* (1962). She did her own singing in this one, though none too impressively.

The death of this doe-eyed beauty off the coast of California's Catalina Island on November 29, 1981, shocked the world. It was called a tragic "accident," but the contradictory statements from the three men aboard the yacht, *Splendour*, have only fueled speculation about one of Hollywood's most enduring mysteries.

DEATH IN A DINGHY
Who Did It?

The news of the still-unexplained drowning of Natalie Wood at the age of 43 off Catalina Island made headlines around the world on November 29, 1981. Her body was pulled from a choppy sea about 30 miles off the southern coast of California and one mile south of the Wagner's 55-foot cabin cruiser, *Splendour*. She became the third star of *Rebel Without a Cause* to die violently, in the wake of, first, the fatal car crash of James Dean in 1955 and the murder of Sal Mineo in 1976.

Her death remains one of Hollywood's darkest mysteries. Not since Marilyn Monroe's death by suicide or murder (take your choice) had Hollywood speculated so wildly about the passing of a movie star. Public interest in Natalie's death was understandable. Many of her fans had grown up with her. After all, she'd made 25 films before she turned 18, including the wildly successful *Miracle on 34th Street* in 1947. Mostly she's remembered for the films she made in the 1960s, the decade of her greatest success at the box office where she reigned as America's second most favorite sexy superstar, bowing only to the champ herself, Elizabeth Taylor. Dubbed "Hollywood's Princess," Natalie had earned three Oscar nominations and had immortalized herself in such films as *West Side Story* in 1961 and *Gypsy* in 1962.

By drowning, Natalie was fulfilling the long-ago prophecy of a Russian gypsy who warned her to "beware of dark water" and death by drowning. Over the years, Natalie had become so frightened of water that she even feared having her hair washed because her head would be submerged.

Her drowning followed a jealous, drunken row with her husband, Robert Wagner, feuding with her over her excessive attention to her on-board guest, Christopher Walken, who was co-starring with her in the sci-fi flick *Brainstorm*, a film nearly completed be-

When **Natalie Wood** first saw **James Dean** and his motorcycle-riding pals pull up at Googie's in Los Angeles, she chased after him. But Margaret O'Brien's overprotective mother, who was chaperoning Natalie at the time, grabbed her by the ear and pulled her away.

Even before the release of his first movie, Dean had acquired a mythical status in Hollywood. Imagine Natalie's surprise when she found herself cast as a rebellious teen opposite Dean in *Rebel Without a Cause*. For Natalie, it was love. Unfortunately he would die in 1955 before the film's release in October of that same year.
But while he was alive, he believed in sharing his body with countless others, both men and women, especially men.

fore her death.

Some of the cast of *Brainstorm* had reported that Natalie had "fallen big" for her co-star, the son of a baker and a former teenage lion-tamer. She said that she "loved his different-colored eyes"—one was blue, the other hazel.

Not all critics agreed with Natalie. Stephen Lemons found that Walken's eyes "looked part cadaver, part Muppet. Those glassy, bulging eyes look like they might entice sex from a bobcat. No one plays the kook, the psycho, the fallen angel, the deadly crime lord, the blood thirsty ghoul better than Walken."

On the set and in her dressing room, they'd talked for hours about acting. He encouraged her return to the stage after *Brainstorm* in which she was going to star in *Anastasia*, the story of the tragic Romanov duchess. Natalie herself was of Russian descent and was eager to play the part. She expressed a dream to friends, "Chris and I might become the Alfred Lunt and Lynn Fontanne of the 90s."

Privately Natalie confessed that she'd been mesmerized by Walken after he played the psychotic Vietnam veteran in *The Deer Hunter*, for which he won the 1978 Best Supporting Oscar. Once she met him, Natalie told him that "no one, but no one, can play the malevolent WASP like you."

Five years her junior, he gave her a renewed feeling for life, awakening a renaissance in her. She'd been putting on weight and had fired a stylist who suggested that she might be getting "a bit too matronly" for the camera. Walken had rekindled a rebellious streak in her and had relit her artistic spirit. She'd already told friends that Wagner was drinking far too much and "becoming even more boring than usual."

Even the second time around, Natalie and her R.J. hardly had a dream marriage. There were rumors of a near fatal suicide attempt, infidelity, a dependence on pills, and the anxiety that every middle-aged actress faces in a search for decent film roles. She was so desperate near the end of her life that she told her sister, Lana, "You know what I want? I want yesterday. Bring back 1960."

Natalie throughout her life, even while married, was promiscuous. As a teenager, friends called her "boy crazy," or perhaps man crazy would be more apt. When she was 15, Frank Sinatra, a ripe 38, had seduced her. On a few occasions, she'd have three heavy dates within a period of 24 hours. "There is nothing wrong with having James Dean in the afternoon, Nick Adams as an after-dinner treat, and Nicky Hilton for midnight champagne." Hilton, of course, was the first husband of Elizabeth Taylor.

Her lovers had ranged from James Dean to Elvis Presley to Warren Beatty. Yet she was not a *femme fatale*. Steve McQueen said, "I never saw what was so great about Natalie. She was short and lousy in bed." Natalie herself could be equally candid about

"The pretty boy with the beach ball," young **Robert Wagner** *(top photo, above)* had already seduced such Hollywood legends as the aging Barbara Stanwyck and Lana Turner. But did he really put out for the notorious gay agent, Henry Willson, who helped launch both his career and Rock Hudson's?

Fan magazines linked Natalie with gay actor Tab Hunter, but Natalie fell big for the young actor and playboy Wagner *(pictured with **Natalie** in photo immediately below)*. They were married on December 28, 1957 in Arizona.

her bedfellows. "Elvis can sing but he can't do much else."

With Walken aboard, Wagner and Natalie set off for Catalina on their ill-fated Thanksgiving sail during a break in the shooting of *Brainstorm*. Natalie may have been deliberately flirting with Walken to make her husband jealous. She was, in fact, furious at him for all the attention he was paying to his *Hart to Hart* co-star Stefanie Powers, following another not sufficiently explained death of her lover, William Holden, only two weeks before.

Wagner had been playing Power's super-rich, private-eye partner, Jonathan Hart, in the crime drama for TV, *Hart to Hart* (1979-1984). His friendship with Powers had actually begun in the late 1950s when the actress was in her teens. "We've coped with the highs," Power reportedly said, "and God knows RJ and I have been through the lows together."

Fans knew little about the marital discord within the Wagner family. "They had to live out the dream the world had imagined for them whether or not it went sour," said Lana Wood, Natalie's sister. Natalie had married Wagner in 1957 but had divorced him in 1962. After a brief second marriage to Richard Gregson, the British producer, she'd remarried Wagner in 1972. To the world at large, she claimed, "My life with RJ," her nickname for him, "never really ended. It was just interrupted. We had each other in our youth, and now we have each other in our prime."

After others turned down the invitation, only four people were on board at the debut of the ill-fated crossing to Catalina—Natalie, of course, plus Wagner, Walken, and the New Jersey captain, Dennis Davern, who would later give conflicting stories of what re-

One of Natalie's most famous movies was *Bob & Carol & Ted & Alice* (1969) about couples who swing. On the *Splendour* sailing to Catalina, could her real life last story be called *Bob & Natalie & Christopher?*

In November, 1981, Wagner invited his rival, **Christopher Walken** *(above)* who was filming *Brainstorm* with Natalie at the time, to sail to Catalina Island with Natalie and him. It would evolve into an explosive, scandal-soaked voyage.

Before and after her first marriage to Wagner, Natalie knew many headline-making lovers.

When she was fourteen, she surrendered her virginity to actor Nick Adams, another doomed actor appearing in *Rebel Without a Cause*. He introduced her to Elvis Presley *(right)*. Elvis wanted to meet her because she'd worked with Dean, his hero. She "became crazy" about **Elvis**, who called her "Mat Nat." He invited her to Graceland but when they got there, he slept with Nick Adams – not her.

The beautiful **Warren Beatty** *(photo below right)* actually abandoned the bed of Joan Collins to make love to Natalie.

Steve McQueen *(photo below)* also succumbed to Natalie's charm.

But despite her formidable allure, Natalie was devastated when she allegedly walked in on R.J. during his involvement with another man, according to Suzanne Finstad, author of the controversial bio *Natasha*.

ally happened that weekend. Both Walken and Wagner were less than candid following Natalie's death, and have mostly remained silent about what really happened aboard the *Splendour*. Most of the participants were so tanked up that their memories, at best, would be unreliable.

The departure just before noon on the Friday after Thanksgiving met cold, gray November skies. Natalie had always liked the island, having honeymooned there with her heartthrob, Wagner, in 1958.

The *Splendour* anchored at Avalon where Wagner, Walken, and Natalie went ashore for a booze-filled afternoon at a Mexican restaurant and later at a waterfront bar, El Galleon.

At one point they went shopping, Wagner buying his wife a one-karat diamond necklace. Halfway through the jaunt, she disappeared, ostensibly to go to the women's room. She was gone for about thirty minutes, later explaining that she had a mild case of Montezuma's revenge.

The reason for her disappearance, if her friend Roddy McDowall was to be believed, was that Natalie had spotted her off-the-record lover (name unknown) who, to her surprise and dismay, had followed her to Catalina for a showdown, since she was trying to drop him now that her outside romantic interest had shifted to Walken.

McDowall had by chance run into Natalie with her handsome young heartthrob only weeks before in Los Angeles. To Rock Hudson, writer Tommy Tompson, and others in the gay Hollywood grapevine, he'd described the stranger as a "combination of Troy Donahue and Tab Hunter as they looked in the 50s." Natalie did not bother to introduce her lover to her long-time friend and hurried on her way. Later, she called McDowall and told him that, "I'm just having a little fling—nothing serious. As we both know, R.J. has his flings. Why not *moi*?"

A waitress at Catalina's El Galleon bar where Walken, Wagner, and Natalie had downed margaritas, said that Natalie had returned unexpectedly with a young, blond-haired man. They'd taken a seat at a concealed table where they had an animated conversation that looked like it was going to break into a violent argument, although they kept their voices down. Even so, a waiter saw Natalie kissing the young man on the lips before she hurried away to rejoin Walken and Wagner.

R.J. & his Natalie became America's sweethearts, generating as much press and as many magazine covers as Brad Pitt and Angelina Jolie today.

In spite of what the magazines said, their first marriage was tempestuous, torn apart by gossip columnists after Natalie's notorious visit to Key West where she shacked up with Warren Beatty during his filming of *All Fall Down*.

The love – and friendship – shared by R.J. and Natalie survived extramarital affairs and even other spouses. The couple came together again for a second marriage in 1972.

That night, Natalie had dinner aboard the *Splendour* with her husband and Davern. Walken, feeling seasick, had retreated to his cabin. Davern recalled that Natalie argued with Wagner about whether to move the *Splendour* to more tranquil waters to avoid the rough waves washing in.

Natalie demanded that Davern take her ashore. She'd decided to spend the night in a hotel, the Pavilion Lodge, where she rented rooms 126 and 219. She asked the captain to sleep with her in 126 because "I'm afraid." Acting as Natalie's bodyguard, he fell into a drunken sleep on the floor beside the star's bed. At some point Natalie must have slipped out of the room, because a maid later told some of the staff at the hotel that she'd seen her coming out of room 219 around four o'clock that morning. About five minutes later a young blond-haired man left the same room. The maid had watched the comings and goings from room 219 through a partially opened broom closet door. When the maid came into room 219 later in the day, she found that the bed had been disturbed. And during her cleaning of the accommodation, she found a semen-filled condom discarded on the floor of the bathroom.

Upon Natalie's return to the *Splendour* the next morning, she tried to wake up Walken, urging him to return with her to the mainland. He refused. Later that morning, she abandoned her plans to go back to Los Angeles and seemed in better spirits as she cooked *huevos rancheros* for Wagner and Walken, "the two men in my life."

Walken was informed that the *Splendour* was being moved over to the Isthmus at Two Harbours on the remote side of the island where the waters were calmer. As the men slept, Davern went for a short ride in the dinghy. It was later speculated that he was delivering a note from Natalie to the young man on shore about their plans to move the craft, but Davern has never confirmed that this was the case.

Buffetted by gusting winds and choppy seas, the *Splendour* moored at Two Harbours with about 55 other pleasure craft. As Wagner slept, Walken and Natalie went ashore, leaving him a note. At a bar/restaurant, Doug's Harbor Reef, Walken and Natalie were seen flirting with each other by Don Whiting, the manager. "It was obvious to all of us that they were in love," he said. Whiting is now dead and, of course, can't be questioned more extensively.

On board the *Splendour*, Wagner woke up and found the note. In a jealous rage, he went ashore to find the pair. As the winds gusted even stronger outside the bar, Wagner joined his wife and Walken. Natalie reportedly continued her "outrageous flirting" with Walken. Whiting, a homosex-

Natalie and **Roddy McDowall**, both former child stars *(pictured in upper photo, above)* were seen together so often that clueless fan mag writers gushed that they were lovers. The pair laughed—"More like sisters," Roddy claimed.

After her death, he shared conspiracy theories with friends about the mysterious drowning. *Below*, **Tab Hunter** *(on the left)* cooks dinner for gay pal **Roddy**. The heavily endowed former child star knew all of Natalie's secrets.

Robert Wagner and **Stefanie Powers** become household words when they appeared in the 1979-1984 TV series, *Hart to Hart*. She became the victim of unfounded but lurid speculation following the mysterious death of her lover, William Holden, whose body was left to rot for days on his living room floor. When Natalie drowned, even more vicious rumors—again, unfounded—were spread about her and Wagner.

ual, later claimed that Wagner, "perhaps to get even with Natalie began flirting with Walken himself, even more outrageously than Natalie had done, making me wonder if those bisexual rumors about him were true. Those rumors go back to the 50s when he was promoted by the king of the casting couch, Henry Willson, who did a lot for Rock Hudson's career."

Whiting said that he was under the impression that Wagner, Natalie, and Walken "were gearing up for a three-way later that night." At the time of their dinner reservations when he ushered them to table at seven o'-clock, he claimed that all three of them were drunk.

The drunken dinner lasted for three hours. At one point Natalie excused herself and was later seen in the women's toilet befriending a young girl and telling her how she missed her own children. It was around this time that Natalie left the restaurant and walked down by the shore.

Whiting, who lived on a boat, had to retrieve something. On his way to the boat, he saw Natalie in what appeared to be a confrontation with a young blond-haired man. He watched the pair from a concealed position. The young man seemed to win the argument, forcing her to disappear with him. Whiting got the impression he was demanding money from her, "but he also seemed to be trying to force her into sex with him at the same time. I wanted to stick around but my presence was due in the restaurant. I noticed that Natalie came back about thirty minutes later. Her hair was in slight disarray, but I don't think Walken and Wagner even seemed to take notice that she'd been gone for a long time."

Walken, Walker, and Natalie closed down the bar at around 10 o'clock and headed back to the *Splendour*. On board, and on deck, Walken and Wagner got into a violent and jealous argument over Natalie. Although allegedly the two actors did not attack each other, Wagner in his fury broke a wine bottle. Natalie ran below to her cabin, and Walken disappeared into his room slightly later.

Here the story gets murky. Apparently, Wagner went below to search for his wife to make up, but he found her missing. He then began a search of the boat, finding that the only dinghy, *Valiant*, was also missing. It seems improbable that he or the captain would not have seen Natalie when she came back on deck and lowered the dinghy into the water. Wagner must have known that

Their yacht, *Splendour (above)* was supposed to bring joy to the "fairy-tale" marriage of Natalie and R.J.

But reporters over the years have filed stories that the "idyllic" couple were "jealous, possessive, and distrustful" of each other. That was certainly true when R.J. sailed the *Splendour* to Catalina with Natalie and Christopher Walken aboard.

Simultaneously, Hollywood gossips were spreading stories that Natalie had fallen for Walken while co-starring with him in *Brainstorm*.

Natalie (above) in a rare photograph aboard the *Splendour's* dingy, a small vessel that would forever be linked to her death. To travel ashore in this dingy, Natalie would have had to overcome her life-long fear of the water. The star was filled with a dread of darkness and a belief— thanks to a gypsy's "prophecy"—that she would die by drowning.

The lonely dingy was found floating in the waters offshore Blue Cavern Point, with scratch marks on its side, as though a doomed Natalie had desperately tried to climb aboard.

there was nothing open at that time on shore, as the only restaurant and bar had closed. Yet he later claimed that Natalie may have lowered herself into the dinghy in the dark, turbulent waters to go ashore for a drink.

Natalie was discovered missing around 10:30pm. But it was not until 1:30am that Wagner radioed for help. Why he waited so long may never be known.

It was "exactly at 11:05pm" that a woman's scream for help was heard aboard a cruiser called the *Capricorn*, which was moored about eighty feet from the *Splendour*. On board were Marilyn Wayne, a commodities broker, her eight-year-old son, Anthony, and her boyfriend, John Payne (not the actor, of course). All three later claimed that they had heard an unknown woman screaming, "Help me! Please help me! I'm drowning!"

All three passengers aboard the *Capricorn* reported that she kept screaming that she was drowning. The trio also reported that they heard either one or two men calling to the woman that they were jumping in to help her. Could those voices have been that of Wagner and Davern? The press would speculate about that for months. Wayne later claimed that the screams for help were coming from the direction of the *Splendour*.

Wayne was discouraged against going into the water herself. There were fears that the drowning victim would clutch her and pull her to her death, and since the waters were cold there was also the fear of hypothermia.

Payne called the harbormaster at Two Harbors but there was no answer. The woman kept screaming for help although her calls grew weaker. Payne turned on the light topping their mast and scanned the area. But the crew aboard the *Capricorn* spotted no one.

In desperation Wayne called the harbor patrol at Avalon on the other side of the island. The harbormaster there promised to send a search helicopter. As time went by and no copter appeared, Wayne placed yet another call to Avalon. Again, there was no answer. Right before 11:30pm, Wayne, her boyfriend, and her son heard no more screams.

The Capricorn crew concluded that someone aboard the *Splendour* had rescued the drowning woman. In testimony the next day, Wagner, Walken, and Davern claimed that they had heard no screams that night. Then who was the man—or men—promising to come to the aid of the drowning Natalie? It was not until the following morning when listening to a radio broadcast that Payne, Wayne, and her son heard that it had been Natalie Wood, the famous movie star, screaming for help in the middle of the night.

The bleak **Blue Cavern Point** on Catalina Island appears tranquil in the pictures to the right, but it silently witnessed the last scene in the mysterious death of Natalie.

Weighed down by a heavy jacket, Natalie, or so it is believed, may have fallen from the deck of the yacht, and then clung to the slippery exterior of the dingy, trying to propel it ashore by kicking her legs and paddling with one arm. She may have been too intoxicated to remove her water -soaked jacket. Had she done so, she might have been able to save herself by clawing her way from the open water into the dinghy.

Although Roddy McDowall apparently never went to the police, he later told friends, including Tommy Thompson, that he felt the young blond man, whom he called Natalie's "stalker/lover," had gone to Catalina for a final showdown. He wanted to prolong the sexual liaison he'd formed with her, but, if not, he wanted a pay-off.

McDowall speculated that the young man was threatening to take a small boat over to the *Splendour* for a confrontation with Wagner if Natalie did not come through for him. "I'm sure the kid would have taken $25,000 in hush money," McDowall said. "Natalie did not have that much, of course, aboard the *Splendour* but she could probably have raised a thousand in cash to hold the kid off until she got back to the mainland. Perhaps she promised him she'd find some cash aboard the *Splendour,* and slip off the boat later that night and deliver it to him."

McDowall, victim of several blackmail attempts during his life, owing to his homosexuality, had been threatened by boyfriends in his time. McDowall also speculated that Natalie's stalker had heard rumors that her husband was a bisexual. "Perhaps he was pressuring Natalie to arrange a three way," McDowall said. "I know R.J. He would never have gone for that."

When he learned that Natalie's body was clad in garments that included a nightgown, McDowall provided what he thought might have been a likely reason: "If Wagner caught her on deck, she could always claim that the dinghy was banging against the *Splendour* and keeping her awake. She could say that she had risen from bed to adjust it. That would explain the nightgown. He would never suspect that she was going to shore in an outfit that included a down-filled jacket, a flannel nightgown, woolen stockings, and no panties."

On his houseboat, Whiting had overheard Wagner's drunken radio call for help to the Harbor Patrol at 10:30pm, 35 minutes before the *Capricorn* crew heard a woman screaming. Knowing the patrol office was closed for the night, Whiting intercepted the call and spoke to Wagner.

Once Whiting determined that Natalie was missing, he agreed to search for her in his own boat. Wagner did not want to call the Coast Guard, fearing "unwanted publicity," a strange reaction from a husband who knew his wife was missing in a dark sea.

In his frantic search onshore for Natalie, Whiting was joined by both Paul Wintler, a maintenance man, and by Wagner himself. Amazingly, all three men seemed to think they might find Natalie on land. Wagner returned empty-handed to the *Splendour* at 2:30am.

It should have been apparent, even to drunken men, that Natalie had been lost at sea. Still Wagner did not want to call Baywatch or the Coast Guard. Whiting and Wintler, however, woke up Doug Oudin, the harbormaster at Two Harbors. Setting out in his own craft, Oudin went aboard the *Splendour* to confront Davern and Wagner, both of whom were still drinking. The men told Oudin that Natalie was attired in her nightgown when she left the cruiser.

How could they have known what she was wearing if they hadn't seen her leave? That comment would later cause much speculation in the tabloids. Rumors spread that Wagner and Natalie had fought on deck and that she'd accidentally fallen aboard. According to that tall tale, he'd been too drunk to rescue her.

Speculation was getting out of hand. A London reporter, Peter Rydin, suggested in an article in *The Globe*

"I don't need to be made to look evil, I can do that on my own," said **Christopher Walken** pictured above as he appeared in *The Comfort of Strangers* (1991). If this talented, handsome actor ever writes a memoir, maybe he will come clean about what really happened to Natalie Wood off the coast of Catalina.

Could the rumors about him having an affair with Natalie be true? Did her husband, Wagner, find out? These questions may never be answered.

that Natalie might have been "murdered" by Walken, with the blessing of Jill St. John, whom Wagner later married. Of course, there was no hard evidence for any of these wild claims, but the public devoured these theories, believing what readers wanted to believe.

If Natalie had indeed fallen overboard in the wake of violence on the deck, that would have accounted for the bruises on her body which were documented during an autopsy.

Even as dire as the outlook appeared, Wagner demanded that Oudin not call the Coast Guard. Oudin left the *Splendour* around 2:45am, continuing the search for Natalie with some local boatmen. He abandoned the hunt within an hour and put through a radio call to the Coast Guard himself. He did not mention Natalie by name, knowing that if someone were listening in, the person might notify the Associated Press, which would immediately send a bulletin around the world and might possibly make headlines in afternoon editions in Europe or in late editions along the East Coast.

The Coast Guard learned at 3:30am that a woman aboard the *Splendour* had been missing since around 10:45pm in shark-infested waters. It was not until 5:16am that Baywatch was notified. As dawn was coming up at 6am, a truly professional search for Natalie at long last had begun. Helicopters with search lights, Harbor Patrol vessels, and Baywatch boats were scanning the coastline in the vicinity of Isthmus Cove.

Trapped in kelp, the empty *Valiant* was discovered at Blue Cavern Point around 5:30am by Whiting himself. Its key was in neutral. The body of Natalie was found at 7:45am, floating face down in the ocean. She was wearing a flannel nightgown and a red eiderdown jacket that, when water-logged, weighed forty pounds. The "coroner to the stars," Dr. Thomas Noguchi, later speculated that this heavy jacket might have led to her death. Had she removed it, she might have been able to climb back into the

"The coroner to the stars," **Dr. Thomas Noguchi**, at the time of Natalie's death, had come under fire for confirming that William Holden's alcoholism had contributed to the actor's death. Frank Sinatra, Natalie's former love, was among Noguchi's severest critics.

Natalie's drowning presented the coroner with a different kind of dilemma. He stated that the police were baffled by the circumstances associated with Natalie's inability to climb into the dinghy, and even more surprised at Natalie's attire.

"It was apparent that she had not dressed for a boat ride – and yet the police believed she must have untied the line which held the dinghy to the yacht. But why had she untied it if she didn't intend to go out in the boat?"

The Mystery of
Natalie Wood

(*Left photo above*) Director Peter Bogdanovich cast **Justine Waddell** (*left*) as Natalie and **Michael Weatherly** as R.J. in his TV biopic, *The Mystery of Natalie Wood*. The director lamented that Wood is likely to be remembered more for her untimely death at the age of 43 than for her memorable performances in such vehicles as *Inside Daisy Clover*, *West Side Story*, and *Splendor in the Grass*.

Bogdanovich himself was drawn into a Hollywood tragedy, the murder of his girlfriend, centerfold-turned actress Dorothy Stratten. Her death inspired two movies of its own.

floating dinghy and safety.

Scratch marks were found on the side of the dinghy, indicating that in her desperation she'd tried to climb aboard but the jacket weighed her down. Her blood contained .14 percent of alcohol and that might have prevented her from thinking clearly. If she were more in control, she might have slipped off the jacket or else swam only a few feet back to the safety of the yacht. In a tantalizing and still-unexplained statement, Dr. Noguchi concluded that, "I don't believe drunkenness caused her to fall into the water."

The announcement of her death launched a media-feeding frenzy. There was almost unprecedented speculation, as various candidates were suggested by Natalie's fans as the possible murderer. At the head of the list of suspects was Robert Wagner himself. Fans also accused Walken of murdering Natalie. And in some of the most outlandish charges imaginable, Stefanie Powers was suggested as the murderer, her motive being that she'd killed her lover, William Holden, and replaced him with Wagner, whose job it now was to do Natalie in. That scenario evoked Hitchcock's *Strangers on a Train* in 1951, starring two bisexual actors, Farley Granger and Robert Walker.

Fans around the world mourned Natalie's death and wanted answers as to how or why she'd died. So-called "official" announcements raised far more questions than they answered. It didn't help that all parties intimately connected with Natalie's death contradicted themselves over the years.

Even as honorary pallbearers such as Frank Sinatra, Fred Astaire, Rock Hudson, Gregory Peck, and Sir Laurence Olivier were attending Natalie's funeral, listening to the strains of a balalaika (in honor of her Russian background), speculation around the world remained rampant.

In spite of all Dr. Noguchi's official reports, he himself admitted that "scandalous stories and weird sexual allegations were spreading like brushfire."

A popular speculation was that Natalie had gone to bed but had awakened later to discover Walken and Wagner making love to each other. In jealousy and frustration, she'd fled the boat, so the story goes. However, Dr. Noguchi himself suggested that Walken and Wagner were far too intoxicated that night to have had sex with each other.

Right after the drowning was reported, there was immediate suspicion that Natalie was the one having an affair.

Dr. Noguchi in his findings postulated that it "could not be ruled out" that Natalie was attempting a clandestine affair on the night of her death.

Although there was an attempt to suppress this evidence, the autopsy found traces of semen in Natalie's genital area. Allegedly, the semen did not match that of Walken, Wagner, or Devern. How Noguchi determined this is not known, as the three men aboard were not asked to provide samples. One report suggested that the coroner, through a court order, obtained medical records of the possible suspects.

If the semen found on her body was not that

At the peak of their beauty, **Natalie** and **R.J.** were two stars who flourished on the Hollywood scene during the closing days of the studio system. As a child star she delivered a legendary performance in *Miracle on 34th Street* (1947).

Natalie's mother, a superstitious Russian immigrant laying her claims to royalty, told her daughter, "You will become a star, the biggest in Hollywood."

R.J., as a teenager, had grown up with such mentors as Gary Cooper and Clark Gable. Gable reportedly told R.J., "You're too handsome not to become a matinee idol. Just keep it zipped for the hundreds of faggots you'll meet in this damn business."

of her husband, Walken, or the captain, then the conclusion was that it had come from this mysterious lover who had shown up on Catalina. During her disappearances from the table with Walken and Wagner, had Natalie engaged in quickie sex with the handsome blond heartthrob? The restaurant manager, Whiting, suspected that she had.

The swabs taken from Natalie's genital area were later "lost" before an attempt could be made to determine who might have had sex with her shortly before her death.

The case of the mysterious semen was never sufficiently resolved, and too many questions left unanswered.

On December 11, the Sheriff's Department told the press that the "case of the accidental drowning of Natalie Wood" was officially closed. The case might be officially closed, but it was hardly closed unofficially. Lurid speculation about what happened that night remains today.

Noguchi, in discussing the role of a medical examiner, talked of the "Five W's." What was the cause of death? Where did it happen? When did it happen? Why did it happen? The last W, of course, is Who—the person responsible."

That final W may never be answered unless there is a death-bed confession from some party.

Frank Salerno of the Sheriff's Department claimed, "We may never figure out exactly what happened."

Long after Natalie gave her life to the sea, Wagner expressed his grief. "When Natalie died, I was embittered. I still get angry about it and I wonder why it had to happen. I have all those feelings of grief and anger that people who've lost someone they love always have. I had lived a charmed life, and then I lost a beautiful woman I loved with all my heart."

As for Walken, he said, "At its best, life is completely unpredictable."
So is death.

One journalist wrote that "the death of Natalie Wood was about as accidental as the shooting of John F. Kennedy in Dallas."

"Every death is a homicide until proven otherwise," Dr. Noguchi said.

In the case of Natalie Wood, her death was never proven otherwise.

NATALIE WOOD   *REST IN PEACE*

At the Westwood Memorial Park, Marilyn Monroe's hard-to-find wall crypt is the most visited attraction.

But after that, the occasional deposit of fresh flowers on her grave attests to the continuing intrigue fans have for the ill-fated **Natalie**.

Years After Natalie's Mysterious Death
DENNIS DAVERN,
CAPTAIN OF *THE SPLENDOUR*, SPEAKS

GOODBYE NATALIE
GOODBYE SPLENDOUR
MARTI RULLI
with former *Splendour* Captain
DENNIS DAVERN

In 2009, the captain of *The Splendour,* Dennis Davern, with his friend Marti Rulli, published a controversial book, *Goodbye Natalie, Goodbye Splendour.* Originally a native of New Jersey, and an enlisted member of the U.S. Navy until 1971, Davern became the California-based captain of *The Splendour,* piloting Natalie Wood and Robert Wagner across the waters of the Pacific. He was in command of the boat the night Natalie died.

Referring to Natalie's death, he said:

*It's the kind of story that never goes away. A year or two can pass, then—**BOOM!**—there she is, walking down the dock, smiling at you when you're ready to fall asleep, and you know you just have to do this for her.*

The book's jacket asserts that "the police investigation was insufficient, that the parties involved received special treatment because of their celebrity status, and that a grave injustic occurred when Natalie Wood's death was brushed under the rug as an accident." It raises additional speculation about the night Natalie died, revives the rumors of the past, and reinforces the suspicions associated with her drowning. Presented as a "confessional," it articulates a damning indictment of Wagner, albeit in a format that would fall short of definitively convincing a jury.

In his book, Davern charges:

My first reaction was that Wagner had everything to do with Natalie's death, and it is my belief to this day that Natalie is a victim of her husband. I saw too much that night to ever believe it was an accident. I witnessed R.J.'s drunkenness. I witnessed R.J.'s anger and outburst. I heard the stateroom fight and saw that it carried over onto the back deck. I know that Wagner was with Natalie when she left the boat. Wagner knows <u>how</u> and exactly <u>why</u> she left the boat.

Yet despite the book's length (335 pages), there is no smoking gun delivering definitive proof of anything. Yet some of its readers, on the

Provocative and insightful, *Goodbye Natalie, Goodbye Splendour*, written by Marti Rulli, with the cooperation of Dennis Davern, the former captain of *The Splendour,* brought new attention to the mysterious death by drowning of a fallen star. The book's stated goal was "to reveal the many truths and misconceptions behind the tragic death of a Hollywood legend."

Lana Wood, sister of Natalie, lived in the star's shadow throughout most of her life. In 1984, she wrote her own book, *Natalie: A Memoir by Her Sister* that remained for six weeks on *The New York Times* Best Seller list. In this sizzler, Lana revealed that she and Natalie sometimes shared lovers: Warren Beatty, Ryan O'Neal, Alain Delon, and Sean Connery. Robert Wagner broke off relations with Lana after the publication of her memoir.

other hand, thought that the book carried an argument that was strong enough to justify a re-opening of the investigation into Natalie's death.

The book is filled with shaky innuendo. For example, it attaches unmerited importance to the fact that immediately after Natalie drowned, a TV episode of *Hart to Hart* was based on a (fictitious) murder victim who, coincidentally, drowned. No final "payoff" in terms of definitive answers ever emerges from a reading of the book.

Many of Natalie's fans, including Peter Winkler of North Hollywood, greeted the book with skepticism. "Suspicion that Robert Wagner threw his wife overboard or intended to murder her is ridiculous. He notified the harbor patrol in enough time to find his wife alive, when she could have conceivably accused her husband of attempted murder."

Actually, Winkler's assessment is not true. As mentioned previously, Natalie was discovered missing at around 10:30pm, but it wasn't until three hours later that Wagner called for help.

Surely, after the passage of three hours, no one expected to find Natalie alive. She would either have drowned or succumbed to hypothermia.

Another reader who identified herself only as "Jeanne," summed up the case logically. "We are supposed to believe that Walken slept through both the loud music and the loud violent fight between R.J. and Natalie. [I'm] not buying that one. If Davern saw/heard the violent fight, why did he not come to Natalie's defense? He could have gotten Walken to help. In another biography, Davern stated that he saw/heard Natalie in the water, crying out for help. Now he says he never saw her in the water. I think everyone involved is still lying. The very sad truth is that there were three men on the boat and not one of them did anything to save Natalie."

Many readers felt that lurid speculation about Wagner's possible involvement in Natalie's death is not fair either to him or to his children. Jason Crawford posted a statement on Amazon.com, saying that he hopes there will be "no more books about the death of Natalie Wood until one of the three men aboard the yacht that night is ready to tell the truth—and all of it."

In the wake of new revelations, Natalie's sister, Lana Wood, has asked the Los Angeles coroner to re-open the case of her sister's drowning.

Lana told CNN that she believed an animated argument between her sister and Wagner on the yacht's rear deck occurred right before Natalie's drowning. Dennis Davern also claims that Natalie's death was a direct result of the fight with her husband.

"My sister was not a swimmer," Lana claimed. "She did not know how to swim. She would never go to another boat or to shore dressed in a nightgown and socks."

In their respective accounts of the drowning, Davern and Wagner gave two very different accounts in their memoirs. But regardless of which account is accurate, the title of the Davern/Rulli book (*Goodbye Natalie, Goodbye Splendour*) evokes its sadness.

In our view, the death of Natalie Wood will forever remain a mystery, evoking the shadowy demise of another screen goddess, Marilyn Monroe, and the legends her passing evoked as well.

Dennis Davern, depicted to the immediate right during happier days, was the captain of the ill-fated *Splendour* on Natalie Wood's final voyage.

"There was a whole lot of tension and jelousy, Davern said, recalling the ill-fated voyage. "R.J. was mad that Natalie had invited Walken aboard. I believe Natalie and Walken were having an affair."

Did Audrey Hepburn Have an Affair with Capucine?

AND WAS THE LESBIAN ACTRESS TRANSGENDERED?

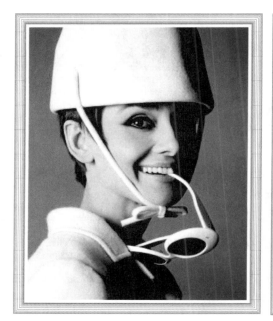 

No she did not

"I used to think I needed a man to define myself—no more."　　　　　　　　**—Capucine**

"Titism has taken over the country. But Audrey Hepburn, single-handed, may make bozooms a thing of the past."　　　　**—Billy Wilder** (Hepburn's director in *Love in the Afternoon*; 1957)

"Audrey Hepburn is the patron saint of anorexics."　　　　　　　　　　**—Orson Welles**

"She is every man's dream of the nymph he once planned to meet."　　**—Theater Critic Walter Kerr**

"For a slim figure, share your food with the hungry."　　　　　　　　**—Audrey Hepburn**

Capucine & Audrey Hepburn

THE TWO MOST BEAUTIFUL FACES OF THE 20TH CENTURY

"She had a face to launch a thousand ships, but she was born too late." That was film director Frederico Fellini speaking, summing up the brief career of the French actress Capucine (1928-90), who in the 1960s and 70s blazed across the screen like a shooting star before flickering out.

The world has more or less forgotten who Capucine was, but her best friend Audrey Hepburn endures. Movie fans may still be watching *Breakfast at Tiffany's* (1961) a hundred years from now.

Just who was this Capucine, whose name translates from the French as "nasturtium?"

Born in Toulon, along the Mediterranean coast of France, on January 6, 1931, she became a fashion model and an actress known mainly today for her roles in *The Pink Panther* (1963) and *What's New Pussycat?* (1965).

With her classic patrician features and a rather non-conformist personality, she appeared in 36 feature films. She was hailed as one of the greatest beauties of the 20th century.

Director Billy Wilder called the bonding of Audrey Hepburn and **Capucine** "one of the greatest female friendships of the 20th Century." In one reckless moment, Audrey told the fabled director, "I'm only half a woman. To know the other half of me, you must know Capucine. She supplies me with my daily oxygen."

For reasons known only to himself, the usually reliable biographer, Donald Spoto, in his tome, *Enchantment: The Life of Audrey Hepburn*, devotes little more than a paragraph to the two dazzling beauties, noting that they shared William Holden as a lover and "were both prone to bouts of serious depression."

In 1967 Susan Hayward appeared with Capucine in the 1967 crime comedy *The Honey Pot*. Hayward claimed that Capucine told her, "Audrey and I on many a night have rescued the other from the brink of suicide."

But Audrey, her best friend, did even better. Evian, whose bottled waters have been purifying people's complexions for decades, named her "the most beautiful woman of all time."

"I was always a dreamer," Capucine said when she was still known as Germaine Lefebvre. "I will go farther in the world than the other girls here in Toulon, because I can dream harder than they do."

She stood an angular five feet, seven inches. With her elegant figure and long straight nose, she thought she'd be ideal as an actress or a high-fashion model in Paris, so she stole some money and ran away from home. "My first photographer compared my high cheekbones to that of an early Picasso painting," she said.

In Paris in the late 40s her features were also compared in a classic sense to the bust of the Egyptian queen, Nefertiti, that rests today in a museum in Berlin.

One of the most enduring legends—call it a rumor—was the accusation that the stunning

French actress was transsexual. The rumor persists to this day, having made its first appearance in print in a 1992 publication called *The Hollywood Death Book.*

There is a certain irony to the transsexual rumor. Nearing the end of her life by suicide, Capucine admitted that she was not only a lesbian—in spite of her affairs with men—but that she was in love with her best friend, Audrey Hepburn.

At the age of nineteen, Capucine made her 1949 film debut in the French picture, *Rendez-vous de juillet.* On the set she met actor Pierre Trabaud. They would marry the following year, although the union was a disaster, lasting for only six months.

Trabaud was brilliant at voices, and was the eternal French-language voice of the cartoon sailor, Popeye. He was also the French-language voice of Daffy Duck and even Marlon Brando in the French release of *On the Waterfront* (1954).

The major source of the transgendered rumor about Capucine came from her one and only husband himself. He never spoke to the press but asserted to his male friends in Paris that when he'd married Capucine, she was a transvestite who later underwent male-to-female surgery in a hospital in Geneva. Although in some ways it appears as a bizarre act of slander, the accusation that she'd been born a male with an undeveloped penis has to be given some credence.

Throughout his life, Trabaud preferred sex with transvestites or transsexuals and was rather frank about his preference. His belief was that drag queens or else transsexuals "give a man a better time in bed than a regular woman. They do more, give more of themselves, know more ways to pleasure a man."

He compared his pursuit of transvestites or transsexuals to studly men in ancient Egypt who preferred to sodomize a man who had had both his penis and his testicles removed. "Those Egyptian men knew that a completely castrated male who could get no enjoyment with the front part concentrated all their sexual energy into their rear door," Trabaud said.

The comparison doesn't quite hold up, but that was his expressed belief.

Death came to Trabaud in 2005 when he was living in France's Hauts-de-Seine region, and he went to his grave maintaining what was either the truth or else an enduring and consistent campaign of slander about his former wife.

Both of them models, Capucine met Audrey in Paris

As an *haute couture* model, **Capucine** *(both photos above)* prepared to confront those Hollywood movie cameras of the future. " The camera has a love affair with her face," said gay director George Cukor.

When she did become a movie star, Capucine said, "Every time I get in front of a camera, I think of it as an attractive man I am meeting for the first time. I find him demanding and aloof, so I must do all in my power to interest him. Men look at me like I'm a suspicious looking trunk, and they're customs agents.

"All the closeted Hollywood lesbians called me for a rendezvous. Did you know that Judy Garland had lesbian tendencies? Well, more than tendencies really."

and almost from the start of their relationship swore to each other "to become best friends for life."

Born in Belgium on May 4, 1929, Audrey was the daughter of a banker and a Dutch baroness, both of whom were Nazi sympathizers.

During their struggling days, Capucine and Audrey shared an apartment while they both pursued careers as models. That presumably was the beginning of their lesbian link, promoted more by Capucine's desires than those of Audrey.

In 1952, Capucine got a two-week job modeling the latest clothes aboard a French cruise ship. She shared a cabin with a stunning 17-year-old dancer, who was working in the chorus of the ship's nightclub. Her name was Brigitte Bardot.

Back in Paris, Capucine modeled for such *haute couture* houses as Dior and Givenchy.

When Audrey or Capucine wandered into "deep, deep darkness, a stairway to a dark gulf," as Audrey characterized it, "Cap and I were there for each other." She referred to Capucine, who was a manic-depressive, by the nickname of "Cap."

Capucine rescued Audrey when actor Ben Gazzara walked out on her. "Obviously I wasn't in love," he claimed. "I was flattered that someone like that would be in love with me. But I didn't know how deeply in love with me until I left her. She told others, not me, that I had broken her heart." After his departure, she wanted to kill herself.

Rumor of an affair between **Gregory Peck** and **Audrey Hepburn** during the making of *Roman Holiday* (1953) have persisted for decades. "I liked her a lot," Peck said. "In fact, I loved Audrey. It was easy to love her."

Biographers have suggested that James Hanson was arriving every weekend in Rome to spend with Audrey, and that Peck was enchanted by his *inamorata*, Veronique Passani, a French journalist whom he took for his second wife.

Director William Wyler dismissed such evidence. "These naïve souls are blissfully unaware of the mating habits of Hollywood stars. Peck himself told me he was fucking Audrey every chance he got. The only problem, at least according to him, was that her honeypot was a bit tight to accommodate him. Ingrid Bergman, on the other hand, had no problem at all in handling it."

Breakfast at Tiffany's was the most famous novel that Truman Capote ever wrote. As Holly Golightly, **Audrey Hepburn** mesmerized audiences. "Truman was my friend, and I was so terribly disappointed when he claimed that I was wrong for the role. He really wanted Marilyn Monroe to play Holly. Sometimes in life, we don't always get our wish, now do we?"

The part became Audrey's signature role, and in a wardrobe designed by her friend Hubert de Givenchy, she became a fashion icon. *Women's Wear Daily* dubbed her "Queen of Chic."

George Peppard, the handsome blond stud, privately known as "Mighty Meat," said, "In my role as a struggling young writer, I was supposed to be the kept boy of the predatory Patricia Neal. I never fucked her, but I can't say the same about Audrey. She was a little vixen."

Long before she actually committed suicide, Capucine made at least four attempts to kill herself. On each of these occasions, Audrey was said to have rushed to her friend's bedside, in each instance strengthening her will to live.

Audrey eventually migrated to Hollywood and, after a few minor pictures, emerged as a big star in the 1953 *Roman Holiday*, playing opposite Gregory Peck. The generous actor insisted she share star billing with him.

Shortly thereafter, at Paramount, Billy Wilder cast *Sabrina* (1954), with Humphrey Bogart, William Holden, and Audrey. Although Bogie seemed to be jealous of the mating, Holden and Audrey fell in love.

Holden told friends, "I was already in love with her screen image before I met Audrey. I fell madly in love with her in spite of my marriage. When Bogart was rude to her, I almost beat the shit out of him. I wanted to protect Audrey—be her guardian, her best friend, her lover. It happened before we could stop it."

On the set of *Sabrina*, it was scriptwriter Ernie Lehman who first discovered the Hepburn/Holden affair. He walked into Holden's dressing room unannounced and caught the stars together.

At one point, Holden planned to leave his wife Brenda (Ardis) Marshall, an actress herself.

Audrey fell in love with Holden, and even told some of her closest friends, "I think we could make beautiful babies together."

Holden had to tell her the truth: He'd had a vasectomy after the birth of the second of his two sons, and could have no more children. She was devastated. She desperately wanted to have children and told Holden she couldn't marry him.

Shortly after this painful separation from "my true love," she met actor Mel Ferrer and fell in love with him.

When **William Holden** first met **Capucine** during the filming of *The Lion* in Kenya, he told his colleagues, "She's so marvously ornamental—when her mouth is shut. Audrey may like her boring stories. I do not."

When Holden's wife Brenda flew out of Kenya, her husband's affair with Capucine resumed in earnest and would last on and off for two years.

At one point she asked him, "Why do you drink so much?" He answered her: "Call it inner turmoil."

Holden eventually changed his opinion of Capucine, telling the crew, "She is the most beautiful woman in the world."

Holden and Capucine are pictured with the lion **Zamba**. "Not one of the Kenya lions would take direction," Holden claimed. "We had to fly in tame old Zamba from Hollywood for the shoot."

On the set of *The 7th Dawn*, **William Holden** looks like he's sodomizing **Capucine**, but he's not. Nevertheless, during the shoot, drunk or not, he invited her to share his bed, and she willingly agreed to it. He was separated at the time from Brenda (Ardis), and he had no reason to conceal his affair with Capucine from the crew. Soon all of Hollywood was talking about the affair, at least those who had learned about it during the making of *The Lion*.

Who was the gossip monger? None other than Brenda's closest friend, **Nancy Reagan**. She and Ronald Reagan had flown to Kenya for a reunion with Holden, Ronald's dear friend, Nancy later claimed, "What was going on between Bill and Capucine was more than just one fling." It was around this time that Holden filed for a legal separation from Brenda. The press was filled with stories that he was set to marry Capucine after the finalization of a divorce from his wife.

As a wannabe star in the Hollywood firmament, Ferrer, born in 1917, might be called an "also ran." He is known mainly today for his appearance in the classic *War and Peace* (1956).

"After Audrey refused to marry me," Holden said, "I fucked my way around the world. My goal was to screw a girl in every country I visited. I'd had practice being a whore. When I was a young actor starting in Hollywood, I used to service actresses who were older than me." He was definitely referring to Barbara Stanwyck, with whom he'd starred in *Golden Boy* in 1939. "I'm a whore. All actors are whores. We sell our bodies to the highest bidders."

Holden was candid in naming some of his biggest conquests, who had included Lucille Ball, Susan Hayward, Grace Kell y, Dorothy Lamour, and Shelley Winters. "But my biggest conquest was the lady herself, Jacqueline Kennedy."

When Holden began a torrid affair with Grace Kelly on the set of *The Country Girl* (1954), he momentarily forgot about Audrey, although they would reunite later.

In 1956, in Paris and bored, Capucine flew to America, where she obtained a job as a model. One night at New York's Pavilion, she by chance met John Wayne and his agent/producer Charles K. Feldman. Feldman was fascinated by this stunning creature and signed her to a contract. She agreed to return to Hollywood with him where he installed her as his mistress and signed her up for English and acting lessons with Russia-born actor Gregory Ratoff, most famous for his role as Max Fabian in *All About Eve* (1950).

"Feldman really launched the career of Capucine," said director George Cukor. "He was not only a great star maker, but a major film producer—*The Glass Menagerie*

The night before this picture was taken on the set of *Sabrina*, **Audrey Hepburn** and **William Holden** were not dressed up. In fact, they were naked in bed together. The other star of the picture, Humphrey Bogart, became so jealous that he made the rest of the shoot difficult. "I wish Cary Grant, my first choice for Bogie's role, had accepted," Wilder said. "Bogie was a pain in the ass. He was incredibly hostile." Wilder had lost relatives during the Holocaust, but Bogie called him "Kraut bastard" or "Nazi."

In front of the cast, Bogie ridiculed Audrey and did devastating impressions of her. On the other hand, Holden fell more deeply in love with her each day. "I wanted to be all things to her," he said. "Most of all, her lover. But also her big brother, even her father, and most definitely her guardian angel."

(1950), *A Streetcar Named Desire* (1951), *The Seven Year Itch* (1955), and the James Bond film adaptation of *Casino Royale* (1967)."

Cukor cited the list of stars and directors Feldman handled—not only Wayne himself, but George Stevens, Claudette Colbert, Irene Dunne, and Charles Boyer. "Let's not leave out Audrey Hepburn, Capucine's closest gal pal."

Cukor said, "Capucine didn't want to go to bed with Feldman any more than I did, but she used him to get ahead."

Feldman engineered a contract for Capucine with Columbia Pictures, landing her the co-starring role in *Song Without End* (1960), with the homosexual English actor, Dirk Bogarde, cast as the 19th-century composer, Franz Liszt.

Although Bogarde and Capucine got off to a chilly start, he later became one of her best friends. She was a frequent visitor at his farmhouse in Provence, France, and they confided their secrets to each other.

One secret was so hot that Bogarde could not keep it to himself. Capucine confessed to him that she was "an occasional lover" of Audrey Hepburn. Bogarde told only trusted gay friends, who were not as discreet as he assumed they'd be. Soon, details of a possible Capucine/Hepburn romance spread across cinematic and theatrical circles in London, making their way via New York to Hollywood.

After *North to Alaska* (1960), with John Wayne, Capucine signed to appear in *Walk on the Wild Side* (1962), in which she played a prostitute and the lesbian lover of Barbara Stanwyck.

Reviewed as "lurid, tawdry, and sleazy" by *The New York Times*, *Walk on the Wild Side* was directed by Edward Dmytryk from a Nelson Algren novel. It starred Laurence Harvey, Capucine, Jane Fonda, Anne Baxter, and Barbara Stanwyck, an all-star cast.

During the filming of *Walk on the Wild Side*, Stanwyck was dating some younger woman. But apparently they had a fight. Stanwyck then turned her attention to Capucine, who seemed more than willing to have an affair.

Capucine and Anne Baxter briefly became friends. "One night when I was drunk I reckless-ly decided to ask Capucine those two questions that insid-er Hollywood had always wanted to know. She did not admit to being a transsexual; however, she did say that when she was a very young girl there was 'a surgical adjustment.' She never explained exactly what that meant."

"She also told me that she'd had a long-running affair with her best friend, Audrey Hepburn," Baxter claimed.

"Audrey is not a lesbian but she gives in to me on occasion," Capucine confided. "Obviously I'm the butch one in the relationship. Audrey is definitely the fem. She couldn't be anything else."

"Right now I'm involved with Stanwyck," Capucine confessed. "Ten years ago it was Marilyn Monroe and Stanwyck."

Capucine was referring to the 1952 film, *Clash by Night* that had starred Stanwyck, Paul Douglas, Robert Ryan, Monroe, and Keith Andes.

"Stanwyck told me that Monroe sometimes allowed herself to be seduced by women," Capucine claimed. "Monroe admitted to Stanwyck that she'd had a brief fling with her friend, Joan Crawford. But Crawford wanted to pursue the affair, and Monroe bolted, or so I heard."

"Crawford also came on to me," Capucine told Baxter, "but I rejected her advances. I find Stanwyck more appealing. There's no kissing called for between Barbara and me in this film. We reserve that for off the set."

The relationship didn't last until the end of the shoot. Stanwyck mistakenly assumed that Capucine, who was spending more and more time with Baxter, was having an affair with her co-star. "There was a bitter fight one after-noon between Capucine and Stanwyck coming from

Peter Sellers appeared in two of **Capucine**'s most successful films, *The Pink Panther* in 1963 and *What's New, Pussycat?* in 1965. The latter film was conceived as a star vehicle for Warren Beatty, the title, *What's New, Pussycat?*, based on his way of answering the telephone.

When producer Charles K. Feldman assigned Woody Allen to write the script, he beefed up his own role at the expense of Beatty's. Beatty then told both Feldman and Allen to "go fuck yourselves."

Sellers showed Capucine erotic photos he'd taken of himself and some of his leading ladies. One of them wasn't exact-ly a leading lady but was widely known throughout Buckingham Palace. She was Princess Margaret.

Stanwyck's dressing room," Baxter said. "All of us on the set could hear it. After that, Capucine and Stanwyck spoke only on camera."

After the filming ended, Capucine probably resented having told Baxter so many personal details of her life. "I encountered Capucine one night at a party," Baxter said. "Even though we'd worked together and had gone out boozing together, she coldly shook my hand. She acted as if she were nobility, and I was being introduced into her royal presence. She was such a bitch to me, that's why I don't mind spilling one or two of her secrets. Call it revenge on my part. After all I played Eve Harrington."

In one of those Hollywood ironies, Capucine was about to go from Stanwyck's bed into the bed of one of Stanwyck's former lovers. This time it was a male, William Holden. Capucine had been cast opposite Holden in *The Lion* (1962). Even though he was still married to the long-suffering Brenda (aka Ardis), Holden fell in love with the French beauty.

Perhaps because she'd heard rumors of an affair, Holden's wife showed up on the set in Kenya, whereupon the crew reported violent arguments between the couple. After Brenda flew back to California from Kenya, the Holden/Capucine affair resumed. The actor felt great guilt. He was not only betraying his wife, but Charles Feldman was one of his best friends. However, he didn't let such guilt keep him from pursuing Capucine.

Whenever he thought about his guilt, he drank even more heavily. He also contracted hepatitis in Kenya. He was taken in a stretcher to Italy for treatment at the Montecatini Terme in Tuscany.

Capucine visited him daily. He later called her "my Florence Nightingale."

In the meantime, Audrey had acquired a new lover, and it was the biggest secret in Washington. The name of her new admirer was John F. Kennedy, and he was the sitting President of the United States.

Kennedy had publicly stated, "My all-time favorite actress is Miss Audrey Hepburn." Privately he told his Boston pals, "Jackie, on the other hand, has the hots for this Warren Beatty."

Capucine lived through every detail of Audrey's new affair, which seemed to have escaped the attention of most biographers.

One year after Marilyn Monroe sang "Happy

Anne Baxter

WALK ON THE WILD SIDE

LAURENCE HARVEY
CAPUCINE
JANE FONDA
ANNE BAXTER
AND
BARBARA STANWYCK

"Hiring Barbara Stanwyck to play a lesbian in *Walk on the Wild Side* was typecasting," said **Anne Baxter** *(top photo, above)*. "But I was horribly miscast as Teresina Vidaverri, a sexually starved Mexican widow who operates a small café. Where was Rita Moreno?"

Walk on the Wild Side was the first A-list film to openly feature lesbianism on the screen. By appearing in the movie, Stanwyck became the first American actress to portray a lesbian character in a feature film.

"The part should have gone to me," Baxter said. "By the way, I was pregnant during the shoot. Capucine had trouble kissing Laurence Harvey. I could also have played her role. I've been kissing gay men on the lips ever since I became a movie star."

Birthday, Mr. President," to JFK, Audrey sang "Happy Birthday, Dear Jack" to him. It was to be his final birthday. The date was May 29, 1963.

In November of that year, when the shots rang out in Dallas, Audrey was portraying Eliza Doolittle in the film version of *My Fair Lady*, which would be released the following year. The news came over a portable radio carried by director George Cukor. "I was too shaken to announce the President's death," Cukor later recalled. "But brave little Audrey did the job for me."

She took a microphone and said, "The President of the United States is dead. Shall we have two minutes of silence to pray or do whatever you think is appropriate?"

Months later, she told Capucine, "I adored the man. I think I made a big mistake. My greatest role should have been First Lady of the land. Many members of the press claim that I have more grace, style, and flair than Jackie herself." This statement represents one of Audrey's rare cases of immodesty.

The year of the President's death, Capucine would enjoy her greatest success when she starred in *The Pink Panther* as the wife of the bumbling Inspector Clouseau (Peter Sellers). Secretly, her character dallies with the larcenous Pantherone (David Niven). Originally Ava Gardner was set to play the role. Capucine said, "Hollywood calls me the new Garbo. Actually I'm the new Ava Gardner." Two weak sequels followed for her, *Trail of the Pink Panther* in 1982 and *Curse of the Pink Panther* in 1983.

Shortly after JFK's death, Holden was apprehensive when he was cast opposite his former lover, Audrey in *Paris When It Sizzles* (1964). Tony Curtis and Marlene Dietrich appeared as guest stars, as did Mel Ferrer, whom Audrey had married in 1954.

Audrey resumed her affair with Holden, telling him that her decade-long marriage to Ferrer was "on the rocks." Friends speculated that she was also trying to make Ferrer jealous.

Capucine had already warned Audrey that Holden's drinking was destroying his life, and Audrey saw up close what alcohol was doing to a man that she still loved, at least in some part of her heart. She didn't seem the least bit jealous that Holden had been involved with her best friend, Capucine.

The *über*-sophisticated English playwright and gossip, Noël Coward, was cast as the third lead in *Paris When It Sizzles*. Coward and Holden bonded and hung out together. Holden knew that the playwright was one of England's stateliest homos, but had no problem with that.

"Like Audrey and Capucine, I too fell in love with Bill Holden during the shoot," Coward said. In his diary, Coward wrote, "Bill, off the bottle and looking 15 years younger,

Stefanie Powers, William Holden's last lover, was gracious enough to invite **Capucine** *(photo above)* for a farewell gathering on the first Sunday after Holden's death.

Robert Wagner showed up with Natalie Wood. Blake Edwards and Julie Andrews were among the guests, as was Patti Davis, the daughter of Ronald and Nancy Reagan. She had been Holden's goddaughter. Close friends James Stewart and Richard Widmark also attended.

Billy Wilder told Capucine, "I really loved Bill, but it turned out I just didn't know him. If somebody had said to me, 'Holden's dead,' I would have assumed that he had been gored by a water buffalo in Kenya, that he had died in a plane crash approaching Hong Kong, that a crazed woman had shot him and he drowned in a swimming pool like I directed him in *Sunset Blvd*. But to be killed by a bottle of vodka and a night table—what a lousy fadeout for a great guy."

absolutely charming. We exchanged confidences and bottles of *eau de cologne*."

Perhaps out of jealousy, perhaps just to be wicked, Coward may have been the first to tell Holden that Capucine was a transsexual. Later he confided in his lover Graham Payn, "Bill showed no surprise. He candidly admitted that once or twice on drunken nights he'd fucked a transvestite, and had received a number of blow-jobs from girly men over his long career."

Holden told Coward, "If Capucine is a transsexual, it'll be my first—and how lucky I am to try one out. A new experience for me. Before the grave, I want to try everything at least once."

Holden was delighted to learn that Capucine would be co-starring with him in *The 7th Dawn* (1964) for United Artists. Their torrid affair resumed.

With Capucine at his side, helping him get through the night, Holden stayed barely sober enough to get through the filming. She later confessed to author Boze Hadleigh that Holden "loved me more than I desired him."

Michael Goodliffe, an English actor born in 1914, befriended Capucine on the set of *The 7th Dawn*. Like her, he too suffered from the most severe bouts of depression. According to him, "We had long talks about our shared darkness," he later said. "I think she was in love with Holden but would have left him in a minute if Audrey had called her."

Goodcliffe admitted that he had discussed suicide with Capucine. "We both planned to do it one day, but the question was when."

While rehearsing for the London revival of the play *Equus* in 1996, Goodliffe had a nervous breakdown and was hospitalized at the Atkinson Morley Hospital in Wimbledon, outside London. On March 20 of that year, he jumped to his death from the hospital fire escape.

At the end of production on *The 7th Dawn*, Holden collapsed from excessive drinking. He was flown to Switzerland, where he was immediately hospitalized.

During the filming, however, and in a drunken state, he delivered a bombshell, telling fellow actor Allan Cuthberton that "I on occasions have a three-way with Audrey and Capucine."

Was this a drunken actor's fantasy, or was he actually admitting to a dark secret that has been rumored about in Hollywood for years?

He also claimed that he "got excited watching Audrey and Capucine get it on with each other."

Cuthberton, a British-Australian actor, was stunned at this revelation, but not to the extent that he kept it to himself. Soon the entire cast was gossiping about Holden's private life.

In 1965, after the flop of the unmemorable *The 7th Dawn*, another hit was in store for Capucine. Written by Woody Allen, *What's New Pussycat?* became one of her biggest films, starring Peter Sellers and Peter O'Toole.

By the mid-1960s, the Hepburn/Ferrer marriage had more or less collapsed, and Audrey in 1969 had married an Italian psychiatrist, Andrea Dotti. Throughout their marriage he maintained frequent affairs with younger women. Dotti died in October of 2007 from complications from a colonoscopy. Ferrer would die the following year, having reached the age of ninety.

In her final years, Audrey was living in Switzerland with the actor Robert Wolders.

In his own final years, suffering from lung cancer, Holden was alone and intoxicated in his apartment in Santa Monica. He apparently slipped on a throw rug, tumbling to the floor and lacerating his head on a night table. Too weak to summon help, he bled to death.

His body wasn't found until November 16, 1981, four days later. He was only 63 years old, but looked in his late 70s because of his long bouts of alcoholism. He was cremated and his ashes scattered over the Pacific.

When his will was read, it turned out that he'd left $50,000 for Capucine.

Two years later, in 1982, Capucine made a softcore movie, *Aphrodite*, appearing in a nude scene. Even those *Pink Panther* sequels had not rescued her flickering career.

Throughout her life Capucine suffered from a bipolar disorder. In 1990, having operated from a base in Lausanne, Switzerland, for a number of years, she committed suicide there at the age of 59, jumping to her death from the window of her eighth floor apartment.

The New York Times reported that her only survivors were three cats she left behind. Before her fatal jump, she left plenty of food out for the felines.

Capucine managed to steal one final heart before her fatal plunge. In the final months of her life, a star-struck young Swiss teenager fell madly in love with her and stalked her. She spurned his advances. After she died, he went into a morbid depression from which he never recovered, eventually committing suicide a year after her death.

Devastated by the death of Capucine, Audrey learned that her own life was drawing to a close. At her home in Tolochenaz, in the French-speaking Vaud region of Switzerland, she fought a brave battle against appendiceal cancer. At the age of 63, she died on January 20, 1993.

"I am too young to die," she wrote to her friends at UNICEF two weeks before death came.

During her final years she had became known for her association with UNICEF, working with them between 1988 and 1992 in disadvantaged communities in Asia, South America, and Africa.

In 1999 she was ranked as the third greatest female star of all time by the American Film Institute.

The "little black dress" she'd worn in *Breakfast at Tiffany's*, designed by Hubert de Givenchy, sold at Christie's on December 5, 2006, for nearly a million dollars, the highest price ever paid for a dress from a film.

The money was sent to the City of Joy Aid charity to help underprivileged children in India. The head of the charity said, "There are tears in my eyes. I am absolutely dumbfounded to believe that a piece of cloth which belonged to such a magical actress will now enable me to buy bricks and cement to put the most destitute children in the world into schools."

William Holden's Other Movie Star Lovers

Barbara Stanwyck (*left figure in photo, right*), who starred with **William Holden** (*right*), in the 1939 *Golden Boy*, was his original "cougar." Once he seduced Stanwyck, he continued a pattern of bedding leading ladies of the screen, including the sarong siren, **Dorothy Lamour,** when he appeared with her in *The Fleet's In (1942)*.

When 1949 rolled around, he was seducing **Lucille Ball** offscreen when they filmed *Miss Grant Takes Richmond.*

Other than Audrey Hepburn, his greatest love was **Grace Kelly,** with whom he had an affair when they co-starred together in *The Country Girl (1954)*.

He also seduced the usually-hot-to-trot **Shelley Winters,** by mutual agreement, every consecutive Christmas Eve for seven years in a row. *(continued on next page)*

I Love Lucille Ball

Dorothy Lamour

Grace Kelly

Shelley Winters

Jacqueline
Kennedy
Onassis

Susan Hayward

Gail Russell

Diana Lynn

Stefanie Powers

(continued from previous page)

Holden and **Susan Hayward** hit the sack together when they shared the same press agent, Jay Bernstein. Both stars had been Bernstein's childhood favorites.

Holden's affair with **Gail Russell**, and also with **Diana Lynn**, was conducted mostly at Lucey's, a one-time speakeasy located beside Melrose Avenue in Los Angeles. Holden's "beard" during his maintenance of those two affairs was Lucey's owner, Steve Crane, the former husband of Lana Turner.

When Holden took up residence in Switzerland in 1959 as a means of avoiding high US income taxes, he became the object of public vituperation. Even the future US Attorney General, Robert F. Kennedy, cited Holden as an example of "the rich who pervert our tax laws." RFK's wife, Ethel, referred to Holden as "a traitor."

Holden confessed to Audrey Hepburn how he got even with RFK. "I had a brief fling with **Jackie Kennedy**," he claimed, "while she was married to Jack but before he was elected President. She had long told friends that she thought I was the sexiest man in Hollywood."

The actor's final affair was with **Stefanie Powers,** a beautiful Polish-American actress. When Holden met her, she was 32 years old. He caught her on the rebound after a failed marriage. "We became soulmates," she later said. "He helped make me back into a human being." Soon, the couple was spotted in Hong Kong, Malaysia, Singapore, Iran, New Guinea, London, Paris, and, finally, Africa. But where was she when his corpse lay rotting on the floor of his apartment for four days?

THE MAN WHO REDEFINED THE ART OF ACTING

Marlon Brando

He Was Bad, So Bad, So Very Very Bad

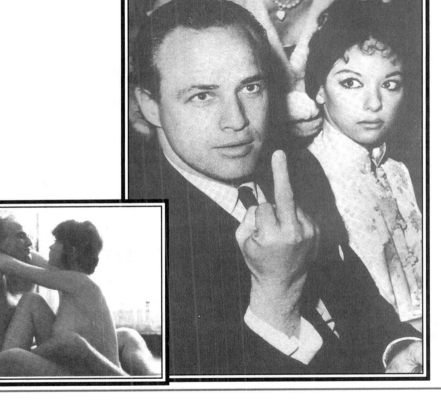

There has never been an actor quite like **Marlon Brando**. If he had as much disinterest in acting as he claimed on so many different occasions, it is baffling why he continued to be so damn mesmerizing, even right up until the end.

Giving a photographer the finger (above), Brando is seated next to actress **Rita Moreno**, who loved him. In the smaller photo on the left, he's naked and in the arms of **Maria Schneider** in his most controversial film, *Last Tango in Paris* (1972).

"I don't think I was constructed to be monogamous," Brando once declared. "I don't think it's in the nature of any man to be monogamous. Sex is the primal force of ours and every other species."

Brando was the "Rebel Without a Cause" who made rebellion hip. He electrified the world in such roles as *A Streetcar Named Desire,* a Broadway play in 1947, a movie in 1951, and in his Oscar-winning turn as Terry Malloy, the boxer who could have been a contender in *On the Waterfront* (1954). He once again electrified the world as Vito Corleone in his comeback picture, *The Godfather* (1972).

Marlon Brando & His (Female)

Fan/Cannibal

A concept that's increasingly in the news involves "celebrity stalking," and it's recognized as the price that many actors and actresses pay for their fame. And although it's an oft-repeated and sinister issue today, it was rarely heard of in the early 1950s.

An exception to that rule during that era revolved around Marlon Brando after his success at portraying Stanley Kowalski in the film *A Streetcar Named Desire*. Based on the smashing Broadway success, the film was released in 1951.

At the time, he had rented a small apartment in New York City on 6th Avenue at 57th Street, where he was constantly pestered by anonymous phone calls. The person on the other end would hang up without saying a word. This continued for three months. Finally, one night, he heard the delicate voice of a woman.

For three full hours, he kept her on the phone, learning that her profession was that of a "stick-up artist." She robbed liquor stores in New Jersey at night, fleeing on a motorcycle piloted by another woman friend who was "deaf and dumb," to quote her words.

She told Brando that for months, she'd had a fixation on him, and that she'd plastered the walls of her bedroom with billboards from *Streetcar*. She kept his picture under her pillow every night, and talked to it. During their marathon first dialogue, she revealed that—with the help of her motorcyclist friend—she planned to kidnap him. They planned to take him to a remote boathouse she'd rented on Long Island, where they'd imprison him and gradually cannibalize him in a scene evocative of the modern-day film *Hannibal*.

At that point, most sane people might have put down the phone and called the police. But not Brando. Years

Scenes off screen (*above*) and on screen (*below*) with **Vivien Leigh** playing her Oscar-winning portrait of Blanche DuBois in Tennessee Williams' *A Streetcar Named Desire*. Playing a sweaty, coarse, rude, and vulgar Stanley Kowalski, **Brando** learns that Blanche finds his smell "objectionable."

During the shooting of the movie, Brando managed to seduce Blanche both on and off the screen, even taking time out to make love to her husband, Laurence Olivier. He wasn't shocked when Vivien told him, "As you'll get to know me, and I hope you will, there is nothing respectable about me. In London, I picked up taxi drivers and fucked them. Don't be surprised—I'm just as whorish as Blanche DuBois." He shot back, "I'm not all that respectable either. I'm every man's whore and every woman's seducer."

later, he recalled the event in interviews, claiming that he knew at the time that the woman was "deadly serious."

In spite of that, he invited her to his apartment. He took the precaution of opening the door with the chain attached. After he'd frisked her, he let her inside, despite the danger to himself.

She identified herself only as "Maria," and begged him to let her wash his feet. As she slowly and sensuously immersed his feet in warm water, he came to realize that in her fantasy, he'd become Jesus to her Mary Magdalene.

Brando later admitted that as she was drying his feet with her long hair, he became sexually aroused. That led to her seduction in his bedroom. In some bizarre (and supremely decadent) kind of reasoning, it became thrilling for him to seduce a women who thought that he was Jesus, and who wanted, literally, to devour his flesh.

After the sex act, he managed to get her out of his apartment, suggesting that she seek psychiatric help. He never let her inside his apartment ever again, although he often encountered her at two or three o'clock in the morning, waiting for him in his hallway. At their last and final meeting, Brando, "as Jesus," commanded her to go away and leave him alone. She did.

When he moved to Hollywood, firmly entrenched in his status as a movie star, he tracked her down to see what had become of her. He finally reached her brother in New Jersey, who informed him that Maria had come home one night covered in blood as if she'd tried to lacerate herself with shards of broken glass. In this condition, she entered her bedroom, gathered up all the *Streetcar* and Brando memorabilia, and outside, in their back yard, ignited them into flames.

Back inside the house, she announced to her family, "Jesus is dead. He will never rise again."

Life imitates art, and there's plenty here to cannibalize. In the top photo, **Marlon Brando** plays the hard-drinking, larger-than-life Stanley Kowalski in *A Streetcar Named Desire*. Below, decades later, he is indeed larger than life. It is nearly impossible to explain to those who have seen Brando only as *The Godfather,* or as a bloated behemoth in his last films, how Brando's uninhibited carnality and skin-tight jeans shocked and astonished audiences in the late 40s and early 50s. He was the living, breathing embodiment of sexual desire in an era when movie censors forbade even the use of the word "virgin" on screen.

THE INCESTUOUS, PSYCHOTIC SUICIDE OF MARLON BRANDO'S DAUGHTER,

CHEYENNE

"The most beautiful, the most intelligent, and the richest girl in Tahiti."

That's how Marlon's daughter, Cheyenne Brando, described herself in 1995, the same year, on April 16, when she hung herself at the Brando estate at Punaauia in Tahiti. At the time of her death at the age of twenty-five, this former model "with the perfect figure" had gained so much weight she was almost as corpulent as her famous movie star father.

Her life was short and tragic. In the final years of her life, she became the focal point of one of the most notorious murders in Hollywood history, based on events swirling around the night of May 16, 1990, when Marlon's 32-year-old son, Christian Devi Brando, Cheyenne's half-brother, shot 26-year-old, Dag Drollet, her Tahitian lover.

Marlon's close friend, George Englund, accurately described Cheyenne: "She was a delicate riddle . . . luminously pretty, not large but with an almost aggressive beauty, black hair, dark eyes, and in those eyes an *anima* pulsing. In Marlon's female child, I was seeing the same penetrating stare, the offhand sexuality, the eyes that know—all the Brando hallmarks."

The story began in 1960 in Tahiti when Marlon met a beautiful Polynesian actress, Tarita Teriipaia, on the set of *Mutiny on the Bounty*. She would become his common law wife and the mother of two of his children, beginning with a son, Teihotu, born May 30, 1963.

When Marlon told Tarita that he wanted another baby to follow the birth of their son, he did not seduce her. Instead he took her to a medical specialist, and the baby was conceived by artificial insemination one hot afternoon in June of 1969. Following the birth of Cheyenne, it would take years for Marlon to officially recognize her and her older brother as his legitimate offspring.

Cheyenne's unusual name came from when Marlon flew Tarita and her baby girl to Washington,

TWO VIEWS OF CHEYENNE: In the top photo, **Marlon Brando** is seen cupping the developing breasts of his teenage daughter, **Cheyenne Brando.** He was on the dawn of beginning an incestuous relationship with her. In the photo below, a cigarette-smoking Cheyenne, fully grown up, has already developed a cynical mask to present to the world.

When Christian shot her lover, Dag Drollet, he got no moral support from his sister, Cheyenne. "My brother murdered Dag," she shouted at the arresting police. "It was pure, cold-blooded murder." What she failed to tell the police was that she had goaded him into the slaying. After the murder, Brando rushed his daughter back to Tahiti and into the hospital. After the birth of her baby, she attempted to overdose on sleeping pills.

D.C. for a convention of American Indians. He'd already asked and had gained permission from the Cheyenne Indians to borrow their name for his newly born daughter. Taking the baby from its mother, who sat near the rear of the hall and who was until then unaware of what he had planned, Marlon carried his daughter to the stage, facing Indians assembled from all over the country. There, he raised his daughter "to the Great Spirit" and announced that henceforth she'd be called Cheyenne Brando in honor of the tribe whose rights he championed.

In the 1980s, growing up in Tahiti, Cheyenne was emerging as a beautiful girl with high hopes for her future. She was good in school and ambitious in her career plans—Painter? Doctor? Actress? She was proud to be the daughter of Marlon Brando, remembering to send him presents on his birthday and on Father's Day, although she ignored her mother on those occasions. When she was old enough, she flew to Los Angeles to be with Marlon. At times he could be extremely affectionate toward her, buying her presents. At other times he could be relatively indifferent as when he refused to pay the bills for her school tuition.

No one knows for sure what happened to Cheyenne, but slowly and then more rapidly she seemed to undergo a major personality change, evolving from a Dr. Jekyll to a Ms. Hyde.

One friend in Tahiti said that Cheyenne as a teenager became hooked on drugs, a dependency she'd maintain until the end of her life. "She went from being a sweet girl to a monster. Although I considered myself as her best friend, I soon abandoned her. If I'd see her coming, I would cross the street to avoid her."

One afternoon in Tahiti, Cheyenne was confronted with a "new sister," Petra, who had been flown in from Los Angeles. She was two years younger than Cheyenne and had been conceived by Marlon with one of his secretaries. Learning that she was on "equal footing" with Petra, Cheyenne exploded in an angry, violent outburst in which she went through the house breaking anything breakable. That afternoon would mark the beginning of violent outbursts that would continue—along with her drug abuse—throughout the rest of her short life.

During one full-moon night in Tahiti—"fired up on angel dust"—Cheyenne met Dag Drollet, a Polynesian man, then only twenty-three years old and very handsome. It was at a disco bordering the sea in Papeete, in May of 1987. The coming together of Dag and Cheyenne would end tragically.

Their relationship quickly became passionate but stormy. Many of their fights were staged in public in local restaurants and dance clubs. One of their most violent public confrontations occurred in August of 1989.

Cheyenne Brando *(left)* is pictured with her lover, **Dag Drollet**, scion of a prominent Tahitian family. He was only 28 years old when Christian Brando murdered him.

In spite of the lies spread by Cheyenne, Dag was actually a gentle man. Christian shot him in the back of the head as he was adjusting the remote control for the TV. "I stood there watching the life go out of this guy," Christian later claimed.

Fleeing from Dag, Cheyenne jumped into a Jeep belonging to Christian Brando. She roared down a night road at 100mph, but lost control of the car, crashing into a ditch. The impact broke her jaw, and part of her ear was ripped off. A section of her face "just caved in."

Marlon didn't want Cheyenne to be operated on by Tahitian surgeons, so he flew her to Los Angeles for better medical care. There, California surgeons put seven metal plates into her head. After a twelve-hour stint on the operating table, Cheyenne's face was saved "but what about her soul?" her mother, Tarita, asked.

Flying back to Tahiti for the continuation of her recovery,

Cheyenne, according to her mother, Tarita, experienced a "degrading of personality." During one intense argument, Cheyenne hurled an ashtray at her mother, causing a severe facial injury.

At school, she physically attacked fellow students, even her teachers. Even though she'd moved in with Dag and his mother, Lisette, Cheyenne claimed that Dag frequently beat her. Because of her heavy drug usage, Tarita suspected that her daughter might be hallucinating.

At one point in 1989, Cheyenne confronted her mother, claiming that she was pregnant with Dag's child. Seven years older than Cheyenne, Dag was already the father of another illegitimate child. During the early months of her pregnancy, Cheyenne became "uncontrollable and unpredictable"—slapping waiters in cafés and shops, assaulting strangers on the street. "If my daughter had lived in a first world country," Tarita claimed, "she would have been judged as certifiably insane."

As Cheyenne's pregnancy advanced, Tarita's concerns grew. Cheyenne would often approach and then strike an innocent passerby. "The doctors told me that her pieced-together face was very fragile. If a stranger who endured an unexpected attack from Cheyenne were to strike her back, it might kill her, I was warned." When Tarita shared her concerns with Marlon, he responded, "My daughter is not sick."

Marlon wanted his grandson to be born in the United States, so he flew Tarita, Cheyenne, and Dag to his home on Mulholland Drive in Los Angeles. Dag (pictured below with Cheyenne) went along for the trip, although even before their child was born, he planned to tell Cheyenne that that he was going to leave her. He could no longer stand her violence and her drug abuse.

At the time, police authorities in Tahiti wanted Dag to return there to face a set of manslaughter charges unrelated to anything associated with Cheyenne. Driving drunk one night, he'd run over and killed an eight-year-old child getting out of a truck on a highway.

On hearing that his half-sister was in town, Christian called Cheyenne and invited her out to dinner at Frank & Musso, a well-known Hollywood restaurant. Dag was pointedly not invited, with the understanding that he'd remain behind and watch television in the den of the house on Mulholland Drive.

In the restaurant, over spaghetti, Cheyenne broke down in tears, falsely claiming that Dag was beating her even though she

TAHITI'S TARITA: THE LOCAL GIRL WHO INSPIRED MARLON TO *Mutiny Aboard His Bounty*

Tarita Teriipaia
Marlon Brando,
mon amour,
ma déchirure

In Tahiti, **Marlon Brando** was very busy the week he met his future wife, **Tarita Teriipaia**. He'd been busy sampling the *vahines* (glamorous Tahitian women) and some olive-skinned Polynesian young men in their teens. "Hetero or homo, all these boys gave in to my desires," he recalled back in Los Angeles. *In Mutiny on the Bounty*, he settled for a nineteen-year-old, Tarita herself, to play Fletcher Christian's South Sea *inamorata*. He bedded her the first night.

Regrettably, Brando had contracted gonorrhea, and he was spreading it around. The disease became so prevalent he had to fly in a doctor, an expert on venereal disease, to wipe out the plague he'd created. "Serum and antibiotics had to be flown in to stop the epidemic, and I regret that sincerely," he said.

was pregnant. Unknown to Christian, she'd only an hour previously, just before she left for the restaurant, told Dag that she was carrying Christian's baby—not Dag's child.

In the restaurant, she also told Christian that she was pregnant with his child. She'd been having intercourse on and off with him, her half-brother, during the previous seven years.

Driving back to Mulholland Drive, Christian stopped off at his girlfriend's house to retrieve an assault weapon, a SIG-Sauer .45 pistol—known as "the Porsche of handguns." After the passage of California's ban on assault weapons, Marlon had demanded, unsuccessfully, that his son bring the gun to the house on Mulholland Drive for safekeeping.

Reportedly, Christian arrived back at the house fuming in his anger at Dag's alleged assaults on his pregnant sister. With his assault weapon, Christian headed for the den. Although he would later claim that he struggled with Dag and the gun went off accidentally, in reality he may have shot Dag in the head without warning. Dag died instantly.

On the night of the murder (May 6, 1990), Tarita remembered waking up to the smell of smoke. She was immediately alarmed because she knew that her increasingly deranged daughter had developed a habit of setting fires, including one recently ignited within a laundry hamper. "She'd just sit back and watch the flames," Tarita said.

Marlon Brando made the cover of *Time* Magazine after the release of his notorious film, *Last Tango in Paris*. "I heard Marlon was doing porn," said playwright Tennessee Williams, "and I couldn't bear to watch it on screen. Poor Marlon. What has he become since the days he played Stanley Kowalski in a *A Streetcar Named Desire?* When he was on stage as Stanley, he was the sexiest man in the history of Broadway. Today, he's become a man no one wants to sleep with. It's good for me that I had Marlon in his prime. I'll always remember that night on the sandy beach in Provincetown. A war was raging around the world, but the only explosion I heard was Marlon blasting into me."

In the right-hand photo above, Marlon got *lei'd* upon his return to Tahiti—"my favorite spot in all the world. No matter how old and fat you get, these young Tahitian kids—boys and girls, are always willing to show a man a good time. Unlike kids in America, these boys and girls respect their elders."

As Tarita wandered through the darkened house, where all the lights uncharacteristically had been turned off, she saw a flickering light coming from the TV room. With trepidation, she entered the room and saw a body sprawled on the sofa. "He was drenched in blood," Tarita said. "I checked to see if he were alive. There was blood everywhere. On my hands, my throat, all over the couch." She began to scream to awaken the household.

Rushing to Marlon's bedroom, she found that Christian was already there, confessing the murder to his father. "Their image was grave," she said. "Marlon ordered me to stop screaming. I fainted dead away."

When she was revived, she remembered the house filled with police officers. She saw two of those policemen leading Christian away in handcuffs.

Surveying the murder scene in the den were homicide detectives, A.R. Monsue and Lee Kingsford, who had been among the first police officers to examine Dag's six feet, five-inch dead body sprawled on the sofa. Barefoot, he was clad in a pair of gray surfer shorts. After a hurried examination, Monsue determined that the fatal bullet had entered Dag's brain through his left cheek.

Kingsford remembered being astonished when he questioned Marlon. Instead of answering questions about what he knew about the slaying, Marlon kept diverting the dialogue for an overview about how he'd tried to be a good father to Christian and Cheyenne. "I've tried to be a good father to all of my nine children," he said. "Four of them are adopted, incidentally."

On the phone "day and night" talking to lawyers in the days and weeks that followed, Marlon was also besieged by the press. Angrily, he addressed this invasion, and Tarita heard his words. "One of the things that's the most difficult to understand is that in the midst of all this chaos, all this anguish, we had to face the press. Men are trying to make money off our family tragedy. In normal times, the press can make you suicidal. But under these circumstances, they become completely impossible."

To defend his son, Marlon hired Robert Shapiro, the famous attorney who would achieve notoriety during the O.J. Simpson trial after the June, 1994 murder of Ronald Goldman and Nicole Brown Simpson.

In a preliminary court hearing, Christian testified that Cheyenne "went off on this bizarre tangent and kinda got me going. Knowing what I know now of her mental state, I doubt whether she was ever beaten by Drollet. I feel like a complete chump for believing her."

Christian was placed in jail for three months while lawyers tried to get him released on bail.

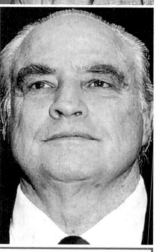

After the killing, Cheyenne flew back to Tahiti. Once on island, legal papers were delivered to her. The Drollet family was suing her as an "accessory" to the death of their son. In the days and weeks ahead, she made several suicide attempts. Complicating matters further, Marlon learned that because Dag's father, Jacques Drollet, had filed a $100 million wrongful death suit against both Christian and himself, he could be detained on Tahiti in the event that he decided to fly back there to comfort his daughter. Simultaneously, Drollet continued to press charges against Cheyenne in Papeete.

In Tahiti, eight months pregnant, Cheyenne found herself caught between Californian and Tahitian prosecutors, both of whom wanted her within their respective jurisdictions for questioning. On June 26, 1990, she gave birth to a baby boy named Tuki. A nurse told the local press, "Tuki was born drug addicted. All during her pregnancy, Cheyenne Brando continued to take drugs. The kid could have been born with brain damage. He had to be sent to detox."

While he was still in detox, Cheyenne wandered into the ward where her child was asleep. With no security guard in sight, she picked him up and carried him into the bathroom where she plunged the infant under a cold water faucet trying to drown him. The nurses rushed in to retrieve the baby, and managed to prevent her from killing the infant. Cheyenne than shifted the focus of her rage from the baby, and started to smash apart the furniture in

WHAT HE LOOKED LIKE AND WHAT HE CAME TO BE: Marlon Brando did not age gracefully, nor did he take care of his once spectacular body. Brando was at ease in his own skin long before even partial nudity was fashionable, and he was often quite the exhibitionist.

Early in his career, he appeared in the Jean Cocteau play, *The Eagle Has Two Heads,* opposite the theater's grande dame and great eccentric, the alcoholic and equally sexually ravenous Tallulah Bankhead. By the time the play was about to preview in Boston, Tallulah and Marlon knew the play was going to be a flop, referring to it as "The Turkey With Two Heads."

On opening night, Marlon showed his disdain for the production during one of Tallulah's long, dramatic monologues. He turned his back to the audience, spread his legs, unbuttoned his fly, and proceeded to urinate against the stage scenery. The audience could clearly see what he was doing, but Tallulah couldn't understand why they were laughing. When she found out what Marlon had done, she had him fired.

her room.

Her doctors committed her to the Vaiami Psychiatric Hospital. A doctor there told Tarita, "Don't worry about the baby. He's doing well in spite of his ordeal. Worry instead about the child's mother. She's the one who needs help."

On November 1, 1990, Cheyenne took a huge overdose of pills to kill herself. Only days before, a French judge in Tahiti, Max Gatti, had demanded that she not leave the country. She was to be tried in local courts as an accomplice to murder.

After having her stomach pumped, she survived that attempt on her own life. But on the night of November 14, she once again attempted suicide by tying a rope to a tree outside her bedroom window, the other to her neck. She then jumped. Miraculously, she also survived this attempt at hanging, although she remained in a coma for one week.

On February 26, 1991, in Southern California, Christian appeared at the Santa Monica Courthouse, telling his father, "I've been coming through these doors since I was a kid." He was referring, of course, to the vitriolic fights staged between Anna Kashfi, his mother, and Marlon over his custody. He pleaded guilty that day to a charge of voluntary manslaughter.

In what must be viewed as incredible understatement, Christian's psychiatrist, Dr. Saul Faerstein, testified: "Once an inquisitive and alert child, Christian has been damaged by his upbringing and chronic substance abuse. Despite the material advantages conferred by the Brando name, neither parent provided a stable, protective, and safe emotional environment for Christian to grow up in."

One of his probation officers took the stand to claim that Christian suffered "brain damage from alcohol and drug abuse as a youth. He was kidnapped several times by one or the other of his parents," the officer said. He also claimed that Christian was "molested by a hired kidnapper, and abused by his alcoholic, mentally ill mother. Christian is unassuming, low-profile, low self-esteemed."

Marlon through his lawyers secured his release, but only after mortgaging his house to post two million dollars in bail money. It was at this point that Marlon walked over to his son in the courtroom and planted a kiss on his head, an image of which was flashed around the world.

Having already pleaded guilty to manslaughter, Christian's trial was set for January of 1991.

Taking the stand, Marlon delivered an Academy Award performance, saying, "You always tend to blame the other parent, but I know that I could have done better."

In a bit of bizarre testimony, Marlon said, "As much as it may not be believed, I loved Dag. He was going to be the father of my grandchild. As they were carrying the boy out, I asked one of the officers to unzip the bag because I wanted to say good-bye to him properly. I kissed him and told him I loved him."

After seventy-five minutes of testimony from Marlon, Dag's father, Jacques Drollet, took the stand. He'd known Marlon for thirty years. "Brando is an actor," Drollet said. "He can cry and lie like a horse can run. He was acting up here on the stand. Does anyone believe a word of it?"

In spite of Marlon's plea for his son, Christian was sentenced to ten years at the California Men's Colony at San Luis Obispo, Christian served half that time before he was released on probation.

In Tahiti, on July 17, 1991, magistrate Max Gatti forced Cheyenne to testify for four hours. At the time, she said that her brother did not see her as a sister, "but as a young woman." The reference was clearly incestuous, which could establish a different motive for Dag's murder.

The judge found her completely irrational and unstable. Taking that into consideration, he granted Marlon's request to let her fly to the French mainland to enter a mental asylum in a western suburb of Paris. He also ruled that her passport should be deposited with the local police station after her arrival on the French mainland.

On the French mainland, Cheyenne underwent treatment for mental illness. During the weeks ahead, she showed some improvement.

Marlon flew to France and in direct defiance of the French court, smuggled her out of the asylum, taking her to a friend's home in the French city of Orléans. In that city, when Cheyenne saw her mother, Tarita, caring for her son, Tuki, after many months of separation, Cheyenne reacted violently. She bit Tarita's finger, practically severing it. Tarita bit her back. When Marlon came into the room, he discovered a mother and daughter at virtual war, and "blood everywhere."

On October 27, 1991 a warrant was issued for Cheyenne's arrest. French police located her living with Marlon in Orléans and arrested her. Marlon was not charged, presumably because at the time, his reputation was so high in France, even greater than it was in America, that French authorities anticipated a public outcry if he were incarcerated. Under armed guard, Cheyenne was flown back on a French military aircraft to Tahiti.

Facing a hearing on April 15, 1992, Cheyenne made the astonishing and headline-screaming charge that, "I am sure that my father asked Christian to kill Dag." It was at this same hearing that she claimed she "detested" Marlon and reported his sexual advances toward her. According to Cheyenne, her father tried to get her to go with him to a sea-bordering hotel in Santa Monica so he could "spend hours making love to me," but she refused to go with him.

Jocelyn Brando always lived in her brother's screen shadow, and she wanted to become a movie star like him. Alas, the dream, like most dreams, never came to be. After her marriage to Eliot Asinof crumbled, she began to drink heavily. "Like mother, like daughter," Marlon said to her.

Jocelyn once landed the single female role in *Mister Roberts*, and *Life* photographed them for a feature. The magazine's writer called Jocelyn "quiet and domestic," Marlon "unpredictable and moody:" Jocelyn was anything but. The night before the shoot, Marlon had invited his sister to see him work out in the ring with a young boxer who had momentarily caught his fickle fancy. His sister was somewhat surprised when Marlon insisted that the boxer join him in the ring in the nude.

In defiance of Marlon's efforts on her behalf, including trying to get treatment for her psychological disorders, Cheyenne constantly made indiscreet remarks to the press about her father. In one interview, she claimed, "Marlon Brando *is* the Godfather in the flesh, capable of manipulating others as he wants."

After endless dramas and international incidents worthy of a feature film, Tahitian Judge Jean-Bernard Taliercio, who had replaced Judge Gatti, dropped all charges against Cheyenne. The judged claimed they lacked merit.

With Christian in prison, Cheyenne no longer faced trouble with the Los Angeles police for fleeing to Tahiti. Marlon encouraged her to return to California. When she arrived, he placed her in a bleak mental asylum in San Francisco, where she languished for two full years before flying back to Tahiti in 1995.

Tarita, along with Cheyenne's son, Tuki, met her at the airport. But upon driving her back to Marlon's home, Cheyenne expressed undying hatred for her mother and threatened to kill her. She lunged at the wheel of the car and attempted to drive Tarita, herself, and her son off the highway as part of a murder/suicide attempt. There was a lot of blood in the car, as Cheyenne bit Tarita and Tarita bit back.

When she finally managed to get Cheyenne home, Tarita called the police and reported the incident. The police came for Cheyenne and hauled her away to the local insane asylum.

But she escaped in April of 1995, returning to Marlon's house. In her bedroom, Cheyenne rigged a rope to a beam in her bedroom ceiling, climbed into a chair, put the noose around her neck, then kicked away the support.

Cheyenne was buried in a granite vault high on a hill over-looking Papeete. Her grave is at the end of a long, arrowhead-shaped valley studded with mango trees and acacia. "Your soul is now in God's hands," said a priest in French over her grave.

Until the end of his life, Marlon claimed, "I'm being haunt-ed." He was so convinced that he was being pursued by the ghost of Dag that close friends thought he might be cracking up. He spoke of "cold ghastly lips" that came in the middle of the night to plant the kiss of death on his own mouth. According to Marlon, the ghost kept whispering in his ear, "I should not have died."

"It's terrifying!" Marlon told his friends. "I know it's Dag's angry spirit."

Eight months after Marlon's death, Tarita burst onto the world scene, publishing in French her autobiography entitled, *Marlon, mon amour, ma déchirure* (*Marlon, My Love and My Torment*). To demonstrate that her former spouse was interested in teenage sex, she maintained that Marlon became her lover when she was very young. However, in her autobiography, she downplayed Marlon's sexual interest in her daughter.

However, Cheyenne left a diary whose passages were wide-ly publicized after her death. In it, she wrote, "He (Marlon) used to like to massage me as if he wanted to pretend we were making love. He presented it as a game, but I was just a child and had no idea what he meant."

Cheyenne also claimed that her father fondled her breasts and "inserted his finger inside me," even after she became involved with Dag. At no point did she ever maintain that there was penile/vaginal intercourse, although she claimed that her father discussed and debated this possibility with her at length.

A friend in Tahiti, who did not want to be named, made the most bizarre charge of all. He said that Cheyenne told him that her father one night claimed that he wanted to become the father of "your next baby."

From a location in Paris, **Edward Dmytryk** directs **Marlon** in *The Young Lions* in which he appeared with bleached blond hair and a Nazi uniform. Marlon, between takes, paraded up and down the Champs-Elysées in full Nazi regalia, eliciting reactions that ranged from *ooh-la-la* sen-sational to outraged.

Playing opposite Marlon in the film was Montgomery Clift, his former lover from the 40s. "When I saw what bad shape Monty is in," he told Dmytryk, "I said to myself. There, Marlon, but for the grace of god go you." Marlon seemed to resent it when Monty spent most of his free time with the third male star of the picture, Dean Martin. "What does a macho man like Martin want with a homosexual like Monty? Monty has always been good at cock-sucking. Dean must be getting quite a workout."

211

BRANDO'S SON, *CHRISTIAN*

THE MURDER HE COMMITTED,
THE INCEST HE CITED,
HIS HIDEOUS CHILDHOOD,
& HIS TRAGIC EARLY DEATH

Christian Brando never wanted to pose for this police photograph. After murdering Dag Drollet, his sister's lover, Christian wanted to flee into the night. Marlon grabbed Christian and held him firmly, trying to calm the drug-induced hysteria that had overcome him. "They'll catch you," he warned his son. "They'll send their most ferocious hound dogs to get you. You might end up dead in a shoot-out. Stay and face them. I'll do everything I can to get you off. It was an accident after all, now wasn't it? Maybe an accident of the heart, but that's just between father and son."

He lived hard and died young. He was Christian Brando, the bad boy son of the late acting icon Marlon Brando and the fiery Welsh actress, Anna Kashfi, Brando's first wife, who had claimed throughout most of her adult life that she was from India.

Marlon met Anna in 1955, telling friends he'd found "the most beautiful woman in the world." He would later say, "In the worst decision of my life, I married the bitch." One outcome of that union was the birth of Christian in Los Angeles on May 11, 1958. He entered the world as the couple was divorcing, launching the most violent and hostile 16-year custody battle in the history of Hollywood.

Initially, Kashfi was awarded custody of her son. But five years later a judge ruled against her, claiming she had a "reliance on drugs and alcohol," which reportedly led to frequent and uncontrollable outbursts of temper. According to journalist Nellie Bly, "Anna left baby Christian alone in her car parked on Wilshire Boulevard while she confronted (Marlon) Brando in his office, beating at him with her fists, in a frenzy of rage." At the age of six, Christian was taken from his mother and brought to live with Brando's older sister, Jocelyn.

It wasn't until 1972 that Brando was granted full custody of

In the courtroom where **Christian** was being tried for the murder of Dag Drollet, **Marlon** kissed him on the head. Their relationship had been intimate, incestuous. He blamed himself for his son's derangement.

During his first interview with the police, Christian was still drunk. "He was fighting with my sister," he falsely charged. "The fucking gun went off. He was beating her, and she's pregnant. Man, death is too good for the guy." That statement seemed to doom Christian's defense.

his son, who had been mostly raised by nannies, servants, and the staff at boarding schools. By then young Christian was in his early teens.

To some of his friends, and only when drunk or drugged (perhaps both), Christian, following in his sister's footsteps, made a wild and reckless charge that has never been proven one way or the other.

He claimed that on three separate occasions, his father came to his bedroom and performed the act of fellatio on him.

"It was never a case of my reporting it to my mother or going to the authorities," Christian said. "In fact, I rather enjoyed it. Dear old Dad was known for being one of the best cocksuckers in Hollywood, and he knew what he was going."

"He never talked about it on the following mornings," Christian said. "I like getting blow-jobs so much that as I grew older I let a lot of Hollywood fags blow me. Why not? They did all the work. I did nothing, because I'm completely straight."

While his father was in Paris filming the notorious *Last Tango in Paris*, released in 1972, Kashfi allegedly "kidnapped" her son and took him to Mexico. The boy eventually was discovered living in a tent and ill with bronchitis. Authorities returned him to Los Angeles and the custody of his father.

By the 11th grade, Christian became a school dropout. He was a virtual alcoholic, using LSD and other drugs. To support himself, he worked at various odd jobs, including being a welder and tree trimmer. He lived for a time in Alaska, Sarah Palin country, piloting a barge for a fish processor during the summer. He even tried to be an actor, but his career went nowhere. Eventually he came to live with his father at his hilltop estate on Mulholland Drive.

Christian's killing of Dag Drollet made headlines around the world. But the press at the time did not know the true motive for the murder. Christian was still in love with Cheyenne, and it's likely that he believed, at least on the night of the murder, that he was the father of the baby growing inside her.

Throughout their short lives, Christian and Cheyenne were lovers. "I took her virginity," Christian sometimes bragged.

After he killed Cheyenne's boyfriend, and in prison, Christian completed his high school equivalency diploma and worked in a vocational education machine shop.

Marlon Brando and his bride look calm but it was merely a lull before the storm. **Anna Kashfi**, a former film actress, spent a great deal of her life trying to convince the public that she was half-Indian, claiming she was born in Darjeeling and reared in Calcutta. Other reporters claimed she was born in Wales, where her family lived. The dispute has never been satisfactorily settled.

The marriage was a failure. Kashfi got even in her memoir, *Brando for Breakfast*. In it she wrote, "I went to bed with Marlon mostly out of curiosity. His seduction technique showed all the subtlety of a guillotine. Physically, Marlon is not well appointed. He compensates for that deficiency by undue devotion to his sex organ. 'My noble tool,' he called it."

The photo is a cover from issue #44 (dated January 11, 1957) of the French movie magazine *Ciné Revue*. The article was entitled "The mysterious personality of the young **Madame Marlon Brando**."

Ironically the couple didn't marry until nine months later on October 11 of the same year. Their marriage was a disaster from the beginning, and they would divorce in April 22, 1959..

In 2004, Christian married Deborah Presley, who claims to be the illegitimate daughter of Elvis Presley. A year later, she sued Christian for domestic violence, claiming that he'd repeatedly beaten her and threatened to kill her in the presence of her teenaged daughter. He countersued, alleging that she broke into his house and beat him after his announcement that he wanted to have their marriage annulled after their first ten weeks together. Both lawsuits were settled in 2006, with undisclosed terms.

Young Brando's name was also connected with another murder, that of Bonnie Lee Bakley, whom he'd been dating. Her husband, actor Robert Blake, at least suggested that Brando—not him—was the killer. After a thorough investigation, the police found no reason to charge Brando in Bakley's murder. However, they did bring charges against Blake, but he was eventually acquitted.

Even so, Christian was summoned to court during Blake's civil trial. He invoked the Fifth Amendment and refused to answer questions about his relationship with Blake's wife. As a consequence, he was fined $1,000 for contempt of court.

A baby girl was born to Bakley in June of 2000, and she called Christian telling him that the baby was his. She even named the girl Christian Shannon Brando. However, a paternity test later established that Robert Blake was the girl's father. Her name was subsequently changed to Rose Sophia Leonore Blake.

Christian spent the last two weeks of his life hooked up to a ventilator in a Los Angeles City Hospital, suffering from AIDS-related complications from pneumonia. During the final years of his life, he reportedly had been seen at more and more gay clubs. He is asserted to have cited a strong dislike of condoms to his sex partners, both male and female, and it is believed that he might have contracted the AIDS virus during any of several barebacking encounters.

News of his death flashed around the world on January 26, 2009.

When he'd entered the hospital he had (accurately) told the staff that he had no money, and that he was living on welfare, despite the fact that the executors to his father's estate were battling over how to divide its more than $20 million worth of assets.

Christian's death has led to an array of charges, including accusations of fraud or possibly

Marlon Brando's divorce from Anna Kashfi was one of the bitterest in Hollywood history. They fought for custody of their son, Christian Devi Brando, born in 1958. As Brando left the courtroom after a hearing, Kashfi attacked him, physically assaulting him until she was restrained. He did not attempt to strike her back.

Kashfi charged that he committed "serial infidelities," and he did not contest her action. She won sole custody of Christian and $1,000 a month for his support, plus another $440,000 over the next decade for her maintenance. The divorce didn't settle anything. There would be more lawsuits, one alleging that Brando broke into her house and "brutally beat and struck me." In time Brando would eventually obtain custody of Christian.

murder. In the wake of threatened lawsuits, one Los Angeles attorney predicted that the estate of Marlon Brando, now complicated by Christian's death, probably won't be settled until 2050—"and I'm being optimistic."

Children of famous movie stars sometimes end tragically. The charismatic quality it takes to achieve stardom is not what is required to make a good parent. Take Joan Crawford, Bette Davis, or Bing Crosby, for example.

Marlon gave his own assessment of his role as a father. In court during his son's murder trial, Marlon told jurors, "I think that perhaps I failed as a father."

Marlon himself died at the age of 80 on July 1, 2004. He could win Oscars, but no "Parent of the Year" awards.

Christian Brando's life was a tragedy almost from the beginning. He once said, "Dad's shoes were too big for me to fill. I always had to live in his long shadow. Most of the world accepted me only because I was his son. Not for any person I was. I was a plaything between my parents, a ball they could bounce back and forth with each other. My father's dad, Marlon Sr., had been cold and brutal to him. My own Dad was a self-indulgent man, often showing me no attention at all. When he did turn his full attention onto me, his behavior was inappropriate. At the time I welcomed it because it showed he loved me. But he should not have loved me that way."

HALL OF FAME

Alas, this book isn't big enough for a comprehensive list of who Marlon actually unzipped for, but reliable sources document some of the lucky ones as having included the following:

Homage to a Satyr
Marlon Brando

Wally
Cox

Vivien
Leigh

Laurence
Olivier

Monty
Clift

Doris
Duke

Rock
Hudson

Truman
Capote

Jacqueline
Kennedy

Cary
Grant

Marlene
Dietrich

James
Dean

Grace
Kelly

Rita
Moreno

Tennessee
Williams

Kim
Stanley

Shelley
Winters

Tyrone
Power

Gloria
Vanderbilt

Greta
Garbo

Leonard
Bernstein

Jean Peters

Joan
Crawford

Bette
Davis

John
Gielgud

Anna
Magnani

Tallulah
Bankhead

Ingrid
Bergman

Ursula
Andress

Edith
Piaf

Hedy
Lamarr

Veronica
Lake

Marilyn
Monroe

Burt
Lancaster

MA KETTLE,
Was a DYKE!

Marjorie Main in the 1930s and 1940s resembled more American housewives than did Norma Shearer or Lana Turner. As Louis B. Mayer, who signed her to a long-term contract, noted, "When she entered the commissary, she attracted more attention than Joan Crawford.

Main was a no-nonsense, "take-no-prisoners" kind of actress, who could play almost any role—Humphrey Bogart's world weary slum mother, a meddling maid, a witty housekeeper, even the town gossip. But her enduring fame rested with those Ma Kettle roles that more or less defined the American country bumpkin. Main played a raucous woman with a potato sack figure who was not afraid to use her broomstick on her unpredictable Kettle brood, or on the chickens.

A New Spin

ON AN
OLD AMERICAN ROLE MODEL

A scene from *Ma and Pa Kettle on Vacation* (1953), which became the sixth of the Ma and Pa Kettle films. Here **Ma** confronts a French apache dancer.

In the City of Love, Pa eyes the French beauties and tries to buy dirty post-cards, and Ma does a bouncy dance number in a night club. (Main had been a hoofer in the 20s).

An endearing, homespun old buzzard, the tall and very large-framed Marjorie Main was born on an Indiana farm in 1890, the daughter of a minister.

From such unlikely beginnings, she became an American legend and one of the most popular character actresses of her day. At the time of her death in 1975, she had appeared in more than 80 films. Nine of them were part of the phenomenally popular "Ma and Pa Kettle" series, which were so successful that they saved Universal International from bankruptcy. (Marjorie worked on loan-out from MGM.) And at least two of the others included major hits wherein she advised, counseled, and empathized with characters played by Judy Garland: *Meet Me in St. Louis* (1944) and *The Harvey Girls* (1946).

Main got her start on Broadway appearing in *The Wicked Age* (1927), a vaudeville comedy and melodrama which had been written by and which also starred Mae West. Risqué and bawdy, it provided a foundation for a friendship between Main and West that would endure till the end of Main's life. Early in their friendship, the savvy but usually tolerant West sensed a "streak of lesbianism" in Main, thereby warning her, "When I reach between my partner's legs, I like to feel something long and thick—not plunge into a hole!"

No one offered Main a long-term contract (it was with MGM) until she was 50 years old. Her real fame came in *The Egg and I* (1947), a hit that garnered an Academy Award nomination for Best Supporting Actress for her role as Ma Kettle.

Main's most visible and gossiped-about lesbian affair was with Barbara Stanwyck, with whom she toured with the Broadway hit *Burlesque* in 1929. Although it seems far-fetched that a good-looking hoofer like Stanwyck would take up with Main sexually, it must be remembered that Main in the 1920s was considered a "handsome"—not a

Ma and Pa Kettle at Waikiki (1955) marked the end of Percy Kilbride's long career. In the role, he tries to run his cousin's pineapple plant with disastrous results. He's even kidnapped by the bad guys, and only Ma can save him.

In the movie, film fans learn that the names of their favorite characters were actually "Phoebe" and "Franklin." Main demanded that her grass skirt number , depicted above, be cut—"It's too risqué for Ma Kettle," she proclaimed.

beautiful—woman who was known for her kindness and charm. In many ways, she was the very opposite of the gruff Ma Kettle she played on the sound stages of Universal.

In New York in the 1920s, Oscar Levant often accompanied Main and Stanwyck (whose birth name was Ruby Stevens) to Harlem. There, they were seen at the Cotton Club on Lenox and 142nd Street, cuddling together between dialogues with performers who included "Bojangles" Robinson, Louis Armstrong, Bessie Smith, and Ethel Waters.

Later, they'd show up together at a lesbian dive known as "The Drool Inn." There Main and Stanwyck would join "Ma Rainey," who in 1925 had spent time in a Chicago prison after having been convicted of arranging a lesbian orgy in her home. One night Main and Stanwyck were seen hanging out at another lesbian hangout, "The Clam House." With them appeared the celebrated Jeanne Eagels and the notorious jazz-age singer, Libby Holman, who were engaged together at the time in some hot female-to-female action.

In 1932, in Hollywood, Main told her co-stars of *Hot Saturday*, Cary Grant and Randolph Scott (she called them "the love birds"), that Stanwyck had dumped her for Joan Crawford. Main admitted that Crawford "is a far better-looking broad than I'll ever be."

Main was reunited with Stanwyck in 1937 when Samuel Goldwyn cast her as Mrs. Martin, the mother of Stanwyck's character in the classic weeper, *Stella Dallas*.

Main's longest-lasting affair, conducted mainly in the 1930s, was with Colorado-born Spring Byington, a sweet-faced character actress who was best known for playing mothers. One of Byington's most famous roles was that of Marmee, matriarch of that brood of *Little Women* in the 1933 movie version. In that film, Byington appeared opposite another bisexual actress, Katharine Hepburn. Main and Byington frequently entertained Hepburn and

Burlesque was a hit on Broadway. Main joined her friend, **Barbara Stanwyck,** and they hit the road together, sharing bedrooms from town to town.

The other cast members claimed they were having an affair. Ironically by 1937, when the movie *Stella Dallas* was released, Main was cast in it as the mother of Stanwyck's character in this classic weepy.

Colorado-born **Spring Byington** fell in love with Main when she arrived in Hollywood. Main introduced her around, and the two women lived together. Their friend, George Cukor, said that they had the most discreet relationship in Hollywood and were loving and supportive of each other throughout their lives. Both Byington and Main had husbands at one time, "but we're not the marrying kind," Main told Cukor.

Marjorie Main and Spring Byington may have lived deep, deep in the closet. Not so **Ma Rainey,** "the Mother of the Blues." She recorded with Louis Armstrong and became known for her vocal abilities and majestic phrasing. She was an "out" lesbian before the term was invented and served time in prison for her activities. She once had a husband, Will Rainey, whom she married in 1904 and toured with him as the "Assassinators of the Blues."

her own long-term lover, Laura Harding, the American Express heiress.

Main and Byington shared a house together in the Hollywood Hills opposite George Cukor, who had directed Byington and Hepburn in *Little Women*.

During her retirement, Marjorie Main outed herself, but in a most subtle way, to Boze Hadleigh in his book, *Hollywood Lesbians*. Like many lesbians of her day, she was once married, in her case, to a Dr. Stanley Lefevre Krebs. Officially, their marital union lasted 14 years, although they seemed to live together only during the first months of their marriage. There was a 26-year age gap between them. The only remaining portrait of him that we know of was taken in the 1890s.

Main's letters to him were destroyed, but one which he wrote to her on August 10, 1934 on stationary from The Langwell Hotel in New York suggests that they were both emotionally involved with a woman named "C" (there's a later reference to Ceil). Nothing is known about this mystery woman, but Dr. Krebs states that "Ceil is the one woman who knows more about you than any other woman on earth."

Main shot most of her nine Kettle films with San Francisco-born Percy Kilbride, who played her scrawny, sad-eyed rube husband, Pa. He stayed with the series until *Ma and Pa Kettle at Waikiki*, shot in 1955, the year he retired.

After that, in *The Kettles in the Ozarks* (1956), the character of Pa was ignored altogether. A year later, in the last of the series, *The Kettles on Old MacDonald's Farm* (1957), Pa was played by Parker Fenn Elly. Main refused to see either of the last two films and retired altogether upon completion of the *MacDonald's Farm* movie.

As she packed her suitcase at Universal, she said, "Without Percy, the films aren't the same any more." Though Main went on her way, she inspired an array of similar hillbilly families riding on her feedsack apron strings: *The Real McCoys*, *Green Acres* (with Eva Gabor of all people), *The Beverly Hillbillies*, and *Petticoat Junction*.

On September 21, 1964, nine years after his retirement, as he was walking across Hollywood Boulevard, a car accident put the original Pa (Kilbride) in the hospital. He survived for some three months before dying on December 11, 1964, at the age of 76, during emergency brain surgery.

Main later told friends that "I cried for a week when I heard the news about dear old Percy." Main herself was to die on April 10, 1975, her personal life a bit of a mystery.

In her somewhat outspoken interview with Boze Hadleigh, Main never revealed the name of "my lady friend," only to say that she was "someone special."

Spring Byington had indeed been someone special. On the set of *Little Women* back in 1933, Byington had informed director Cukor that, "I'm the lady in the relationship. Marjorie has to do all the manly things."

Marjorie Main met the two homosexual lovers **Randolph Scott** (left) and **Cary Grant** (right) when she appeared with them in a movie called *Hot Saturday*. When Main and Byington invited Katharine Hepburn and her lover, Laura Harding, the American Express heiress, over for dinner to "meet the two fellas," Kate asked. "You're not trying to fix us up with anybody, are you?"

"These two guys are already fixed up with each other," Main told Kate.

Dumbing down a sophisticated woman like **Marjorie Main** to play a raucous hillbilly housewife took makeup, wardrobe, and damn good acting.

Marjorie Main—A Life on Film

Spying on James Craig in *Gentle Annie* (1944)

Advising Clark Gable in *Honky Tonk* (1941)

As a rich spinster in *Tish* (1944) with ZaSu Pitts

Eyeing Katharine Hepburn in *Undercurrent* (1944)

A tense moment with Stanwyck in *Stella Dallas* (1937)

The Bugle Sounds (1941) with Wallace Beery

"A BETTER LOVER THAN ELVIS," CLAIMED A GROUPIE

The Sex Tape and Mysterious Death of
Jimi Hendrix

"When I die, I want people to play my music, go wild, and freak out an' do anything they wanna do."
　　　　　　　　　　　　　　　　　　　　　　　　　　　—Jimi Hendrix

Music critic Anthony DeCurtis described **Jimi Hendrix**'s strange legacy:

"Despite a personal and aesthetic style that reveled in his blackness, Hendrix never spoke out on the pressing civil rights issues of the day either in his lyrics or in interviews. His audience was overwhelmingly white. He came of age backing up the likes of Little Richard on the so-called chitlin' circuit, but some African Americans saw him as pandering to white stereotypes of black superstuds and resented his reverence for white artists like Bob Dylan, The Beatles, and Eric Clapton. What seemed subversive and provocative coming from someone like Mick Jagger was seen as unacceptable, a little embarrassing really, coming from a black man."

A Hardcore Look at an
Iconic Rock Legend

Sylvester Stallone, Paris Hilton, Colin Farrell, and Pamela Anderson, among many others, have found themselves unwitting sex tape stars. This illegal and unauthorized pornography has turned into a lucrative business, making somebody millions.

Along comes *Jimi Hendrix: The Sex Tape* released in 2008 by L.A.-based Vivid Entertainment, the porn purveyor behind XXX-rated superstars Jenna Jameson and Tera Patrick.

Executives there reported that the 40-year-old tape came to them as part of a memorabilia collection.

The footage features the guitarist engaging in various sex acts with two foxy women (names unknown) in a dimly lit room. Vivid officials claim they went to great trouble to authenticate the footage before the release of this controversial and invasive sex tape.

The release of the sex tape caused quite a stir, catalyzing widespread coverage by the tabloid press. Of course, the estate of Hendrix denies that the man in the video is actually Jimi Hendrix. Even Hendrix's British girlfriend, Kathy Etchingham, claimed that the film is not authentic.

Vivid Entertainment has offered $100,000 if anyone can prove that the man depicted in the video is not Jimi Hendrix.

Many of the late rock star's close associates claim the central character in the film is definitely Hendrix.

Neville Chesters, Hendrix's road manager during the late 60s, claimed, "It's the real thing. We were all jealous of Jimi's sex life at the time, and we were accustomed to seeing him frequently go to his room at night with an entourage of women we called 'Band of Gypsies,' the same name as the 1969 recording."

Hendrix is pictured above with his British girlfriend, **Kathy Etchingham.** As anticipated, she denied that the man in the sex tape was her former lover. "It's not him. His face is too broad and nose and nostrils too wide for Jim. Also the hair is too low on the forehead. He would never have allowed anyone to see that. In private he was very shy and would cover up."

"The 60s were socially, sexually, and politically changing times," Chesters said. "The footage in the movie looks as if it were shot about 1968. It would have been difficult to get explicit film like that processed commercially in the U.S. back then, no less a biracial sex act. So this film was probably developed in Germany and kept hidden because of how incendiary its release would have been."

"Plaster Caster" Cynthia Albritton looked at the footage and pronounced that the man in the porno was Hendrix. She should know, as she once made a plaster cast of his cock, which was about eight inches long and somewhat thick, but not in the category of John C. Holmes.

"Plaster Caster" confirmed that she made a plaster mold of the star's penis on February 25,

1968. She also claimed that he had an orgasm while in her cast for the mold.

She spoke about the clay Jimi penis she crafted: "Jimi's pubes got stuck in the mold because I didn't lube them enough. I spent the next 15 minutes pulling out each individual hair one by one, while he had intercourse with just the right sized repository—his negative impression! This unexpected delay made him late for his show that evening, where he was seen scratching his crotch a lot onstage."

Albritton continued: "Judging from having cast Jimi's cock, in addition to looking at some old photos of him recently, I'm convinced that he is indeed the man seen in this film. Facial aspects such as the muscle around his mouth, his lips, eyebrows, and mustache, look like those of Jimi. Also, the hairstyle, body mass, and absence of acne scars make me think that the film was made during the final year of his life."

The footage demonstrates that Hendrix was fabulous in bed and really wanted to please his partner," said Pamela Des Barres, author of *I'm With the Band: Confessions of a Groupie.* "The 1960s was a time of exploring bodies, music, drugs, and the coming together of like-minded souls who thought they would change the world," said Des Barres.

Curtis Knight, author of the 1973 book, *An Intimate Biography of Jimi Hendrix*, said, "He went really crazy about cinefilming. He would also get friends of his to film naked women running around his room. I think Kathy Etchingham still has a hard time talking about Jimi doing all these things and facing the fact that he had other women. It sounds to me that she is still smarting from the pain of memories that he was not always faithful to her."

Watching Hendrix's "performance," there's little doubt that had he not played such a great guitar, he could have made it as an adult film star. His enthusiasm about returning pleasure to the two slim brunettes appears to be boundless.

The Jimi Hendrix estate disputed the film's authenticity and said, "We have not authorized distribution of this film. Further, we deplore the obvious exploitation of Jimi Hendrix, and we are highly offended by the disgraceful portrayal."

In the spring of 2010, *Valley of Neptune* came out, the first album of previously unreleased studio recordings. Because he never authorized a will, lawsuits are still being filed as to who controls Hendrix's estate. Contested ownerships of his recordings, Dickensian in their

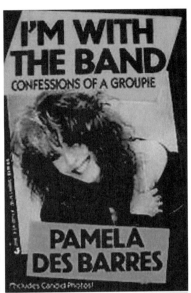

Pamela Des Barres was known as the original groupie. She had not only a taste for rock 'n' roll, but for the men who made the music. She listened to their music and, after the show, seduced them one by one.

Her list of conquests became famous—Jimmy Page, Keith Moon, Mick Jagger, Jim Morrison, *et al.* As her infamous book (see above) proclaimed, she had a set of fundamental rules—no one-night stands, hands off married men, and only one conquest per band.

Cynthia Albritton made a widely publicized contribution to the world of rock 'n' roll, earning the nickname "Plaster Caster" when she got many famous rock stars to agree to have a mold made of their erect penis. Many rock stars didn't want to immortalize themselves in plaster, fearing they'd look "too small." Even so, some went along with Albritton's request, although claiming as part of the process that she could have made them bigger.

She had no trouble getting Jimi Hendrix to model, although the actual casting was fraught with a few hazards.

227

complexity, abound. For the 40th anniversary of Hendrix's death, the estate of Jimi Hendrix is staging a sort of comeback for their idol, even though he never really went away. The event was commemorated with the release of a new CD, a "freshening up" of his classic titles, a tribute tour, and a video game named *Rock Band* devoted to him. In addition to music that's a part of the 2010 release, the estate is said to have 10 more years of "lost music" squirreled away within its vaults. Like both *The Beatles* and *The Rolling Stones*, Hendrix lives on as a rock artist of Olympian stature.

FOXY...AND REALLY DIRTY!: These images were associated with the sales trailers for the Hendrix sex video.

Was Jimi Hendrix
Murdered?

The year 2010 marked the 40th anniversary of the death of Jimi Hendrix, guitarist, singer, and songwriter. Today he is hailed as the greatest electric guitarist in the history of rock music. He's even the singer most closely associated with the iconic Woodstock Festival in 1969.

His early death at age 28 on September 18, 1970 remains the source of lurid speculation.

On the eve of his death, he was shacked up with Monika Dannemann, who presumably was the last person to see him alive. A German figure skater and painter, she was also Hendrix's last girlfriend, who had momentarily, perhaps, split with Kathy Etchingham. An obsessive fan, Monika had begun her relationship with Hendrix by stalking him.

For his final night on earth, Hendrix was driven to Monika's flat in Lansdowne Crescent in London's neighborhood of Notting Hill.

That night within her flat in the Samarkand Hotel, Hendrix consumed red wine. He desperately needed rest, and Monika gave him *nine* of her prescribed Vesperax sleeping pills. That is not a misprint. Vesperax was a German drug unknown to Hendrix. He trusted Monika and swallowed all of them, even though her doctor had instructed that she should take only half a tablet at a time. Surely she knew that.

Did she deliberately decide to kill Hendrix—if so, what was her motive? Or else was she instructed to do so after receiving a pay-off from

Although the rock chick, German blonde **Monika Dannemann**, and **Jimi Hendrix** look cozy in this photograph, they rarely saw each other. Engaged for two years, they spent only three weeks together during that entire period.

In 2006, 36 years after the sinister death of Hendrix himself, Monika was found dead inside her fume-filled Mercedes sports car at her thatched home in Seaford, Sussex (UK) The artist and former skating champ had received death threats ever since Hendrix died.

Her long-time companion, musician Uli Jon Roth, insisted that her death was "suspicious—she used to get death threats over the phone." Could an avid Hendrix fan have killed her? The question may never be answered for certain.

Monika Dannemann

Artist of the Inner Light

Monika devoted the rest of her life to Hendrix's memory. On the left, above, she is depicted as the "Artist of the Inner Light," and on the right, she poses in 1994 with one of her paintings of Hendrix, wherein she depicted him in "guitar ecstacy."

Her cottage in Sussex became a virtual shrine to his memory. Paintings of Hendrix, some of them depicting him as a young god descended to Earth, lined every wall of her home. In one, skulls, occult signs, and flowers dance in a circle around the rock star's head.

someone else? Did someone else enter Jimi's room that night?

The examining surgeon, Dr. John Bannister, claimed that Hendrix had become asphyxiated in his own vomit, mainly from the huge consumption of red wine that night. The sleeping pills apparently finished him off. They had also induced him to vomit, at which time his air supply was cut off.

Monika never offered a satisfactory explanation of what happened on that mysterious night. In testimony, she claimed that she did not discover that Hendrix was unconscious until after 9am. For some reason she did not summon an ambulance until 11:27am. She later said that she was afraid to call an ambulance because she feared that it would cause a scandal and Hendrix would beat her.

A medical emergency team arrived only about 20 minutes after being summoned. They wrapped Hendrix and carried him up from the garden apartment to the street level and put him in an ambulance.

Monika later claimed that Hendrix was alive when he entered the ambulance and perhaps died on the way to the hospital. The attendants accused her of lying, claiming that Hendrix was dead when they arrived in the apartment. The door was open but Monika had mysteriously disappeared.

In another bizarre twist, James (Tappy) Wright in May of 2009 published a book claiming that Michael Jeffrey, the artist's manager, admitted to him that he killed Hendrix because the guitarist had threatened to end their management contract. Fearing that was so, Jeffrey had taken out an enormous life insurance policy on Hendrix.

Jeffrey was almost as controversial a business manager as Col. Tom Parker, who swindled millions from Elvis Presley. Jeffrey had also managed the British band, "The Animals." Many members of that group blamed Jeffrey for breaking up their band. He was also charged with appropriating most of their royalties.

In a reckless disregard of his own legal position, Jeffrey told some associates that he hired Monika to ply Hendrix with pills and alcohol on the night of his death. His stories have never been independently confirmed.

At this point, the truth will probably never be known. On March 5, 1973, aboard an Iberian Airlines DC-9 above the city of Nantes in

Michael Jeffrey *(photo above)* managed Jimi Hendrix and is often referred to as "the man who made him a star." But did he arrange to have him killed when Hendrix was set to end their business relationship?

Author David Henderson, in his book, claimed that Jeffrey confessed Hendrix's murder to him. The death allowed Jeffrey to cash in on a life insurance policy he held on the star's life. Wright claimed that Jeffrey "came clean" during a drinking session together the year after Hendrix died. The manager said he entered the star's bedroom, with some assistance from Monika Dannemann, and forced several bottles of red wine down his windpipe until he drowned.

GROUPIES AT WAR: The two former girlfriends of Hendrix battled it out, often in court. A Sixties sex siren, **Kathy Etchingham** (left photo above) was the guitarist's first British girlfriend. She met Hendrix when he was spending money as quickly as he earned it, indulging himself buying jewelry, heroin, cocaine, hash, and LSD, and lavishing or squandering enormous sums on clothes for many of the "birdies" who flew toward him.

Monika Dannemann (right) became Hendrix's London girlfriend when the relationship between Etchingham and Hendrix cooled. Hendrix's death catalyzed a saga of obsession, jealousy, and (perhaps) love, and decades of pointless fretting and grieving over a man that neither of them knew very well.

France, Jeffrey was killed in a mid-air collision. He went to his grave claiming that he had murdered Hendrix, using Monika as an accomplice.

In a shocking book, *Scuse Me While I Kiss the Sky: The Life of Jimi Hendrix*, author David Henderson claimed that Monika deliberately waited several hours before she called an ambulance for the star. If that were true, and it appears to be so, then she knew that Hendrix was already dead long before she summoned emergency aid.

An attendant from the hospital claimed that he untied a red scarf that had been tied around Hendrix's neck, cutting off his breathing. That added yet another twist to the death of the rock legend.

In the aftermath of Hendrix's death, the two rival girlfriends, Monika and Kathy, launched a war of words that eventually brought them before the British High Court to settle charges of libel. Backing up author Henderson's charge, Kathy accused Monika of waiting hours before calling for an ambulance. Monika countered that Kathy was both a "liar and a cheat."

Hauling Monika into court, Kathy won a £1,000 fine against her plus an agreement never to repeat the allegation about her being a liar and a cheat. There was peace in London until 1996, when Monika repeated the charge in a book. Once again, Kathy sued and once again she won. This time Monika was hit with a £30,000 fine for libel. Kathy had wanted her jailed, but the English judge found that a bit draconian.

April 5, 1996, two days after the court case, Monika was found dead in her Mercedes, allegedly having sucked fumes from the exhaust pipe, which had filled her lungs and poisoned her.

Although officially designated as a suicide, Monika's death also continues to be the subject of lurid speculation. Was it a suicide? Since Hendrix's death, she had received numerous death threats.

In the aftermath of Monika's death, her last and final lover, Uli Jon Roth, made accusations of foul play.

Monika's death is complicated, murky, and associated with lots of unanswered questions. Her name continues to resurface in any probe into who or what killed Jimi Hendrix. Dr. John Bannister, the attending surgeon who attempted to resuscitate Hendrix after his death, later added an alarming note to the investigation. In a quote attributed to him, he said that there was "a strong possibility that Jimi actually died from 'forced' inhalation of copious amounts of red wine."

But who forced him? Was it really Jeffrey, or could it have been someone else? That is the question that remains unanswered to this day.

Monika Dannemann (left) is seen looking haggard and depressed as she leaves a London courtroom in 1996, where for the second time she would lose a libel judgment to **Kathy Etchinham** (right figure in photo above). Monika had only hours to live.

A trimphant Etchingham is seen leaving the courtroom with her husband, Nick, a doctor. Kathy is a woman in middle age today, and the mother of two sons. Even so, she is still drawn into the controversy surrounding Hendrix's death, as well as the recent release of his sex tape. What is not known is what her respectable husband thinks about all of this.

The Fine Art of Screwing Your Guitar

In an act he repeated regularly on stage, **Jimi Hendrix** set his guitar on fire. He didn't so much play his guitar as attack it, waving it suggestively between his legs and even picking its strings with his teeth. He was so skilled he could even play it behind his back.

At every performance, he performed a simulated sex act with the unfortunate instrument. He would then set it on fire, like a rapist who decides to kill his victim after a brutal attack. If the fire wouldn't blaze, he would get down on his knees before it and coax it with voodoo gestures he learned in Haiti. If the voodoo didn't work, he'd spray it with lighter fuel before picking up the charred remainder and smashing it to bits.

Too bad he did that. A Jimi Hendrix guitar could command at least a million dollars on the market today.

Revealing far more than Jimi Hendrix's death certificate (above), was a report from John Bannister, who said it was "plausible" that Hendrix was killed by having red wine and sleeping pills foced down his throat.

Bannister was on duty at London's St. Mary Abbots Hospital when Hendrix's body was brought in. "The amount of wine that was over him was just extraordinary," Bannister said. "Not only was it saturated right through his hair and shirt, but both his lungs and stomach were absolutely full of wine. We had a sucker that you put down the trachea, the entrance to his lungs, and to the whole of the back of his throat. We kept sucking and it kept surging and surging. He had already vomited up masses of red wine, and I would have thought there was half a bottle of wine in his hair. He had really drowned in a massive amount of red wine. We worked very hard for half an hour, but there was no response at all. Our work was really an exercise in futility. Somebody said to me, 'You know who that was? That was Jimi Hendrix.' I said, 'Who's Jimi Hendrix?'"

Jimi Hendrix's body was laid to rest in Greenwood Cemetery, in Renton, Washington State. He was buried here on October 1, 1970, after a memorial service at Dunlap Baptist Church. The inscription on the gravestone *(top left photo above)* reads: "FOREVER IN OUR HEARTS. JAMES M. ("JIMI") HENDRIX, 1942-1970."

In 2003, the body was moved to a new location in the same cemetery, this time under the huge monument depicted in the lowest of the three photos above. Fans making a donation had their names inscribed on tiles positioned around the edge of the tomb. For $25, these fans were sold a stone unearthed during the ground-breaking ceremony at the new memorial. For $250, they were sold a CD-shaped piece of granite from the block used to make the mausoleum. Much was made about the fact that a plaque on the tomb bore a likeness of Hendrix's "authentic" autograph.

Many of Hendrix's fans attacked the relocation of the body as "crass and vulgar'. Noel Redding, the British bass player and former friend of Hendrix, said, "This is the most awful thing I've ever heard. Why don't they just leave the man alone?" Kathy Etchingham also responded in horror. "Jimi always said that people would eventually wrap him up in cellophane and sell him, and he was right. The next thing the family will do involves putting his remains in a glass case and taking him out on tour again."

To the chagrin of nearly all his fans and friends, the Estate of Jimi Hendrix then proceeded to license a Hendrix brand of red wine, the drink on which the star choked to death.

The bronze statue of Jimi depicted in the top right photo, above, is located in front of the corporate offices of AEI Music Networks, at 900 East Pine Street, in Seattle, WA, a city that claims Hendrix as a native son.

The Jimi Experience

METRO. TORONTO JAMES M. HENDRIX 2199/69 MAY 3/69

A shy and sensitive boy, **Hendrix** knew poverty in the slums of Seattle. He's pictured with his father *(upper right)* during a rare happy moment. His parents divorced when he was nine, and his mother died in 1958. Elvis Presley and Little Richard had a powerful influence on the burgeoning musician, who acquired his very first guitar at the age of 14. It had only one string.

His first gig was in a synagogue in which he was fired between sets—"You're just too wild," said the rabbi.

Hendrix had a bad record in the Army, "taking dope" and getting caught deserting his post to masturbate in the latrine. The police photos above were taken on May 3, 1969, when Hendrix was arrested at the Toronto Airport. He'd stowed heroin and hashish in his luggage. At his trial, he convinced the jury that a "crazed" fan had planted the stash on him.

Vincent Sherman

DIRECTING, SEDUCING, AND GOSSIPING ABOUT
Movie Stars

The world took little note of the passing of Vincent Sherman on June 18, 2006, one of the last survivors among Hollywood's studio era directors. He passed on only days before reaching his one-hundredth birthday. He's pictured above with two of the Hollywood hotties he seduced—**Rita Hayworth** (left) and **Joan Crawford** (right).

For a little boy growing up in Vienna, Georgia, in the years before World War I, it's hard to imagine that he would end up directing and having affairs with some of the most legendary actresses of the silver screen.

He became known as a "woman's director," a title he hated, pointing out that he'd also directed Errol Flynn, Humphrey Bogart, Richard Burton, and Paul Newman. In his crusty old age, he reflected, "Woman's director. That's bullshit. The last time I checked out their dicks, Errol, Bogie, Ronnie Reagan, that drunk, Richard Burton, and that Paul Newman boy with the baby blues were men."

Although at least by reputation, Southern gentlemen aren't supposed to kiss and tell—think Rhett Butler—Sherman did just that in both interviews and memoirs, the latter appropriately called *Studio Affairs*.

As he grew older, he adopted a "what-the-fuck" attitude and made even more startling revelations about Hollywood legends, going much farther than he did even within his "tell-all" memoirs.

You name the legend, and Sherman had plenty to say about the star. Take, Humphrey Bogart for instance....

Vincent Sherman Gossips About
HUMPHREY BOGART

"Women are funny. Just because of that little triangle they have, they think they can get away with anything."

Humphrey Bogart

Vincent Sherman directed Bogie in such films as *The Return of Dr. X* in 1939 and *All Through the Night* in 1942. For the most part, these two strong egos got along well together.

"I really got to know Bogie when I directed *Crime School* in 1938, in which he appeared with the Dead End Kids. Maybe the casting of Bogie as a do-gooder instead of as a villain was a mistake. The guy was not like his screen persona. He was no staggering macho—in fact, I think he was a coward. He was the kind of guy who would run from a fight."

"Because of that lisp, many people at Warners, but not me, thought he was a faggot. He wasn't. In fact, he was a ladies' man and had seduced many of the leading lights of Hollywood, including Joan Crawford, Bette Davis, Jean Harlow, and Barbara Stanwyck. Of course, he'd had his cock sucked a few times by a guy, I'm sure. But that could be said about nearly any actor in Hollywood. Getting your cock sucked comes with the business."

"When I was assigned Bogie as one of the leads in *Dr. X*, I was told by the honchos at Warners to 'get him to play something besides Duke Mantee.' That was a reference to the role that Bogie had played both on the stage and on the screen in *The Petrified Forest*."

"The thinking was that Bogie would always be cast as a heavy, not as a romantic leading man," Sherman said. "I bought into that. It was inconceivable to me that he'd become a romantic lover on the screen, appearing opposite Ingrid Bergman in *Casablanca*. But he became the idol of millions, more dashing to some fans than Errol Flynn himself."

"When I directed Bogie I never knew if he'd show up beaten, stabbed, or bloody," Sherman recalled. "He was married to this vixen named Mayo Methot. They were known as

Miscast as Marshall Quesne, **Bogie** had to play "second banana" to two forgotten stars of yesterday, Wayne Morris and Rosemary Lane, in *The Return of Doctor X*. Mercifully, the Sherman-directed film ran only 62 minutes.

The plot has Bogie executed and buried but brought back to life through a mad doctor's discoveries. To sustain life, Bogie must relentlessly search for fresh blood.

In *All Through the Night*, another Sherman-directed film, **Bogie** co-starred with German actor Conrad Veidt, with whom he'd appear in the fabled *Casablanca*. Bogie played "Gloves" Donahue, a big-shot Broadway gambler in search of a killer.

The year the picture was made (1942) included the darkest months of WWII, so films from that time had a Nazi spy around every corner.

'The Battling Bogarts.'"

"She showed up on the set one day looking for her man," Sherman said. "She rightly suspected he was having an affair with the script girl. I was ahead of her. I sent Bogie to my studio office to fuck the girl, because the first place Methot looked was Bogie's dressing room."

"To get one up on Bogie, who thought he was so damn smart, I came up with an idea," Sherman said. "Since she couldn't find her straying husband, I invited the bitch for a drink. Before the night ended, I screwed this hot-to-trot harridan. Bogie was none the wiser. He showed up the next day, looking like the cat who swallowed the canary. But I was the one who got his whore. I went back to directing him in his cornball role in this hokey picture, and no one was ever the wiser. What Bogie didn't realize was that Methot was getting as much on the side as he was."

"I was paid a lousy three hundred dollars a week to direct Bogie in another picture," Sherman said. "It was called *All Through the Night* (1942), an anti-Nazi film. Our picture was filmed before Bogie shot *Casablanca*. After our little film together, I ran into Bogie on several occasions. We were drinking buddies for a while."

"Let me get one thing straight about Bogie, Bergman, and *Casablanca*," Sherman said. "Forget all those stupid biographies that claimed Bergman and Bogie didn't have an affair. He fucked her all during the making of *Casablanca*, and fell madly in love with her."

"In spite of her saintly look, that cold Swede was hot to trot once you got her pants off. Alfred Hitchcock, who was one of her directors, told me 'she'd do it with doorknobs.'"

"She liked to seduce her leading men," Sherman claimed. "You name them—Joseph Cotten, Gary Cooper, Bing Crosby, Gregory Peck, Omar Sharif, and Bogie himself. I never got to the bitch, but my old buddy, Victor Fleming, scored a bull's eye when he directed her in *Dr. Jekyll and Mr. Hyde*. In that one, Bergman was fucking both the director and its star, Spencer Tracy."

"Incidentally, that thing Bogie and I made during the war, *All Through the Night*, is still around," Sherman said. "I see it every now and then on TV. It's become a Bogie favorite like *Casablanca* and *The Maltese Falcon*."

In this instance, the director was exaggerating a bit.

Screen success did not come early to **Bogie**. Although he made 75 feature films in his career, his busiest period ranged from 1936 to 1940, during which time he averaged a film almost every two months. Except for *The Petrified Forest* (1936) with Leslie Howard and Bette Davis, this series of programmers were the most undistinguished of his long career. In most of the films of this period, he had only supporting roles, enough to earn him a reputation as the screen's "Number One Bad Boy."

Casablanca (1943) with **Ingrid Bergman** marked the turning point in Bogie's career. It opened at the Hollywood Theatre on Thanksgiving Day, 1942, just 18 days after the Allied landing at the real Casablanca. The picture was still running in January, 1943, at the time of the Casablanca conference. Talk about timing. The role of "Rick," owner of Rick's Bar, made Bogie an A-list romantic star and brought him an Oscar nomination. It also made him "The King" of Warner Brothers.

Vincent Sherman Gossips About
BETTE DAVIS

"Until you're known in my profession as a monster, you're not a star!"

Bette Davis

"My most difficult star to direct was not Bogie, nor even Ida Lupino, who wanted to take over the direction herself," Sherman said. "It was Miss Bette Davis. When we shot *Old Acquaintance* at Warner's, a picture released in 1943, I had not only to direct her, but act as referee between her and Miriam Hopkins. I was once told that Hopkins had lesbian designs on Davis, and was bitterly rejected. Could that have been the cause of such animosity?"

At the end of the shoot, Davis, while having a hamburger with Sherman, told him she loved him. Stunned, Sherman claimed he was flattered.

At this moment of confession, Davis was married to her second spouse, Arthur Farnsworth, and Sherman was married to his long-devoted wife, Hedda. She knew of his many extramarital adventures, but obviously tolerated his dalliances, sticking with her errant husband for fifty-three years until her death in 1984.

Before the start of their next picture together, *Mr. Skeffington*, Sherman heard over the radio that Davis's husband, "Farney," had died, apparently of a brain hemorrhage he'd suffered while walking down Hollywood Boulevard. The report claimed

"That bitch," **Bette Davis** (left figure in top photo), told Vincent Sherman, her director. "**Miriam Hopkins** (right) keeps getting younger while I keep getting older!" The script had both of them aging as time went by. Before filming ended on *Old Acquaintance* (1943), Bette wasn't speaking to her rival.

Throughout the filming, Miriam had been a scene stealer, doing little bits to distract the audience's attention from Bette's performance. Bette later revealed how she dealt with Miriam. "I never blew up at her because if you let her get to you, you'd be the loser. But I'd go home and just scream my head off afterward."

Later, she got even with Miriam by having an affair with her estranged husband, director Anatole Litvak.

that the hemorrhage may have come from an accidental fall he suffered that summer at home with Davis in New Hampshire.

She later gave a false confession to Sherman, claiming that she pushed Farney off the platform of a moving train when he went to confront her about her trip to Mexico, where she'd invited the director. "His head injury that day caused the hemorrhage," Davis said.

To certain friends, including Tennessee Williams during the stage production of *The Night of the Iguana*, Davis told quite a different story. She claimed that late one afternoon she came home early from the studio with a headache. She caught Farney in bed with the Oomph Girl, Ann Sheridan, and struck his head with a wrought-iron lamp on a nightstand. The story she told a Grand Jury about his fall at their New England home, she admitted, had been completely fabricated.

While filming *Mr. Skeffington*, Sherman made love to Davis for the first time at her home called "Riverbottom." He vividly recalled the night. "As she walked away from me, nude, with a cigarette in her hand, her two well-rounded buttocks moving in tandem with the Bette Davis hip swivel, I could not help but be amused."

Weeks into the relationship, Davis demanded that Sherman get a divorce from Hedda and marry her. He told her that he could not do that, that he was still in love with his wife.

As he headed for the door, her angry words, delivered in that distinctive voice known around the globe, echoed in his head for years.

"You're not going to leave my bed like I was some whore!"

But that's exactly what he did.

After *Mr. Skeffington*, Sherman vowed never to get involved with another actress he directed.

But vows are made to be broken.

Even such a great actress as **Bette Davis** couldn't achieve the impossible, that of playing "the most beautiful woman in town."

"I had to think beautiful, be beautiful, and act beautiful—all at the same time," she said.

The role of Mrs. Skeffington was originally offered to Tallulah Bankhead, who demanded $50,000 to film it. She was turned down. Next it was offered to Ruth Chatterton, who nixed it, as did Claudette Colbert. Jack Warner then asked Greta Garbo to return to the screen in the vehicle. She didn't respond. Finally, Bette Davis was offered the part and immediately rejected it too…at least at first.

During the shoot, Bette's second husband, **Arthur Farnsworth**, (right figure in photo above) collapsed on Hollywood Boulevard and died soon thereafter in a mysterious death.

Virtually everyone in insider Hollywood surmised that Bette's earlier blow to his head with a blunt object led to a blood clot and his ultimate death.

During the making of *Mr. Skeffington*, **Bette Davis** was her most difficult. On several occasions, she actually threatened to shut down the picture unless **Vincent Sherman** went to her dressing room and made love to her.

Bette particularly objected to the heavy rubber mask she had to wear in the aging scenes. She had to arrive early at the studio and spend four tedious hours in make-up.

After she removed the mask at night, she went dancing to entertain the servicemen at the Hollywood Canteen. She often invited the more attractive sailors, marines, airmen, or soldiers to visit the *Mr. Skeffington* set. To make Sherman jealous, she often "auditioned" the more virile servicemen in her dressing room.

Vincent Sherman Gossips About
ERROL FLYNN

"I'm just a goddamn phallic symbol to the world."
Errol Flynn

"There's a little bit of Don Juan in every man, but since I am Don Juan, there must be more of it in me!"
Errol Flynn

When Sherman agreed to direct *The Adventures of Don Juan*, a film eventually released in 1948, Errol Flynn was still Warner Brothers' biggest moneymaker, but his star was starting to flicker out in the Hollywood sky.

Alcohol, beautiful women—and sometimes teenage boys—had taken their toll on his once-fabulous face and physique. The script by George Oppenheimer was a bit too Walt Disney for Sherman's taste. Some of the brass agreed with the director. "In a Flynn film, he's got to be either fighting or fucking on the screen," Jack Warner told him. Other writers were called in "to toughen up" the Oppenheimer script.

On the first day of shooting, Sherman encountered trouble with Flynn in the wardrobe department. The costume department had designed jackets for the star that fell to a point three inches below his crotch line. Flynn did not like them, wanting the hems raised so that at least half of his crotch was exposed to view.

Sherman was leery about showing Flynn's celebrated endowment on screen. He suggested that he follow the custom of ballet dancers. "Pull your thing up and put a piece of tape across it, then put on either a jock strap or the cod piece."

"My dear, boy," Flynn said. "I've done many things for Warners over the years, but I'm damned if I'll tape up my cock for them."

"Flynn was always putting people on," Sherman said. Once, Flynn invited Sherman into his dressing room, ostensibly to discuss an upcoming scene.

Throughout the 40s Errol Flynn managed to project the aura of a *roué* or libertine on screen, even if he wasn't playing such a character.

Following his rape trial in 1943, the viewing public was not turned off by Flynn, but went in greater numbers than ever for a view of his onscreen exploits. According to Vincent Sherman, "His scandalous amours, drunken brawls, alimony problems, and reports of heavy drinking only made him a more intriguing figure."

"During our love scenes," said Swedish actress **Viveca Lindfors**, "he pressed his erection against me, and it was an impressive package, but I wasn't interested. I was more interested in looking ravishing in those Oscar-winning costumes I had to wear."

Director **Vincent Sherman** (right) got to know **Errol Flynn** (left) rather well during the shooting of *Adventures of Don Juan*. "Flynn had a complicated regard for women, Sherman said. "It possibly stemmed from his relationship with his parents. He spoke with great respect of his father, but he expressed a son's love for his mother. It's easy for gossips to dismiss him as a Don Juan, A philanderer, but I think he basically feared women and distrusted them. He once told me he enjoyed a close companionship with men that he could never achieve with women."

Sherman encountered Flynn sitting almost naked, with a small towel covering his privates. Suddenly, he ripped off the towel to reveal a phallus at least a foot long," Sherman claimed. "I stared at it in amazement until I realized the costume department had created this enormous phallus from plastic. But Flynn didn't have to use a fake penis. On three different occasions, he pulled down his pants and exposed his cock to onlookers on the set if he detected the slightest interest. I'd never seen an actor do that before."

"He had many strange theories about sex," Sherman claimed. "He once told me he secretly hated women and preferred the company of men. 'The reason I perform oral sex on a woman is to debase her,'" he told me.

"I would call it worship, not debasement," Sherman countered.

Sherman had heard the stories about Flynn being a bisexual, but he claimed he had no evidence of that during the making of *Don Juan*. However, Sherman was sophisticated enough to admit, "There is in the Don Juan character an incipient homosexuality, but Flynn was not a practicing homosexual."

It was only when Sherman talked to gay director Edmund Goulding that he learned Flynn had had sex "from 12,000 to 14,000 times [Flynn's words] and that his male conquests had included Howard Hughes, Laurence Olivier, and Tyrone Power. Flynn later told Goulding that "Ty disgusts me with the filthy things he wants me to do."

Sherman was not entirely candid in his assessment of Flynn's sexuality. He knew far more than he cared to write about. Perhaps he was protecting what was left of Flynn's reputation.

Flynn's biographer, David Bret, wrote: "Much of the camp content in *Don Juan* stemmed from the fact that Errol and the scriptwriter, George Oppenheimer, 'spoke the same language.' Between them, they were reputed to have slept with every one of the muscular young actors who portray Don Juan's fencing students in the film, and Oppenheimer several times 'put on shows' beneath the see-through mirror in Errol's bedroom for the benefit of those voyeurs [positioned silently behind it] in the 'jerk-off' room."

During the shoot, Errol became sexually intrigued with Robert Douglas, who portrayed the villain of the piece, the Duke de Lorca.

Bret revealed what was obvious to everyone on the set. "Errol got involved with his on-screen enemy, Robert Douglas—not exclusively in a homosexual affair, but to 'augment' his sex life. He was fascinated by the slightly younger actor's pale, extraordinarily beautiful eyes."

Robert Douglas was suave, sophisticated, and urbane but destined not to play the leading man in Hollywood. According to reports, Flynn found him a "sexy number" and came on to him strong.

A bisexual himself, Douglas was flattered by Flynn's attention. "At my home you can participate in the best orgies in Hollywood," Flynn told his co-star in *Don Juan*." Douglas was eager to take him up on his offer...and did.

In *Don Juan*, **Errol Flynn**, who was often photographed in green tights, wanted to show off his famously ample crotch, which brought him into conflict with several of his directors. "We're not making that kind of movie," Vincent Sherman told him.

"As far as *Don Juan* is concerned, I'd call it a two-hour piss-take," Flynn told his director. During filming, Flynn came down with sinus trouble. A doctor prescribed drops. Returning to work, the actor was seen shoving the nozzle up his nostrils throughout the day. He was actually inhaling a mixture of cocaine and vodka.

After seducing Douglas in his dressing room, Flynn invited him to join the young men in his 'jerk-off' room at his home on Mulholland House. Douglas gladly agreed, performing in front of the mirror for the voyeurs looking in. Soon Douglas became a regular at these get-togethers, making love to a woman while watching two men having sex or else masturbating a man, perhaps Flynn himself, while watching two lesbians go at it.

For reasons known only to himself, Sherman in his memoir, *Studio Affairs*, left out one of the most evocative stories.

One day Flynn brought to the set a beautiful young girl who looked the epitome of innocence. "Flynn introduced her to me, but I paid no attention to her name," Sherman said. "I met dozens of hopeful starlets every week. I thought she was pretty but nothing sensational. They disappeared into his dressing room, and I practically had to send two grips to haul him out two hours later. The girl came out adjusting her clothes. I thought no more of the incident."

"Years later I ran into my friend John Huston," Sherman said. He told me he was directing a beautiful young blonde in a movie and that she was going to be a big star sooner than later. He said this girl knew me. I didn't recall her."

"She said Flynn introduced her to you on the set of *Don Juan*," Huston told me.

"I vaguely remember he brought some young model by," Sherman said.

"That girl, my dear man, was Marilyn Monroe," Huston said. "You should have signed her on the spot."

When ***Studio Affairs: My Life as a Film Director,*** by Vincent Sherman, was published in 1996, the director's revelations shocked Hollywood. Despite the fact that he'd included many scandalous details about his life, he held back, avoiding some of the more lurid scenes and involvements he'd either witnessed or experienced with Hollywood's biggest stars.

For the book's front cover, he selected a picture of himself in his undershirt, with a very youthful **Ida Lupino** snuggling up to him. He had directed her in the 1942 release, *The Hard Way*, but this future director became notorious for trying to direct the scenes herself.

"Finally," Sherman later said, "I realized that what the insecure Ida really needed was a good fucking in her dressing room at three o'clock every afternoon. That lasted until she received news of her father's death. He was Stanley Lupino, a famous actor of his day. I also threw my back out on the set and that stopped my amorous visits."

Vincent Sherman Gossips About
RONALD REAGAN

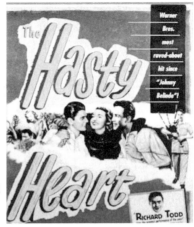

"He's about as good in bed as he was on the screen."

Jane Wyman

Released on December 2, 1949, *The Hasty Heart* was directed by Vincent Sherman and starred Ronald Reagan, Patricia Neal, and the British actor, Richard Todd, a newcomer to the screen.

Although Sherman had known Reagan for a number of years, he became much better acquainted with him in London during the shooting of *The Hasty Heart*. "He was still heartbroken over his recent divorce from the Oscar-winning actress Jane Wyman," Sherman said.

Reagan admitted that he knew of her affair with co-star Lew Ayres, during the 1948 making of *Johnny Belinda*, in which she played a deaf mute who is raped.

"I can overlook an affair here and there," Reagan said. "She's been very tolerant of me when I get Leadingladyitis. I'd heard about Lew and Jane. She very much needs to have a fling, and I intend to let her have it. If she'd stayed with me, we could have worked things out. I'm sure of that."

"He told me he was stalking her, and often would park his car across the street from where she lived," Sherman said. "Sometimes, according to him, he'd wait in his car until two or three o'clock in the morning to see who she was bringing home."

"When I later talked to Patricia Neal, I learned that she too was a lovesick puppy," Sherman said. "She wanted to get back to Hollywood and the arms of Gary Cooper, with whom she'd fallen in love."

Away from the studio, and out and about in London, Reagan was seen frequently with Neal, his co-star. "We would have dinner and even go dancing at one of the local dance

"**Reagan** had a lot of complaints while making *The Hasty Heart* in England," according to **Richard Todd**. "After the war, England froze the amount of money a producer could take out of the country. Reagan felt that was a total lack of grace considering that the United States 'had saved England from Hitler's Nazi grip'—his words."

"Although shot in England, *The Hasty Heart* was actually set in Burma," Todd said. "On those cold sound stages, we had to wear light tropical garb. Reagan complained constantly about the chill and dampness of an English winter. Nothing was heated after the war. Reagan told me, 'I'm freezing my balls off, and the gals back in Hollywood won't like that.' That was the first time I realized Reagan could talk like a regular bloke if he wanted to."

"**Reagan** gave a great massage," said British actor **Richard Todd** (*figure on right in photo immediately above*). "If he hadn't become president, he could have hired out as a masseur. If I recall, he gave me an erection." We assume Todd was joking, but perhaps not. According to Todd, "It wasn't all love on Reagan's part. I know he wanted to play my plum role of Lachie himself and ended up in the duller part. The guy could be jealous. I hear he came out with some rumblings when I received an Oscar nod in reference to 'the role that belonged to me.'"

halls," Neal later said. "He was a good dancer. People may have been shabbily dressed and their food rationed, but at night they sang and danced with all their hearts. They were so happy the war was over."

Reagan, according to Neal, missed his American steaks and had a dozen flown in from "21" in New York. But when he invited Neal to a steak dinner at the Savoy Hotel, the chef came out and apologized. "The steaks, Mr. Reagan, have gone bad."

"Ronnie knew differently," Neal said. "The chef probably had eaten them himself."

"Both Neal and Reagan were depressed about their respective affairs of the heart," Sherman said. "I had to put up with them and that bitter London cold."

Reagan had originally wanted to play the role of the prickly young Scottish lad, Lachie, in *The Hasty Heart*, but that went to the young and handsome Dublin-born actor Richard Todd, although Reagan had been promised star billing. "Reagan was cold to me at first, and I knew he resented me," Todd claimed. "But when he heard I was cast in *Stage Fright*, he suddenly became so warm and cozy I thought he was a poof. Later on, I found out the real reason for the friendship."

Todd was set to star in the Alfred Hitchcock film, *Stage Fright*, co-starring Jane Wyman and Marlene Dietrich. "I think what Reagan really wanted was for me to be a go-between, running messages to Jane on the set. He told me he thought there was a good chance that if she would agree to meet with him, there could be reconciliation with Jane."

"I didn't think so, but I humored Reagan," Todd said. "To be honest I was screwing Jane in her dressing room, and she told me I was much better at it than her former spouse. Not only that, I got a blow-job from Miss Dietrich herself. Fellatio was her specialty."

Todd delivered a bombshell. He claimed that Reagan approached him only weeks before his marriage to Nancy Davis, and asked him to go see Jane Wyman once again on his behalf.

"He told me that if Jane would remarry him," Todd claimed, "that he'd call off the upcoming wedding to Nancy. I found this astonishing, because the grapevine claimed that Nancy was already carrying Reagan's baby on her long route to the altar with him."

Virginia Mayo, who had made *The Girl from Jones Beach* with Reagan, attended a Royal Command Film Performance of the

When Reagan met **Richard Todd**, he was on the dawn of what looked like a brilliant career. But clouds were on the horizon. His biggest professional disappointment occurred when Ian Fleming asked him to play James Bond in *Dr. No*. A scheduling conflict prevented that, the role eventually going to Sean Connery.

Todd's greatest private pain involved the suicides of his two sons—Seamus Palethorpe-Todd in 1997 and Peter Todd in 2005. Both men shot themselves. Todd, suffering from cancer, died on December 3, 2009.

"The image of **Jane Wyman** hovered over the set of *The Hasty Heart* like she was the co-star in the picture," Richard Todd said. "Reagan was still in love with her, although having dates—perhaps affairs—with the likes of Doris Day and the up-and-coming Marilyn Monroe bombshell. I jokingly asked him one time if he got back with Jane, would he give me his cast-offs? He had no answer for that. While shooting the film, he spent a lot of time calling Jane in California. He was eager for news of not only her but also of the children."

While in London, although they had already been divorced, Reagan was invited to accept an award for Jane from the *London Daily Express* Film Tribunal, which had declared her as the year's best actress for her appearance in *Johnny Belinda*.

movie, *Scott of the Atlanta*, starring John Mills. "Our party in London included Alan and Sue Ladd," she recalled, "along with Larry Olivier and Vivien Leigh. Vivien fell asleep during this dull movie, and her right breast popped out. I nudged Ronnie to awaken her and inform her of her tit malfunction. Instead of watching John Mills, he spent the rest of the movie staring at that exposed breast of Scarlett O'Hara, which he didn't get to see in *Gone With the Wind*."

During the making of *The Hasty Heart*, Sherman claimed that Reagan was "very thin skinned when I critiqued his performance. In his memoir, *Where's the Rest of Me?*, he had good words for everyone but failed to mention me."

During the four months that Reagan worked in London, Sherman noted a radical shift in his politics, as Reagan moved away from the Democrats and into the camp of the Republicans. As he'd later put it, "I spent those months in England while the Labour Party was in power. I saw firsthand how the welfare state sapped incentive to work from many people in a wonderful and dynamic country."

Sherman claimed that Reagan tried to get over Wyman by having a secret affair with a script girl on the set of *The Hasty Heart*. "She was sort of a mousey looking creature with glasses but had bit tits," Sherman recalled. "I heard that she joined him for shack-ups when he took a vacation after filming. They were seen together in Wales, Ireland, and France."

When Sherman returned to Hollywood, Jack Warner told him, "I want to get rid of Reagan. Most of his pictures are lousy. Did you see crap like *That Hagen Girl* and *Night Unto Night*. He was a pretty boy when he was running around Hollywood in the early 40s fucking Betty Grable and Lana Turner. But he's getting jowly and mov-

Back to back, **Richard Todd** (left) and **Ronald Reagan** (right) posed for this famous shot on the set of *The Hasty Heart*.

Todd had pub drinks with Reagan one night, and the future president shared a poignant moment with the emerging young actor. "I feel my career is about over and yours is just beginning. I envy you. But one thing I don't envy is your trying to make it in post-war Hollywood. It was always a vicious place. But the deadly rattlers have been replaced with man-eating dinosaurs. I may go into politics on a national level, although my involvement in film industry politics has damaged my career. I made enemies of directors and producers who might have hired me."

Long before the ex-Mrs. Ronald Reagan—**Jane Wyman** (left)—appeared with **Marlene Dietrich**, there was speculation that these two actresses, each with a super-sized ego, would clash. Jane told reporters, "If I worked for forty years I couldn't be a glamour girl like Marlene Dietrich." Already fifty, Dietrich was billed as "The world's most glamorous grandmother."

In the film, Dietrich played herself, a dazzling star, and Jane appeared as a dowdy maid. Every time Jane saw the rushes of herself alongside Marlene, she burst into tears.

Even though he was still pining for Jane Wyman, **Ronald Reagan** "settled for **Nancy Davis**," according to Vincent Sherman. "He told me he'd never get over Jane, but had to move on with his life. Nancy definitely got Reagan on the rebound." *Hellcats of the Navy* was Reagan's first and only film with his second wife. Nancy played a navy nurse.

As an actress, Nancy turned out to be no Jane Wyman. All she could do was look loving and supportive. An aging Reagan was going nowhere with his screen career. For Nancy, *Hellcats* more or less doomed a film career that never really got off the ground.

ing into middle age. I'll throw him in crappy films and maybe he'll break the contract."

"Although Reagan didn't really like me," I visited him in the hospital," Sherman said. "He'd sustained multiple fractures to his right knee when he was playing with other film stars in a fund-raising baseball game."

"I felt sorry for the guy who was down on his luck," Sherman said. "A fading Hollywood star going into oblivion. But when this beautiful nurse—she looked about eighteen—came to check on him, I didn't feel so sorry for him anymore. After she'd gone, he told me she was bathing him and including a quickie blow-job as part of the package."

Believe it or not, **Ronald Reagan** was viewed as a male pinup during his early years in Hollywood. In the left-hand photo, he poses with **Jane Wyman**, a young starlet he was pursuing, among several others. "In my early Hollywood days, I was too busy and too scared to collect phone numbers." he said. As far as it is known, that was the first lie he ever told the press. He was indeed collecting phone numbers, especially of hot blondes like young Betty Grable and young Lana Turner. Soon, he was bedding that sultry redhead, Susan Hayward. To William Holden, later his best friend, he said, "I never intended to marry Jane. It was too exciting playing the field. In Hollywood, you didn't have to call up women for dates. They called you. Jane was pretty and pert, and I think she set her hat for me. What chance did I have?"

In the center photo, "**Ronnie and Jane**" were photographed on their wedding day in January of 1940. Parents Nelle and Jack Reagan showed up for the wedding, and Louella Parsons hosted the reception at her home in Beverly Hills.

On the right, **the Reagans** hold hands with their daughter, **Maureen**, and their son, **Michael**. They lived in the "dream house" they built overlooking Sunset Boulevard, but their marriage was slowly crumbling as both of them engaged in extramarital affairs.

Born in Kentucky, reared in Tennessee, **Patricia Neal** became recognized as one of the most talented actresses in Hollywood. She met **Ronald Reagan** when they co-starred in *John Loves Mary* (1949), the same year *The Fountainhead* was released. That teamed her with her alltime love, Gary Cooper. Ironically, also configured for release in 1949, was *The Hasty Heart,* which teamed her once again with Reagan.

It was her first time in England. The year was 1948. "I hated it, just hated it. Everything went wrong, the picture just went on forever—four months. Men referred to their wives as either 'old girl' or 'old sausage.' I was bored and homesick."

Neal later claimed that Reagan never made a pass at her, although they were occupying adjoining suites at the swanky Savoy Hotel. "I was a young, pretty girl, but I was wildly in love with Gary Cooper, and Reagan was still in love with Jane."

Vincent Sherman Gossips About
JOAN CRAWFORD

"That terrible, vulgar woman with the pop eyes beats her children. But what do you expect from that class? A cheap tap dancer."

Marlene Dietrich

When Vincent Sherman met Joan Crawford, he swore to himself that he would not get involved sexually with her the way he had with her rival, Bette Davis. He also wasn't that turned on by her. With a director's steely sharp eye, he noted, "there were lines in her face, crow's feet around her eyes, and her neck was beginning to show wrinkles."

Crawford, however, had other plans. She invited him to a screening of her 1946 movie, *Humoresque*, in which she'd co-starred with John Garfield.

"Midway through the movie, when I complimented her on a very sexy scene, she took my hand, held it against her breast, and soon followed it by placing her other hand on my knee and moving it up my leg. I was stunned but aroused."

Before he knew what was happening, she had pulled off her clothes and a pair of red silk panties and demanded that he take her on the carpeted floor of the projection room. "I confronted a female who went after what she wanted, and was very masculine in her approach to sex."

When he seduced her again days later in the shower of her luxurious home, she told him, "The ideal wife is a lady in the living room but a whore in bed."

The first picture Sherman directed with Crawford, originally known as *The Victim*, underwent a title change and became *The Damned Don't Cry* (1950). Marketed by Warner

Looking like a "lipstick lesbian," this is the most imperial photograph ever taken of **Joan Crawford.**

"She was the ultimate star—magnetic and glamorous," Vincent Sherman said. "She had won an Academy Award for her performance in *Mildred Pierce* and had replaced Bette Davis as Warner's number one female. I had never thought of her as a great actress, but she was certainly talented and had a vivid personality, and I admired her drive and determination to better herself. So I was not unhappy when that next assignment would be to direct her."

Columbia Pictures hired Vincent Sherman to direct **Joan Crawford** in the 1950 *Harriet Craig*, the story of a neurotic perfectionist who makes life miserable for everyone around her. That was especially true for her husband Walter (Wendell Corey).

A right wing Republican and amateur politician, Corey, a New Englander, like Joan, was alcoholic. He would die at the age of 54 of cirrhosis of the liver. Joan complained about the casting of Corey opposite her. "There's no chemistry between us," she told Sherman. "One night I tried to seduce him. He took off his pants and I laughed at it. He quickly put on his pants and left."

Brothers as "the Flaming Stars of *Flamingo Road* meet in Scarlet Shadows Again," it co-starred David Brian, Steve Cochran, and Kent Smith.

When not in bed with Sherman, Crawford was attracted to the ruggedly handsome Cochran, who had been the lover of Mae West. He was fabled in Hollywood for the size of his appendage.

The crime writer, James Ellroy, was to make more fans for Cochran thanks to references to him in his novels *American Tabloid* and *L.A. Confidential*. The actor, who had one of the largest penises in Hollywood, bore the nickname "Mr. King Sized." Ellroy referred to Cochran with the sobriquet "*The Shvantz*."

Virile and swaggering, with a tendency to drink, Cochran told Sherman that he was only plugging Crawford because he hoped she'd give him a role in her next picture.

Like Rita Hayworth, Crawford wanted Sherman to divorce his wife and marry her. But he turned her down.

There were many mishaps before Sherman's relationship with Crawford came to an end, including two more pictures with her—*Harriet Craig* in 1950 and *Goodbye, My Fancy* in 1951. There was even a suicide attempt when Crawford called him with what seemed at the time like a final good-bye. He rushed to her home to discover she'd overdosed on sleeping pills.

The relationship definitively ended in 1952 after Crawford called Sherman's wife, Hedda, and told her, "I'm sending Vince back to you."

He assumed that everything had ended between Crawford and himself until he received a phone call from her in 1963, just before the filming of *Hush, Hush Sweet Charlotte*, starring herself and, once again, Bette Davis, her co-star in the wildly popular *What Ever Happened to Baby Jane?* (1962).

Reportedly, Crawford became seriously ill during the shooting of the film, and was sent to the hospital, where Sherman visited her. From her hospital bed, Crawford told him there was nothing wrong with her. She claimed that she'd faked the illness as a means of getting out of the movie because Davis had been maneuvering with director Robert Aldrich "to get my part cut down to nothing."

Then, to Sherman's surprise, Crawford wanted him to seduce her in her hospital bed. "I obliged the lady. My heart wasn't in it, but fortunately my hard-on was."

The last time he ever heard from Crawford was in 1977, when a call came in from her in New York. She'd heard that Sherman had turned down an invitation to the Life Achievement Award banquet for Davis.

The Damned Don't Cry

(*Top photo*) Caught between two guns, **Joan Crawford** comes between **Steve Cochran** (left figure in photo above, and again on left in photo below) and **David Brian** (right figure in photo above) when they shot *The Damned Don't Cry*.

Unlike some of the other men she worked with, Crawford interpreted both Cochran and Brian as "two hotties, especially that Cochran. I've had most of the big ones in Hollywood, but he's right up there with the best of them. They don't come much rougher or tougher on screen or off than Steve. He's screwed everybody from Mae West to Jayne Mansfield."

Joan went on to say, "David [Brian] is also every inch a man if you get my drift. Can you believe he had to put up with me in 1949 on *Flamingo Road* and that same year appeared with that psycho, Bette Davis, in *Beyond the Forest*. David told me he didn't fuck Davis, saving it all for me." She burst into laughter. "Should I believe that?"

248

"Vincent, darling," Crawford said, "I'm so happy you're not going to the dinner for Bette. She's such a bitch. She made my life miserable on *Baby Jane*."

Crawford urged Sherman not to change his mind. He assured her he was standing firm in his decision not to attend.

"Are you okay?" I asked her, as he sensed something might be wrong with her.

"Yes, darling," she said. "Goodbye and God bless."

Unknown to him at the time, Crawford was dying of cancer.

Death came to Lucille Fay LeSueur (her real name) on May 10, 1977. TV broadcasters interrupted their regular shows to notify the world that Joan Crawford had died. Much of America had grown up watching her emote on the screen.

When the press called Sherman for his reaction, he said, "If anyone asked me to define the words 'movie star,' I'd simply say **JOAN CRAWFORD**."

On the set of *Goodbye, My Fancy,* director **Vincent Sherman** places a possessive hand on **Joan Crawford**, a public display of affection. The entire cast knew she was having an affair with her director. By the end of this film, relations between Sherman and Joan had cooled. "The on-screen romance between Joan and **Frank Lovejoy** *(photo, above, right)*, as I had predicted, did not work," Sherman said. "She complained about having him cast as her leading man."

"'Lovejoy,' he calls himself," Joan said. "He has no love of joy or anything else. I put his hand on my breast, but that didn't get a rise out of him. Don't tell me he's not gay. How could he resist me?"

At the end of this disaster, Sherman was asked to move on from Warner's. Joan would make one more film for them and then depart as well. "Joan and I also moved on from each other," Sherman said. "What we had together was never made to work out."

Vincent Sherman Gossips About
CLARK GABLE
& AVA GARDNER

LONE STAR

"Some people say Liz and I are whores, but we are saints. We do not hide our loves hypocritically, and when in love we are loyal and faithful to our men."

Ava Gardner

"I can't stand a man who has fake store teeth and doesn't keep his uncircumcised cock clean under the foreskin. I hear he shoots too soon and messes himself all the time."

Bette Davis, referring to Clark Gable

Ava Gardner claimed she never bedded **Clark Gable** (left), although there was speculation. No one even suggested that she went to bed with her other co-star **Broderick Crawford** (right).

Ruth Waterbury, a Hollywood journalist, disputed Ava's claim. Calling on her for an interview at her London residence in 1953, she found Ava cooking bacon and eggs for someone. The voice in the adjoining bedroom sounded familiar. "In a minute, Clark Gable walked into the kitchen wearing nothing but a grin," claimed Waterbury.

Wearing a pair of blue jeans and a man's work shirt, Ava Gardner, with her feet propped on her dressing table, confronted Vincent Sherman. "If you're such a hot shot director, why are you directing this piece of shit?" She was referring to MGM's *Lone Star*. Released in 1952, and starring Clark Gable, it was a big-budget, loosely historical epic which MGM advertised as "The Battle for Texas, and the Battle of the Sexes."

She was contemptuous of her role as a newspaper editor who opposes Texas' entry into the Union. "Cast me as a hooker. I can play that. A fallen woman. But a god damn newspaper editor! Hell, I don't even look like I can read a newspaper, much less edit one."

She was romantically involved with Frank Sinatra at the time, who was at the low point of his career. "Frankie was washed up," said Broderick Crawford, another co-star in *Lone Star*. "You couldn't give that fucker away free to any director. I saw him visiting the set every now and then but staying way in the background. He was no doubt making sure that Ava didn't start fucking Gable again like she did on the set of *The Hucksters* back in 1947."

"Sinatra was not the only one washed up," Sherman said. "Once the biggest star at MGM, Gable was also washed up. His box office smashes were behind him. This picture was slated for release in 1952. It was a hell of a long time since he'd played Rhett Butler in *Gone With the Wind* (1939)."

Once, while Sherman was in the hospital, someone tipped Gable off that his director was a card-carrying communist and listed on the infamous Red Channels List.

[The Red Channels List, aka "The Report of Communist Influence in Radio and Televison," was an anti-Communist pamphlet published on June 22, 1950, listing 151 writers, musicians, broadcast journalists, actors, producers, and directors who were allegedly manipulating the American entertainment industry with Communist propaganda.]

Broderick Crawford claimed that Gable, a Right Wing American patriot, "didn't want to be directed by a commie pinko."

Only when Sherman signed a loyalty oath did Gable agree to let him direct him in *Lone Star*. Sherman was forced to do that, even though he opposed loyalty oaths, because *Lone Star* might otherwise have become the target of a boycott, which neo-Fascist American groups were willing to organize.

"The script needed a massive overhaul, and Borden Chase was brought back to rewrite his own piece of crap he'd given us earlier," Sherman said. "We were like a rattlesnake and a chicken coming together. He was practically a Nazi. He even felt that Texas should not have joined the Union. He was also a son of a bitch. He was later accused of incest with his stepdaughter."

"He also wanted to transform the story into a subliminal love story between two super-macho men, Gable and Broderick Crawford," Sherman said.

"Women are mere sex objects," Chase told Sherman. "To be fucked and discarded. The only real love bonding in life is between two guys. I've talked this over with John Wayne, and he agrees with me."

Finally, near desperation, Sherman was forced to shoot Chase's script. He tried to eliminate what corny dialogue he could, but later claimed, "I could not make a silk purse out of a sow's ear."

In shooting footage of Gable, Sherman was faced with another problem—the star's "creeping" Parkinson's disease.

Ava Gardner with **Vincent Sherman** (right) knew what kind of movie *Lone Star* was. In spite of the big names, Ava said it could pass for a Grade B western at Republic, one that might have starred Vera Hruba Ralston and Forrest Tucker. "Both Ava and I wondered how we got stuck in this lemon," Sherman said. "It was a rotten picture. But, you know, you need to get paid, and you're under contract so there isn't much choice. My three stars were drunk. Ava and Gable, old pals from way back, were tippling. Broderick Crawford went through the picture in an alcoholic stupor."

MGM had warned Sherman to calculate his shots carefully, and to avoid any scene that ran too long. In longer shots, Sherman was told, "Gable's head will start to shake."

Although Gable would not die until 1960, it was obvious to Sherman that he knew he was nearing the end of his trail. "They say life begins at forty," Gable told his director. "I'm past fifty. They've got no fucking slogans for after fifty."

Gable was still sexually active, but even during his prime, he'd been referred to as "less than able Gable" by women he'd seduced. Even his once-beloved former wife, Carole Lombard, told anyone willing to listen, "God knows I love Clark, but he's the worst lay in town. I should know. I've had them all."

During the shooting of *Lone Star,* Gable spent many a drunken night with Sherman, and the director found him honest and even self-deprecating about his sexual allure.

"That Mexican spitfire, Lupe Velez, once tried to get me to plug her," Gable told Sherman. "There was no way I was going to do that. That Montana Mule, Gary Cooper, is a tough act to follow. Actually, I prefer whores. You can fuck 'em, pay 'em, and get rid of 'em. They go away and keep their mouths shut."

After *Lone Star* was wrapped, Sherman ran into Gable only very sporadically. "I tried to get in touch with him when I heard he'd signed to do *The Misfits* with Marilyn Monroe," Sherman said. "But I never got through to him. I felt I should warn him about something. When Tallulah Bankhead hit Hollywood, she claimed she'd come here for only one reason: '*To fuck that divine Gary Cooper, dahling.*' Marilyn told me she came to Hollywood for two reasons— 'to become the biggest movie star there is and to fuck Clark Gable, my idol.' I thought I'd better warn Gable to eat his Wheaties before encountering Marilyn."

Later in life, Sherman reflected on the regrets of his career. "I have two biggies—I didn't get to direct Bogie in *Casablanca,* and I didn't fuck Ava Gardner when she asked me to on the set of *Lone Star.*"

Vincent Sherman Gossips About
RITA HAYWORTH

"All I ever wanted to be was myself. Every man I've ever known has fallen in love with Gilda and wakened up with me."
Rita Hayworth

Rita Hayworth, screen goddess of the 1940s, was nervous facing the camera again after a long absence. But Columbia's primary honcho, Harry Cohn, who had constantly pursued her for sexual favors, convinced her he had a great property lined up for her.

The picture came to be called *Affair in Trinidad*, and it was released in the autumn of 1952. Her return to the screen after three years caused worldwide anticipation, even though the actual movie didn't merit such press fascination.

The director she'd been assigned was Vincent Sherman. Her co-star was her former lover, Glenn Ford, who had created box office magic with her in *Gilda*. Cohn assured her that *Affair in Trinidad* would be greater box office than *Gilda*, although after reading its script, she wasn't convinced.

She'd been a princess during her ill-fated five-year marriage to a real-life Muslim prince, the Aly Khan, but at this point in her life, their relationship was over. "I think he started fucking other women on our honeymoon," she later confessed to her former husband, Orson Welles, during their reunion.

Princess Rita had danced onscreen with both Fred Astaire and Gene Kelly. She'd had affairs with everyone from Howard Hughes to Victor Mature, from Robert Mitchum to Tyrone Power.

Her co-stars had included a former married couple, Joan Crawford and Douglas Fairbanks Jr., both of whom had successfully maneuvered to seduce her. She played onscreen with Fredric March, who also seduced her. She'd starred with James Cagney in *The Strawberry Blonde* (1941), but he didn't even try to seduce her.

Along with Betty Grable, she was the most popular

Meeting on the set of *Affair in Trinidad*, **Rita Hayworth** and **Vincent Sherman** *(right)* were all smiles. But within minutes, each of them confessed to the other that the Trinidad picture had an "absolutely awful script."

Harry Cohn had rushed Rita into the picture at Columbia to take advantage of the massive publicity she was receiving following the breakup of her marriage to Prince Aly Kahn. Earlier that day, Cohn had told Sherman, "even a bad picture with Princess Rita in it can clean up at the box office."

"Rita seemed to drift in and out of men," said Vincent Sherman, "including myself. But she always went back to **Glenn Ford**, her co-star in *Gilda*, her most famous picture."

One of the screen's great love teams, Glenn and Rita made the screen sizzle in their sado-masochistic affairs in both *Gilda* and *Affair in Trinidad*. They became part of the pantheon of romantic teams like Greta Garbo and John Gilbert or Jean Harlow and Clark Gable.

Glenn later admitted that in *Gilda* he was playing a latent homosexual. "But I wasn't gay off screen, especially during those visits to Rita's dressing room."

pin-up of WWII—dubbed "The Love Goddess." Most ironic of all, her likeness had been taped to the atomic bomb that destroyed Hiroshima and changed the course of world history forever.

Long before Grace Kelly, she was the first Hollywood star to become *real life* royalty when, in 1948, she married Prince Aly Salomone Khan (1911-1960), heir at the time to the spiritual legacy of millions of members of the Shia Muslim Ismailian community, on the French Riviera. As part of their spectacularly publicized wedding ceremony, thousands of Ismailian Muslims paid homage to their spiritual leader, and the swimming pool of the French Riviera's Château de l'Horizon overflowed with champagne. The marriage officially ended five years later, in 1953, although for all practical purposes its life had been extinguished several years before.

She had everything, or so it seemed. But she lacked the one thing she so desperately wanted. Someone to love her as much as she loved back.

During the filming of *Affair in Trinidad*, Sherman had no idea of any sexual interest which Hayworth might have had in him. "It seemed that Glenn Ford was balling her every afternoon. They had rekindled their old affair. Like myself, Glenn had also seduced Bette Davis and Joan Crawford. Or, rather those two broads had seduced him."

After the shoot, Hayworth accepted an invitation to an Italian dinner with Sherman. When he drove her home, she invited him in for a nightcap. Leaving him in her living room, she went upstairs to say good night to her children.

When she returned, she was barefoot, clad only in a silk nightgown. After a glimpse or two, he determined she was wearing nothing underneath. That became even more obvious when she sprawled across her sofa, putting her feet up on his lap. He gave her a seductive foot massage, which produced an erection.

Sensing this, she told him she wanted to take a warm bath and invited him to come up and help her with that chore. "It was no chore," Sherman later said. "What red-blooded man could turn down Rita Hayworth?"

He admitted that, "I bathed her like a child. Her body was firm and voluptuous. I dried her off and undressed myself and got into bed with her. I held her for an hour before making love to her."

She came to his office the next day, and he sensed that she was desperate for someone to love and cherish her. But he had to turn her down. "You're a lovely, talented lady, and it would be easy to fall madly in love with you, but I have a devoted wife, plus two beautiful children."

There were tears in her eyes as she kissed him goodbye. They would never see each other again.

After Sherman rejected her attempt to establish a long-term relationship, Hayworth began to date at random. Victor Mature called, hoping to ignite their old fires from the 40s.

Kirk Douglas arrived on her doorstep for a brief romance. He quickly broke it off. "I felt something deep within her that I couldn't help—loneliness, sadness—something that would pull me down. I had to get away."

"I had $300,000 in the bank when I married Prince Khan, but I came back from the marriage broke," **Rita Hayworth** said. "That's why I agreed to do that turkey, *Affair in Trinidad*. Of course, I loved being back in Glenn Ford's arms."

The impassioned romantic scenes between Rita and Glenn still worked their magic on screen—reviewers referred to them as "scorching." Rita later confessed that Glenn off screen was "even more of an experienced lover during the shoot of *Affair in Trinidad* than he had been on the set of *Gilda*, and he was pretty terrific then. He must have been taking lessons with someone while I was abroad."

253

Her affair with the agent-producer Charles Feldman ended violently when she kicked him in the balls.

When she appeared in *Salome* in 1953, she had a torrid affair with her co-star, the British actor Stewart Granger. "When he wasn't fucking me, he was fucking Michael Wilding," she said. "You remember him? One of Elizabeth Taylor's husbands."

A new husband, the Argentinian singer Dick Haymes, was waiting in the wings. "Rita was a steep, steep toboggan ride," Orson Welles said of his former wife. "Especially when she met and married that singer."

When Hayworth met Haymes in 1953, he was known as "Mr. Evil," and had blown four million dollars of his earnings, a vast fortune in the 1940s.

"Haymes found what he perceived to be his meal ticket when he married Rita," Welles charged.

The singer used and abused her until her marriage to him ended in the divorce courts.

There would be one final husband, producer James Hill (*Vera Cruz;* 1954, and *Sweet Smell of Success;* 1957).

That marriage, like all the others, was stormy. It ended when the forty-two-year-old actress entered a courtroom for her final divorce on September 7, 1961. Her voice was so hoarse it was barely audible in the courtroom.

As she walked out of court to breathe in the last days of summer, she did not know that a mysterious and degenerative disease would soon after find a permanent home in her body.

Alzheimer's disease would eventually take her life. After a long, hard struggle that would last for years to come, Rita Hayworth—born Margarita Carmen Cansino—called it quits on May 14, 1987.

Headlines blared: **GILDA IS DEAD.**

Later reflecting on her role in *Affair in Trinidad*, **Rita Hayworth** said, "It wasn't really a movie. It was a culmination of compromises made by everyone from the gateman at Columbia right up to Harry Cohn himself."

At the time of her marriage to Prince Aly Kahn, Rita told the press that she probably would never make another film. At least that was her intention at the time. *Affair in Trinidad* represented her comeback after four long years off screen. After endless delays and script revisions, none of which pleased Rita, the picture became known as *Compromise at Columbia*. At one point Rita was suspended when she walked off the film, calling it "shit wrapped in a turd." Actually *Affair in Trinidad* ended up outgrossing *Gilda* by a million dollars.

Sensational Stanwyck

BISEXUAL AFFAIRS WITH THE A-LIST

A tough little girl from Brooklyn, Ruby Stevens – later renamed **Barbara Stanwyck** *(photo above)*– grew up the hard way. Like Marilyn Monroe, she was shunted from one uncaring foster home to another.

Later in Hollywood, she brought that same toughness, adding glamour and a sexiness to the silver screen. She even married heartthrob Robert Taylor, who turned out to be more romantic on screen than off.

Her greatest love affair – and the most enduring – was with Joan Crawford. The young love of her autumnal years was Robert Wagner.

Aboard the Titanic in 1953, There Was More to Worry About Than Icebergs and Frostbite

Poor Robert Wagner. During the making of *Titanic* in 1953, he was pursued by both of its older stars, Clifton Webb and Barbara Stanwyck. Webb told his friend, Noel Coward, "Getting into Bobby's pants would be the peak achievement of my life. I can hope, can't I?"

Stanwyck, 45, was far luckier, though she completely denied to the press that she was involved in a May-September romance with the handsome young stud, then in the blush of his early twenties. Her biographer, Axel Madsen, said that Wagner "had a kind of gauche innocence and capacity for bursting into flames that flattered her and reminded her of Bob when they first met."

The above-noted reference to "Bob" referred to her second husband, the bisexual actor, Robert Taylor. Perhaps because of Stanwyck's domineering, take-charge personality, Taylor became impotent with his wife, who was constantly accusing him of homosexuality. Not that she was one to talk. "Talk about the pot calling the kettle black," said Lana Turner, one-time rival for Taylor's affections.

"Ah, that woman," Taylor told his friend, Andy Devine about Stanwyck. "She always wants to run the fuck."

Taylor had no trouble getting an erection when he met another Taylor—Elizabeth, that is—on the set of *Conspirator* (1949). He was 38 years old, appearing with the young violet-eyed beauty in her first adult role. "To be kissed on the screen by Robert Taylor means I will never again be considered a little girl."

For the kissing scene, Elizabeth, also already of full bosom, wore a black *négligée*. Embracing the nymphet, Taylor (Bob, that is)

Robert Wagner *(right)*, young and beautiful, was "discovered" by gay casting couch agent, Henry Willson, who was known for finding handsome, well-built hunks and fashioning careers for them in the movie industry. Willson also claimed to have discovered Rock Hudson, Tab Hunter, Tony Curtis, Rory Calhoun, and Guy Madison. Wagner was a particular favorite of Willson's, but the young actor had other plans, going on to seduce the likes of Joan Collins, Linda Christian, Terry Moore, Lori Nelson, Mona Freeman, Jean Peters, Debbie Reynolds, Lana Turner, and even Tina Sinatra.

TITANIC

Barbara Stanwyck's sometimes rival, Bette Davis, had only kind words about **Stanwyck** *(top photo)* but constantly condemned her best friend, Joan Crawford. "I certainly agree with all those who find more sex appeal in Barbara Stanwyck and her ankle bracelet in *Double Indemnity* (1944) than in all those naked bodies rolling around on the screen today." So spoke the chain-smoking Mother Goddamn herself.

When Stanwyck appeared with costar Clifton Webb *(photos above)* in the 1953 version of *Titanic*, she knew that the aging actor was hopelessly in love with the young, incredibly handsome Robert Wagner. But Webb's loss was Stanwyck's gain--at least until Wagner moved on to other conquests.

developed a hard-on and couldn't get rid of it. It was like one of those Viagra doses men take in the post millennium where the erection lasts for hours and won't go down. Finally, the actor told the cameraman he had to shoot him from the waist up.

None of his other lovers complained that Taylor was impotent. If only they had talked, eye-witnesses would have included Errol Flynn, Tyrone Power, Ava Gardner, Howard Hughes, Yvonne De Carlo, and Eleanor Parker. He struck out with Greta Garbo who found him "so beautiful . . . yet so dumb," but scored a bull's eye with her former lover, John Gilbert.

In a rare moment of congeniality on the set of *Undercurrent* (1946), Taylor told co-star Katharine Hepburn that his first real love was Thelma ("Pat") Ryan, with whom he'd had a brief fling with when she appeared as an extra in his film, *Small Town Girl*, released in 1936. "Pat" later confessed that "I had an awful crush on Bob Taylor," but gave no more details.

"Pat lost her virginity to me," Taylor claimed a decade later to Hepburn. "I think she never got over me."

"You're so vain," Hepburn chastised her co-star. "But aren't all men, especially actors?"

Of course Pat later became known as Patricia Nixon, wife of President Richard Nixon.

It wasn't until November of 2004 that Wagner at the age of 74 finally revealed the truth about his affair with the legendary Stanwyck. He admitted that he was only 22 years old when he embarked on a five-year romance with Stanwyck. Because of the stigma attached to such relationships at the time, both stars agreed to deny their involvement.

"At that time, it could never have been revealed," Wagner said. "It wasn't public. It was hidden. It just couldn't come out. Today, it wouldn't have made any difference. Then it made a difference and it made a big difference for her. She was an absolutely wonderful, wonderful woman and it was so great for me. It was a wonderful time. It was really great and I loved her very much."

Barbara Stanwyck died in 1990, and in her later years she knew a string of young male lovers in addition to Wagner. As she got older, the boys with beautiful faces and athletic bodies—each a candidate for a Calvin Klein underwear ad—got younger. These flings were brief.

Apparently in her later years, she did not have lesbian relationships of the type that she enjoyed in the 1920s and 1930s except for Marilyn Monroe, with whom

Robert Wagner *(above, right)* rekindled memories of another Bob, her husband **Robert Taylor**, pictured together with **Stanwyck** on the left. Wagner also reminded her of a young William Holden whom Stanwyck took under her wing and into her bed during the filming of *Golden Boy* in 1939
.
Still in his 20s, Wagner fell in love with Stanwyck as she was approaching a glamorous 50. "She is a sensitive lady beneath her tough outer shell," he said. "She convinced me that as an actor I could be more than just another pretty face on the screen." In the 1950s Wagner lied to the press about their affair, but admitted it later in life.

she'd become sexually involved when they made *Clash by Night* in 1952, a year or so before she took up with Wagner.

"From Monroe to R.J.," said Henry Willson, Wagner's former agent. "Not bad. Stanwyck was a true bisexual, although very closeted about her lesbianism. She fucked everybody from Glenn Ford to Gary Cooper, but I suspect she had her hottest times with the gals, especially Marlene Dietrich and Joan Crawford. Crawford was her real love, the friendship enduring a lifetime."

Elizabeth Taylor and **Robert Taylor** *(together in the left photo, above)* grace the cover of *Picturegoer* magazine.

Elizabeth was only sixteen when she sailed to London in October of 1948 to play a naïve 21-year- old American debutante who marries a man who's secretly a communist spy. That spy was played by none other than the right-wing Taylor himself – then thirty-eight years old. Together they made a box office bomb. In the photo above, young Elizabeth looks beautiful but Taylor with his mustache appears a bit sleazy.

The public wasn't quite ready to accept Elizabeth in her first romantic lead. Taylor had some advice for her: "If you don't shave those legs, I'm going to shave them for you."

For young **Thelma Ryan** *(photo, above right)*, Robert Taylor was her dream man. But after seducing her, he dumped her. She later married a man named Richard Nixon, changed her name from Thelma to Pat, and became the tormented First Lady of the land. As such, because of her husband, she endured endless public humiliations.

Dietrich

Stanwyck

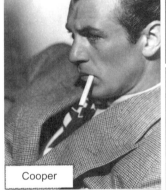

Crawford

The Loves of Barbara Stanwyck

According to Jerry Asher, a gossipy confidant of **Joan Crawford**: "Joan and 'Missy' (a reference to Stanwyck) had a sexual relationship. Both of them were interested in men and women alike." Crawford and Stanwyck, as well as Bette Davis, were each sharing the sexual favors of **Glenn Ford**.

Stanwyck had a brief fling with **Marlene Dietrich**, but soon after she ended it abruptly. Crawford said that the reason the Stanwyck/Dietrich affair didn't work out was that "each of them wanted to be the man in the relationship."

Stanwyck began a torrid affair with **Gary Cooper** in 1942 when they made *Balls of Fire* together at RKO. A biographer once wrote, "Cooper, known to have affairs with his leading ladies, did not attempt one with Barbara. "

Crawford would have laughed at that. She told gay pal William Haines, "Barbara told me that Cooper shares a lot in common with those bulls he used to see on the ranch in Montana."

Cooper

In 1939, Robert Taylor was left to date his boyfriends after Barbara Stanwyck laid eyes on **William Holden** *(right)* with whom she co-starred in *Golden Boy*. Although the bisexual actors, Tyrone Power and Alan Ladd, had been in line for the role of the young boxer, Stanwyck wanted Holden, a handsome hunk, who was at the time only 22 years old. When the director wanted to fire the nervous, inexperienced Holden, Stanwyck wouldn't hear of it. She spent endless hours rehearsing him in her dressing room. "If there's any way I can help you, for God's sake, let me know."

The rather blunt Holden responded, "You can let me fuck you. That will steady my nerves."

Stanwyck welcomed him to go at it. Regrettably, she regularly offered him booze to steady his nerves, a gesture which contributed to a lifelong habit of alcohol abuse that would eventually take his life.

Ford

Stanwyck with Holden

The Night Barbara Stanwyck Seduced Bogie

When Joan Blondell and Humphrey Bogart were still getting their starts in talking pictures during the early 1930s, Blondell called Bogie, "I ran into an old friend of yours from New York. I gave her your number. You definitely will not be lonely tonight."

"Who is it?"

"And spoil the surprise?" Blondell asked. "Have fun, duckie."

Within the hour, his phone rang, and Bogie, with some reluctance, picked up the receiver.

"This is Barbara Stanwyck," the voice said. "Is this the one and only Humphrey Bogart?"

"Joan said you were an old friend of mine," he said. "But we've never met. Of course, I'd be honored to take you out."

"Never met?" she said, mocking him. "In Brooklyn, where I come from, when a man fucks a woman, he's met her. I'm Ruby Stevens, that hot jazz baby from the chorus line. You told me I was the greatest fuck of your life."

Later that night, at 3am, at the conclusion of a double date with Bogie's best friend and confidant, Kenneth MacKenna and the lesbian actress Kay Francis, Stanwyck drove Bogie back to his apartment. After he staggered inside, she slammed the door and locked it. "Let's get one thing straight, Bogart. When I take you to bed, I run the fuck."

She was right about that. Twice, she mounted him. Both times, he'd lain on his back as she did her gymnastics over him. At dawn's light, he woke to find her standing in front of his bedroom window, which opened onto a brick wall. She wore only a brassiere, highlighted with the glow of her cigarette.

He bolted up in bed. "My God, I must be sobering up. It's come back to me. I remember you when you were dancing at the Strand."

"Great!" she said in a harsh voice. "So you aren't a retard. That proves that even as a teenager, I could make a lasting impression on a drunk."

"You were one of the Keep Cool Cuties," he said. "You did that number with Johnny Dooley. 'A Room Adjoining a Boudoir,' if memory serves."

"So finally you know who I am," she said, "even though I had to fuck you twice to jar that pickled brain of yours."

"I miss the Twenties back in New York," he said when she crushed out her cigarette and returned to bed. "Speakeasies, dirty dancing, bootleg hooch, plunging necklines, red hot jazz, flapper clothes."

"And big-dicked New York men," she chimed in. "Don't forget them."

"I didn't know too many of those," he said.

Bogart related this story to Kenneth MacKenna, who gossiped about it widely to whomever would listen. "Ruby Stevens," Bogart later said, "is one tough, sassy broad, but she has class. She's hard-boiled yet soft and vulnerable, a free-spirited woman who takes no crap from any man. And she's one of the sexiest women I've ever met."

Despite that assessment, he suspected that in her heart, Stanwyck was a lesbian.

Later, when they were shooting *The Two Mrs. Carrolls,* released in 1947, she told him, "I save my real loving, my gentle side, for women. With men, things immediately revolve around power games."

Hollywood Bazooms

A Mammary Roll Call

"Chesty" Morgan starred opposite Harry Reems (co-star of *Deep Throat*) in a film called *Deadly Weapons* in 1974. It was billed as "seeing is believing." In the film, Chesty played "Zsa Zsa" as in Zsa Zsa Gabor. She was cast in one of the most unintentionally hilarious pieces of dementia ever to hit the screen. She suffocated her victims between her knockers in this sleazy movie.

Despite the on-screen presence of porn star Harry Reems, there were no sex scenes in the movie. One critic said, "Chesty's chest is the only redeeming factor of her performance. Director Doris Wishman tries to make her look erotic, but her body is a mess, her hair is gray, she has weird teeth, and her face is a wrinkled prune. But I love you, Chesty, don't get me wrong!"

But to return to the world of more normal female mammals, here are some noteworthy quotes about the feminine torso from movie icons who knew a thing or two about them, followed by a compilation of Blood Moon's favorite breasts. Most of these have already been displayed, sometimes frequently, on the screen; others have been more frequently concealed than not. And whether they're the real thing or, in one or two cases, created altogether by a plastic surgeon, is something you'll have to figure out for yourselves.

261

"We live in a tit culture."

Bette Davis

"Miss United Dairies herself."

David Niven, in reference to Jayne Mansfield

"I say, you Americans are positively obsessed with mammaries!"

Terry Thomas

"There's nothing wrong with my tits, but I don't go around throwing them in people's faces."

Joan Crawford, in reference to Marilyn Monroe

"Look at these breasts. Aren't they beautiful?"

Elizabeth Taylor in *Ash Wednesday* (1973)

"I was Ava's first husband and the taker of her virginity. She had big brown nipples, which, when aroused, stood out like some double-long, golden California raisins."

Mickey Rooney

"You can't sho' yo' bosums 'fore three o'clock!"
Hattie McDaniel, lecturing Scarlett O'Hara in *Gone With the Wind*

*"**Ursula Andress**' emergence from the sea in Dr. No is still unsurpassed in cinematic sexiness."*

The Washington Post

*"**Ann-Margret** comes through dirty no matter what she plays. She does most of her acting inside her mouth. She gleams with built-in innuendo.*

Men seem to have direct-action responses to Ann-Margret. They want to give her what she seems to be asking for."

Critic **Pauline Kael**

Cindy Adams

Rick Solomon with Paris Hilton

Pamela Anderson

*"**HOLLYWOOD'S NEWEST DO-EST TWOSOME?** Pamela Anderson and Rick Soloman This is the sweet young man who, after ending a few-months marriage to Shannon Doherty, sold a sex tape he had made with Paris Hilton for enough money to buy a house.*

And we all know Pamela Anderson, whose brains may well be in her bra. Repeat breast implants, Playboy layout."

Columnist **Cindy Adams**

Jugs, bazooms, and big knockers have flashed across the screen with ever-increasing frequency since the release in 1943 of Howard Hughes' *The Outlaw*, which was forever associated with its provocative ad "How'd you like to tussle with Russell?"

Julie Andrews, of all stars, even bared her breasts in Blake Edwards' wicked *S.O.B.* in 1981.

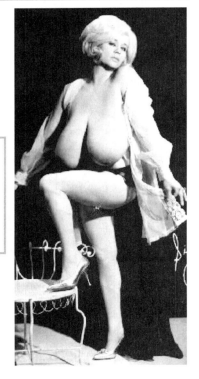

The all-time winner, of course, is **"Chesty" Morgan** *(right)* as she appeared in *Deadly Weapons* in 1974. With a 73-inch bust, her cups *doth runneth over.* For a big-boobed bimbo, she was enough for six women...and more.

"Chesty" starred opposite Harry Reems, who went on to immortality when he was cast opposite **Linda Lovelace** *(left)* in *Deep Throat.*

Filmed in only six days, *Deep Throat* (1972), cost $22,000 to make and so far has grossed $600 million. It is the most culturally influential porn film ever made, and was one of the first hard-core sex films to be shown in mainstream movie theaters.

Some sociologists assert that it even helped define its era.

Celebrity Breasts...Guess Who?

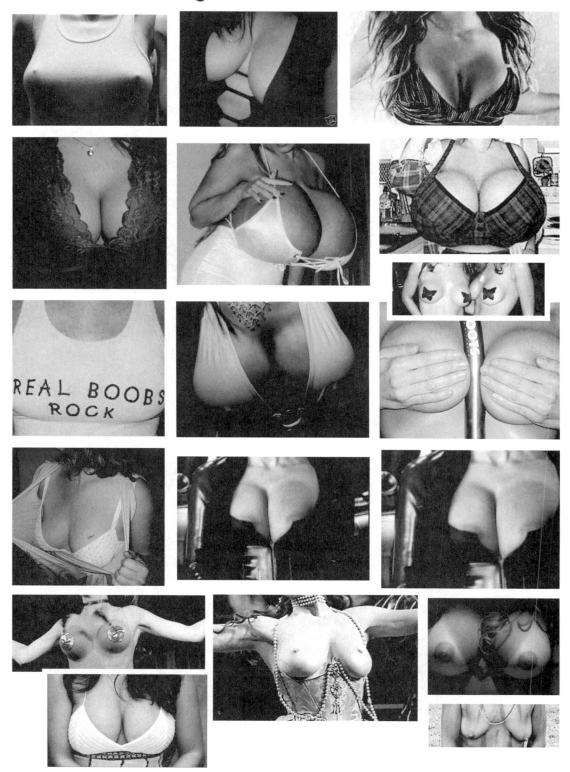

Ann-Margret   36 1/2"

"She was a lady, everybody's wet dream," said Steve McQueen. Elvis Presley once had a round bed, painted "pussy pink," made just for her. Actress Maureen Stapleton attended a mostly male audience for a screening of *Bye Bye Birdie* (1963). "I'm the only person in this room who doesn't want to fuck you," she said to Ann-Margret during the reception that followed.

Stapleton, a great friend of Tennessee Williams, should have known better. At least half the audience, maybe more, was composed of gay men. "When a man tells me I'm sexy, it's the biggest compliment he can pay me," said Ann-Margret. The Swedish star—actress, singer, and dancer—was often called "the female Elvis," at least when she wasn't being referred to as a "sex-kitten."

Steve McQueen

267

Pamela Anderson   36"

It's no secret that until around the age of 22 Pamela had a breast size of 23. Then she had her first implants, and her breast size grew and grew until tapering off at the age of 29. Then came the shocking news: Pamela was downsizing her implants. Fortunately, this rash decision lasted less than a year before she came back like two ripe melons. She became famous for her many appearances on the cover of *Playboy* and gained a nationwide audience with her appearance on *Baywatch* (1989).

As an animal rights activist, she posed naked in 2006 in the window of Stella McCartney's store in London to protest against the use of fur for making clothes.

Pamela's greatest star turn was in the honeymoon sex tape she filmed with Tommy Lee, which became the best-selling celebrity porn video of all time. On a sizzling TV special in 2001, Pamela revealed her sex secrets. She claimed that she'd love to have sex in public and that she loves anal sex and even had a three-in-a-bed romp. She also confessed to collecting vibrators and said that she loved porn movies. The gorgeous actress revealed, "My wildest sexual dream is to have sex in an elevator."

Ursula Andress   38"

"If the role demands it, then naturally I will remove my clothes." So said Ursula Andress. Often referred to as the definitive Bond Girl because of her appearance in *Dr. No* (1962), Andress was chosen by *Empire Magazine* as one of the 100 Sexiest Stars in Film History, ranking #53 in 1995.

Her white bikini from the Bond flick was sold at auction for $61,500. The costume was made from one of Andress' own bras.

Andress dated actor James Dean, but not much came out of that so-called romance. Between 1957 and 1966, she was married to actor John Derek, with whom she had co-starred in *Once Before I Die* (1967). She later had a child with actor Harry Hamlin, their romance blooming on the set of that kitschy fantasy *Clash of the Titans* in 1981.

One movie critic referred to Andress as "Lynx-eyed, vivacious, the nearest thing to a cartoonist's version of a sex symbol."

John Derek

Brigitte Bardot   36"

The breasts of the French sex kitten, Brigitte Bardot, were on ample display in 1957 in the film *And God Created Woman (Et Dieu Créa La Femme)*, directed by her first husband, Roger Vadim. Today the film looks like a lame excuse to show Bardot naked on a beach in St-Tropez.

Although her breasts became familiar around the world, one critic claimed she also had "the world's most beautiful armpits," as illustrated by the countless glam shots of the sex goddess with her arms stretched over her head.

"I have always adored beautiful young men," Bardot once said. "Just because I grow older, my taste doesn't change. So if I can have them, why not?"

Des Amis de B.B.
(Top to bottom, above)
Raf Vallone,
Sean Connery,
Stephen Boyd,
Louis Jourdan,
Mick Jagger.

Halle Berry   36"

The world got treated to the breasts of Halle Berry in the movie, *Swordfish* (2001), in which she co-starred with John Travolta. The former model and beauty queen, who has an African-American father and a Caucasian mother, never wanted to do nudity, fearing that it would type-cast her. "I wouldn't read scripts that had nudity in them before, but now that I've done it I realize that it's actually very easy."

Berry also appeared in a full frontal nude scene in a steamy sex romp, making love to Billy Bob Thornton in *Monster's Ball* (2001). She was rumored to have been paid an extra $1 million for this daring scene, but later denied that she got this bonus.

Pierce Brosnan found playing love scenes in *Die Another Day* (2002) with Berry disappointing. "I hated it," he said. "These love scenes sound so seductive. Here you are with this beautiful woman rolling around in the sack. But you've got this director under the sheets with you, trying to get the shot. There are also cameras on either side of you, while you're attempting not to show your dick, especially when it's hard."

Berry has claimed that sex appeal is power. "It's most empowering to a woman to know she's sexy and to be able to use that to get what she wants, and to win—that's our secret weapon."

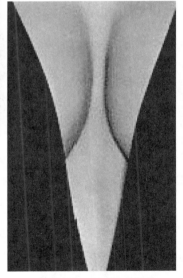

Jacqueline Bisset 37"

"Miss Goodthighs," a role she played in *Casino Royale* (1967), aptly describes Jacqueline Bisset. Because of her name, the stunning beauty is assumed to be French. Actually, she was brought up in England. She made quite a splash in *The Deep* (1977). Her underwater swimming scenes inspired the worldwide wet T-shirt craze. *Newsweek* called her "the most beautiful film actress of all time." But she hated those wet T-shirt scenes and later claimed that she felt exploited.

She's the godmother of Angelina Jolie. What part of a man's anatomy fascinates her the most? "The twinkle in a man's eye."

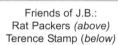

Friends of J.B.:
Rat Packers *(above)*
Terence Stamp *(below)*

Joan Collins   38"

Vogue claimed that "Joan Collins displays her breasts on *Dynasty* as if bra-cup size was a measure of personal magnificence."

Author Jackie Collins, her sister, once said that "Joan always lived her life like a man." Did Jackie ever get it wrong. Just ask Warren Beatty, Robert Evans, Nicky Hilton (well, he's dead), Dennis Hopper (he's dead too), Ryan O'Neal, Robert Wagner—and the beat goes on.

Her first husband, British actor Maxwell Reed, tried to get her to bed a fat, old Arab sheik, who was willing to give Reed 10,000 pounds. (Sounds like the plot for an old Robert Redford movie.) Joan said NO and divorced the ungallant Reed. "I've got a great body," Joan once said. "Sometimes it looks terrific. If it's photographed right, it can look absolutely great."

Bo Derek   35"

This blonde bombshell has often asserted that Americans are prudish about nudity. A naturalist, she said that the country "has a big problem with nudity—not vulgarity, violence, and cheapness, just simple nudity. You can have these really heavy-duty sex scenes with half-clothed actors doing really vulgar things on a kitchen table or in a bathroom or on an airplane. But take your clothes off and suddenly it's a big problem."

She was 30 years the junior of actor John Derek, whom she met in 1974, and who, in 1948 had been declared as "the handsomest man in Hollywood." John filed for divorce from his wife, actress Linda Evans. He moved to Germany with Bo to avoid being charged with statutory rape under U.S. law. His new love was only 16.

The actor and Bo remained married for almost a quarter-century, until his death in 1998.

Bo burst onto the screen in the 1979 Blake Edwards film, *10*, in which Dudley Moore's character is torn between his love for Julie Andrews and his sexual attraction to Bo. Overnight she became a sex symbol. Her beaded and plaited cornrow hair style was widely copied by women across America.

She made the first of many appearances in *Playboy* with its March 1980 issue. Her most dubious achievement? In 2000 she was voted "Worst Actress of the Century." Other dubious accomplishments were campaigning for Daddy Bush in 1988 and 1992 and for Baby Bush in 2000 and 2004.

Baby Bush (left) with
Daddy Bush (right)

274

Cameron Diaz   34"

A photographer who took topless pictures of Cameron Diaz before she became famous was convicted in July of 2005 on three counts. A jury convicted John Rutter, 42, of forgery, attempted grand theft, and perjury. He tried to sell back the pictures to Diaz that she'd posed for 11 years previously. Rutter confessed to the jury that the model release form giving him ownership of the photos was forged, but that he didn't do it.

He also admitted that he asked Diaz to pay him $3.5 million, or else he'd sell the candid snapshots around the world to coincide with the 2003 release of her film, *Charlie's Angels: Full Throttle*. In September of 2005 Rutter was sentenced to 3 years and 8 months in prison for extortion. Diaz admitted to posing for the candid shots when she was a 19-year-old model hoping to break into Hollywood.

In May of 2007, the co-star of *Holiday*, with Jude Law, almost went topless on *The Ellen DeGeneres Show*. To borrow a term from Janet Jackson, the culprit for the dirty deed was "wardrobe malfunction." Diaz's loose-fitting top slipped down, exposing her right breast. "Excuse moi," said Diaz when DeGeneres alerted her to the problem. "I went through so many foolproofs on this too," Diaz said. "I hate double-stick tape. You can always see double-stick tape." Comedienne DeGeneres responded, "Well, we saw something else!"

"I'm very proud of my breasts, as every woman should be," said the Swedish bombshell, Anita Ekberg. "It's not cellular obesity. It's womanliness." Awarded the title "Miss Sweden" in 1950, the model and actress became a cult sex symbol when Federico Fellini cast her in her greatest role in *La Dolce Vita* (1960) in which she played the unattainable dream goddess of Marcello Mastroianni. Her uninhibited cavorting in Rome's Trevi Fountain remains one of the most celebrated cinema images of all time. "It was I who made Fellini famous—not the other way around," said Ekberg. The lesbian actress, Ethel Merman, dubbed buxom Ekberg "the thinking man's dunce cap—two of them."

...with Marcello Mastroianni

Betty Grable   36"

The Pinup Girl of World War II, Betty Grable was married twice, first to Jackie Coogan, the child actor and her co-star in *Million Dollar Legs* (1939). "Coogan taught me more tricks than a whore learns in a whorehouse," she later said. She later married Harry James, bandleader and trumpeter. But that didn't stop her from "knowing" (in the Biblical sense) an array of actors, dancers, and chorus boys, plus rough guys she met at truck stops. She once said, "I'm a truck driver's delight."

Many of her lovers among the chorus boys and dancers, such as Dan Dailey, were gay but went to bed with Grable anyway. "The rougher they are the better I liked to fellate them," she once told Robert Stack, another one of her lovers. Betty was attracted to bisexual men like Rory Calhoun, Desi Arnaz, Victor Mature, and George Raft. According to Betty, Raft never touched her during their so-called "affair," except to beat her up. "George was probably a latent homosexual," she later said. She once had a condom embedded in her and didn't know what was the cause of her bad vaginal odor until it was discovered by a doctor during a routine medical exam. Tyrone Power broke off with her because "I couldn't stand the smell."

(Above, from left to right): George Raft, Victor Mature, Rory Calhoun, Desi Arnaz, Tyrone Power

Salma Hayak   36"

Her mother was a *mexicano* opera singer, her father a Lebanese-Mexican businessman. At the age of 12, Hayek was sent to a Catholic boarding school in Louisiana. But she terrorized the nuns and was sent home again. Fleeing to Hollywood, she made it big, both as an actress and a sexpot. *FHM,* the men's magazine, ranked her 8th among the 100 Sexiest Women in 2001.

She is one of the most outspoken women in Hollywood when it comes to men. She dated actor Edward Norton between 1999 and 2003 and then Josh Lucas in 2003. But she said, "I keep waiting to meet a man who has more balls than I do." She also claimed that, "I find feminine men unbelievably sexy."

She also says that she needs a man who is strong enough to handle her personality. "I come from a strict Catholic upbringing where sex was a taboo subject. That makes you crave sex 10 times more for the rest of your life."

Jennifer Love Hewitt   33 1/2"

In Waco, Texas, where she was born, friends called her "Love." That's not a bad name for an actress who hit it big on TV in *Party of Five* (1994). She's made a lot of "Sexiest Girls" polls, coming in #7 in *FHM*'s survey in 2002. However, the producers of *Lolita* (1997) turned her down for the role of the sexy nymphet, bait for a child molester. She's been romantically linked to Joey Lawrence, Enrique Iglesias, and even Alec Baldwin.

In 1999 she briefly dated actor Wilmer Valderrama who "immortalized" her on Howard Stern's morning radio program in 2006. He rated Hewitt an "eight" out of 10 when it came to sex. *That 70s Show* star also talked about his own sexual prowess, claiming that he'd been with two women at once and had also engaged in anal sex with a famous actress whom he refused to name. Valderrama also claimed that he is "blessed" when it comes to penis size, "cocking in" at "slightly bigger" than eight inches. He also revealed that he has videotaped his sexual escapades.

Hewitt admitted that she was horrified when she first sprouted breasts until she noticed how good they made her T-shirts look. "When I first got my boobs, I was so insecure," she recalled. "I was 11 years old with this chest. It was like, 'Who, what's going on here?' Then I finally went, 'Wow, what a great accessory.' My T-shirts have never looked so exciting. A girl just has to embrace her boobs."

In spite of these remarks, the perky actress claims that she finds the fascination with breasts bizarre. "To be honest, I think it's hysterical. I mean they're just . . . fat. There's nothing interesting about them. Sure they look good in the right dress, but why obsess about it? Every time I go out in public they post a new picture and write things like, 'Does the left one look bigger than the right?' It's ridiculous!"

Wilmer Valderrama

Enrique Iglesias

Joey Lawrence

Scarlett Johansson   34"

In 2006, *FHM* magazine readers voted *Lost in Translation* actress Scarlett Johansson the world's sexiest woman. She dethroned previous winners, the anorexic Angelina Jolie and the two Jessicas—Alba and Simpson. In 2007 *Playboy* magazine named her the "Sexiest Celebrity."

But does she like to bare breasts? "I always check in the mirror to make sure nothing is see-through." I like to look nice, but I think that there's a way of doing that is more tasteful than just wearing a bikini wherever you go." That's what she said a few years ago. But read on about her current views on nudity.

Sometimes she doesn't have to look in the mirror to see her image. "I was driving through Los Angeles and I look up and see the biggest photo of me I have ever seen in my life on a massive ad space. I screamed and slammed on the brakes. I couldn't believe it. It's very strange to see my cleavage the size of a Brontosaurus. My breasts were huge. I had long hair and my goodness, I couldn't get past the cleavage."

While Johansson was filming *The Island* (2005), director Michael Bay was horrified when the actress wanted to go topless in a love scene because the romance is rated PG-13. Calling Bay to her trailer, Johansson allegedly claimed, "I'm not fucking wearing this cheap ass black bra, okay? I'm going naked." She not only fought over wardrobe, but questioned co-star Ewan McGregor's kissing prowess. She sniped, "He kissed like a 16-year-old schoolboy."

Scarlett (front), sprawls as Tom Ford "necks" with Keira Knightley.

Ashley Judd   34"

Voted one of *People Magazine*'s Most Beautiful People in 2002, Ashley Judd is the daughter of country music singer, Naomi Judd. She has a half-sister, Wyonna Judd, who is also a country music singer.

Although she refused a nude scene in *Kuffs* (1992), Ashley's nude scenes in such movies as *Norma Jean and Marilyn* (1996) and *A Normal Life* (1996) have drawn attacks from her family's southern, conservative base. During the 2000 Oscar presentations she walked across the stage wearing "a dress split up to Honolulu"—and no panties.

An eighth-generation Kentuckian, Ashley is a self-proclaimed feminist. She has dated everybody from Robert De Niro to Matthew McConaughey.

The Judd family may be conflicted over the nudity issue but not the staunchly Catholic Hollywood actor Jim Caviezel. He refused to strip off his clothes for a hot sex scene with Ashley—in fact, threatened to walk out unless director Carl Franklin shot the scenes for the thriller, *High Crimes* (2002), with both parties wearing their panties. "There are times where sex is appropriate, but I've yet to see butts and breasts act themselves out of a scene!" said Caviezel.

It went very differently with Hugh Jackman in a scene from *Someone Like You* (2001). Ashley and that handsome hunk stripped to their underwear. His underwear had a big flap in front. Hugh asked Ashley, "Did you see everything God gave me?" She answered, "Not this time, but two takes before, I saw *everything*." So Ashley knows what all the gay men on Broadway who flocked to see *The Boy from Oz* don't know. Just what does Hugh Jackman's dick look like?

Jim Caviezel, playing Christ

Hugh Jackman

Gina Lollobrigida 36"

Born to a working-class family in Italy during the Mussolini era, this stunning beauty was nicknamed "Lollo," a French word meaning "beautiful breasts."

Her sultry looks thrilled men around the world, even Fidel Castro, whom she interviewed (she's also a journalist). Howard Hughes and Frank Sinatra were captivated by her. John Huston cast her in *Beat the Devil* (1953). During that shoot, Truman Capote gave the star, Humphrey Bogart, his famous blow-job.

Gina earned her nickname, *The World's Most Beautiful Woman,* after her signature 1955 movie. What does Gina think of her image as an international sex symbol? "I get very irritated when people think I must be the same woman I portray on the screen."

...with Dr. Christiaan Barnard

Friends of Gina

Fidel Castro

John Huston

French actor Jean Sorel

Yul Brynner

282

Traci Lords   34"

This American film actress, producer, director, writer and singer, was born in Steubenville, Ohio of Ukranian parents. She changed her name from Nora Louise Kuzma to Traci Lords in honor of the Katharine Hepburn character, Tracy Lord, in *The Philadelphia Story*.

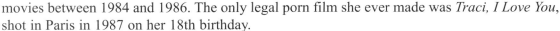

In 1983 at the age of 13, while still in high school, she paid for an abortion herself, later running away from home.

Lying about her age to porno filmmakers, she broke into the industry, making 80 to 100 X-rated movies between 1984 and 1986. The only legal porn film she ever made was *Traci, I Love You*, shot in Paris in 1987 on her 18th birthday.

The Federal government has tried to prosecute filmmakers who hired Traci for porn, but the case fell apart when it was proven that Lords used a U.S. passport issued by the government as her ID.

Nonetheless, it is still illegal to own Traci Lords movies which are officially classified as child porn. She was the centerfold model for the same issue of *Penthouse* magazine that "exposed" Miss America of 1984, Vanessa Williams. However, because Lords was underage, it is today illegal to own this notorious issue.

Lords became the most successful of all porn stars to make the transition into mainstream movies. "I'm successful in spite of my past and not because of it," she said. A singer and advocate of gay rights, Lords was critically hailed for her 1995 appearance as a sneering sociopath, Rikki, on *Melrose Place*. She has often played villains and psychotic characters.

In summing up her infamous life, she said, "At the age of 10 I was raped. I came to Los Angeles and used drugs and got involved with the wrong people. So in the end I found myself in front of the camera."

She later said, "Men are my favorite topic. I've always said that if a man can get inside my head, he can get inside my pants. I don't have a type. I don't go for drop-dead gorgeous guys. I am also an equal opportunity fucker. I love life. I love food. And I love sex."

Sophia Loren   38"

"It's like being bombed by watermelons," said Alan Ladd, her bisexual costar in *Dolphin* (1957). Gay actor and composer Noël Coward almost sounded straight when he pronounced, "She should have been sculpted in chocolate truffles, so that the world could devour her." Did Cary Grant seduce her when he starred with her in *The Pride and the Passion* (1957)? Grant went to his grave without ever confirming that. Actually, he probably would have preferred a handsome hunk instead.

Born in a ward for unmarried mothers, Loren went far in the world, cooking her famous spaghetti for Marshal Tito of Yugoslavia or dining with the Queen of England. She charmed Charlie Chaplin, Marcello Mastroianni, William Holden, and Vittorio de Sica, but Marlon Brando hated her.

"Your bosom?" asked a British journalist of Sophia. He mimed two half-moons on his chest. "Bigger than Lollobrigida's? Y'know. *Molti grande*?"

"It's true, *si*," Loren said. The reporter later wrote, "Sophia is great, aren't they?"

...with Jayne Mansfield

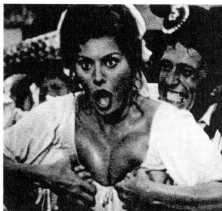

Friends of Sophia

Alan Ladd

Marshal Tito,
Resistance Fighter and
President / Dictator of
Yugoslavia

Rosanna Brazzi

Cary Grant

Peter Sellers

Omar Sharif

Marcello Mastroianni

Gig Young

Anthony Perkins

Jayne Mansfield   40"

Jayne Mansfield called her vagina "Suzi," but most men knew her for her two greatest treasures, her breasts, each of which was revealed in the February, 1955 issue of *Playboy*. The Rev. Billy Graham once said, "The country knows more about Jayne's statistics than about the Second Commandment."

Jayne herself made some revelatory statements. "I'm a big girl and I have to have a big guy." She also said, "Men are those creatures with two legs and eight hands." How about this comment? "Men want women pink, helpless, and to do a lot of deep breathing."

Jayne's lovers ranged from John F. Kennedy to Ronald Reagan. Her biggest thrill was the Dominican playboy Porfirio Rubirosa. Jayne was brutally killed on June 29, 1967 when her car crashed into the rear of a tractor-trailer. Rumors that she was decapitated are untrue.

...with Mickey Hargitay

Friends of Jayne

John F. Kennedy

Porfirio Rubirosa

Ronald Reagan

Steve Cochran

Rose McGowan   36"

"I'm a man with really nice breasts," admits Rose McGowan who was reared in Florence in a Children of God commune, the same cult into which both River and Joaquin Phoenix were born. She legally emancipated herself at the age of 15, and went to Hollywood where in 2007 she was ranked #44 on *Maxim Magazine*'s "Hot 100" list.

She's given to making controversial statements: "It's my job to spread deviance to the American youth." She also said, "I think if I had lived back in Salem, I would have burned at the stake."

Rocker Marilyn Manson moved to Hollywood hoping to meet her. In 1999 she announced their engagement on Howard Stern, but broke it off in 2001, citing lifestyle differences. She claimed that "I always thought I was more satanic than Manson." She delivered one of her best performances as Ann-Margret in the mini-series *Elvis* (2005). Ann-Margret made *Viva Las Vegas* with Elvis in 1964, during which time they had an affair, while teen jailbait Priscilla was waiting back at lonely Graceland.

One final tantalizing quote from McGowan: "I'm so guilty of doing every single male thing—not calling, not showing up, leaving at four in the morning."

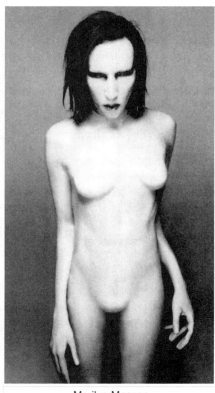

Marilyn Manson

One of America's most popular film actresses of the late 1950s, Kim Novak is best known today for her performance in Alfred Hitchcock's *Vertigo* (1958). In her heyday, she was also known for her scandalous love affairs, if only in rumor. She sampled some of the "biggest" boys around, including actor John Ireland and Frank Sinatra—even the Dominican playboy, Porfirio Rubirosa.

Her affair with Sammy Davis Jr. made tabloid headlines. Her boss at Columbia, Harry Cohn, was said to have called out the mob to break up the relationship. Kidnapped, Davis was driven into the desert outside Las Vegas. One hoodlum told him, "You've got only one eye now. Wanna try for none?" Novak also became notorious in Hollywood for turning down several great roles: the 1961 *Breakfast at Tiffany's*, which went to Audrey Hepburn; the 1961 *The Hustler* (Piper Laurie); the 1962 *Days of Wine and Roses* (Lee Remick), and the 1965 *The Sandpiper* (Elizabeth Taylor).

Above, Sammy Davis Jr.; right, with Alfred Hitchcock

Rebecca Romijn   35"

That *X-Men* beauty, Rebecca Romijn (pronounced Romaine, like the lettuce), famously wed *Full House* heartthrob John Stamos in 1998. The couple divorced in 2005. On July 14, 2007, she married Jerry O'Connell. The same year she made her first appearance on the ABC series *Ugly Betty*. She plays Alexis Meade, a male-to-female transsexual.

In her own life, she allegedly did some sexual experimentation to clear up some confusion. WENN reported in the spring of 2002 that the sexy actress has enjoyed several lesbian relationships to cure her curiosity. She appeared in steamy lesbian scenes in her movie, *Femme Fatale*. "In my 20s," she admitted, "I wondered whether I was interested in women—so I did my homework." After those episodes, she apparently figured out that she was straight after all.

That same year Romijn revealed all in the pages of the then-new *Jane* magazine. She donned a sheer Chanel chiffon dress for an underwater shot. It left nothing to the imagination.

She admitted to the press that she gets "into the mood" by watching celebrity porn. Her extensive DVD collection of underground films features some of today's superstars in early porn roles. Her favorite star is Sylvester Stallone, who can be seen in his pre-Rocky days in *Italian Stallion*.

John Stamos

Jane Russell 39"

"Christians can have big tits, too," or so claimed Jane Russell, who became an international sensation in Howard Hughes' *The Outlaw* (1943).

Contrary to rumors, the billionaire aviator and movie producer never seduced Jane—but not for lack of trying. Actually, he was hot for her co-star, hunky Jack Buetel. He did design a special brassiere for Jane. After all, Hughes was an engineer.

He didn't know it, but she didn't wear that bra in *The Outlaw*. She wore her regular bra and smoothed out the seams and hid the straps. But the legend continues.

Married three times, Jane is not known for sleeping around, although affairs with co-stars Robert Mitchum and John Payne are rumored.

(left photo) with Marilyn Monroe in *Gentlemen Prefer Blondes*; *(above)* with Robert Mitchum in *Macao*.

Jill St. John   35"

This incredible piece of eye candy from the 1960s might have a large bust measurement but is always known for her IQ (162). How else could she indulge in pillow talk with Henry Kissinger? Except for the former Secretary of State, most of her guys were Hollywood studs, including Frank Sinatra.

Once married to Lance Reventlow (son of Woolworth heiress Barbara Hutton), she is today the soul mate of Robert Wagner, whom she married in 1990. As a girl, she studied ballet with Natalie Wood (twice Wagner's wife) and his friend Stefanie Powers. Jill was also famously married to Jack Jones.

Bond fans still remember her as a Bond babe in *Diamonds Are Forever* (1971) where she played the ridiculously named "Tiffany Case."

Long past her bimbo (on screen) stage, Jill is no longer cast in brief bikinis today (she was born in 1940). She still refuses to answer that all-important question: Who was the biggest thrill ever? Wagner? Sinatra? Sean Connery?

Pillow Talk

Henry Kissinger, Frank Sinatra, Robert Wagner, and *(bottom)* with Sean Connery

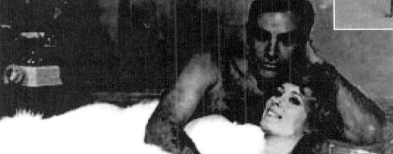

Jessica Simpson   36"

"I had doors slammed in my face as a 14-year-old because my boobs were too big," said Jessica Simpson on being a curvaceous Christian pop star. Named as #16 in *FHM's* "100 Sexiest Women in the World," the singer/actress is famous for having retained her virginity until her wedding night. Simpson and Nick Lachey were married in 2002 and subsequently starred together in the MTV reality TV series, *Newlyweds: Nick and Jessica*. But they filed for divorce in 2005.

The American pop singer and actress rose to fame in the late 1990s, eventually generating seven *Billboard* Top 40 hits. The big-busted star recorded "These Boots Are Made for Walkin'," that Nancy Sinatra hit from 1966. But the video was banned in some countries for its overtly sexual content. Featured as Daisy Duke, Simpson is seen washing her car in a pink string bikini.

Nick Lachey

Raquel Welch   36"

Raquel Welch was one of the leading sex symbols of the 1960s and 70s. When she posed for a publicity still, clad in a furry animal-skin bikini for *One Million Years B.C.*, it became the best-selling poster of its day. And although she consistently refused to appear nude, those boys at *Playboy* dubbed her "The Most Desired Woman" of the 70s.

The famous makeup man, George Masters, claimed, "She's silicone from the knees up." The British author, Donald Zee, said, "The art of Raquel Welch is her flair for looking nude with her clothes on." Regrettably, Raquel claimed that "I've never found a man who can satisfy me."

The actress assumed Marilyn Monroe's title and forever wiped away the notion that enduring sex goddesses came only in one form—bottled blondes. Raquel turned down the lead in *Barbarella* (1968), which subsequently (and notoriously) went to Jane Fonda. Playing a trannie, Raquel had a backstage feud with the indomitable Mae West on the set of *Myra Breckinridge* (1970), Gore Vidal's most salacious and gender-bending novel.

"There's no question Mae West was a comedic genius but I did, in person, actually feel like she was some kind of dock worker in drag," Raquel said.

Actor/musician **David Cassidy** wrote a book, published in 1994, entitled
C'MON, GET HAPPY: FEAR AND LOATHING ON THE PARTRIDGE FAMILY BUS

Here is a paragraph excerpted from chapter 10:

Now gone

"Women began to ask me, after they met me, if the rumor about my dick was true: that I happened to have been rather well endowed, they told me. My penis became sort of legendary, in an undergournd sort of way. My brothers call me 'Donk.' It's their nickname for me. One fellow even published a book on the Hollywood scene that described me as pulling down my pants, and an impressed female fan gasping, 'Oh man, oh man, You really have been blessed with a rock-and-roll cock.' Well, I don't know if I *had* been blessed with a rock-and-roll cock or not. But I decided that if I had it, there wasn't any point in just keeping it in the holster all the time. I'd have to let it out. And let it out I did. I also never thought I'd be writing all this private, embarrassing shit about it, either!"

History's First Tabloid "Outing" of

Hollywood's Golden Homos

Hollywood Machos Who Climbed the Lavender Ladder

| Rudolph Valentino | Clark Gable | John Wayne | Gary Cooper |

During the Silent Screen era, Hollywood homosexuals lived mainly without fear of media exposure. Even as late as 1959, the word *homosexual* could not even be spoken on the screen. When Marlon Brando and Vivien Leigh made Tennessee Williams' *A Streetcar Named Desire*, Blanche wasn't even allowed to reveal that her former husband had been gay. *Time* magazine once wrote: "Hollywood, with its dozens of gay stars, its hundreds of gays in positions of creative and executive power, prefers to reside in one huge, beautifully appointed celluloid closet. Or a gilded birdcage with a cover over it."

As author Boze Hadleigh put it, "Hollywood is where the truth *lies*... especially about gay stars."

How To Live in the Hollywood Closet?

BECOME A LEGENDARY WOMANIZER, LIKE DON JUAN

In in the late 1960s, superstar Steve McQueen was riding high above the heap of other Hollywood stars, but one morning at breakfast with his long-suffering wife, Neile, he learned, once again, the price of fame. It was a different era. Studios no longer had most stars under contract, and there was no department to cover up embarrassing incidents such as a male star running over and killing someone while drunk, or another male star getting caught in bed having sex with an eight-year-old boy.

With fame came an increasing attention focused on Steve's background, which to some observers was notorious.

In January of 1968 an underground book, *Hollywood Homos,* was published and distributed under the counter at newsstands along Hollywood Boulevard and other places. It was an exposé of gay Hollywood, and its editors ran pictures and identified "The Top Homos of Hollywood." As of this writing, the author of that book is still alive, and, for reasons associated with an FBI investigation at the time, still denies authorship or any involvement with it at all, for that matter.

Many of the names which appeared on that list of Hollywood homos did not surprise *tout Hollywood*. After all, the noctural habits of Rock Hudson, Montgomery Clift, Roddy McDowall, Sal Mineo, James Dean, Errol Flynn, Tyrone Power, Cary Grant, Van Johnson, and others were well known.

One of the biggest surprises, however, was the appearance of the name of Steve McQueen (above), who was said to have to have two women a day "to keep me sane."

No closet had a thicker door and a stronger padlock than that of McQueen, even though he had secret affairs with men, especially bikers and race car drivers.

An anonymous call came in to Steve the morning the book hit the stands. In her memoirs, Neile quoted the caller as telling Steve: "I thought you'd like to know that your name is on the list." The caller abruptly hung up.

Sometimes the wife is the last to know. Neile wrote, "No one in his right mind would ever think of Steve as gay. I mean, *Steve*!!" Yet, some of the great womanizers of Hollywood had secret gay liaisons, including the likes of Errol Flynn and others.

But instead of letting the book die on the grapevine, "Steve became possessed" in Neile's words. "His ego couldn't handle the innuendo. It seemed to violate everything he stood for—most notably his macho image."

During earlier, more naïve eras, it was presumed that gay men were effeminate—never macho. That myth, of course, was exploded decades ago, but not where Steve was concerned. He ordered his attorneys to track down the source of the publication. It was traced to a mailbox in West Hollywood.

The list, in no particular order, included the following celebrities:

ROCK HUDSON
TAB HUNTER
MONTGOMERY CLIFT
RODDY McDOWALL
PAUL NEWMAN
STEVE McQUEEN
SAL MINEO
YUL BRYNNER
MARLON BRANDO
JAMES DEAN
FARLEY GRANGER
RORY CALHOUN
GUY MADISON
TROY DONAHUE
PETER LAWFORD
ROBERT WALKER
TOM DRAKE
CARY GRANT
RANDOLPH SCOTT
GENE KELLY
FRED ASTAIRE
GEORGE CUKOR
DAN DAILEY
TYRONE POWER
ERROL FLYNN
ROBERT TAYLOR
WALT DISNEY
NICK ADAMS
VAN JOHNSON
JEFFREY HUNTER
JOHN DEREK
ANTHONY PERKINS
CESAR ROMERO
SPENCER TRACY
CLIFTON WEBB
GEORGE NADER

In Hollywood of the 1940s and 50s, or even today, homosexuality remained the love that dare not speak its name. "I wouldn't call the actors named in that homo exposé gay," said gay casting agent Henry Willson. "Bisexual might be a more apt term. Even if an actor had 2,000 affairs with women and only two or three liaisons with a guy, Hollywood labeled him gay. James Dean was the 'chief Bad Boy of the Bad Boy Brigade.' He seduced Sal Mineo, Rock Hudson, Paul Newman, Steve McQueen, Marlon Brando, Nick Adams, etc., etc., etc."

The first detailed biographies of the private lives of Paul Newman and Steve McQueen—both by author Darwin Porter—were *Paul Newman, the Man Behind the Baby Blues: His Secret Life Exposed*, and *Steve McQueen, King of Cool: Tales of a Lurid Life*. Each was published by Blood Moon Productions in 2009, thereby casting new light on the concealed private lives of these two film icons.

Newman's bisexual history included off-the-record trysts with Marlon Brando, James Dean, Anthony Perkins, and Sal Mineo, among others.

McQueen's early life included stints as a tawdry teenage hustler, "blue movie" star, and toy boy escort. His affairs ranged from Marilyn Monroe to Paul Newman himself.

Each of the names ran with a picture, often a nude, and a small profile, outlining the gay relationships and activities, however provocative or illegal in some cases, of each of the stars named. In Steve's case, it cited his intimate relationship with certain male stars, including Sal Mineo, Montgomery Clift, Paul Newman, and Marlon Brando.

The book that caused such consternation at the McQueen family's breakfast table so long ago also described Steve's involvement in Cuban porno, his work in three different bordellos (suggesting that he might have been for hire himself), and his former role as a male hustler to both men and women.

Its writer ended his book with a postscript: "This is only the tip of the iceberg," the back page read. "Many more stars—both on the A-list and B-list—will be exposed in a subsequent edition. YOU KNOW WHO YOU ARE!"

The date of that publication marked the beginning of speculation on the closeted homosexuality of both Paul Newman and Steve McQueen. From that date forth they would be labeled as "Friends of Dorothy" in the underground press throughout the 70s and 80s. "Dorothy," of course, was a reference to the character that Judy Garland played in *The Wizard of Oz* and was a code word for gay. So prevalent was the gossip that from that moment onward, all McQueen biographers, if only to deny it, had to deal with the subject of his potential homosexuality.

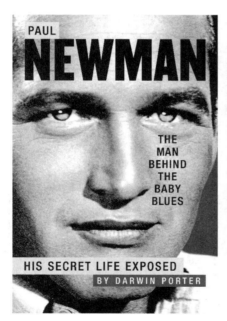
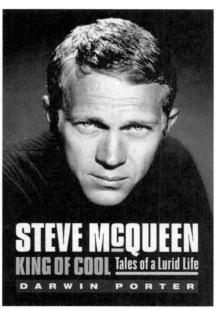

The first detailed biographies of the private lives of **Paul Newman** and **Steve McQueen**—both by author Darwin Porter—each published by Blood Moon Productions in 2009. Each of them cast new light on the concealed private lives of these film icons.

Newman's bisexual history included off-the-record trysts with Marlon Brando, James Dean, Anthony Perkins, and Sal Mineo, among others. McQueen's early life included painful stints as a tawdry teenage hustler, a "blue movie" porno star, and male escort for both men and women. His affairs included ongoing sexual intimacies with Marilyn Monroe and Paul Newman himself.

1968: The Underground Press "Outs" Hollywood Homos

| Rock Hudson | Tab Hunter | Montgomery Clift | Roddy McDowall |

| Paul Newman | Steve McQueen | Sal Mineo | Yul Brynner |

| Marlon Brando | James Dean | Farley Granger | Rory Calhoun |

| Guy Madison | Troy Donahue | Peter Lawford | Robert Walker |

| Tom Drake | Cary Grant | Randolph Scott | Gene Kelly |

| Fred Astaire | George Cukor | Dan Dailey | Tyrone Power |

| Errol Flynn | Robert Taylor | Walt Disney | Nick Adams |

| Van Johnson | Jeffrey Hunter | John Derek | Anthony Perkins |

| Cesar Romero | Spencer Tracy | Clifton Webb | George Nader |

With full recognition for the importance in lovemaking
of a man's thoughtfulness, consideration, good manners,
and his ability to sweet-talk, here's a rundown *(blush)* of historic

Hollywood Shortcomings

(Losers in the Battle of the Bulge)

"Now that I see you, let me ask you something. Does that come in an adult size?"

Whoopi Goldberg
in *Fatal Beauty* (1987)

"Why is it that a woman always thinks the most savage thing she can say to a man is to impugn his cocksmanship?"

William Holden
in *Network* (1976)

The Size of Things

All Hollywood hunks aren't incredible studs. Not at all, according to both their girlfriends or their boyfriends. Some of these guys, though lady killers on the screen, just don't measure up in private life. Some of the biggest romantic stars of yesterday and today were no match for Gary Cooper, known throughout Hollywood as "The Montana Mule."

Maybe in the next lifetime of these men, God will be more generous when she hands out sexual endowments.

To spare embarrassment, we didn't name certain stars of today who are big only on the screen. ***But you know who you are!***

Ginger Rogers with Fred Astaire

"Fred once told me, 'I make love with my feet,'" said his dancing partner of the 1930s, Ginger Rogers. "He didn't have much else to make love with, so I guess he had to use his feet." To best friend Lucille Ball and others, Ginger described her "extreme disappointment" in having gone to bed with Astaire when they'd shot *Flying Down to Rio* in 1933.

Joan Crawford tried to seduce Astaire when she appeared with him as a high-stepping duo in *Dancing Lady* (1933). But he turned her down. "I hear you devour men," he told her in rejecting her. "I don't want to be your dinner."

"Don't flatter yourself," she said to him. "You wouldn't make dinner, my friend. From the looks of you, a light snack if that!"

A talent scout at Paramount looked at Astaire's first screen test and wrote, "Can't act. Can't sing. Balding. Can dance a little."

Astaire actually could dance a whole lot, and did so spectacularly with such partners as Ginger herself, but also with Eleanor Powell, Rita Hayworth, Judy Garland, Leslie Caron, Cyd Charisse, Vera-Ellen—and so many others. He reportedly had several affairs with actresses of his day, including Marilyn Miller.

A bisexual, Astaire indulged in an affair with Randolph Scott when they filmed *Roberta* together in 1935. In Astaire's autobiography, *Steps in Time*, all the dancer would admit was that he and Randy "became close friends." According to George Cukor, Astaire offered his beloved Randy "much comfort" when his other lover, Cary Grant, abruptly walked out on him.

Over the years, even though he led a very closeted life, the gay underground press has "outed" Astaire on many an occasion. Privately, and without knowledge of family and friends, he often seduced handsome, well-built young dancers who came to pay homage and also to dance for him.

Pandro S. Berman, a big-time producer at RKO, cast Astaire in *Follow the Fleet* with his best buddy, Randolph Scott. Ginger Rogers was the female star, and Lucille Ball and Betty Grable had bit parts. That's the film that introduced the song, "Let's Face the Music and Dance."

During the making of the film, Berman conflicted with Astaire and later made several disparaging remarks about his star. "I heard that his sister, Adele, used to call him 'Moaning Minnie' because he was such a sad sack during dress rehearsals, fearing we were going to fail."

The producer claimed that Astaire fell for several hunky extras on the set of *Follow the Fleet*. These men with their imposing bodies had been hired to perform as dancing sailors.

"From what I found out, I had every reason to call Fred 'Moaning Minnie' all over again, but for a different reason," Berman said. "He sampled quite a few of the extras, from what I heard, and those moans were of pure joy. As you might have expected, Fred was a bottom."

Montgomery Clift

The Nebraska-born actor wanted to become the greatest in the world. In that, he did not succeed but he left a number of powerful, sensitive, and magnetic performances as best evoked by the 1951 *A Place in the Sun* or the 1953 *From Here to Eternity*. Regrettably, he turned down what might have been his signature role, that of Joe Gillis starring opposite Gloria Swanson playing Norma Desmond in *Sunset Blvd.* (1950).

Montgomery Clift

Back in the 40s, his chief rival on Broadway was Marlon Brando. Both actors were bisexual, although for most of his life Clift was almost exclusively gay. Brando was later dismissive of Clift, calling him "Princess Tiny Meat." Although Clift had a number of affairs, ranging from playwright Thornton Wilder to heiress singer Libby Holman, he was always embarrassed by his small penis.

Deborah Kerr, who appeared with Clift in *From Here to Eternity*, once said, "He wanted to love women, but he was attracted to men. He crucified himself for that." Bedeviled by his guilt over homosexuality, the actor turned to liquor and drugs, both of which would eventually destroy him as his career faltered.

In a confession, Paul Newman told Brooks Clift, Monty's brother, "When I wake up in bed with him, I find myself battered and bruised. He sure likes to be the dominant one."

"Monty's just high-strung and filled with nervous energy," Brooks said. "You need to restrain him a bit. He doesn't know what limits are. Don't let him dominate you. You should be the controlling factor. I love my brother dearly. Help him! He's disturbed."

During his too-short life, Monty got around to seducing most of the other bad boys of Hollywood, including Steve McQueen and James Dean. For a while, he lived in a cozy nest with none other than a young Merv Griffin.

At one time Clift was celebrated for his beauty, and *Empire Magazine* named him one of the 100 Sexiest Stars in Film History. However, one night during the filming of *Raintree County* (1957), co-starring Elizabeth Taylor, Clift visited her hilltop home for dinner. Leaving her house later that night drunk, he drove his car into a ravine and smashed his face. Plastic surgeons could never restore his beauty. Elizabeth stood by him and tried to salvage his career, insisting that he be cast as her husband, a closeted homosexual, in *Reflections in a Golden Eye* (1967). But Clift died before shooting began, and Marlon Brando stepped into the role.

On July 23, Clift was found dead in his townhouse in New York by his companion Lorenzo James. The actor was lying nude on top of his bed, dead from an "occlusive coronary artery disease." When asked earlier in the evening if he wanted to see *Red River*, a picture he'd made with John Wayne in 1948 on TV, Clift responded: "Absolutely not!"

Those were his last words. He was only forty-five when he died.

Kirk Douglas

The son of Jewish Russian immigrants, Kirk Douglas became more famous for his cleft chin than for his sexual prowess. Some of the stars of Hollywood's Golden Age didn't file good reports on him.

Early in his career he "auditioned" for Mae West for an appearance in her stage show. Ms. West insisted that all her actors strip down to their skimpy briefs for an inspection.

The heavy hung Steve Cochran passed her test. "With a name like that, why wouldn't he?" West later said. However, after inspecting Kirk Douglas in his panties, Ms. West informed him, "You don't pass the grade, junior."

Studio mogul Harry Cohn couldn't resist quizzing Evelyn Keyes ("Scarlett O'Hara's Younger Sister") about her affair with Kirk Douglas.

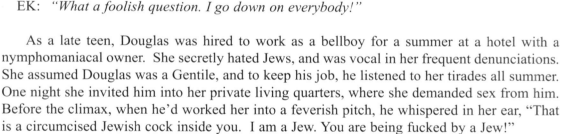

Kirk Douglas

HC: "A big cock?"
EK: *"It's just about the right size."*
HC: "I suppose you let him go down on you?" Cohn asked.
EK *"Let him? Why on earth would I want to stop him."*
HC: "You go down on him?" Cohn asked.
EK: *"What a foolish question. I go down on everybody!"*

As a late teen, Douglas was hired to work as a bellboy for a summer at a hotel with a nymphomaniacal owner. She secretly hated Jews, and was vocal in her frequent denunciations. She assumed Douglas was a Gentile, and to keep his job, he listened to her tirades all summer. One night she invited him into her private living quarters, where she demanded sex from him. Before the climax, when he'd worked her into a feverish pitch, he whispered in her ear, "That is a circumcised Jewish cock inside you. I am a Jew. You are being fucked by a Jew!"

One night, Douglas seduced Joan Crawford, or rather, she seduced him. "We went back to her house. We never got past the foyer. The door closed and she slipped out of her dress. She had a beautiful, trim body. There we were on the rug. In the middle of our lovemaking, she murmured, 'You're so clean. It's wonderful that you shaved your armpits when you made *Champion.'* A real conversation stopper. I don't shave under my arms. A strange comment to make; a stranger time to make it. The [bad] breath which she uttered it blew away all my fantasies about Miss Crawford."

Douglas once said, "An erection is a mysterious thing. There's always that fear, each time one goes, that you won't be seeing it again."

In spite of those self-doubts, Douglas managed to seduce Linda Darnell, Marlene Dietrich (who preferred to give blow-jobs), Rita Hayworth, Gene Tierney, and Lana Turner.

"I've been close to Bette Davis for thirty-eight years—and I have the cigarette burns to prove it!" That was Henry Fonda speaking about his longtime relationship with Davis at a Dean Martin roast. Fonda and Davis, the stars of the 1938 *Jezebel*, had actually met when she was only seventeen when he went out on a date with her and gave her a peck on the cheek.

When she got home, Davis wrote Fonda. "I've told my mother about our lovely experience together in the moonlight. She will announce the engagement when we get home."

Joan Crawford with Henry Fonda

"Holy shit!" Fonda said. "One kiss and I'm engaged!" As it turned out, Davis was just playing the imp to the naïve 20-year-old attending a football game at Princeton.

When Davis finally managed to seduce Fonda when they appeared in the 1937 picture, *That Certain Woman*, it was not a memorable experience. "He was a premature ejaculator like my first husband." The husband she was referring to was Harmon Oscar Nelson. "I was able to train him but was too busy in the mid-30s to take on another pupil like Fonda. Nonetheless, I remember his seduction of me as the easiest 30 seconds I've ever spent with any man."

Fonda's first marriage was to Margaret Sullavan. It lasted from December of 1931 until their divorce the following year. It was not a successful marriage. She pronounced him a "fast starter and a lousy finisher." Fonda responded in a quote sometimes wrongly attributed to Sullavan's third husband, agent Leland Hayward. "She castrates a guy—she makes him feel like two cents—and two inches," Fonda said.

Both Hayward and Fonda learned that Sullavan liked to attend plays in New York and then follow handsome actors home where she'd offer her sexual services. She also cruised at night picking up young men. "Hell, Maggie knew all about highway pickups before they became fashionable—or, rather, infamous," Hayward said.

Sullavan broke Fonda's heart by picking up young men during their brief marriage and having an affair with producer Jed Harris, "the beast of Broadway." In a restaurant, Sullavan responded to Fonda's accusations of infidelity. "Hell, I'm not satisfied with your little prick and I have to get it from somebody."

When Joan Crawford tried to seduce Fonda when they were co-starring in *Daisy Kenyon* in 1947, he stripped down. She sized up the jock strap he was wearing and burst into laughter. "Hank," she said, "you don't need a jockstrap to hold up that package. A thimble would do."

Homosexual rumors are still spread about Fonda but only in connection with his longtime friend James Stewart. Director Josh Logan knew both men when they were struggling actors in New York in the 1930s. "They definitely had a thing going between them," he said. "They did more than share a bed in that rooming house rat-hole they lived in."

Fortunately, Fonda will not be remembered for his off-screen sexual dalliances.

"One inch less and Clark would be the queen of Hollywood." So spoke his doomed spouse Carole Lombard, who died in a plane crash in 1942. Gable's less than adequate cock never got good reviews. Yet, when seeing a group photo of MGM's leading ladies, he told his friend, Spencer Tracy, "They're all beautiful and I've had every one of them!"

Clark Gable with Carole Lombard

His longest-running affair was with the bisexual actress, Joan Crawford. "He wasn't a satisfying lover. I often tried to distract him from the bedroom."

Gable never admitted to it, but his own bisexuality manifested itself during his early years in Hollywood, based on affairs he conducted with gay actor William Haines and others. He even let Lionel Barrymore go down on him. He'd originally married Josephine Dillon, a much older acting teacher and a lesbian.

Gable suffered from a bad case of phimosis, a condition where, in men, the foreskin cannot be fully retracted from the head of the penis, and which sometimes causes acute pain and in some cases, bleeding. It was a condition he detected when he was just fifteen years old in Cadiz, Ohio, and lost his virginity to a fat, 55-year-old widow. As a result, he developed a bad smegma odor.

The gay director George Cukor is said to have delivered to him a bottle of Listerine and a cake of red Lifebuoy soap. "Clark dear, the soap is to clean the cheese beneath your foreskin and the Listerine is to take away the smell." Perhaps that contributed to Gable's ire against Cukor, and what eventually prompted MGM to fire Cukor as director of *Gone With the Wind*.

Gable even managed to seduce gossip maven Louella Parsons, but struck out with Bette Davis. However, he scored with Grace Kelly, Ava Gardner, Mary Astor, Hedy Lamarr, Lana Turner, and Marilyn Monroe, to name only a few.

Gable never liked to strip down before the camera, not even wanting to bear his chest in *It Happened One Night*. But earlier he was persuaded to don Tarzan's loincloth and take a screen test for the role. His body wasn't considered buffed enough, and he lost the role to the Olympic swimming champion, Johnny Weissmuller.

At one point, Gable had hoped to jump-start his early career by going away for a weekend with the bisexual aviator and movie producer, Howard Hughes. Gable had told Haines, "I'll do anything to become a star—and I mean *anything*." Gable wanted the role of the newspaper reporter, Hildy Johnson, in *The Front Page*, a movie that Hughes was financing. Initially Hughes liked Gable and flew him aboard a plane he was piloting to San Francisco as a means of getting to know him better.

The actual events of that weekend will probably never be known. But when Hughes returned, he told his director, Lewis Milestone, that Gable wasn't going to get the part. "His ears are so big they make him look like a taxi with both doors open wide," Hughes said. Then, just before ending the dialogue, Hughes made a final enigmatic comment before dropping the subject forever. "Besides, his tits are too small!"

Cary Grant

Smooth, classy, and debonair, the English-born Archibald Alec Leach was virile, charismatic, and charming on the screen. When the American Film Institute compiled its list of the all-time great male stars, Grant came in second, having been bested only by Humphrey Bogart.

Cary Grant

One of Hollywood's top box attractions for decades, Grant could do both comedy and drama and was the favorite actor of Alfred Hitchcock, who was notorious for disliking actors.

The debate still rages over Grant's sexual preference, but he was clearly bisexual. He had long-enduring affairs with both Randolph Scott and Howard Hughes. Insights into many of these romances are detailed in Darwin Porter's pioneering biography of Hughes—*Howard Hughes: Hell's Angels*. Details about the secret affair between Marlon Brando and Cary Grant are revealed in another of Darwin Porter's books, *Brando Unzipped*.

During the 1930s, two of Grant's very hip blonde co-stars knew immediately that he was gay. "I had no romantic feelings for Grant," said Marlene Dietrich. "He was a homosexual." Mae West personally chose him to star opposite her in one of her first films, *She Done Him Wrong* (1933).

In that historic film, she invited him to "come up sometime and see me." Also in 1933, he appeared opposite West in *I'm No Angel*. West later referred to Grant as "one of the boys." She claimed, "He never came up to see me, not even sometime. Cary had Randy Scott during the filming of *Hot Saturday* back in '32. They became an item for years. Those boys were hot for each other."

Grant married five times, most famously to Woolworth heiress Barbara Hutton. He also seduced such stars and celebrities as Noel Coward, Gary Cooper, heiress Doris Duke, Grace Kelly, Clifford Odets, Ginger Rogers, Fay Wray, and George Orry-Kelly (the fashion designer).

At least twice he came close to getting arrested by the police, once in a department store toilet when he was caught performing fellatio on a handsome male employee. He bribed his way out of that one. He was also questioned by the police again in 1969 when a mother filed a complaint that Grant picked up her 14-year-old son on Santa Monica Boulevard and offered to give him a twenty-dollar bill if the kid would unzip his pants. No charges were ever filed.

Grant always remained hypersensitive about gay charges, especially in November of 1980 when Chevy Chase on NBC called him a "homo" and referred to him as "Whatta gal!" Grant sued for $10 million but the case was settled out of court.

In spite of his many affairs, with both women and men, Grant was never known for his endowment. As former girlfriend Maureen Donaldson revealed in her memoir, *An Affair to Remember*, she had known many men better hung.

Grant's less than adequate penis never bothered his lover, Howard Hughes. As Hughes told his pimp, Johnny Meyer, "As far as Cary is concerned, I've got enough for the both of us."

Burt Lancaster

Known as "Mr. Muscles, Mr. Teeth," Burt Lancaster, a former circus performer, blazed across the Hollywood screens in the post-war era. He was also a "serious, compulsive womanizer," in spite of his somewhat modest endowment.

Burt Lancaster

That didn't stop Shelley Winters from falling for him. Nor did it prevent everybody from Yvonne De Carlo to Marlene Dietrich going big for Lancaster. "I guess I'm the guy who went to bed with the girl—even if it was after the movie had finished."

Lancaster was also a bisexual, especially in his early days, and he posed for gay porn. He also had a penchant for hiring homosexual secretaries. "They're the best," he told his buddies. "On the nights when you don't want to go out and look for a woman, they'll always open their rosebuds for you. Good boys. I like 'em."

If Lancaster didn't have big balls in real life, he had *cojones* when it came to taking public, liberal stands. He was the only matinee idol type male star to publicly support Rock Hudson when it was revealed that the mega-star was dying of AIDS.

Lancaster's most famous male seduction was a brief affair he had with Marlon Brando. Lancaster was the first choice to play Stanley Kowalski in *A Streetcar Named Desire* on Broadway, but he turned it down. The role in the Tennessee Williams play went to Brando—and the rest is history. Actually Lancaster was more interested in starring in the movie version than he was in the stage version.

Unknown to Lancaster, Brando had a habit of seducing his competition, including James Dean and Montgomery Clift. As Brando's agent later discovered, Brando got his man . . . namely, Burt Lancaster. Brando also got the role in *The Godfather* that Lancaster wanted.

From a poor kid who grew up in East Harlem, Lancaster knew *The Sweet Smell of Success*, the name of his 1957 movie. He won an Oscar for his 1960 *Elmer Gantry*.

As the cult goddess Liz Renay once said, "I have gone to bed with men with heavier endowments than Burt, but he sure made good use out of what God gave him."

Opinions about him differed. "In Italy, Burt is known as bisexual," said Idalah Luria, an Italian dialogue coach. "Masculinity was oozing from every pore," said gossip columnist Sheilah Graham, the former lover of F. Scott Fitzgerald.

After Lancaster turned down Monty Clift's invitation for sex while they were co-starring in *From Here to Eternity* (1953), Monty called Lancaster "a big bag of wind and the most unctuous man I ever met."

"Burt was an exhibitionist," said Tennessee Williams. "When I visited his hotel suite while we were filming *The Rose Tattoo,* he stripped jaybird naked in his living room, telling me he had to take a shower. Fortunately, I was never a size queen."

Liberace

"Lee" to his friends, Wladziu Valentino Liberace was born in 1919 in Wisconsin to a Polish mother and an Italian immigrant father. A twin died at birth.

A closeted homosexual, he became one of the most famous entertainers of the 20th century. For decades, he was known for his piano music, his pompadoured toupées, his candelabra, his rhinestones, and his dazzling costumes.

Believe it or not, he was a romantic idol to middle-aged, blue-haired women of the 1950s. His fans uttered *oohs* and *ahhs* when he appeared on stage in outrageous drag, including on one occasion in a Norwegian blue shadow fox cape with a train 12 feet wide and 16 feet long. "There's only two of these in the world," he giggled, "and I've got both." At all appearances, he was all gooey smiles and dimples, wavy hair, and outrageous rings on each finger.

Liberace

His piano playing, like his clothing, was showy and sentimental with such hits as "The Impossible Dream" or "Send in the Clowns."

In 1956, he was outed by a British tabloid which described him as a "deadly, winking, sniggering, snuggling, chromium-plated, scent-impregnant, luminous, quivering, giggling, fruit-flavored, mincing, ice-covered heap of mother love." The writer concluded that Liberace was "the biggest sentimental vomit of all time."

He successfully sued the tabloid for libel, claiming he had never indulged in homosexual practices. "I am against the practice because it offends convention, and it offends society." When he died of AIDS in 1987, London's *Daily Mirror* requested a refund of the $24,000 libel that they had been forced to pay back in 1959.

"I don't want to be remembered as an old queen who died of AIDS," was Liberace's last moan on his deathbed. But the corpse was not cold before tabloids outed him as a homosexual who died of what was then called "the gay plague."

Although not heavily endowed, Liberace was a voracious lover, at least according to Scott Thorson, his companion of five years. Thorson sued for palimony when kicked out by Liberace but the case was settled out of court for $95,000.

In a tell-all book, Thorson revealed one of Liberace's darkest secrets: To maintain his small erection, he had to have a penile implant.

Liberace made a lot of claims, including that he'd been engaged to women three times. That we don't believe. But he told best friend Merv Griffin that the first man he ever had sex with was a member of the Green Bay Packers.

Some of his A-list seductions included Elvis Presley ("I taught him how to dress"), Rock Hudson (a "mercy fuck" on Hudson's part), and even composer/conductor Leonard Bernstein For the most part he preferred blond, blue-eyed young men with strong physiques and large endowments.

Once, he told Rock Hudson, "Mae West and I are fighting over which one of us is the real Queen of Hollywood.".

(Lord) Laurence Olivier

Producer David Lewis said, "Larry would sleep with anyone." That almost—but not quite—excluded his first wife, Jill Esmond, who was a lesbian. Their marriage was not consummated for a long time, and from all reports their first sexual encounter was not satisfactory for either of them.

Seduced by another boy at the age of fourteen, Olivier spent most of his youth with men. When he entered the theater, he enjoyed sexual intimacies with actors who included Richard Burton in England and Errol Flynn when he got to Hollywood.

Other male lovers included Kenneth Tynan, the British theater critic, and director James Whale. Olivier also had a brief affair with Douglas Fairbanks Jr. And Olivier's wife, Jill Esmond, was in bed with Fairbanks' wife, Joan Crawford.

Laurence Olivier

Olivier's female seductions included Claire Bloom, Elissa Landi, Sarah Miles, actress Jane Welsh, Jean Simmons (his co-star in the 1948 version of *Hamlet),* and Dorothy Tutin, his co-star in *The Beggar's Opera*, in 1952.

Larry Cole, a close friend of Noël Coward, claimed, "Noel adored Larry. There is no other word for it."

Olivier's most famous marriage was to Vivien Leigh, Miss Scarlett O'Hara herself. "I was barely out of my teens when Larry started fucking me," she said.

Olivier and Vivien were anything but faithful to each other. She seduced everyone from Sir Alexander Korda to Rex Harrison—and, in later life, Warren Beatty, her co-star in Tennessee Williams' *The Roman Spring of Mrs. Stone* (1961).

When her director pal George Cukor indiscreetly told her that her husband was having an affair with Greta Garbo, Vivien shot back, "I hope poor Larry knows what to do."

Other than "Her Ladyship" (Leigh), Olivier's long-running affair was with the bisexual actor, Danny Kaye. Kaye's nickname for Olivier was "Lala." After years and years of making love to Kaye, Olivier suddenly dropped him. Jilted, Kaye became almost suicidal.

In his desperation, he telephoned "the competition," Vivien herself, asking her to intervene "to get Larry to come back."

"Oh, dear heart," she said, "you'll get over it. The best way to do that is to take on a new bloke. I hear Rock Hudson is up for grabs." Then she slammed down the phone.

During the time that Marlon was making *A Streetcar Named Desire* with Vivien, actor David Niven discovered Brando and Olivier nude in the swimming pool kissing. "I turned my back to them and went back inside to join Vivien. I'm sure she knew what was going on, but she made no mention of it. Nor did I. One must be sophisticated about such matters."

When Olivier made *The Prince and the Showgirl* in 1957 with Marilyn Monroe, she seduced him the first night they were alone together. It was not successful. "I fear I've sadly disappointed you," he said. "All my life I've suffered from premature ejaculation. I disappointed Vivien too. Strangely my male lovers never complained. After I quickly ejaculated, they could always turn me over and bugger me. I suppose women can't do that."

Marilyn was quick on the comeback. "Yes, we can. Ever hear of a dildo?"

Brad Pitt

Emerging into the light of day on December 18, 1963 in Shawnee, Oklahoma, Brad Pitt went on to become a world famous movie star and *People Magazine*'s "Sexiest Man Alive." On the way to the top, he supported himself by driving strippers around in a limo to their next gig. At one low point, he dressed as a giant chicken to advertise El Pollo Loco.

Married to actress Jennifer Aniston in 2000, he abandoned her for the skinny arms of Angelina Jolie . . . and lots of children.

Brad Pitt

When Pitt first broke into movies in the late 80s, he was hailed as "the most beautiful man ever to appear on the screen." Before his marriage to Aniston, he was romantically linked to Geena Davis, his costar in *Thelma and Louise* (1991). He was also involved with Uma Thurman, Jill Schoelen (costar in *Cutting Class*, 1989), Shalana McCall, Juliette Lewis (costar in *Too Young to Die*, 1990), and most famously with Gwyneth Paltrow, costar in *Seven* (1995). Under the category of "What Was He Thinking?" he was also involved with both Robin Givens and Courtney Love.

He is dismissive of his romantic image, however. "Heartthrobs are a dime a dozen," he said. Even though he's settled down (at least at the moment) with Jolie, he once said, "I'm not about to settle down with one woman. I don't care what they say about me—it's my life."

Although there are many nude pictures out there of Pitt on the Internet, he has a dim view of filming scenes in the buff. "It's a long day when you're running around with a patch on your personals," he said. On the set of *The Curious Case of Benjamin Button* (2008), Pitt told the director that he'd have to "get another bare butt."

From all reports, there is nothing wrong with Pitt's current butt. However, he told producers he was not mooning it and that they had to find a body double to replace his ass. In 2004 Pitt showed off his ass in *Troy* (in more scenes than one), but he refused to do it again. A casting call went out for an actor who could "impersonate" Pitt's butt.

In spite of the fact that Pitt's body is still in good shape, the Hollywood hunk, when he turned 43, told the press that he feared that he was losing his looks. He claimed that the "trials and tribulations" of his life during his 30s contributed to his sudden aging. "One thing sucks," he said. "Your face kind of goes. Your body's not quite working the same either. But you earned it. You earned that, things falling apart."

In spite of all the adoration heaped on Pitt as the "perfect male specimen," the actor himself has his doubts. He spent a year getting in shape to play Achilles in *Troy*. When he posed nude for *Vanity Fair*'s Nick Knight, he left women and gay men swooning.

However, Pitt assured the jealous men of America that they could relax. According to him, he's no leading man in one important measure. "I'm hung like a hamster," the star was quoted as admitting to Britain's *Sun*.

Edward G. Robinson

Although Edward G. Robinson came to personify the Prohibition gangster, he was actually born in Bucharest, Romania in 1893. He came to New York when he was 10 years old.

Edward G. Robinson

Growing up in New York's Lower East Side, he dreamed of becoming a rabbi but turned to the stage instead, although he felt his 5' 5" stature would work against him.

"I remember just before going onto the stage, I'd look in my dressing room mirror and stretch myself to my full height to make me appear taller and to make me able to dominate all the others and to mow them down to my size," he later told several of his costars, including Bette Davis. "I feel my legs are very beautiful and I never mind wearing tights. However, I think God could have given me another 3 inches, or at least 2 ½."

Puffing on a cigarette, Davis turned to him and looked somewhat startled. "Mr. Robinson," she said, "Are you wanting more inches in your stature? Or, are you talking about somewhere else?"

"That's for you to find out if you're interested," he said provocatively.

"I prefer, Mr. Robinson, that we keep our relationship professional. If I want personal statistics about you, I will ask Lupe Velez."

Producer Hal Wallis claimed that "Eddie's attack, his vigor, his electric energy, made you forget that he was a small and ugly man."

"Some people have youth, others beauty," Robinson said. "I have menace." He also said, "My whole life has been for women, and I've never ceased being frightened by them. They have a weapon against which there is no defense. Unpredictability."

A gruff-talking gangster on screen in the 1930s and 40s, Robinson in private life was called a Renaissance man and was an art collector. Along with Bette Davis herself, he remains one of the most parodied actors of the Golden Age.

Comedian Richard Jeni jokingly claimed that, "I love the new trend of women smoking cigars. In a romantic situation, I want my woman to remind me as much of Edward G. Robinson as possible. 'Look, here's how it's gonna go, see? You're gonna make love to me . . . see?'" Jeni delivered those lines in his best Robinson-esque voice.

Robinson's most famous female seduction was Marlene Dietrich, with whom he appeared in the 1941 *Manpower*. In it, he sparred with George Raft both on and off the screen for her affections. "Raft was the skilled seducer," Dietrich told her friends, "but occasionally, I like to go to bed with a very ugly man like Robinson. They are always so grateful."

One night when Bessie Mona Lasky, wife of studio head Jesse Lasky, visited Robinson's palatial Hollywood estate, she asked why he didn't have a swimming pool like other movie stars. "I have a dreadful fear of water," he told her. "My son, Edward Jr., was only seven years old when he almost drowned my first wife." He was referring to Gladys Cassell Lloyd.

Summing up Robinson's sexual allure, screenwriter Aben Dandell said, "I'm not a trained psychologist, but I don't think Eddie was very sexually oriented."

Roy Rogers

At the pinnacle of a fame that began after World War II and lasted through the 1950s, Roy Rogers was the most popular Western star in America, replacing Gene Autry and William ("Hopalong Cassidy") Boyd. In a 1945 survey of American boys, kids were asked to name the hero they most wanted to emulate. The vote was more or less a tie among Franklin D. Roosevelt, Abraham Lincoln, and Roy Rogers.

Rogers became the "King of the Cowboys," his third wife, Dale Evans, "The Queen of the Cowgirls." The crinkly eyed Rogers was a familiar figure at Saturday matinees across America, wearing his double-creased 10-gallon white hat and flowing kerchief knotted at the side of his neck. His dress—a gabardine cowboy shirt, western cut trousers, and shining pointed cowboy boots—

Roy Rogers with Dale Evans

was imitated across America. He evoked a time when men tipped their hats to the ladies and (at least theoretically) sat around campfires warbling sentimental ballads at night.

Politically, Rogers was to the far right of John Wayne, as was his wife, Dale Evans. Labeled "homo haters" in the press, they joined the notorious "Orange Juice Queen of Florida," Anita Bryant, in her denunciation of gay men and lesbians in the late 70s. Rogers and Evans viewed homosexuals as an "abomination." Reportedly, Rogers told some close friends that he felt "homosexual men should be castrated." Even Anita Bryant herself didn't go that far.

It is doubtful if gay men would have been much interested in Rogers. Seemingly he had little to fear from them. George (Gabby) Hayes, his garrulous, bewhiskered sidekick, once said, "If judged on dick size, my pal Roy would be called Queen of the Cowboys. There wasn't much there. Trigger, of course, had him beat by a country mile."

Rogers was such a narrow-minded conservative that he even refused to kiss his wife on screen. "I'm a role model for millions of children, and I don't want to lead them astray." Dale suggested a kiss on the forehead instead.

"Who do you want to be?" he responded. "A replacement for Betty Grable? You stick to what you're doing."

"Roy," she protested, "a kiss on the forehead is not pornography."

"If I want to kiss someone, I'll kiss Trigger," he said.

Reportedly, Roy had been sensitive about the size of his penis ever since he had a bad first seduction with a prostitute in Ohio, where he was born Leonard Slye in 1911. When he pulled off his trousers, the battle-hardened older whore mocked his small size. Reportedly, after that, he never fully undressed in front of a woman again—and even had sex with his wives while half dressed.

Robert Taylor

Wavy-haired actor Robert Taylor came from the great American heartland, Nebraska, where he grew up as Spangler Arlington Brugh. Little wonder he changed it to Robert Taylor.

A bisexual, he was dogged by rumors of homosexuality from the outset of his career. That was no surprise. He was having affairs with the likes of Howard Hughes, Errol Flynn, and Tyrone Power. The press called him a pretty boy. He resented the label, claiming "I am a red-blooded man and I resent people calling me 'pretty.' For your information, I've got hair on my chest."

He begged studio mogul Louis B. Mayer to give him rugged, he-man parts and to engineer a macho image for him off-screen. To prove his masculinity, he was a frequent visitor to the whorehouse that MGM ran for its male employees at Culver City.

Barbara Stanwyck with Robert Taylor

In the 40s he would seduce glamour queens and best pals, Ava Gardner and Lana Turner. Neither goddess was impressed with his love-making skills. In 1938 the MGM publicity department released these measurements for Robert Taylor: Chest 42", waist 30", hips 37", thighs 23", calf 15", biceps, 14¾", forearm 12", wrists 7", and neck 16". What they didn't release was his penis size, which reportedly was little more than 4½ inches.

His friend, character actor Andy Devine, was urinating with Taylor in the woods on a hunting trip. Checking out Taylor's penis, he said, "that doesn't look like it belongs to the world's greatest lover." Taylor sighed, "I know, but don't tell my wife. She thinks they're all the same size."

Taylor in 1939 had married the most closeted lesbian in the history of Hollywood, Barbara Stanwyck. During their marriage, which lasted until 1951, "Babs" might have spent more time with her lifelong friend, Joan Crawford, than she did with her husband.

A bisexual herself, Stanwyck, even in front of friends, constantly hounded Taylor about his homosexuality. Eventually, he became impotent with her. His problem was said to have begun when she had an affair with Gary Cooper, her costar in *Meet John Doe* in 1941. Stanwyck taunted Taylor that Cooper's penis was three times the size of his own.

So, Stanwyck did know that cocks came in small, medium, and economy size, in spite of what Taylor had told Devine.

When he could no longer produce an erection for her, she kicked him out of her bed. He was never to return, although their marriage would endure for years. With other men or women, he was not impotent. "Ah, that bitch," he said to Andy Devine one day on yet another hunting trip. "She always wants to run the fuck, except now there is no fuck to run."

314

John Wayne

Here is the testimony of a former soldier from World War II who went skinny-dipping with the Duke.

John Wayne

"I met John Wayne when I was in the South Pacific during World War II. We were tent-mates for a month during his USO tour. While we were on Arawe Island, the two of us decided to visit a native village. We paddled across the bay in a rubber raft, visited the village, and enjoyed a sing-sing. On our return trip, we came across a secluded beach where we decided to skinny-dip for a while. It was my first time to see the Duke completely nude, and I must confess I was a bit surprised to see that he had a very small (conservative even in that respect) uncut penis. However, it was very capable of expansion to a comfortable working size. I have a postcard from him on which he wrote: 'That junket to Arawe stands out as a most thrilling experience in my life.'"

The only problem we have with this testimony is this: How did the soldier know that Wayne was capable of expanding to working size?

Wayne flew to the South Pacific theater of the war for three months in 1943 and '44, touring U.S. bases. While there, he did undercover work for OSS commander William J. (Wild Bill) Donovan. Although Wayne was a celluloid war hero in several patriotic films, he was exempted from service because of his age. He was 34 at the time "the dreaded Japs" (as he called them) attacked Pearl Harbor. He was also classified as 3-A (family deferment).

As a hot stud, Wayne did better on screen than off. "He walks like a fairy," said director William Wellman. "He's the only man in the world who can do that—and get away with it."

Joan Crawford, after seducing Wayne, claimed, "Get him out of the saddle and you've got nothing." Marlene Dietrich, upon first spotting him, said to Tay Garnett, her director of *Seven Sinners* (1940), "Baby, buy me some of that." But after going to bed with Wayne, the German claimed "it was *veek* (i.e., weak) *lemonade*." Amazingly Wayne later told director John Ford that "Marlene was the best lay I've ever had."

"Women scare the hell out of me," Wayne confessed. "I've always been afraid of them." He once seduced Clara Bow, who later said, "After Gary Cooper, Wayne felt like a mere pin-prick. Place the emphasis on pin—not prick!"

Wayne seduced his costars, including Claire Trevor in *Stagecoach* (1939). He fell for Paulette Goddard, his costar in *Reap the Wild Wind* in 1942, but she dumped him after the picture was completed. Other seductions included Sigrid Curie, his costar in *Three Faces West* (1940) and Martha Scott, his co-star in *Old Oklahoma* (1943). He fell bigtime for Guy Madison's wife, Gail Russell, his costar in *Angel and the Badman* in 1947, but the affair ended tragically.

When he made *The Alamo* in 1960 with Laurence Harvey, the British bisexual actor tried to seduce him. "Please, Duke. Tonight. Just one time. I'll be the Queen if you'll be the King." The Duke turned him down, even though Harvey, according to Orson Welles, was known for having "The most talented rosebud in all of Hollywood."

Marlon Brando's
NOBLE TOOL

From *A Streetcar Named Desire*

Named the fourth greatest male star of all time by the American Film Institute, Brando was another movie great to come out of Nebraska, following in the footsteps of Henry Fonda and Montgomery Clift. Although each of them was a towering figure in cinema, all three actors show up on our Shortcomings list

Critics from around the world have hailed Brando's screen presence, but he did not always get good press. Gossipy Louella Parsons, whom Brando called "the fat one who pees on people's sofas," said, "As far as I am concerned, he can drop dead! He has the manners of a chimpanzee, the gall of a Kinsey researcher, and a swelled head the size of a Navy blimp."

Tennessee Williams, who created Brando's most memorable character on Broadway and on the screen, the role of Stanley Kowalski in *A Streetcar Named Desire*, had a different evaluation. "He was just about the best-looking man I had ever seen, with one or two exceptions. And I have never played around with actors. It is a point of morality with me. And anyhow, Brando was not the type to get a part that way."

That was the playwright's attempt to tell why he didn't sample Brando's charms. To intimate gay friends in Key West, Tennessee related in great detail how he'd first seduced Brando on a beach in Provincetown at the tip of Cape Cod as early as 1943.

As documented in Darwin Porter's tell-all biography, *Brando Unzipped*, published after the actor's death, there has never been an actor like Brando—impassioned, iconoclastic, imaginative, impulsive, and indomitable. A bisexual, the man led an X-rated private life which began when he arrived to conquer Broadway where he was called "lightning on legs" by the critics of 1947.

For many, it is difficult to remember the man decades before the tragedies of Brando's personal life overshadowed his early accomplishments. After three tempestuous marriages and countless other relationships that produced 11 children (five from his wives; three from his former maid; one adopted; two from affairs), the fiercely private Brando was shocked and grief-stricken after his son Christian shot and killed the *fiancé* of his troubled daughter, Cheyenne, in 1990. He blamed himself for Cheyenne's lifelong unhappiness and never recovered from her suicide by hanging in 1995.

It is nearly impossible to explain to those who have only seen Brando as *The Godfather* in

1972, or as a bloated behemoth in his last films, how Brando's uninhibited carnality and skin-tight jeans shocked and astonished audiences in the late '40s and early '50s. He was the living, breathing embodiment of sexual desire in an era where movie censors even outlawed use of the word "virgin" on-screen.

No one who swooned for Brando in his early years would have dreamed that he would end his days as an obese recluse in his home in the Hollywood Hills, before dying at age 80 of congestive heart and lung failure on July 1, 2004.

While in his final days, Brando replaced his voracious appetite for sex with food. In his heyday, he wielded what he happily called his "noble tool" with deliberate impunity. Women (and a fair share of men) literally fell at his feet.

Perhaps Brando's "noble tool" provided some measure of oblivion; perhaps he was merely a sex addict. After all, he did say, "All my life I've never been interested in someone else's sex life—only my own. My noble tool has performed its duties through thick and thin without fail!"

One of his wives, Anna Kashfi, wasn't impressed with Brando's tool. "Physically, Marlon is not well appointed. He screens that deficiency by undue devotion to his sex organ."

The list of his lovers was a *Who's Who* of Hollywood and high society: One-night stands and brief relationships with Marlene Dietrich, Grace Kelly, Jacqueline Kennedy (who claimed, "Marlon is one of the most interesting men I've ever met"), Ingrid Bergman, Leonard Bernstein, Ursula Andress, Edith Piaf, Faye Dunaway, Bianca Jagger, Kim Stanley, Veronica Lake, Hedy Lamarr, Joan Crawford, Bette Davis (her first words to him were, "I've done everything a woman can do in life but meet Mr. Marlon Brando"), Jean Peters, Gloria Vanderbilt, Doris Duke (then the richest woman in the world), John Gielgud, Burt Lancaster (originally intended to play Stanley in *Streetcar*), even Princess Margaret, and hundreds if not thousands of other bit players, the rich and famous, as well as complete strangers.

Brando was at ease in his own skin long before even partial nudity was fashionable, and he was often quite the exhibitionist. Early in his career, he was appearing in the Jean Cocteau play, *The Eagle Has Two Heads*, opposite the theater's grande dame and great eccentric, the alcoholic and equally sexually ravenous Tallulah Bankhead. By the time the play was about to preview in Boston, Tallulah and Marlon knew the play was going to be a flop, calling it "The Turkey with Two Heads." On opening night, Marlon showed his disdain for the production and his costar during one of Tallulah's long, dramatic monologues. He turned his back to the audience, spread his legs, unbuttoned his fly, and

A studio publicity shot

Viva Zapata!

Guys and Dolls

proceeded to urinate against the stage scenery. The audience could clearly see what he was doing, but Tallulah couldn't understand why they were laughing. When she found out what Marlon had done, she had him fired.

After that, Marlon was lucky in that his talent was so immense producers took a chance on him anyway. Still, you'd think he'd have learned his lesson—but he was too much the prankster to care. When his first film, *The Men*, was trounced by critics, Brando took the train back to New York from Hollywood, displaying his buttocks through the window at railway stops across America. "I made an ass of myself in *The Men*, so before America sees it, I wanted them to look up close and personal at the real thing."

Several years later, he took a girlfriend to a screening of *The Wild One*. Ever his own worst critic, he couldn't bear to watch himself. Before running out, he shouted at the audience, "Look at Marlon Brando's fat ass!"

Brando was also an equal opportunity lover. Perhaps most surprising is the casualness of his bisexuality, switching easily as he did between male and female lovers with equal ardor. Streetcar co-star and life-long friend Kim Hunter said, "Marlon told me some of his deepest, darkest secrets, including his fear of being forever a mama's boy." Marlon also told her that after a particularly intense affair with a man, he'd go crazily promiscuous: "screwing every girl who will go to bed with me—and very few of them say no."

His agent, Edith Van Cleve, explained Marlon's penchant for going after men. "Instead of being hostile to actors with whom he was competing, Marlon tried to seduce them," she said. "It was as if the act of seduction gave him the edge. Take poor Monty (Montgomery) Clift, for instance. Instead of being leery of Monty, Brando overpowered him sexually. At any rate, when I combed all of New York for Brando to tell him he was on again for the part of Stanley, he was screwing Burt Lancaster. If I had been a man, I too would have wanted to screw Burt Lancaster."

"I have guilt about sleeping with men, and, almost to atone for it, I go in the opposite direction," Brando claimed. "The more the merrier. That way, I manage to convince myself I'm a *bona fide* heterosexual, until the queer side of me comes out again."

As well as countless casual encounters, Brando had much more complicated relationships with Rita Moreno (whom many said was the one woman he should have married and didn't); Tyrone Power (with whom he frolicked in a *ménage à trois*); playwright Tennessee Williams; and Shelley Winters.

"Marlon's friendship with Monty Clift—dare I call it an

As Superman's Father

*Last Tango in Paris
(with Maria Schneider)*

*The Men
(with Teresa Wright)*

Mutiny on the Bounty

affair—was brief and intense," his acting teacher Stella Adler said. "So intense that it was destined to burn out quickly. It was rivalry that tore them apart. They were both the two young geniuses of 1940s Broadway and later the two young geniuses of Hollywood."

Years later, Brando told Clift's dearest friend, Elizabeth Taylor, "Your friend Monty and I were alike in only one regard. Both of us had desperate hopes and nursed unspeakable desires."

When Elizabeth asked him to explain himself, Marlon said, "Both Monty and I have human hearts. But they beat in the wrong places."

Brando's heart often seemed to beat in many places at once. Elia Kazan was blunt: "During the months he appeared under my direction as Stanley Kowalski, Marlon was a 'fuck machine.' He became a phallic dream for both gay and thousands of female theatre-goers. Later he would become the wet dream for millions of film fans around the world. He was, in essence, the male sex symbol of the '50s, with Marilyn Monroe wearing the crown for women."

Kazan ought to know. Brando had first met Marilyn Monroe at a bar in New York in 1946, when she was so strapped for cash that she was turning tricks in between modeling gigs.

"I wouldn't call her a rising starlet," Brando said, when she came to "entertain" him several years later in Hollywood. "Seems to me she spends more time on her back."

Yet they became great friends, more than occasional lovers, and confidantes, sharing the same intense drive. "I know a lot of gals arrive in Hollywood dreaming of becoming a movie star," Monroe told him. "But I have one up on them. I can dream harder than they can." They were also sexual kindred spirits, for Monroe was quite a lot more complicated and pragmatic than the vulnerable girly-girl of legend.

"A girl should use sex like a weapon," she told Brando with characteristic candor. "I think this is the only way a girl can get ahead in a town ruled by men." Over the years, she and Brando stayed in touch, often falling into bed when the urge struck. When he was filming *Viva Zapata!* in Mexico, Monroe showed up to visit director Elia Kazan, with whom she was having an affair. When Kazan's wife unexpectedly arrived, Monroe happily took to Brando's bed, which made his own affairs with co-stars Rita Moreno and Mexican actress Movita (who later became his second wife) a tad complicated.

Kazan later told Tennessee Williams that "the most outrageous event took place," claiming that, on a lark, Brando and Monroe slipped away and got married under assumed names. "When she was sleeping with me," Kazan claimed, she called herself Mrs. Brando, and told me that since I was married and she was married we were committing adultery. I told her I had no problem with that!"

Brando obviously had no problem with adultery either. He flatly denied having an affair with *Streetcar* co-star Vivien Leigh in his autobiography, *Songs My Mother Taught Me*, claiming that her husband, Sir Laurence Olivier, was such a "nice guy." In truth, however, he had already spent some time under the covers with the bisexual Olivier, who'd been captivated after Brando's small but electrifying role onstage in *Antigone*.

Like Monroe, Vivien Leigh was sexually uninhibited. She quite surprised Brando when she introduced herself by saying, "Her ladyship is fucking bored with formality." Then she went on: "As you'll get to know me, and I hope you will, there is nothing respectable about me. In London, I pick up taxi drivers and fuck them. Don't be surprised—I'm just as whorish as Blanche DuBois."

Director Kazan referred to the couple as the pairing of "a gazelle with a wild boar." The jungle did become a bit overcrowded during the filming of *Streetcar*, when Brando was invited to stay with the Oliviers in their Hollywood home. He spent nights playing musical beds, even though Olivier was then having a well-known affair with the actor Danny Kaye. At one party, when Brando showed up on the arms of Leigh and Olivier, Kaye, whose hair had been dyed a bright red for a film role, saw them and flipped. He slapped Brando full in the face. Brando, who'd had no idea about Kaye's relationship with Olivier, merely said, "Like your hair color."

Then he went back to the house and packed his bags, leaving a note for his hosts: "Dear Vivien and Larry," it read. "Thank you for your hospitality. You were both wonderful to me. But it is time to move on now, and I'm heading back to New York to resume my life. My regret is never having gotten to know either of you. But, then, I have always depended upon the kindness of strangers."

The Nightcomers

One famous stranger he soon met was Cary Grant, with whom he had a brief relationship. "Spending some time with Cary Grant has convinced me of one thing," Brando said. "Of all the possibilities for me in all the world, I don't want to be a fucking movie star. Let me out of this cage!"

Another was the young James Dean, who approached his idol after Brando gave a talk at the Actors Studio. "I'm confused about a lot of things," the bisexual Dean told him. "Very confused. But not confused in my admiration for you." The two spent quite a lot of time together in the winter of 1951. "He was completely in charge of our lovemaking," Dean reportedly said. "He told me what he wanted, and I went along for the ride."

On the Waterfront

But Dean quickly became obsessed, showing up unannounced at Brando's apartment, often spending the night outside in the cold, hoping to be let in. Brando sometimes took pity on Dean—and sometimes ignored him completely before telling a mutual friend, "You'd better get your boy to a psychiatrist right away. He's an emergency case. One crazed sicko! If you only knew what he wants me to do to him."

Later, after he learned that Dean had died, he commented: "The trouble with Jimmy is that he wanted to be me. I don't know why. Even I, myself, don't want to be me."

Finally, Brando got a much-deserved Oscar for Best Actor in 1954 for his role in *On the Waterfront*. "Thank you very much," he said graciously after accepting the award. "It's much heavier than I imagined. I had something to say and I can't remember what I was going to say for the life of me. I don't think that ever in my life have so many people been so directly responsible for my being so very, very glad. It's a wonderful moment, and a rare one, and I am certainly indebted. Thank you."

Later that night, he left a star-studded party. "I've got a date with a blonde," Brando said. "And there are still those people who spread the rumor that I don't like blondes."

The blonde was Grace Kelly, that year's Best Actress Oscar-winner for *The Country Girl*, who couldn't resist Brando's

The Young Lions

charms, even though she'd been having an affair with her co-star, Bing Crosby. What happened in Grace's suite around three o'clock that morning is still not known in exact detail, but Bing Crosby arrived for a showdown with Grace. Instead of that, he found a nude Marlon in her bed.

The affair was short-lived. Kelly went on to marry Prince Rainier, and Brando went on to make a string of films, many of them less than stellar. Although vowing never to wed, he nonetheless fell for the actress Anna Kashfi, a beautiful, troubled actress whose real name was Joan O'Callaghan, marrying her in 1957 when she was pregnant with Christian. "She was probably the most beautiful woman I've ever known, but she came close to being as negative a person as I have met in my life," Brando said.

Quiemada!

"Marlon attracts women like feces attracts flies," Kashfi retorted.

Viva Zapata! co-star Movita (born Marie Casenada) became his second wife in 1960. "I know my reputation for preferring jailbait, but I often throw a mercy fuck to older women," Brando had said when he met her. "I think Movita is funny—she makes me laugh. She's also beautiful in her own kind of way, smart and very sympathetic to my problems when I lay my head on her breast at night."

That union barely lasted two years. While filming *Mutiny on the Bounty* in Tahiti, Brando fell in love with the young and lovely Tarita Teriipaia, married her in 1962, and bought a private Tahitian island. It became his retreat from the pressures of Hollywood and his own tormented, contradictory nature.

The Wild One

Although Brando again astonished filmgoers when *The Godfather* and *Last Tango in Paris* became blockbuster hits in 1972 and 1973, respectively, his passion for acting gradually dissipated and his eccentricities became more pronounced.

The most embarrassing encounter Brando ever had on film was during the making of *Last Tango*, when he agreed to be photographed frontally nude. "My penis shrank to the size of a peanut," he related in his memoirs. "I paced back and forth around the apartment stark naked hoping for magic, trying to will my penis and testicles to grow. I even spoke to them. I was humiliated. I simply couldn't play the scene nude, so it was cut." After he died, his ashes were mixed with those of his best friend and longtime lover, Wally Cox, then scattered to the winds of the California desert. "Now we'll be united for eternity," Brando said.

Even in death, he had not wanted to be by himself. Still, the glory that was Brando in his prime will live on forever.

As Napoléon in Desirée

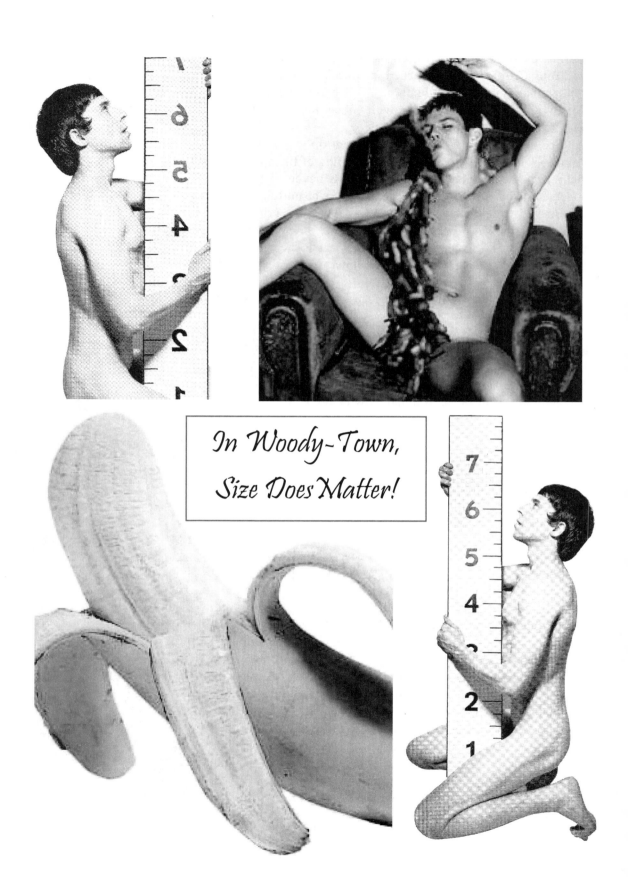

In Woody-Town,
Size Does Matter!

Index

BLOOD MOON PRODUCTIONS

Entertainment About How America Interprets Its Celebrities

Blood Moon Productions originated in 1997 as *The Georgia Literary Association*, a vehicle for the promotion of obscure writers from America's Deep South. Today, Blood Moon is based in New York City.

Our corporate mission involves researching and salvaging the oral histories of America's entertainment industry--those "off the record" events which at the time might have been defined as either indecent or libelous, but which are now pertinent to America's understanding of its origins, its values, and its cultural roots.

Since 2004, Blood Moon has generated at least nine different literary awards. They've included both silver and bronze medals from the IPPY (Independent Publishers Assn.) Awards; four nominations and two Honorable Mentions for BOOK OF THE YEAR from Foreword Magazine; and Honorable Mentions from both the Hollywood and the New England Book Festivals.

For more about us, and the books we're planning, click on our website, or refer to the pages which immediately follow.

Thanks for your interest, best wishes, and happy reading.

Danforth Prince, President
www.BloodMoonProductions.com

Salvaging the unrecorded
oral histories of the Entertainment Industry's
"off the record" past

And its affiliate, the Georgia Literary Assn

THE GEORGIA LITERARY ASSOCIATION
ENTERTAINMENT YOU WOULDN'T NECESSARILY EXPECT FROM THE DEEP SOUTH

The Private Lives of **Vivien Leigh** *and* **Laurence Olivier**

by **Darwin Porter** *and* **Roy Moseley**

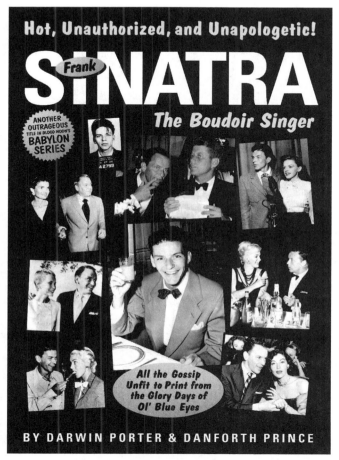

Finally--A COOL Biography that was too HOT to be published during the lifetime of its subject. TALES OF A LURID LIFE!

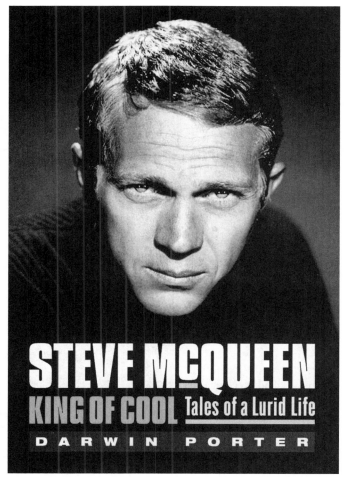

The drama of Steve McQueen's personal life far exceeded any role he ever played on screen. Born to a prostitute, he was brutally molested by some of his mother's "johns," and endured gang rape in reform school. His drift into prostitution began when he was hired as a towel boy in the most notorious bordello in the Dominican Republic, where he starred in a string of cheap porno films. Returning to New York before migrating to Hollywood, he hustled men on Times Square and, as a "gentleman escort" in a borrowed tux, rich older women.

And then, sudden stardom as he became the world's top box office attraction. The abused became the abuser. "I live for myself, and I answer to nobody," he proclaimed. "The last thing I want to do is fall in love with a broad."

Thus began a string of seductions that included hundreds of overnight pickups--both male and female. Topping his A-list conquests were James Dean, Paul Newman, Marilyn Monroe, and Barbra Streisand. Finally, this pioneering biography explores the mysterious death of Steve McQueen. Were those salacious rumors really true?

Steve McQueen   King of Cool   Tales of a Lurid Life
by Darwin Porter

ISBN 978-1-936003-05-1   Hardcover $26.95

PAUL NEWMAN

THE MAN BEHIND THE BABY BLUES, HIS SECRET LIFE EXPOSED

by Darwin Porter

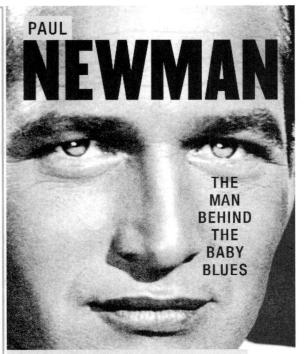

THE MOST COMPELLING BIOGRAPHY OF THE ICONIC ACTOR EVER PUBLISHED

Drawn from firsthand interviews with insiders who knew Paul Newman intimately, and compiled over a period of nearly a half-century, this is the world's most honest and most revelatory biography about Hollywood's pre-eminent male sex symbol, with dozens of potentially shocking revelations.

Whereas the situations it exposes were widely known within Hollywood's inner circles, they've never before been revealed to the general public.

If you're a fan of Newman (and who do you know who isn't) you really should look at this book. It's a respectful but candid cornucopia of information about the sexual and emotional adventures of a young man on Broadway and in Hollywood.

WINNER OF AN HONORABLE MENTION AT THE **2009** NEW ENGLAND BOOK FESTIVAL

This is a pioneering and posthumous biography of a charismatic American icon. His rule over the hearts of American moviegoers lasted for more than half a century. Paul Newman was a potent, desirable, and ambiguous sex symbol, a former sailor from Shaker Heights, Ohio, who parlayed his ambisexual charm and extraordinary good looks into one of the most successful careers in Hollywood.

It's all here, as recorded by celebrity chronicler Darwin Porter--the giddy heights and agonizing lows of a great American star, with revelations never before published in any other biography.

Paul Newman, The Man Behind the Baby Blues
His Secret Life Exposed
ISBN 978-0-9786465-1-6 $26.95
Hardcover,   520 pages, with dozens of photos.

"One wonders
how he managed
to avoid public scrutiny
for so long."

BLOOD
MOON
Productions, Ltd.

MERV GRIFFIN
A Life in the Closet

by Darwin Porter

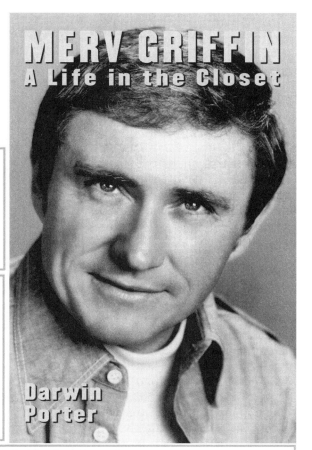

> "Darwin Porter told me why he tore the door off Merv's closet.......*Heeeere's Merv!* is 560 pages, 100 photos, a truckload of gossip, and a bedful of unauthorized dish."
>
> **Cindy Adams, The NY Post**

> "Darwin Porter tears the door off Merv Griffin's closet with gusto in this sizzling, superlatively researched biography...It brims with insider gossip that's about Hollywood legends, writ large, smart, and with great style."
>
> Richard LaBonte, BOOKMARKS

Merv Griffin, A Life in the Closet

Merv Griffin began his career as a Big Band singer, moved on to a failed career as a romantic hero in the movies, and eventually rewrote the rules of everything associated with the broadcasting industry. Along the way, he met and befriended virtually everyone who mattered, made billions operating casinos and developing jingles, contests, and word games. All of this while maintaining a male harem and a secret life as America's most famously closeted homosexual.

In this comprehensive biography--the first published since Merv's death in 2007--celebrity biographer Darwin Porter reveals the amazing details behind the richest, most successful, and in some ways, the most notorious mogul in the history of America's entertainment industry.

Most of his viewers (they numbered 20 million per day) thought that **Merv Griffin**'s life was an ongoing series of chatty segués--amiable, seamless, uncontroversial. But things were far more complicated than viewers at the time ever thought. Here, from the writer who unzipped **Marlon Brando**, is the first post-mortem, unauthorized overview of the mysterious life of **the richest and most notorious man in television**

HOT, CONTROVERSIAL, & RIGOROUSLY RESEARCHED

HERE'S MERV!   Hardcover, with photos

ISBN 978-0-9786465-0-9 $26.95

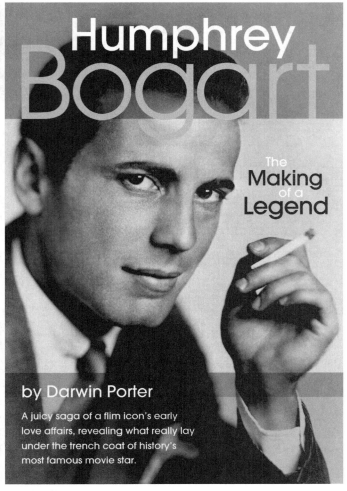

This "entertainingly outrageous" (FRONTIERS MAGAZINE) biography provides a definitive,
blow-by-blow description of the "hot, provocative, and barely under control drama" that was the life
of America's most famous Postwar actor.

Brando Unzipped

by Darwin Porter

"Lurid, raunchy, perceptive, and certainly worth reading...One of the ten best show-biz biographies of 2006."   ***The Sunday Times (London)***

"**Yummy**. An irresistably flamboyant romp of a read."
Books to Watch Out For

"Astonishing. An extraordinarily detailed portrait of Brando that's as blunt, uncompromising, and X-rated as the man himself."
Women's Weekly

"This shocking new book is sparking a major reassessment of Brando's legacy as one of Hollywood's most macho lotharios."
Daily Express (London)

"As author Darwin Porter finds, it wasn't just the acting world Marlon Brando conquered. It was the actors, too."
Gay Times (London)

"*Brando Unzipped* is the definitive gossip guide to the late, great actor's life."
The New York Daily News

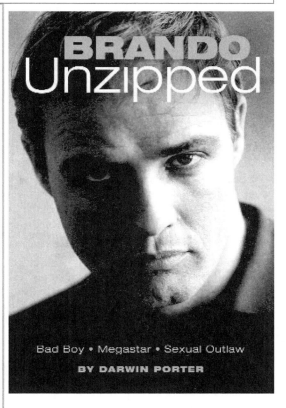

Bad Boy • Megastar • Sexual Outlaw

BY DARWIN PORTER

Hardcover, 625 indexed pages,
with hundreds of photos.

ISBN 978-0-9748118-2-6. $26.95

This is one of our most visible and most frequently reviewed titles. A best-seller, it's now in its fifth printing, with French, Portuguese, and Dutch editions selling briskly in Europe. Shortly after its release, this title was extensively serialized by THE SUNDAY TIMES in the UK, and in other major Sunday supplements in mainland Europe and Australia.

Katharine the Great
(KATHARINE HEPBURN)
A Lifetime of Secrets Revealed

A softcover that fans of old Hollywood find fascinating.

by Darwin Porter
569 pages, with photos $16.95
ISBN   978-0-9748118-0-2

Katharine Hepburn was the world's greatest screen diva--the most famous actress in American history. But until the appearance of this biography, no one had ever published the intimate details of her complicated and ferociously secretive private life. Thanks to the "deferential and obsequious whitewashes" which followed in the wake of her death, readers probably know WHAT KATE REMEMBERED. Here, however, is an unvarnished account of what Katharine Hepburn desperately wanted to forget.

"Behind the scenes of her movies, Katharine Hepburn played the temptress to as many women as she did men, ranted and raved with her co-stars and directors, and broke into her neighbors' homes for fun. And somehow, she managed to keep all of it out of the press. As they say, *Katharine the Great* is hard to put down."
The Dallas Voice

"The door to Hepburn's closet has finally been opened. This is the most honest and least apologetic biography of Hollywood's most ferociously private actress ever written."
Senior Life Magazine, Miami

"In Porter's biography of Katharine Hepburn, details about the inner workings of a movie studio (RKO in the early 30s), are relished."
The Bottom Line, Palm Springs

Katharine
The Great

Darwin
Porter

"Darwin Porter's biography of Hepburn cannot be lightly dismissed or ignored. Connoisseurs of Hepburn's life would do well to seek it out as a forbidden supplement."
The Sunday Times (London)

Katharine Hepburn was the most obsessively secretive actress in Hollywood. Her androgynous, pan-sexual appeal usually went over big with movie audiences--until those disastrous flops when it didn't. This book tells the how and why of Kate Hepburn's most closely guarded secrets.

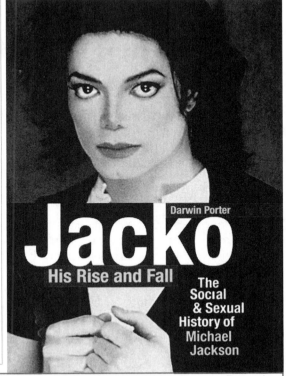

A DEMENTED BILLIONAIRE:

From his reckless pursuit of love as a rich teenager to his final days as a demented fossil, Howard Hughes tasted the best and worst of the century he occupied. Along the way, he changed the worlds of aviation and entertainment forever. This biography reveals inside details about his destructive and usually scandalous associations with other Hollywood players.

Howard Hughes
Hell's Angel by Darwin Porter

Set amid descriptions of the unimaginable changes that affected America between Hughes's birth in 1905 and his death in 1976, this book gives an insider's perspective about what money can buy--and what it can't.

"Darwin Porter's access to film industry insiders and other Hughes confidants supplied him with the resources he needed to create a portrait of Hughes that both corroborates what other Hughes biographies have divulged, and go them one better." ***Foreword Magazine***

"Thanks to this bio of Howard Hughes, we'll never be able to look at the old pin-ups in quite the same way again." ***The Times*** **(London)**

A BIG comprehensive hardcover, Approx 814 pages, with photos, Available in August, 2010
$32.95
ISBN 978-1-936003-13-6

Hughes--A young billionaire looks toward his notorious future.

"The Aviator flew both ways. Porter's biography presents new allegations about Hughes' shady dealings with some of the biggest names of the 20th century"

New York Daily News

Billie Dove-- duenna of the Silent Screen. She gave him syphilis.

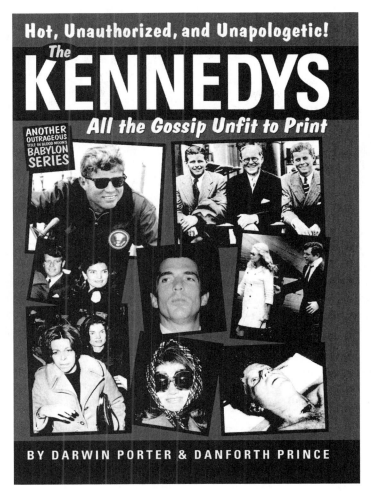

Get Ready
for what's going to rock the country
just before Christmas
of 2010

The Kennedys, All the Gossip Unfit to Print,
Another startling title from Blood Moon's BABYLON series
Hardcover, approximately 400 pages, with hundreds of photos.
$25.95
ISBN 978-1-936003-17-4

OUT OF THE CELLULOID CLOSET
HOMOSEXUALITY IN THE MOVIES

A Reference Source for Private Homes and Libraries
Softcover, 524 pages, with film reviews, gossip, and hundreds of photos

ISBN 978-1-936003-09-9 $25.95

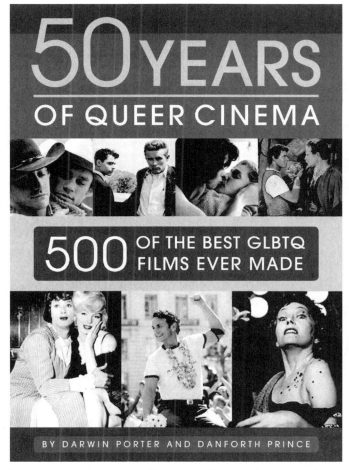

"In the Internet age, where every movie, queer or otherwise, is blogged about somewhere, a hefty print compendium of film facts and pointed opinion might seem anachronistic. But flipping through well-reasoned pages of commentary is so satisfying. Add to that physical thrill the charm of analysis that is sometimes sassy and always smart, and this filtered survey of short reviews is a must for queer-film fans.

"In part one, Porter and Prince provide a succinct "A to Z romp" through 500 films, with quick plot summaries and on-point critical assessments, each film summed up with a pithy headline: *Yossi & Jagger* is "Macho Israeli Soldiers Make Love, Not War.

"The films surveyed in part two are quirkier fare, 160 "less publicized" efforts, including—no lie—*Karl Rove, I Love You*, in which gay actor Dan Butler falls for 'George W. Bush's Turd Blossom.'

"Essays on Derek Jarman, Tennessee Williams, Andy Warhol, Jack Wrangler, Joe Gage and others—and on how *The Front Runner* never got made—round out this indispensable survey of gay-interest cinema."

RICHARD LABONTÉ
BOOK MARKS/QSYNDICATE

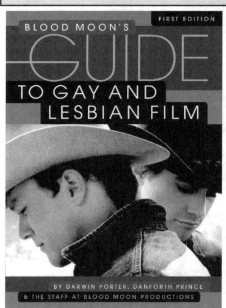

360

Midnight in Savannah

Sexual Eccentricities in the Deep South
Perversity in Extremis

by Darwin Porter

Trade Paperback   498 pages   **$16.95**
ISBN   978-0-9668030-1-3

After its publication in 2000, Darwin Porter's **Midnight in Savannah** quickly established itself as one of the best-selling gay novels in the history of the Deep South.

Eugene Raymond, a filmmaker in Nashville, writes, "Porter disturbs by showing the world as a *film noir* cul-de-sac.   Corruption has no respect for gender or much of anything else.

"In MIDNIGHT, both Lavender Morgan (at 72, the world's oldest courtesan) and Tipper Zelda (an obese, fading chanteuse taunted as 'the black widow) purchase lust from sexually conflicted young men with drop-dead faces, chiseled bodies, and genetically gifted crotches. These women once relied on their physicality to steal the hearts and fortunes of the world's richest and most powerful men. Now, as they slide closer every day to joining the corpses of their former husbands, these once-beautiful women must depend, in a perverse twist of fate, on sexual outlaws for *le petit mort*. And to survive, the hustlers must idle their personal dreams while struggling to cajole what they need from a sexual liaison they detest. Mendacity reigns. Physical beauty as living hell. CAT ON A HOT TIN ROOF's Big Daddy must be spinning in his grave right now."

"If you're not already a Darwin Porter fan, this novel will make you one!   We've come a long way, baby, since Gore Vidal's The City and the Pillar."
Time Out for Books

"An artfully brutal saga of corruption, greed, sexual tension, and murder, highlighted by the eccentricities of the Deep South. Compulsive Reading."
The Georgia Literary Assn.

"I've just booked the next flight to Savannah! Nothing like a good Georgia boy on a chilly night in Dixie!"
Out!

Wild, orgiastic nights in pre-code Hollywood

Hollywood's Silent Closet

by Darwin Porter

Trade Paper 7" x 10" 746 pages. 60 photos $24.95

ISBN 978-0-9668030-2-0

"The Little Tramp" **Charlie Chaplin** (above) was one of the most recklessly debauched players in Hollywood.

Disillusioned In her later years, **Mary Pickford** (left) declared herself a recluse and virtually never left her bedroom.

An anthology of star-studded scandal from Tinseltown's very gay and very lavender past, it focuses on Hollywood's secrets from the 1920s, including the controversial backgrounds of the great lovers of the Silent Screen.

Valentino, Ramon Novarro, Charlie Chaplin, Fatty Arbuckle, Pola Negri, Mary Pickford, and many others figure into eyewitness accounts of the debauched excesses that went on behind closed doors. It also documents the often tragic endings of America's first screen idols, some of whom admitted to being more famous than the monarchs of England and Jesus Christ combined.

The first book of its kind, it's the most intimate and most realistic novel about sex, murder, blackmail, and degradation in early Hollywood ever written.

"The *Myra Breckinridge* of the Silent-Screen era. Lush, luscious, and langorously decadent. A brilliant primer of **Who Was Who** in early Hollywood."

Gay Times, London

A banquet of information about the pansexual intrigues of Hollywood between 1919 and 1926 compiled from eyewitness interviews with men and women, all of them insiders, who flourished in its midst. Not for the timid, it names names and doesn't spare the guilty.   If you believe, like Truman Capote, that the literary treatment of gossip will become the literature of the 21st century, then you will love *Hollywood's Silent Closet.*

Millions of fans lusted after **Gary Cooper** (background) and **Rudolph Valentino** (foreground) but until the release of this book, **The Public Never Knew.**

BLOOD MOON
A sexy, horrifying spellbinder

by Darwin Porter

In 2008, this title was designated as one of the ten best horror novels ever published in a survey conducted by **Boiz Who Read**

ISBN 978-0-9668030-4-4

A controversial, compelling, and artfully potboiling paperback $10.99

Blood Moon exposes the murky labyrinths of fanatical Christianity in America today, all within a spunky context of male eroticism. If you never thought that sex, psychosis, right-wing religion, and violence aren't linked, think again.

"In the gay genre, Blood Moon does for the novel what Danielle Steele and John Grisham have been publishing in the straight world for years."
Frank Fenton

Rose Phillips, Blood Moon's charismatic and deviant evangelist, and her shocking but beautiful gay son, Shelley, were surely written in hell. Together, they're a brilliant--and jarring--depiction of a fiercely aggressive Oedipal couple competing for the same male prizes.

*"**Blood Moon** reads like an IMAX spectacle about the power of male beauty, with red-hot icons, a breathless climax, and erotica that's akin to Anaïs Nin on Viagra with a bump of meth."*
Eugene Raymond

Rhinestone Country
A novel about Love and the Music Industry

by Darwin Porter

All that glitter, all that publicity, all that applause, all that pain...

The *True Grit* of show-biz novels, *Rhinestone Country* is a provocative, realistic, and tender portrayal of the Country-Western music industry, closeted lives south of the Mason-Dixon line, and three of the singers who clawed their way to stardom.

Rhinestone Country reads like a scalding gulp of rotgut whiskey on a snowy night in a bow-jacks honky-tonk.
-Mississippi Pearl

"Beautifully crafted, Rhinestone Country sweeps with power and tenderness across the racial, social, and sexual landscapes of the Deep South. This is a daring and dazzling work about trauma, deception, and pain, all of it with a Southern accent."   **Peter Tompkins**

"A gay and erotic treatment of the Country-Western music industry? Nashville has come out of the closet at last!"
The Georgia Literary Assn.

BUTTERFLIES IN HEAT

by Darwin Porter

A compellingly retro softcover expressing some eternal truths about love, hate, greed, and sex.   ISBN 978-0-9668030-9-9 $14.95

Tennessee Williams, who understood a thing or two about loss, love, and drama, had this to say about **Butterflies in Heat:**

"I'd walk the waterfront for Numie any day."

"The most SCORCHING novel of the BIZZARE, the FLAMBOYANT, the CORRUPT since Midnight Cowboy. The strikingly beautiful blond hustler, Numie, has come to the end of the line. Here, in the SEARING HEAT of a tropical cay, he arouses PASSIONS that explode under the BLOOD-RED SUN."
Manor Reviews

"A well-established cult classic. How does Darwin Porter's garden grow? Only in the moonlight, and only at midnight, when man-eating vegetation in any color but green bursts into full bloom to devour the latest offerings."

James Leo Herlihy, author of
MIDNIGHT COWBOY

This title, a cult classic now in its **16th printing**, has sold steadily to a coterie of Darwin Porter fans since its inauguration in 1976, when it was the thing EVERYBODY in Key West was talking about, and the inspiration for the movie (The Last Resort/ Tropic of Desire) that EVERYBODY wanted to be in.

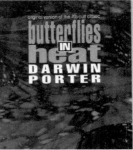

"Darwin Porter writes with an incredible understanding of the milieu--hot enough to singe the wings off any butterfly."
James Kirkwood, co-author of *A CHORUS LINE*

"We know from the beginning that we're getting into a hotbed that has morbid fascination for potential readers. The novel evolves, in fact, into one massive melée of malevolence, vendetta, and e-v-i-l, stunningly absorbing alone for its sheer and unrelenting exploration of the lower depths."
BESTSELLERS

BLOOD MOON PRODUCTIONS ANNOUNCES THE RELEASE of the 75-minute documentary it filmed in late May from the floor of America's world-famous and most important bookselling event, BEA 2010.

BOOK EXPO 2010: BLOOD MOON'S VIEW FROM THE FLOOR, represents history's first attempt to capture—close, in-your-face, uncensored, and personalized—the interactions, alliances, scandals, and dramas that explode for a small book publisher during a bookselling mega-event devoted to the marketing, pricing, and sale of its literary products.

Defined as a hybrid between a documentary and an infomercial, the film was conceived as a publicity and promotion piece by Blood Moon's founder and president, Danforth Prince: "Book publishers operate in a state of barely controlled hysteria, especially in this economic climate," he said. "Within this film, we've captured some of the drama of how books are promoted and hawked at a highly competitive event where everyone from Barbra Streisand to the Duchess of York was shaking his or her bonbon to sell something."

"At BEA 2010, enemies, competitors, and authors evoked Oscar night in Hollywood before the awards are announced," Prince continued. "This film is the first attempt to depict, on video, how a small press swims in the frantic, shark-infested waters of the book trade. It's a documentation of a specific moment in America's mercantile history, with implications for America's reading habits and how consumers will opt, sometimes through digitalization, to amuse and entertain themselves in the 21st century."

During the footage he shot from within and near his booth #3784 at BEA, Mr. Prince was assisted by members of Blood Moon's editorial staff, and directed by Polish-born Piotr Kajstura, winner of several filmmaking awards and grants for his work with, among others, the tourism board of South Carolina.

BOOK EXPO 2010, BLOOD MOON'S VIEW FROM THE FLOOR.
© Blood Moon Productions, Ltd. Available now, electronically and without charge, from the home page of **BloodMoonProductions.com**

WHAT BOOK-INDUSTRY CRITICS SAID ABOUT THIS FILM:
Blood Moon Productions, which specializes in books about Hollywood celebrity scandals of the past--many of which were hushed up at the time--offered a feature-length video on BookExpo America 2010, which aims to give "nonprofessional book people an insight into book fairs"--while highlighting some Blood Moon titles. The narrator is Blood Moon president Danforth Prince, who interviews, among others, Carole Stuart of Barricade Books, Philip Rafshoon, owner of Outwrite Bookstore and Coffeehouse, Atlanta, Ga., Graeme Aitkin of the Bookshop in Sydney, Australia, Eugene Schwartz of ForeWord Reviews, and a what seems like half of the staff of National Book Network, Blood Moon's distributor.

Shelf-Awareness.com August 3, 2010 (volume 2, issue #1247)

ABOUT THE AUTHORS

This, Volume Two of Blood Moon's Babylon Series, represents the latest in dozens of previous collaborations between **Darwin Porter** and **Danforth Prince**, who share emotional and journalistic links through their long-standing co-authorship of many past and present editions of THE FROMMER GUIDES, North America's most respected travel authority. Since 1982, their shared responsibility has included editorial coverage of the travel landscapes of Europe, The Caribbean, and America's Deep South.

Darwin is also the respected author of at least twenty celebrity biographies and film guides, some of them award-winners, about Hollywood. Each of them outlines, often with glaring clarity, the sometimes bizarre sociology of America's entertainment industry and the corrosive effects of fame.

Danforth, a former employee of the Paris bureau of *The New York Times*, is founder and president of The Georgia Literary Association, Blood Moon Productions, The Porter & Prince Corporation, and other media-related firms.

For more information about upcoming titles from Blood Moon Productions, and for access to Porter and Prince's ongoing roster of hot, juicy newsletters and videotaped book trailers, click on

WWW.BLOODMOONPRODUCTIONS.COM